Josephine

Also by Carolly Erickson and published by Robson Books:

Bonnie Prince Charlie
To the Scaffold: The Life of Marie Antoinette
Our Tempestuous Day: A History of Regency England
Bloody Mary: The Life of Mary Tudor
Her Little Majesty: The Life and Times of Queen Victoria
Great Catherine: The Life of Catherine the Great, Empress of Russia
Great Harry: The Extravagant Life of Henry VIII
The First Elizabeth

Josephine

A Life of the Empress

CAROLLY ERICKSON

ROBSON BOOKS

This paperback edition first published in Great Britain in 2004
by Robson Books, The Chrysalis Building, Bramley Road, London W10 6SP

An imprint of Chrysalis Books Group plc

First published in the United States of America by St. Martin's Press

British Library Cataloguing in Publication Data
A catalogue record for this title is available from the British Library.

ISBN 1 86105 637 0

Printed by Creative Print & Design (Wales), Ebbw Vale

Contents

Josephine

Into the Wind-House

*T*here was a stillness in the heavy, humid air and smoke from the cooking fires rose slowly straight upward into the cloudy sky a long way before drifting off sharply to the north. The trade winds had ceased. No comforting puff of air stirred the thick leaves of the breadfruit trees, and in the cane fields, where a hundred near-naked slaves bent to the work of harvest, slashing at the cane stalks with long sharp knives, the heat by mid-morning was like an oven.

It was the thirteenth of August, 1766, a month into the *hivernage*, the season of storms and rain. On the craggy, mountainous island of Martinique in the western Antilles, four hundred miles from the Guinea coast, clouds were piling up and an eerie darkness was gathering. In the slave quarters there were whispers that a bad storm was coming, for the Carib chiefs had announced that the skies were ominous and everyone knew that on the night before, at sunset, a blood-red light had been glimpsed at the horizon in place of the usual emerald green—a portent of death.

"It is the *ioüallou*," the slaves told one another and their creole masters repeated the warning in their own tongue. "It is the *ouracan*."

Out in the wide bay of Fort-Royal, the clear turquoise water had turned opaque, and by noon the ocean was choppy with whitecaps and an angry surf crashed noisily on the beach. Ships riding at anchor at the harbor mouth began to dance crazily in the swell, and nearer the shore, fishermen hurried to bring their boats ashore, dragging them up far from the beach and tying them to the wide stalks of palm trees with thick ropes.

By early afternoon a leaden twilight had descended, and a harsh wind off the ocean had begun to whistle through the cane fields. Cows bellowed and pawed the earth restlessly, chickens deserted their coops to seek refuge amid the rocks on the mountainside. Seabirds flocked together and flew toward the center of the island, away from the coast, and the brackish streams were full of fish swimming up from the ocean, seeking protection from the churning waters.

Though the overseer had not yet given the order to stop work the field hands paused in their labors and sniffed the air. It reeked of sulphur. They looked up, and saw, threaded among the thick dark clouds, fine streaks of silver lightning. Then the first large drops of rain began to fall, spattering on the red earth with a sound so loud it made talk impossible.

In the plantation of Trois-Ilets on the lower slopes of Morne Ganthéaume, Joseph Tascher decided that it would be unwise to wait any longer. He had to get his family to safety. His wife Rose-Claire was in no condition to undergo hardship of any kind. For several weeks she had been in bed expecting to deliver her third child—a child Joseph fervently hoped would be a son. The black midwives were in attendance, prepared to deliver the child if the doctor from Fort-Royal was unable to arrive at the plantation in time, and both the baby's grandmothers, the aristocratic Françoise Tascher and the iron-willed Irishwoman Catherine Brown, who on her marriage had become Catherine des Sannois, had made the trip to Trois-Ilets in order to be in attendance when Joseph's heir was born.[1]

Joseph ordered a cart brought from the stable and helped his anxious wife into it, along with his daughters Yeyette and Catherine, aged three and not quite two, who clutched their slave nursemaids in fear, and his mother and mother-in-law, and the six-year-old boy Alexandre who had been living with the family since his birth. Into the cart went a few belongings, the women's jewelry and the few heirlooms they had thought to snatch hurriedly on their way out. Joseph took one last look around, then ordered the driver to go as quickly as possible to the wind-house.

Every plantation in Martinique had a wind-house, an all but impregnable structure with stone walls six feet thick and no windows, built deep into the hillside where no storm, no matter how fierce, could penetrate. Massive wooden doors, made from hardwood cut in the rain forest higher up on the slopes, opened into a dark, cavernous room that could hold several dozen people and supplies of food and water. In this refuge, secure behind the stout wooden doors, they would wait out the storm.

In the high watchtower at the edge of the cane fields, the bell began to ring, sounding the alarm. Work ceased, and the field hands rushed at once to their huts, gathered their children and a few provisions, and made their way to the sugar mill. The other buildings on the plantation were dilapidated and neglected, but the stone-walled sugar mill, built several generations earlier in more prosperous times, was still sturdy. It would stand up to the *ioüallou*.

More cartloads were sent to the wind-house, full of candles and lanterns, baskets of salted fish and cassavas and loaves made from manioc flour, large red earthenware vessels full of fresh water and molasses beer. The midwives brought their knives and cords and charms made of dried palm leaves, blessed by the healers, to ward off zombies.

By early evening the plantation was in total darkness, and the rain was falling in sheets, swelling the streams and flooding the fields. Hour by hour the wind grew in force and violence, churning the bay into high waves and surging breakers. In the shelter where the Tascher family and their house slaves were waiting out the storm, the thick wooden doors began to bulge outward and tug against the ropes that restrained them. Joseph and the other men took turns pulling on the ropes with all their force, fighting the terrible outward sucking of the wind.

So loud was its roaring that they could barely distinguish the sounds of destruction outside—the crashing of the huge trees as they fell to earth, the flying apart of the two-story plantation house, the mowing down of the cane fields and plantation gardens. The wind had become a great scythe, sweeping across the land, cutting down everything in its path, while rain lashed at the devastated earth and washed the debris into the swollen rivers.

Joseph, nearly at the end of his strength, listened to the thunderous noise of the wind and despaired. Everything he owned was being carried off, and there was nothing he could do to prevent it. He had no money, he was deeply in debt and his health had been poor ever since the previous year when he had nearly died of a malignant fever. He was only thirty-six, but felt much older, worn down by the weight of his failure, and by the continuing nagging disappointment of his unhappy domestic life.

He had been struggling fitfully since his marriage five years earlier to make the plantation a success. Trois-Ilets, its buildings and its hundred and fifty African slaves had been a wedding present from Rose-Claire's parents; Joseph had an obligation to make it profitable. But well-intentioned though he was, he was ineffectual; he lacked the energy and capability to manage a large estate. Neither manly nor masterful, as his younger brother Robert was, Joseph could not seem to find the discipline or the skill to increase the plantation's output of sugar. He was reasonably intelligent, but pleasure-loving and easily distracted. He preferred spending time at Fort-Royal to meeting with his overseer Blacque or listening to the complaints of his unhappy wife, whose task it was, in his absence, to run the plantation.

Life was so much easier at Fort-Royal, the chief town of the island and the center of its social life. There he could sleep until noon, meet with his friends in the evenings to dine and play cards, visit his beautiful mulatto mistresses and pretend that he was a man of substance and breeding instead of a near-bankrupt and the son of a disreputable father. In recent years he had been spending less and less time at Trois-Ilets, letting his responsibilities go. Times were hard, what with the British blockade making it all but impossible to sell what sugar the estate produced; it hardly seemed worthwhile to keep trying. And the longer Joseph stayed away, the more run down Trois-Ilets became, the buildings falling into disrepair, the fields only partially cultivated, the slaves dwindling in numbers as their absent master failed to provide for them.

Now, of course, none of that mattered. The hurricane was sweeping everything away. Everything but his family, that is. He still had his daughters, and the son he and his wife were expecting. At least the family name would be carried on, even if there was only a ruined plantation and a thick sheaf of debts to go with it.

There was a boy attached to the family already, of course. Little

Alexandre, who had lived with them for all of his six years, was a sort of surrogate son. A tall, dark-haired, good-looking child, well-spoken and good at his lessons, Alexandre had been born in Martinique and given to the Tascher family to raise—a temporary arrangement, it was understood, but one that did not seem likely to end soon. Alexandre was the son of François de Beauharnais, former governor of the Windward Isles, who now lived in Paris with his married mistress, Joseph's sister Edmée. Alexandre's mother, who was in poor health, also lived in France but apart from her husband, and apparently did not mind living apart from her son as well. So little Alexandre continued to be raised as a creole, along with the Tascher children Yeyette and Catherine, spending time with grandmother Tascher and grandmother de Sannois as well as at Trois-Ilets, never having known his parents. In every respect but that of blood kinship, he was one of the family.

Throughout the night the storm continued, save for an hour of unnatural calm—the eye of the hurricane—when the wind dropped suddenly and all was still. For that brief interval the victims of the storm, crowded together in the wind-house, tried in vain to rest. But the respite was brief. Soon the assaulting gusts returned, and so greatly did their force build that for a time it seemed as if the mountains themselves would be shaken into the ocean. Once again the doors of the wind-house bulged outward, and the weary occupants, exhausted from their long vigil, said their prayers and clutched each other in fear.

Not until dawn did the ceaseless roaring and shrieking of the wind begin to die down, and it was mid-morning before Joseph Tascher cautiously opened the thick wooden doors and peered out at the blasted landscape.

A pale sun shone down on a sea of mud that had been the plantation of Trois-Ilets.

No trees were left standing. The two-story plantation house, with its wide veranda and its straggle of outbuildings, had vanished, along with the rose garden and the wide courtyard with its fine avenue of tamarisks. The bell tower had gone, the rows of slave huts had been demolished, and in the fields stretching away from where the plantation house had been, no stalk of cane was left upright.

The quiet was unnerving. There were no birds to sing, no frogs to croak, none of the everyday animal and human sounds that were the familiar backdrop to plantation life. Even the hum of insects had been stilled, for the clouds of mosquitoes, which had been unable to escape the cruel wind, had perished in their millions.

One building still stood. The refinery appeared to be untouched by the storm, and when Joseph and his family left the wind-house and made their way to it, they found within its spacious interior, amid the machinery and rows of barrels and freshly cut cane stalks, most of the field hands and their families.

Over the following weeks the slow, dispiriting work of restoration began. Debris was sorted and cleared away, fallen trees were chopped into timber to build new sheds and huts and carts and a new bell tower. Dead cattle were buried, along with a number of slaves, for as always happened following a severe storm, there was an outbreak of fever and many did not survive it.

Gradually news reached Trois-Ilets from other plantations, and from Joseph's brother Robert in Fort-Royal. The devastation had been island wide. Fort-Royal itself had been badly damaged, and many smaller settlements had all but disappeared. Out in the bay, hundreds of ships had sunk, with a very high loss of life. It had been, everyone agreed, the worst storm anyone could remember.

In the refinery, Rose-Claire Tascher lay on a makeshift bed, watched over by her mother and mother-in-law and the black midwives. She was past her time.

She had no privacy. The entire population of the plantation slept in the same large but crowded room, the master and his children and other relatives, the slaves, many of whom lay stricken with fever, the overseer and the few visitors who arrived with supplies and messages from outside.

On the oppressively hot night of September 2, three weeks after the storm struck the island, Rose-Claire went into labor. She was prayed over, massaged, protected with amulets and given rum to drink when the pains became too great to be endured. Finally, on the following day, her baby was born. Everyone in the community, caught up in the drama, listened for the cries of the newborn infant, and smiled when they heard its first thin wails. The birth was an omen of better times to come, they told one another. The hurricane had brought death, yet despite its ravages, new life was coming into the world.

But Joseph, haggard and careworn, turned his face away from his child and tried to hide his tears of disappointment. He had another daughter.

2

The Scent of Sugar

ive years after the hurricane destroyed the Trois-Ilets plantation, the Tascher family was still living in the refinery. Some of the land had been cleared and replanted, and the slaves had built themselves new huts from scrap lumber and bits of debris. But the old, gracious plantation house was not rebuilt, because Joseph Tascher did not have the money to rebuild it, and what with the tremendous losses he suffered in the storm, and his ever increasing debts and continuing poor health, the state of his finances worsened year by year.

Rose-Claire, who greatly disliked making her home amid the clanking of machinery and the crunching of cane stalks, resented her husband's financial failure and resented as well his constant stays in Fort-Royal. She had hoped that if they had a son Joseph would spend more time at Trois-Ilets, but no son arrived, and she was losing hope of having any more children.

Fortunately the three girls, eight-year-old Yeyette, six-year-old Catherine and five-year-old Manette, had all survived the perils of infancy. Of the three, Yeyette was especially promising, a sturdy, smiling little girl with wide dark eyes and a musical voice whose sweet nature and natural kindness were very appealing. Pleasing as she was, however, it did not appear that Yeyette would be a beauty, and at least one of the three girls would have to be beautiful so that she could marry well and salvage the family fortunes.

Marrying well was, after all, how the Taschers had managed to stave off ruin for at least the past two generations. Gaspard Tascher, Joseph's father, had been an impoverished nobleman who emigrated to Martinique from France four decades earlier and had married an heiress who brought him an estate in the nearby island of Santo Domingo as well as lands in Martinique. Joseph's own marriage had brought him wealth in property. Now his daughters would have to be groomed to find rich husbands.

Joseph's attractive blonde sister Edmée, who had attached herself to no less than a marquis, was the family expert in securing matrimonial advantages, though her own situation was complex and not quite respectable.[1]

At nineteen, Edmée had become the mistress of the forty-two-year-old François de Beauharnais, a man of modest wealth and considerable rank. Such liaisons were common, but socially acceptable only if both the lovers were married; consequently Beauharnais supplied Edmée with a husband, Alexis Renaudin, a young officer with a shadow over his past and an inclination to violence.[2] Renaudin understood that in marrying Edmée he was doing a favor for a senior officer, and that she was to be his wife in name only; he could be counted on not to object to her relationship with Beauharnais.

Edmée had secured for herself most of the advantages of marriage to the marquis, and after his wife died, she became, in fact if not in law, stepmother to Beauharnais's son Alexandre, the boy who had been born and raised in Martinique, then sent to France at the age of nine.[3]

Edmée wrote urging Joseph to send his daughters to her in Paris to be educated, instructed in the refined ways of the French capital, and readied for marriage. Joseph wrote back to say that he couldn't afford to send them. There was no money to pay for the long sea voyage, the trunks and clothing, the tuition and tutors—the whole panoply of a first-class education. Edmée wrote again—and went on writing, year after year, as the little girls grew older. Joseph's response was always the same. He could not find the money. The girls would have to be given what education and polish Martinique could offer.

It was a fateful decision. Instead of being groomed in France as miniature Frenchwomen, taught to speak correctly and assume the erect posture required by court gowns, their manners trained and their minds furnished with the rudiments of civilized knowledge, they were raised amid a natural environment that was part French, part African. Their speech was creole French, but they also knew the soft, musical dialect the slaves spoke; unconsciously they imitated the languid, graceful movements of the slave women, and the formal education Yeyette and Catherine received, at the convent of the Dames de la Providence in Fort-Royal (Joseph could not afford to send his daughters to the best school in Martinique, the Ursuline convent school at Saint-Pierre), was rudimentary at best.

Their real education was acquired in and around the plantation, where they watched, from under their parasols, the cane being cut in the fields, took refuge from the oppressive midday heat in dim shuttered rooms, strolled in the cooler evenings under the young trees planted in the years following the great hurricane. They learned the rhythms of life in the tropics: to rise late and eat nothing before noon, to sleep after the noon meal, never to hurry, or to take really long walks, lest the body become too agitated and succumb to fever. To avoid the perishing heat and the intense, glaring light of the sun.

At the convent school they learned to read and write, to dance and draw and do embroidery, but at Trois-Ilets they learned about the natural world, how the large black ants were harmless but the venomous small red ants had a stinging, painful bite, what to feed the land crabs kept in large barrels and fattened for the cooking pot, how to avoid the huge foot-long centipedes and the dreaded poisonous snake called the *fer-de-lance* that came out at night in large numbers. They learned to name the plants that yielded curing infusions and those that induced sleep or hastened the labor of women in childbirth. They learned to watch the sky for signs of the daily rain showers, and to anticipate the storms of the *hivernage* season and the epidemics that followed them.

They learned that life is fragile, and fleeting. Of the hundreds of emigrants from France who came to Martinique each year, hoping to establish themselves in time as plantation owners, many contracted malignant fevers and died within a very short time. Many of the slaves imported from Africa each year died too, along with a large number of the babies, both black and white, born on the plantations.

More funerals than christenings were held in the church at Trois-Ilets, and the Tascher girls all had black dresses, black hats and black stockings kept in readiness for the sad yet inevitable seasons of mourning.

Life in Martinique was precarious, but it was lived in surroundings of rare beauty. Visitors to the island were astonished at the sparkling, translucent turquoise ocean, so clear that ships in the harbor seemed to float in pale green air, at the vivid, luxuriant plant life, the wide-leafed bananas, draping liana vines, and palm trees, the brilliant yellow and crimson and purple flowers and the expanses of yellow-green cane. Dramatic high mountains dominated the island landscape, soaring above the white beach and green fields. Mount Pelée and Mount Vauclin were volcanic peaks, from whose flanks radiated lesser mountains and hills on whose steep slopes dense rain forests grew.

Profusion, that was the word for Martinique: everything that grew there was produced in abundance, especially the sugar cane that gave the island its importance. Except in years following devastating storms, every spring a hundred thousand barrels of sugar were shipped from Fort-Royal to the ports of Europe, yielding millions of livres in revenues, and making Martinique, along with the other islands of the Lesser Antilles, France's most important colonial possession.

It was impossible to get away from the odor of sugar. It clung to buildings and clothing, it hovered over villages and towns, it even floated out over the ocean, so that incoming ships could smell their way to Martinique before they saw it. Sugar was added to milk, baked into bread, used as flavoring for vegetables, rice and meat. Beer and wine had large quantities of sugar, and the local dishes were overwhelmingly sweet.

All the children of Martinique had toothaches from eating too much sugar, and Yeyette, Catherine and Manette grew up with a dread of the tooth-extractor with his cruel pincers and tongs. To be sure, there were charms one could buy to ward off toothache, and particular saints one could pray to, and everyone knew that Good Friday water—rain caught in a flask on Good Friday—could ease the pain of swollen gums.

Belief in magic was part of everyday life on the island. The slaves constantly invoked spirits, demons, tribal gods to aid them and protect them from harm. Amulets hung around their necks, fetishes made from palm leaves and other natural objects hung from the walls of their huts. The influence of the supernatural was everywhere, and creole children, raised by slave nannies, grew up with a strongly developed sense of the otherworldly.

Many times a day the Tascher children were given messages about links between the real world and the world of the unseen. When they heard the yowls of cats fighting, they felt a chill of fear, for their nannies told them that sound was a sure sign that death was coming. If they sat down on the threshold of the refinery they were scolded, for it was bad luck to sit in a doorway; it ensured that they would take on themselves the pains and troubles of all who passed by. When a moth flew near a candle they shuddered, for they had been told many times that flying insects carried the spirits of the wicked dead.

Most of all the children were taught to fear the black sorcerers, the *quimboiseurs,* whose powers were vast and terrible (far more terrible, it was implied, than any power possessed by the Christian priests to counteract their evil).[4] The sorcerers could make rain, stop the wind from blowing, or bring on thunder and lightning. They had the gift to see into the future, to predict when ships would arrive, when sickness or misfortune would come. Some were said to have the ability to cause the heart of a man or woman to shrivel and dry up, causing a lingering, painful death. All knew the secret of creating zombies, fearsome entities half dead, half alive who walked by night and disturbed the dreams of everyone on the plantation.

A quiet terror descended with the night on Martinique. No one knew when or where the demonic visitors would appear, only that it was impossible to be safe from their visitations, for they could slip past barred doors, through shuttered windows, even through strong stone walls. The manner of the visit was often the same: the startled victim awoke, screaming, to see an ominous figure at the foot of the bed, a figure not quite human, that suddenly grew taller and taller until it loomed as high as the ceiling.

Night terrors, witchcraft, poisonous snakes and fear of the unseen: of such was a creole childhood made, and the Tascher girls were susceptible. They went to mass, they learned to say the rosary and to pray to the saints, but a stronger conditioning compelled them to believe in fate, destiny, and the power of magic.

And there was another force at work in their lives, a subtle but pervasive one, stronger than the teachings of the nuns at the convent school, stronger than the moral admonitions of Rose-Claire and the girls' two grandmothers. It was the force of bodily sensuality, instinct in grain, largely unfettered by custom and reinforced by the easy amorality of the slave culture and by the environment itself, the jasmine-scented air and rich blossoming foliage, the cool winds and warm sand, the urgent ripeness of all things that called forth primal appetites.

Amid such influences the Tascher sisters spent their childhood, in surroundings of great beauty and considerable risk, living in privilege but with uncomfortable financial constraints, their heads filled with magical lore and the scent of sugar always in their nostrils.

Meanwhile, as the girls grew into their teens, Joseph Tascher's ever-increasing debts were a continuing source of anxiety at Trois-Ilets. Three successive years of poor cane harvests were a major setback, and then in 1776 and 1777, the British navy blockaded Martinique's harbors and interrupted the export of sugar to Europe. It was not the first time Martinique had been a pawn in the perennial battle between the British and French; in the early 1760s, British troops had attacked Fort-Royal and for a time it appeared that all the islands of the Antilles would be conquered. Fortunately for the French, the attack could not be sustained and the British soldiers, their ranks thinned by disease and heatstroke, withdrew.

Now, however, the British threat was renewed and no one could say how long the blockade would last. For the Tascher family, it could well last long enough to cause complete financial ruin.

News of the family's difficulties was sent to Joseph's sister Edmée in France, and once again the question of arranging marriages for the three girls arose. Yeyette, whose baptismal name was Marie-Rose, was now a smiling, sweet-voiced girl of fourteen, avid for life, generous and good-hearted, with dark eyes and dark hair, a striking, likable girl but hardly a beauty. Visiting French officers who met her at balls in Fort-Royal were struck by her flirtatiousness, and captivated by her charm. One of them, remembering her many years later, wrote that she was "graceful, more fascinating than beautiful, already note-worthy for the suppleness and elegance of her bearing, dancing like a nymph, and amorous as a dove."⁵ Capricious, extravagant, surprisingly provocative for one so young, Yeyette was memorable—yet without a dowry, she was not an attractive prospect as a bride.

Yeyette's youngest sister Manette, though only eleven, was a pretty child who might grow into a lovely young woman, but any betrothal for her would have to wait several years. And twelve-year-old Catherine was not only too young but too ill to be considered as a possible candidate for marriage.

In fact, Catherine was dying. She was brought home from the convent, along with Yeyette, and put to bed in the refinery, where she languished in the late-summer heat. Prayers were said over her, and charms placed under her pillow while she lay burning with fever, the last of her strength ebbing. In mid-October of 1777 she died, her funeral held in the village church, her small coffin interred in the family vault.

Some two months after Catherine's death a letter arrived from Paris. François de Beauharnais (induced by Edmée) was formally requesting Catherine as a bride for his younger son Alexandre, the boy who had spent his childhood with the Taschers in Martinique. There was no need for Joseph to provide a dowry with his daughter, the marquis said, for the income Alexandre would begin receiving when he married—forty thousand livres a year at least—would be more than large enough to support a lavish household.

It was a macabre suggestion; of course the marquis had not known, when he wrote the letter, that Catherine was in her grave, for it took at least several months for news to reach France from Martinique. Still, the marquis's letter left the door open for a substitution. "The respect and attachment he [Alexandre] feels for Madame de Renaudin," the marquis wrote, "makes him eagerly desirous of becoming united with one of her nieces." One of her nieces, Joseph read eagerly. Perhaps it didn't matter too much which one.

"I wish your oldest daughter was a few years younger," the marquis added, "she would certainly have had the preference . . . but I assure you that my son, who is only seventeen and a half, believes that a girl of fifteen is too close to him in age."⁶

In fact Yeyette was only fourteen, but never mind; there was always Manette, prettier than Yeyette and at eleven, certainly not too old. Would Alexandre be willing to wait for her? Perhaps not. A letter from Edmée arrived along with that from the marquis, stressing the urgency of the situation. Young Alexandre's eagerness to marry had less to do with the "respect and admiration" he felt for his de facto stepmother than with the legal restriction under which he was chafing; he wanted his inheritance, and to obtain it, he had either to reach his majority, which was far off, or to marry. He wanted his money, therefore he wanted a wife.

And there was another reason for haste, one understood in the family but spoken about only in whispers. The marquis was aging, his health failing. Although his finances were sound, his moderate income was dropping, and when he died, all that he had would go to his sons. Edmée might well find herself in want. Far better to ensure, through a marriage connection between the two households, that Alexandre's inheritance would benefit all the Taschers, Edmée included, before this calamity happened.

It was a proposition worthy of Edmée's talent for advantageous matchmaking. If Alexandre married Manette, she would have a rich husband, Alexandre would have his forty thousand livres a year, Edmée would not have to worry about what would happen to her when the marquis died, and Joseph would be able to call on Alexandre to shore up his finances. What was more, there would be no troublesome adjustment to make, no in-laws to deal with, for Alexandre and Manette were not unlike cousins, bound by their common ties to Edmée; although she had never met Manette, who had been born after Edmée left Martinique, still they were aunt and niece, and Alexandre regarded Edmée almost as his mother, since she was the only mother he had ever known.

It only remained to obtain the marquis's agreement to substituting Manette for Catherine.

Yet Joseph hesitated. What if Alexandre objected to Manette, either because of her extreme youth or for some other reason? To be sure, she was pretty, she combined "health and gaiety of character with a figure that will soon be interesting."[7] Yet something might go wrong, and then the windfall of Alexandre's fortune would be lost to all the Taschers. Joseph reconsidered, then wrote to the marquis offering to send both his remaining daughters to France, so that whichever one seemed most suitable could be married to Alexandre.

He made the assumption that Manette would be the one chosen, and began preparing her to make the long sea journey to France, along with Yeyette, who was delighted at the prospect, having wanted to go for years. But before they could leave, Joseph had to spend some time on his other estate on St. Lucia, and in his absence, everything went wrong.

Rose-Claire, having lost her second daughter Catherine only a few months earlier, was rebelling against the thought of sending Manette away. She was firmly supported in this by Grandmother de Sannois. And Manette who, unlike her older sister, had never felt any curiosity about visiting France, began to plead tearfully not to be sent away from her family. So severe was her distress that she caught a fever and languished in bed for three months.

Joseph returned from St. Lucia to find his household in turmoil.[8] Manette was weak and slow to recover, Yeyette was upset by all the emotional disturbance around her, there were more letters from France urging haste. ("Come to Paris," the marquis wrote. "Bring one daughter or both. Whichever you like will be agreeable to us. We must have one of your daughters!"[9] Clearly, Joseph had to make an immediate decision. If he did not act quickly, the golden opportunity to salvage the entire family's future would be lost. His wife and mother-in-law were adamant: Manette must not go. Very well then, it would have to be Yeyette.

Joseph wrote once again to the marquis, explaining that because of Manette's illness, he would prefer to send Yeyette, who was about to turn fifteen. (Surely a three-year gap between bride and groom was a wide enough difference in age, he implied.) Besides, Yeyette was beside herself with eagerness, had an excellent character and an agreeable figure. "She is very advanced for her age," he added—perhaps unwisely, for it was youth and obedience, not precocity, that Alexandre wanted in a wife.

"She is well formed for her age, and sufficiently matured in the last six months to pass for eighteen," Joseph went on. She was sweet-natured, played the guitar a little—she had had special lessons at the convent—sang, and had a gift for music.[10] As for her looks, she had "very good skin, good eyes, and good arms." Joseph knew that the marquis, Edmée and Alexandre would all be reading carefully between the lines, and would realize that in effect he was telling them that his daughter was not beautiful, but that her good inner qualities (he hoped) would compensate for whatever was outwardly lacking.

"It is a pity," Joseph added, "that she has not the advantage of an education in France." Here too he was giving an unwritten message: Alexandre must not expect Yeyette to be sophisticated, to project the cold, proud polish of the graduate of a Parisian finishing school. She was naive, fresh, uncorrupted, uninformed about the ways of the world. Joseph, who had himself spent three years at the French court as a page, knew how awkwardly, painfully provincial a young girl from the country or the colonies would seem to a wellborn young Parisian gentleman like Alexandre—as well as how cruel the sophisticates of the capital could be to a newcomer.

But surely Alexandre knew what his future wife would be like, having been raised in Martinique himself. He would not be expecting urbanity and refinement in his bride-to-be, but authenticity, innocence, candor and a trusting nature. All would be well.

Arrangements were made, agreements finalized. All that remained was for Joseph to book passage on a merchant ship bound for France.

As for what Yeyette thought, imagined, hoped for, dreamed of, for that we must read between the lines ourselves. Joseph's letters contain almost nothing about her—not that she wept at the thought of leaving home, or that Rose-Claire wanted to keep her in Martinique (a significant omission), or that she was busy readying herself for the coming journey. Only that she wanted badly to go to France, and to see her aunt Edmée.

It was not as if she would be marrying a stranger. She remembered Alexandre as a boy, much bigger and older than she was, fair and blue-eyed, a boy much admired for his good looks. Aunt Edmée wrote that he had grown into a good-looking young man, witty and intelligent, with a true heart and a fine character. "He is beloved by all who surround him," she assured the family in one of her letters.

Knowing that he was a lieutenant in the Sarre regiment, Yeyette may have thought Alexandre would be like the charming, ebullient young officers she danced and flirted with in Fort-Royal, and that life in Paris would be an unending round of balls and parties, more lavish and more exciting than any she had ever attended. In her imagination she may have seen herself, dressed in a gown far finer than any she had ever worn, with jewels at her throat and in her hair, dancing with her handsome, adoring husband.

At fifteen, she was too young to imagine much more than this. She knew, of course, what marriage entailed—lovemaking, children, a household, servants, responsibilities. But the giddy, flirtatious girl who enjoyed herself so much at balls, who danced like a nymph and was as amorous as a dove, could not have spent much time daydreaming about the more taxing side of marriage. Instead she no doubt thought of the dazzling world she would be entering, of growing up quickly and being adorned, like the finest ladies she had glimpsed in Fort-Royal, in satin gowns and diamonds. Perhaps she dreamed of the wedding trousseau Aunt Edmée had promised to provide, of the ceremony itself, of the tender way Alexandre would look at her when they repeated their vows.

In her mind's eye she must already have been saying farewell to sleepy Martinique, and embarking on the journey that awaited her, the first long journey she had ever made, toward a far country and an unknown fate.

3

A Troubled Passage

Abruptly, in the fall of 1778, Yeyette's dreams were interrupted by war.

The British blockade had turned into a much more serious threat, for France had come to the aid of the rebellious American colonies and that made all French colonies fair game to be seized by the British as prizes of war.

Martinique was at risk, Fort-Royal was full of naval vessels and to attempt a journey to France would have been dangerous folly.

So Yeyette's wedding voyage was postponed, and Joseph Tascher, who despite his frail health had responsibilities as a captain in a dragoon regiment of militia, had to join his men to meet the advancing British threat. In December British troops succeeded in overrunning St. Lucia, and confiscating all French properties on the island. Dreading the capture of Martinique, the militias assembled there in haste, and prepared to wait out the coming siege.

For a time it looked as though Yeyette's future husband would join Joseph Tascher there. Hundreds of the men in Alexandre de Beauharnais's regiment had been shipped to the Caribbean, and he knew that he might well be sent there himself. The knowledge troubled him, because although he was no coward—indeed he looked forward to someday gaining glory in war, through his skillful command of troops—he was reluctant to leave Brest, where he was stationed. He had come to feel very attached to the rather bleak, windswept coast of Brittany, and more particularly to an estate near the town. For the first true love of his life lived there, and she had recently told him that she was expecting their child.

He was not yet nineteen in December of 1778, but already Alexandre was a man—and a man of the world. Handsome, articulate, well aware of his personal attractions and boldly confident in advancing himself, he had shown an admirable ability to get on. Educated with his older brother François at the prestigious Collège du Plessis in Paris, he went on to further study at Heidelberg, where he was exposed to genuine learning (as opposed to mere pedantry or persiflage, always the bane of the half-educated) and where his intellectual tastes began to be shaped.

To his credit, Alexandre had a quick if shallow mind, and instincts which, if not entirely noble, at least led him in humane, forward-looking directions—as long as his own personal advantage and comfort did not have to be sacrificed. But because he was overwhelmingly narcissistic and vain, he tended to view ideas in the same way he looked on military uniforms and insignias—as personal adornments; true discernment was lacking.

The tutor provided for Alexandre and his brother, a conscientious but prosaic schoolmaster named Patricol, did little to rein in Alexandre's innate tendencies (as Yeyette would later say of him, Alexandre had "a taste for liberty and an inflexible will"), but when by chance Patricol was offered a position in the household of the Duc de la Rochefoucauld, wider horizons beckoned.

No more cosmopolitan finishing school could be imagined than the duke's vast, richly appointed château of La Roche-Guyon, where, amid a lush natural setting of tall trees, spreading lawns, and carefully manicured wilderness, highminded aristocrats and distinguished guests discussed lofty concepts and envisioned a better world.

Studying with Patricol while living on the margins of this remarkable establishment, young Alexandre absorbed the influences of the Enlightenment, becoming enamored of the American ideals of liberty and democracy—ideas unthinkably radical in the stratified society of France, where the church, the monarchy and the aristocracy held nearly all the wealth and virtually all the political power. He learned that Americans had begun to speak about the rights of man, to have a vision of human betterment in a world where privilege was abated and institutional oppressions abandoned. He began to espouse these ideas as his own, partly because they were appealing and because the duke and his companions were models of thoughtful, tolerant humanitarianism and partly, perhaps, because his older brother François did not espouse them, and Alexandre was eager to differentiate himself from François.

The château of La Roche-Guyon was not only a school of enlightened ideas, it was a model of worldly manners where amorous liaisons were looked on as one of life's pleasures, like fine wine or good conversation; among truly cosmopolitan people, Alexandre observed, a certain moral fluidity prevailed, and gallantry was not only tolerated but subtly encouraged.

Certainly gallantry was rampant among Alexandre's brother officers in the military. From the age of fifteen he was attached to the Sarre regiment, whose colonel was the Duc de la Rochefoucauld, and earned rapid promotion thanks to the duke's patronage. Six months out of every year he spent with his regiment, though his duties were light, and left him plenty of time to pursue a variety of women, from chambermaids to titled ladies.

By the time the Marquis de Beauharnais wrote to Joseph Tascher asking for one of his daughters as a bride for Alexandre, the young officer was well launched on a career of romantic adventure. The fact that he was successful with women, most of whom were considerably older than himself, flattered his self-esteem, according to his friend the Marquis de Bouillé, to whom Alexandre displayed his collection of love-trophies. He was "completely preoccupied" with flirtation and sexual possession; he kept well-organized lists of the women he had slept with, noting down the names and titles (if any) of each one together with her distinctive attributes. Alexandre was nothing if not analytical.

That Alexandre had a calculating, manipulative streak in his nature was apparent to everyone around him. Patricol took sad note of another prominent quality: his pupil's carefully nurtured detachment and dissimulation. "What astonishes me most," the tutor wrote when Alexandre was sixteen, "and greatly displeases me in the young man is the extreme care which he takes to hide, the ease with which he disguises, the sentiments of his heart."[1] To be sure, there was more to him than this; his dispassionate manner and obsessive sexual greed masked a strong-willed dynamism, a profound desire to distinguish himself and a notable quickness of mind. His erotic adventurism apart (and it was typical, in kind if not in degree, of his age and class) Alexandre was promising, and his merits were evident.

Now, however, as he awaited the birth of his child, the eighteen-year-old Alexandre was aware that he had entered deeper emotional waters. He had met Laure de Girardin, the twenty-nine-year-old wife of another naval officer, at her country house where she was accustomed to entertaining men from the Brest garrison. Like Alexandre, she had been born in Martinique, and was in fact related to the Tascher family, but the passion she inspired in Alexandre had nothing to do with family ties.

Alexandre knew from the start that the feelings he had for Laure were unique. In a letter to Edmée, to whom he often confided details of his amorous liaisons, he wrote of the "violent passion" she aroused in him, of the tender affection she felt for him and of his surprise and delight at having discovered true love. Laure's husband was away for several weeks, and in that blissful interval the lovers indulged their passion. By the fall of 1778 Laure was pregnant, and Alexandre was certain the child was his. He also knew that he might soon have to leave France in order to take part in the hostilities with England, and the thought pained him. "It is with the deepest despair that I see the moment approaching when I must part from her for a long time," he wrote to Edmée. But at least he would be leaving something of himself behind with Laure. The child she carried would be a lasting memorial to his true love.

"The word Juliette may intrigue you," Alexandre told Edmée. "It is the name we have chosen for the one who will be very dear to us."[2]

Alexandre saw nothing odd or awkward in the fact that, having discovered true love with one woman, he was about to marry another. His marriage would be one of convenience alone; that was understood. He was marrying for three reasons—because his father was insisting on it, because he was impatient to receive his inheritance, and because, given his age and rank, it was appropriate that he acquire a wife. It was what young men with aspirations to distinction did—

they married, usually for money. No one expected infatuation between husband and wife, merely civility and, in the wife, complaisance and well-bred subordination.

"Juliette" was born in the summer of 1779, and she turned out to be a boy, who was given the name Alexandre. How often the infant's father visited him, what he thought of him, whether his birth brought Alexandre and Laure closer is unknown. However, before little Alexandre was more than a few months old, Yeyette and her father were aboard the small store-ship *Ile de France*, making their way slowly across the Atlantic, bound for Brest.

The journey, in that storm-season of 1779, was long and particularly arduous, taxing to both body and spirit. Yeyette, her father, her aunt Rosette (Joseph and Edmée's unmarried sister) and Yeyette's mulatto maid Euphémie were confined for three months in a tiny cabin, barely large enough to contain their trunks and narrow, uncomfortable bunk beds. The ceiling was so low they could barely stand upright, while the narrow width of the cabin made wearing the wide petticoats then fashionable impossible. The extreme pitch and roll of the small ship must have made them all ill, with Joseph suffering the most; as the weeks passed he declined alarmingly.

But then, no one was really well, especially after they had been at sea for several weeks and all the fresh fruits and vegetables were gone and there was little but salt meat and ships's biscuits to eat and wine and tea to drink. The stored water, kept in large barrels on deck, was all but undrinkable; green algae coated the insides of the barrels and the foul liquid drawn from them by the bucketful was rank and full of bugs and worms.

Green slime appeared on the walls of the cabins as well, its growth encouraged by the sea-damp that kept all the passengers' clothes limp and wilted and that worked its way into trunks and cupboards. At night, the passengers slept under cold, wet bedclothes, breathing stale air in the confining cabin, the constant rolling of the ship making sleep difficult.

Added to the daily misery of the journey was everpresent fear— fear that the winds would rise and the waves would crash over the ship and sink her, fear of catching a fever, above all fear of capture, either by pirates or by a British gunship.[3] The *Ile de France* was part of a convoy, guarded by a French frigate, the *Pomona*. But convoys were often attacked, and the *Ile de France*, with its store of provisions and military equipment, was a particularly valuable prize.

The long weeks dragged by, the *Ile de France* drawn off course at times, her progress slowed by bad weather. Under ideal conditions the travelers should have made landfall early in September, but it was not until October 12 that, weary and spent, they went ashore at Brest and took refuge in the nearest inn.

There was no one to greet them. Joseph had not had time, before leaving Martinique, to send a letter to the Marquis de Beauharnais or to Edmée informing them that he was making definite arrangements for the journey. Now, weak and ill, he sent a letter to Paris, but two weeks passed before Edmée and Alexandre arrived to greet the visitors. For Yeyette, worried about her father and impatient to see her future husband, the two weeks must have been interminable.

At last a cabriolet drew up to the inn, and out stepped the blonde, still attractive Edmée and the tall, fair Alexandre in his dapper white uniform, his black tricorn hat under his arm, his sword at his side.

Yeyette's reaction to Alexandre has not been preserved, but presumably she reacted as many other women did to his striking presence—with a quickening heartbeat and a revealing smile of inward pleasure. He loomed over her, well mannered, well spoken, taking her hand with a gentlemanly bow and brushing his full lips against it. Most likely his blue eyes betrayed little emotion, only a grave correctness, and a maturity far beyond her own.

At first sight Alexandre was surprised and displeased with Yeyette. He remembered her well, of course, and recognized her at once. But the girl he had known had not grown into the pretty woman he had hoped to see. Clearly she had been overpraised by her relatives.

To be sure, Alexandre was hardly an unbiassed observer, and he was so obsessed with the lovely Laure de Girardin that any other woman might have looked unattractive to him. But Yeyette, with her slightly exophthalmic eyes, her somewhat shapeless nose, too large for beauty, and her thin, bow-shaped lips, puckered in a semi-smile but held tightly shut to conceal her unsightly teeth, seemed plain, quite ordinary in her figure, and entirely lacking in style.

Her clothes and bearing marked her at once as a provincial, and this alone the fastidious Alexandre found hard to overcome. But there was another quality about Yeyette, an almost feral avidity and appetitiveness, that was so arresting it prevented him from putting her in the same category as Laure or the other wellborn women he knew. It was as if she was continually perched on the edge of something, and impatient to dive in. She quivered with eagerness, setting up a constant tension in herself and everyone around her.

She had sweetness, that he could see at once, and she spoke with a soft, soothing voice. But she was too alert, too galvanic, too intense to be pleasing as a woman; when added to her evident mediocre intelligence and rudimentary education, Alexandre found this eager alertness almost offensive. He must have known, even in the first moments they spent together, that intimacy with Rose, or any sort of comfortable familiarity with her, would require a great, perhaps an impossible, effort on his part.

Of course Alexandre was holding Yeyette to a high standard, and he was not in the best of moods; for the past several months he had been ill, and had spent a good deal of time away from his garrison, recuperating at a country château.

Alexandre swallowed his deep misgivings and turned his attention to immediate concerns. The wedding would not take place for some weeks yet, and he felt confident that his father would not force him to marry anyone with whom he was genuinely incompatible. "Surely it is not your intention to have me marry this young lady if she and I should have a mutual repugnance for each other," Alexandre had written to his father.[4] Even though it would be a marriage of convenience, there ought to be a reasonable degree of amiability on both sides, to make the arrangement a pleasant one. If such amiability did not develop, then Alexandre would appeal to his father to release him from what promised to be an unsatisfactory alliance.

What was most apparent to Alexandre was that Yeyette and her entourage were woefully ill-equipped. Joseph was weak and ill, and needed medicine, the women needed warm clothes and boots and a variety of other things. Alexandre took charge.

"I have been dashing about ever since I got up," he wrote to his father soon after meeting the wedding party. "The number of things our new arrivals need and the meager resources of this gloomy town we hope to leave soon have given me a lot of trouble."[5] Clearly his focus had not been on his bride-to-be, but on the forlorn state of the Taschers and on his own inconvenience and expense. Because of

Joseph's condition there could be no question of taking the public coach to Paris; consequently a vehicle had to be bought, a driver found and horses rented for the journey. The doctor who examined Joseph strongly advised that he ought not to make the trip to Paris all at once, but slowly, over a number of days, so that he could rest as much as possible.

In his letter to his father Alexandre did add a brief positive sentence about Yeyette. "I think I can tell you that her integrity and good nature will exceed anything you have been told." She might not be pretty, she might repel him, but she was solid, trustworthy and pleasantly candid, and these qualities he appreciated.

It took nearly a week for Alexandre to outfit the visitors, but finally, on November 2, all was in readiness and they started out. Traveling only a few hours each day, they had a good deal of time to become acquainted with one another. Alexandre warmed to Yeyette slightly, and wrote to his father of the pleasure of being with her. The choice of words was almost certainly disingenuous; Alexandre was saying what he thought his father wanted to hear. But Edmée too wrote positively to the marquis. Yeyette, she said, "has all the feelings that you could wish her to have toward your son, and I have observed with the greatest satisfaction that she suits him. . . . He is busy, yes, very busy, with your daughter-in-law."[6]

These were faintly hopeful signs. But even as Edmée watched the young couple talking together, she must have been thinking of Laure, and of the baby, knowing that Alexandre's affections were all with them, and knowing that in time her niece would learn that her husband was deeply attached to another woman.

On a brisk, raw day in mid-November Yeyette had her first glimpse of Paris. Cold, damp and dirty as the city was, crowded and noisy, the boulevards full of carriages and the dim, narrow alleyways full of the stench of open sewers and rotting garbage, still it must have thrilled her to see at long last the place of her dreams. She had heard about its wonders from her father, now she saw for herself the grand mansions and old stone churches, their towers rising into the leaden sky, the gilded carriages, footmen in livery and soldiers in every sort of uniform, workmen and market-women and beggars without number.

The sheer size of the city must have been overwhelming to Yeyette, who had never seen any town larger than the modest settlement of Fort-Royal and the small garrison town of Brest. Slowed by the traffic and by the mire in the streets, the cabriolet rolled through district after district, finally entering a neighborhood of run-down large houses that had clearly seen better days. A strong, unfamiliar odor permeated the area—it was the reek of the tanneries nearby, where the carcasses of horses and cows were hoisted into rendering vats and their hides treated with chemicals.

The carriage turned into the rue Thévenot and stopped before a rather undistinguished two-story house faced with stone. They had arrived.

Over the next several weeks, as she settled into the house where she and Alexandre would live along with the Marquis de Beauharnais and her aunt Edmée, Yeyette came to realize that the marquis, like his rented house, had come down in the world and was in decline. Aged and ailing, he presided over a small staff of servants, but his house was cold and comfortless and had none of the opulence Yeyette had seen in the homes of the rich creoles in Martinique. The grand staircases needed repair, the large rooms were sparsely furnished and the entire establishment had a temporary air about it—perhaps because everything was expected to change once Alexandre's income rose.

For the next three weeks Yeyette and Edmée occupied themselves ordering Yeyette's trousseau, attending fittings, receiving visits from hairdressers and wigmakers. Edmée paid for everything—and Yeyette needed a great many things, not only gowns and petticoats but corsets and chemises, stockings and slippers and high-heeled shoes, muffs and cloaks and shawls. When the final bills were presented, the total rose to some twenty thousand livres.[7]

Yeyette had known all her life that Paris was the center of fashion. The dressmakers on Martinique had copied the Paris modes as best they could, but the wealthiest of the creoles had sent away to Paris for their gowns. Yeyette knew that ever since the young King Louis XVI came to the throne five years earlier, and his beautiful wife Marie Antoinette became queen, styles had changed. The queen set the fashion: when she developed a passion for feathers, all the well-dressed women of Paris put feathers in their hair; when she wore Turkish bonnets, Turkish bonnets were seen in abundance in all the best drawing-rooms. And when the queen decided to pile her hair high on her head, adding cushions and lengths of false hair to make elaborate foot-high structures ornamented with flowers, fruits and diamonds, all the women of her court did the same—until the queen tired of the fad and returned to wearing her own ash-blonde hair, elaborately curled and powdered and pouffed around her small face.

In the winter of 1779, when Edmée and Yeyette were ordering Yeyette's trousseau, women were wearing the ankle-length gown called a polonaise in the afternoons and formal long gowns in the evenings, with thick quilted petticoats underneath them for warmth. Most of the cost of a trousseau came from the expensive hand-woven, hand-painted fabrics of which the gowns were made, China silks and silk taffetas, embroidered brocades with floral sprays painted on them, shimmering iridescent silks with silver metallic stripes, all in the pale pinks, pale blues, ivories and creams then in style.

Because Edmée's funds were restricted and Yeyette's wedding was to be a quiet affair, most likely her trousseau was limited in size and relatively modest in style; even so, it must have seemed very splendid indeed to the poorly dressed newcomer from Martinique. The expert dressmakers with their entourages of seamstresses, the drapers with their gleaming lengths of silk and taffeta, the corsetiers and shoemakers, the suppliers of ribbon and silk rosettes and lace, all calling her "Madame la Vicomtesse"—for that would be her title once she was married—must have made the eager Yeyette feel exalted and important, and she had not been in France long before it was clear to her that she herself, as Alexandre's bride, was the key personage in the household. Without her there would be no wedding, and without a wedding there would be no inheritance.

Whether or not Yeyette grasped the full import of this fact is unknown, though it may safely be presumed that Edmée, who was from first to last the architect of the marriage, did her best to make it clear to her niece how vital it was that she play her part well. She must show herself capable of being Alexandre's agreeable, pleasant wife, of fitting in to her father-in-law's household with no friction, of holding her husband in appropriate wifely awe, and of taking her place in Paris society—not high society, not court society, but in the echelon of respectable minor nobility where the Beauharnais family found itself.

Yeyette had much to learn if she was to mold herself into the partner Alexandre deserved. She had, in effect, to remake herself, to put aside the slow-paced, natural, earthy, sensually avid persona she had brought from Martinique and become a cool, self-possessed, chic Parisienne who reined in her instincts and impulses as firmly as the whalebone in her corsets reined in the curves of her plump young body. She had to learn to match her rhythms and manners to those of her talkative, energetic husband-to-be. From now on, he would be the ruling influence in her life, his expectations her commands, his tastes her governing preferences. No standards but his would have any force for her, and if anyone, even a near relative, clashed with her husband over anything, she would be expected to take her husband's side.

Advised and cautioned, mindful of all that was being asked of her, as attentive as she could be to her role, elegantly gowned and coiffed, sixteen-year-old Yeyette Tascher prepared to take her wedding vows, well aware that the bond she was about to forge with Alexandre de Beauharnais would be for life, for there was no divorce in France and she would be Viscountess de Beauharnais forever.

4

A Cankered Bond

hile Yeyette's trousseau was being made, lawyers were drawing up the marriage contract that would govern the property agreement between Alexandre de Beauharnais and (to give her her legal name) Marie-Josèphe-Rose Tascher de la Pagerie.

The banns were read on December 5, and five days later, on December 10, family members and other witnesses gathered in the house on the rue Thévenot to observe the signing of the contract.

Alexandre's last opportunity to back out of the engagement had come and gone. Whether he had decided on his own to grit his teeth and go through with the marriage, or whether he had had a long talk with Edmée about his adverse reaction to Yeyette and she had persuaded him to marry her in spite of it, or whether, more likely, the Marquis de Beauharnais had asserted his parental authority with ultimate force and insisted that Alexandre make the best of things and face up to life with a less than perfect bride, will never be known. But by persuasion or force, Alexandre was present, composed and dutiful, at the signing ceremony, prepared to undertake his responsibilities and receive his rewards as a husband.

It was a solemn occasion, as important as the wedding ceremony and almost as consequential. The bride, called Rose by her new relatives, was in theory bringing her husband a substantial dowry, which the contract spelled out in detail. Her father pledged to give her a large sum of money at some point in the future, her aunt Edmée added another large sum (payable, it was understood, on Edmée's death), and Rose herself brought fifteen thousand livres. In actuality, Rose came to her marriage virtually penniless, for no one expected Joseph to pay her any money in the future, Edmée's pledge was shadowy at best, and Rose's fifteen thousand livres was not a sum of cash but an estimate of value of furniture and other goods belonging to her which she left behind in Martinique.

Alexandre, for his part, was well endowed with incomes from his late mother's and grandmother's estates, lands in Santo Domingo worth eight hundred thousand livres and estates in France yielding another three thousand annually in rents.[1]

As a wedding present Edmée gave Alexandre and his bride the furnished house she owned in the village of Noisy-le-Grand east of Paris. This was, no doubt, a quid pro quo, part of the bargain she had struck as a matchmaker. If Alexandre married her niece, she would give him a house of his own, a pied-à-terre, where his children could be raised and where she, Edmée, could live rent-free after the marquis died.

In the presence of the notary, Alexandre and Rose signed the document, as the marquis and Joseph, Edmée and a distant relative of the Taschers, Louis-Samuel Tascher, a cleric who had the position of almoner in the household of the Duc de Penthièvre, looked on. Aunt Rosette was not present, but two members of Edmée's social circle were, two unmarried sisters named Cecconi. There were several Beauharnais relatives: Alexandre's older brother François, who was now captain of a dragoon regiment, the marquis's brother Claude, another military man, and his son, Alexandre's cousin Claude, also a lawyer, Michel Bégon.

Three days later the same group gathered once again in the church in Noisy-le-Grand for the modest wedding ceremony. Rose's two aunts stood with her, and Alexandre had as his groomsman a friend, a naval officer. Joseph Tascher was too ill to be present, so the Abbé Tascher took his place and handed Rose over to her husband.

No record survives to tell us how Rose looked on her wedding day, whether she was joyful or subdued, whether the atmosphere in the little church at Noisy was festive or solemn. Alexandre had given

Rose some heavy jeweled earrings in a branching design, some brace-lets and a diamond watch on a chain, and perhaps she had some keepsakes from her Tascher or Sannois grandmothers, or from her mother. No doubt Edmée did her best to be both mother and father to Rose, helping her to get ready for the ceremony, offering advice, answering questions.

If Rose had any questions about lovemaking, no doubt Edmée answered these too, but as to what passed between husband and wife on the wedding night, only they knew, and neither of them wrote about it afterward. Presumably Alexandre had no reason to doubt his wife's sexual innocence, or, if he did doubt it, he made no complaint. Most likely he was thankful when the distasteful task of ridding his bride of her virginity was past, and he could look forward to the keener pleasures of Laure de Girardin's erotic companionship.

So Marie-Josèphe-Rose, Viscountess de Beauharnais, embarked on her married life, with her father and Aunt Rosette staying on in the marquis's house and the newly affluent Alexandre paying the bills for everyone. Winter closed in, the season of balls and parties, but al-though Alexandre went out in the evening and enjoyed himself to the full, he did not take his bride with him. She was too young, too raw; she lacked suavity and finesse. If something pleased her—as her new jewelry did—she was too quick to say so, and display it with girlish pride. If something bored her, she did not hide her boredom, as a more socially adept young woman would, behind a mask of well-bred indifference. She did not know how to conduct herself, how to speak with assurance and mingle deftly. She moved well, and she was likable, but not teachable. She knew no one, was ignorant of everyone and everything, and was far too forthright in making her ignorance known.

Quickly becoming impatient with Rose's social shortcomings, Al-exandre went his own way, enjoying his newfound wealth, spending lavishly and running up debts. He had new contacts to make, new worlds to conquer; he could not be encumbered with a gauche young wife from the provinces.

And, as always, he sought pleasure. He drank, he caroused with fellow officers, he stayed out half the night and came home in a stupor, ready to collapse.[2] Then he slept until mid-afternoon, whereupon he roused himself and prepared to go out once again.

Meanwhile Rose was left on her own, a sixteen-year-old girl-wife, bursting with a hunger for all the good things Paris had to offer, stuck in a house full of middle-aged and elderly people, conforming to the rules of her father-in-law's household and prevented from enjoying, as her husband so flagrantly did, the delights of the capital. She became accustomed to adopting the routines of a leisured, privileged woman, rising late, sipping coffee, remaining in her boudoir, *en négligée*, until noon, then attending to her complex and time-consuming toilette for several hours. In mid-afternoon, with her face rouged and her hair powdered, teased, and twisted into a complicated design, dressed in one of her striped silk gowns, she went out, usually with Edmée, for an hour's drive. In the evening, after supper, she played cards or engaged in frustratingly tedious conversation with her family, waiting for bedtime to arrive.

And all the time she watched Alexandre, the full force of her intense vigilance trained on him, noted when he went out, when he stumbled in, how late he slept. He spoke to her less and less, and when he did, it was to criticize her and correct her.

After a few months of married life Alexandre left the house on the rue Thévenot to join his regiment—and Laure de Girardin—in Brittany, stopping on the way for a lengthy stay at the Duc de la Rochefoucauld's estate.

He was in a quandary, filled with annoyance and mortification. For he had learned, probably shortly after his marriage, that Laure had become a widow; had he waited a few months longer to take the fateful step of marrying, he might have been able to persuade Laure instead of Rose to become his bride.[5]

To be sure, she might not have agreed. Still, the thought of his extreme misfortune, that with Laure within his grasp he had allowed himself to be yoked for life to an ill-conditioned, immature girl he found personally repugnant, filled him with chagrin. Self-centered and self-dramatizing as he was, Alexandre felt cheated by fate—hence his eagerness to drown his sorrows and his reluctance to keep company with Rose.

When his six months' obligation to his regiment was over, Alexandre did not return to his wife and family, but found ways of avoiding them. The situation was unsatisfactory for everyone, Rose most of all. Joseph and Rosette were still living in the marquis's house, delaying their return to Martinique, most likely, in the hope of being present at the birth of Rose's first child—of which there was as yet no sign. Edmée was forced to acknowledge that the match she had made had soured. Rose was discontented and querulous. Why, she demanded to know, was Alexandre spending so much time with others and so little with her?

Finally Edmée acted. She had a talk with Patricol, who knew Alexandre as well or better than any of his relatives did, and asked him to confront Alexandre with his neglect of his wife and discover the cause.

What Alexandre told Patricol—or, at any rate, what Patricol chose to pass along to Edmée, which may well have been an elaborate fiction—was that Rose was simply too far below him in intelligence and education to make living with her tolerable. Alexandre was not only verbal, but unusually articulate; Rose could only chatter vapidly, and her chatter had dried up or turned to reproaches under Alexandre's disdainful glare.

Rose had nothing to say to him, Alexandre told his old tutor—or at least, nothing he found worth listening to. So he left. At first, he admitted, he had thought that he could learn to live with her by becoming her teacher, filling in the startlingly wide gaps in her education, coaching her in the ways of the world, replacing her provincial assumptions with broader views and more refined manners. But he had not found her to be cooperative, indeed, she had not been willing to put herself in his hands to the extent necessary to remake her mind and behavior. She had rejected his efforts to improve her. So he simply gave up.

But there was more. Rose had not turned out to be either obedient or amiable. She made demands. She would not leave him alone. She insisted that he spend all his time with her, and when he was away from her, she wanted to know what he said and did, even what he told others in his letters. Jealous and suspicious, she hounded him unbearably.

Rose and Alexandre were mismatched; that was clear. Alexandre was a sensualist and a sophisticated freethinker in need of reassurance and approbation. Volatile and precipitate, he could find nothing in Rose to gratify his desires or his intellectual tastes, and his attitude toward her wavered between impatient condescension and indignant disdain. Though not devoid of dutiful, even noble instincts he was irascible and easily exasperated; with Rose he was constantly either thwarted or revulsed, and he felt only increasing alienation.

Rose, on the other hand, was a sweet, well-meaning girl, solid, earthy and relentlessly shallow, constantly driven to gratify her own sharp appetites and with a disconcertingly strong will and well-developed instincts for self protection. She was put off by Alexandre's efforts to change her, and by his verbose intellectuality, and his dissipated habits both frightened and angered her. Given their temperaments and expectations, clashes were inevitable.

The second year of the marriage brought a respite of sorts. Patricol drew up a plan of study for Rose, and enlisted the help of all the relatives in tutoring her. Her drawling provincial speech would be improved, he suggested, if she learned to recite speeches from the classic plays of Racine and Corneille. Her father could instruct her in history. Edmée could coach her in how to conduct herself at social gatherings, even the marquis could take a hand.

Patricol urged Edmée to remember that Alexandre had a passionate heart and (this was questionable) genuinely wanted to find a modus vivendi with Rose. But for this to happen, Rose would have to become an appropriate companion for him, a companion for life, with the capacity to share his interests on all levels.

There was one family member unusually well equipped to improve Rose as a wife for Alexandre. Fanny de Beauharnais, wife of the Marquis de Beauharnais's brother Claude, was a productive writer of novels and verse, who entertained other writers and poets at her salon in the Rue de Montmartre. Separated years earlier from her husband, she devoted herself to her art and to her lovers, and she welcomed the seventeen-year-old Rose into her circle. Whether or not Rose's appreciation of literature improved (which is doubtful, as neither Fanny nor her writer friends were very distinguished), she did learn from Fanny, who was an example of a woman on her own, without encumbering family ties, indulging her creativity and acquiring celebrity in the process. It cannot have escaped Rose's notice as significant that both of the contented, reasonably happy women she knew in Paris, Edmée and Fanny, were separated from their husbands and living life on their own terms.

While Rose was attempting, albeit without enthusiasm, to furnish her mind she was also struggling through her first pregnancy. By the spring of 1781 she was able to send word to her mother and sister in Martinique that her baby was expected in late summer, and no doubt the relatives on both sides of the family felt relieved. A child would provide stability and ballast to the shaky marriage, motherhood might settle Rose down and give her something to occupy herself with during Alexandre's prolonged absences.

Alexandre was not at Rose's side when she went into labor, and so missed the birth of his son on September 3. He was present at the baptism, however, and gave the baby the names Eugène-Rose.

Unfortunately, the birth of little Eugene did not have the calming effect everyone had hoped for. Quarrels erupted, and the rift between the spouses widened, with Alexandre complaining that Rose was "brusque and dictatorial" with him and Rose feeling ignored and neglected. Once again Edmée stepped in, and suggested that Alexandre remove himself from the household for a while and make a tour of Italy, as many wellborn young men did. It would give Rose time to adjust to motherhood while allowing Alexandre a chance to further his education in art.

By now there was no disguising the fact that the marriage between Alexandre and Rose was a disaster. The vague efforts to fill in the defects in Rose's faulty education had done nothing to increase the couple's compatibility, and it was hard to see what other remedy could be applied. As he grew older Alexandre became more high-strung and quick-tempered, while Rose, more self-assured at eighteen than she had been as a bride of sixteen, was maturing but hardly mellowing. Before Eugene was two months old Alexandre had left for Italy, and Rose, deeply offended and hurt, was in no hurry for his return.

Another winter season passed, another spring came and went. Rose turned nineteen, little Eugene thrived and crowed, Joseph and Aunt Rosette returned to Martinique and, in a belated response to Alexandre's increased income, the marquis and his household moved to a pleasanter neighborhood, to a house near the church of Saint-Philippe du Roule on the rue Neuve-Saint-Charles, away from the stink of the tanneries and closer to the fashionable world. Rose attended Fanny's soirées, but did not appreciably widen her acquaintance beyond the people she met there. Still, Paris seems to have agreed with her. She could have returned with Joseph and Rosette to Martinique, but she chose to stay, waiting for Alexandre's long-delayed homecoming from Italy. Possibly she still hoped for a reconciliation, or perhaps her spirits were too low to permit her to do anything other than wait for fate to take a hand and deliver her from the worsening situation.

Precisely when, and under what circumstances, Rose learned of Alexandre's involvement with Laure de Girardin is unknown, but by the third year of her marriage she must have been informed about Laure—and about the little boy she and Alexandre had together. Rose was shrewd enough to realize that Alexandre had married her for financial and familial reasons, and not for herself. Whatever romantic illusions she may have had on first arriving in France had all but disappeared—as she told her Aunt Rosette in a letter, she had "cured herself" of her feelings for Alexandre. But at the same time that Rose was coming to terms with the truth of her circumstances, she was observing that she was far from unique, that many women were married off to serve the interests of their relatives, and that they survived, and even flourished, in spite of this disadvantage.

Besides, when she reflected on her life in Martinique, Rose must have realized that had she remained on her father's plantation, she would have married far less well—or possibly not at all. She was, after all, a dowerless girl from a provincial backwater; what hope could she ever have had of finding a desirable husband? Alexandre was presentable, well off, with an exceptional career and valuable social contacts. Many women would consider themselves lucky to share such a man's life, despite the resentment and heartache that came with it.

Sobered by these thoughts, disabused of her remaining illusions about marriage and with a hardened attitude toward her intractable husband, Rose waited for Alexandre to return from his long sojourn, and when in July of 1782 she learned that he was in Paris, she left Noisy, where the family was spending the summer, to join him there.

For a few brief weeks there was a flicker of hope for the future. Husband and wife behaved themselves, were outwardly affable to each other, even seemed to take pleasure in each other's presence. Italy had changed Alexandre, or so it appeared. When he and Rose returned to Noisy together, he adapted to the quieter life of the village. He did not become restless and run off to Paris to spend long evenings with friends. Indeed he gave Rose no cause to complain, and, without her reproaches, there was no friction. As proof of their newfound harmony, Rose conceived another child, which Alexandre declared would be a second son.

But the apparent harmony was illusory. Alexandre was able to tolerate a brief domestic interlude because he knew that it would soon end. Even before his return from Italy he had formed a plan of action that would keep him away from Rose for many long months to come. He had decided to join the fighting in the Americas, and had written to the new governor of the Windward Isles asking to be appointed his aide-de-camp. Alexandre had risen to the rank of major, and stood on the threshold of military renown. All he needed was an opportunity, men to lead, glory to gain.

While in Noisy he waited with increasing impatience for a reply to his request, only to discover that the governor had never received it. If Alexandre wanted to serve, he would have to go to Martinique on his own, and offer himself for any post still available.

Laure de Girardin too was planning to make the long trip to Martinique, on family business. She had not remarried, she would be sailing with only an older relative for company. Having Alexandre with her would no doubt relieve the boredom of the voyage.

Without telling Rose of his plans, Alexandre made quiet preparations to leave Noisy—and to coordinate his travels with Laure. Taking one of the servants into his confidence, he made arrangements for a secret escape, and on the night of September 6, when everyone in the household was asleep, he stole into the courtyard and rode off along the high road to Paris. When Rose awoke the following morning, she found him gone.

If Rose had been inclined to trust Alexandre, even a little, this abrupt and cowardly departure must have destroyed that sliver of trust once and for all. He had deceived her in not telling her of his plans, he had abandoned her and their unborn child, he had shown once again that he had little or no regard for her wellbeing or for family life. When Rose learned, shortly after Alexandre's departure, that he and Laure de Girardin were to be on the same ship bound for Martinique, she must have felt utterly betrayed.

Nor was she at all mollified by a letter that arrived shortly after Alexandre left.

"Will you forgive me, my beloved, for leaving you without saying goodbye, for having taken my departure without letting you know, for having gone without telling you one last time that I am entirely yours? Alas!" In language reminiscent of the melodramatic classical dramas Patricol had wanted Rose to memorize, Alexandre went on, writing in the early hours of the morning, no doubt under the dual influence of lack of sleep and euphoria at having left his wife and her entire menage behind.

Alexandre posed as a man torn between duty to country and duty to loved ones. "Love of my wife and love of glory: both rule supreme within my heart.... The day will come, my dearest love, when you will thank me for having had the bravery to make so many sacrifices. Adieu! My heart is yours, and always will be."[4]

Reeling from the shock of Alexandre's abandonment, her stomach churning with morning sickness, unsure what would become of her and her children should Alexandre fail to return from Martinique, Rose remained unmoved by her husband's specious rhetoric. His words proclaimed one thing, his actions another, and she had learned by now that his deeds were all that mattered.

Injured and angry, feeling ill-used, Rose did not outwardly flinch or withdraw under this latest blow to her pride. She would not forgive what Alexandre had done. She would not lend wifely support to his feigned campaign for military honor. She knew better.

In the privacy of her own room, however, Rose must have given way to tears. She was only nineteen, and would soon have two children. In nearly three years of marriage, she had spent only a few months with her husband, and much of that time she had been miserable. With no one to notice or value her, she was maturing, outgrowing the overeager naiveté she had shown as a bride, her face losing its chubbiness and her features acquiring definition, her petite body blossoming as her pregnancy advanced. All these changes, and the melancholy understanding she was acquiring along with them, were going unappreciated.

She, Marie-Rose Tascher, creole of Martinique, was alone, wasting away in a house tantalizingly near the great world of Paris society, where all was glitter and blazing light and frivolity, beauty and comfort and ease of heart. While her husband, fresh from his Grand Tour of Italy and looking ahead to ever greater attainments, was off on a journey halfway around the world, with his mistress by his side.

5

"The Vilest of Creatures"

Rose's pregnancy did not go well. She was ill much of the time, the stress of her deeply unhappy marriage making her illness worse. Alexandre, waiting in Brest for his ship to depart for Martinique, wrote her peevish, petulant letters, full of reproaches tempered, occasionally, by affectionate outbursts.

"I begin to fear our marriage [is] turning out decidedly badly," he wrote. "You have only yourself to blame." He accused her of spoiling Eugene, of wavering in her feelings toward him, of complaining too much and of neglecting him.

Even his relatively complimentary messages were rebarbative. "I am excessively sad and melancholy," he declared. "The most effective means of driving out the blackness of my spirit, you possess. With your assurance of tenderness I would destroy one part of my suffering and would acquire the strength to rise above the other. Adieu, ma chère amie. I have promised not to speak of love. I must then, do no more than move my lips as if to kiss you a thousand times."[1]

He needed Rose's "assurance of tenderness" to rise out of his black mood—yet Rose, understandably enough, was slow to provide that assurance, given Alexandre's recent behavior. She answered his letters, but far less often than he felt was his due. He complained that he was "forsaken" by her (an exact reversal of the truth), that other officers of his acquaintance received far more letters than he did, though they were less "deserving" than he was.

Again and again Alexandre raised the banner of his own heroism, and waved it melodramatically. "Amid the risks of war and of the seas," he wrote, "where I go to seek death, I shall, without sorrow and without regret, see a life taken from me whose moments will have been reckoned only in misfortunes. Adieu!"[2]

Such callow effusions might have been forgiven had they not been absurdly exaggerated. In fact, as Rose well knew, her husband had no specific military assignment in Martinique—despite having been promoted to the rank of major in the Sarre regiment—and if he suffered from black moods, he had Laure nearby to console him.

In all, Alexandre and Laure waited more than three months for their ship, the *Venus*, to begin its journey to the West Indies. During that time Laure's two children, her son by Alexandre and her daughter by her late husband, were placed in the care of nuns at a convent in Paris. Alexandre wrote to Edmée and Rose asking them to look in on the children—a request Rose was in no hurry to comply with— but Edmée, at least, did as he asked.

Rose continued to feel unwell, even after the early months of her pregnancy had passed. Alexandre claimed, in his pompous way, that he suffered along with her, undergoing "the torments of the spirit," but this was small consolation. The baby, whom Alexandre referred to playfully as "little Scipio," was restless and caused Rose many sleepless nights. As she fretted uncomfortably in her bed, she must have wondered whether Alexandre was sleeping alone or with Laure, her distressing thoughts worsening her bodily discomfort.

The *Venus* left La Rochelle, where more delays had arisen to detain its departure, in the last days of December and embarked on a tempestuous voyage. Storm after storm arose to endanger the small vessel, and for six weeks Alexandre, who was not a good sailor, lurched queasily from bunk to rail and back again. In the intervals between spells of seasickness he played lotto with Laure, and wrote to Rose about what amusing company she was.

When at last the high volcanic cone of Mount Pelée rose into view above the horizon, and the *Venus* anchored in the harbor of Fort-Royal, Alexandre was weary, jaundiced, and out of temper. He had not eaten or slept properly for six weeks, and instead of resting he plunged into the social life of the capital, attending balls and suppers, overtiring himself and risking his health further.

His efforts did win him a post as aide-de-camp to the governor, but his already low spirits plummeted when he learned that the fighting in the Americas was all but at an end. Diplomats were already at work negotiating peace. There would be no battlefield glory for Major Alexandre de Beauharnais in the New World any time soon.

Alexandre's dispirited mood affected his every thought and impression. Although he had spent most of his childhood in Martinique, and was in some ways a product of its environment himself, he now saw it through new eyes, and was repelled by what he saw. Instead of a lush and abundant landscape and an easy, earthy culture free of artificial moral constraints Alexandre saw only material and moral decay. The predominantly African culture repelled him; in his letters to France he expressed amazement at the indecent dress, sexual license and "evidences of debauchery" among the slaves. The squalor in which they lived, their flimsy, insect-ridden huts with dirt floors, their illiteracy and superstitious beliefs offended his educated, fastidious tastes; he responded with snobbery, revulsion and genuine horror.

When he went to the plantation at Trois-Ilets to pay his respects to the Tascher family, he received another shock. The Taschers still lived in the sugar refinery, with much of their land fallen out of cultivation. A small number of slaves were in the fields, and so desperate were the family's finances that Joseph himself, thinner, older and more ill than ever, was at work alongside them. Clearly the Taschers had gone down in the world, and although he was not devoid of sentiment for these in-laws who had nurtured him as a child and whose daughter he had married, Alexandre could not afford, given his social and career ambitions, to be associated with them.

Hiding his misgivings, Alexandre presented himself to the Taschers and was received with warmth. He presented a portrait of Rose, and no doubt he had one of Eugene as well. He brought Joseph a handsome forty-volume edition of the works of Voltaire (a singularly inappropriate gift; a bank draft would have been much more welcome). He also brought another gift—an offer of marriage for Manette, now sixteen, from a fellow officer in his regiment.

But Manette was in no condition to marry anyone. Languid and pale, she was suffering from scurvy and spent most of her time lying on a couch, resting. Her mother and grandmother resisted the suggestions of their doctor that Manette be inoculated against smallpox and that she take a mercury cure. They feared that inoculation would make her even more ill, while the mercury cure carried a stigma with it, since it was most often used in cases of syphilis. Alexandre urged inoculation, but he was not heeded. Given Manette's weakness, and the high mortality rate on the island, it was clear to Alexandre that her prospects for survival were poor.

Rose had ceased to write to Alexandre, though she did send letters to her family. He wrote to her, reminding her that on his return they would set up housekeeping in their own house at Noisy, though he was, as he frankly admitted, "unsuited" to running a household.

"I recommend you above all to keep busy," he wrote. "This will banish laziness which has always been the first cause of forgetting one's duties."[5] This rather impersonal advice suggests a certain absence of mind; had he thought about it, Alexandre would have realized that his letter would arrive in France just as Rose was about to give birth, and would need, not activity, but rest. His thoughtlessness was a symptom, slight yet ominous, of a rising pique.

At the best of times Alexandre was poised to become irritated with Rose, his emotions balanced as if on a knife-edge, quick to resent what he perceived as her insults to his dignity. As the weeks passed and she sent him no letters, he felt slighted, injured, especially when a letter from Rose to Aunt Rosette was read aloud to him in which Rose announced that she had "cured herself" of her feelings for him.

Hearing this, and knowing that Rose's entire family knew it, was a blow to Alexandre's ego. It made explicit what everyone felt, but no one discussed openly—that the marriage had failed, and, by implication, that Alexandre had failed. Narcissistic as he was, Alexandre could not but feel Rose's declaration of emotional independence as an assault on his worth. And when his worth and dignity were questioned, he became not only angry but malicious. How dare Rose, a woman to whom he had been so unsuitably yoked, a woman unworthy of him, toward whom he had never felt anything but revulsion, no matter what false flowery sentiments he professed in his letters to her, bring him into dishonor? He looked around for a weapon with which to fight back.

He didn't need to look far. Martinique seemed to him a swamp of depravity, where illicit liaisons flourished without regard to the carefully respected unwritten codes by which sexual immorality was governed in Paris. Rose had been formed in this licentious environment. Rose no longer cared for him. Perhaps Rose had never cared for him. Perhaps Rose was anything but the innocent girl he had believed her to be when she became his wife.

"I recall, ma chère amie," Alexandre wrote to Rose in April of 1783, "that you once predicted that if ever you should be untrue to me I would perceive it either by your letters or by your conduct towards me. This moment has surely come, for during the three months that I have been here, vessels have arrived from every port and not one brings a single word from you."[4]

Simmering with anger, and feverish—he was exhibiting the first symptoms of typhus—Alexandre suffered a second blow. Rose wrote to her relatives to tell them of the birth of her daughter, Hortense, on April 10. But she did not send any letter to Alexandre.

So the baby was a girl, and Rose chose her name—and her god-mother, Fanny de Beauharnais—without consulting Alexandre or even informing him directly. Such insults could only mean one thing: Rose was revealing her true self, a self he knew only in part. He must find out who and what she really was.

Laure de Girardin, who had been occupied since her arrival in Martinique with settling her father's estate and visiting various plantations, now provided fuel to Alexandre's fiery anger at his wife. Baby Hortense, she pointed out, was born not quite nine months after Alexandre's return from Italy. Ignoring what all women knew, that not all babies were carried to term and many were born earlier than expected, Laure claimed that the date of Hortense's birth was proof that Rose had conceived the child with someone other than Alexandre.

Since no one in Martinique knew exactly when Alexandre had returned from his trip abroad, there was no refuting this damaging allegation, and soon scandal spread across the island. Old tales of Rose's grandfather's dissipated habits were revived. Rose, it was said, took after him. Rumormongers in Fort-Royal recalled how flirtatious Rose had been as a girl of fifteen, how precociously mature she had seemed, how she had danced with exceptional lightness and grace with the officers in candlelit ballrooms. Tales were revived, invented, elaborated. Rose's reputation for propriety, which seems never to have been questioned before, now became clouded and compromised. Her family, aghast and scarcely able to believe what they were hearing, protested that their beloved child was being victimized. But the damage was done.

And there was much worse to come. Fighting off fever, and with Laure to help him, Alexandre was systematically collecting evidence with which to convict Rose, not of adultery (that was self-evident, to his half-deluded mind), but of sexual impurity before her marriage.

Ignoring or denying to himself what he knew at first hand about Rose's sexual inexperience as a bride of sixteen, and choosing to disregard as inconclusive the fact that Hortense had his fair hair and blue eyes, Alexandre threw his energies into investigating Rose's past behavior.

What he found, or claimed to find, made him even more frenzied in his campaign to blacken his wife's reputation. With the caustic Laure by his side, he interviewed spiteful gossips in Fort-Royal and uncovered stories of Rose's romantic intrigues with several officers, tales of midnight trysts and secret meetings, of love letters and love tokens given and received. At Trois-Ilets Alexandre attempted to force Rose's slave Brigitte to "confess" to having helped her young mistress slip away to meet her lovers, and when Brigitte stoutly refused, and insisted, even when Alexandre offered her money, that Rose had never engaged in any impropriety, he threatened her with death should she reveal their conversation to anyone.

Another slave, Maximin, was more cooperative. When Alexandre gave him a large bribe, he corroborated every accusation Alexandre and Laure made—and Alexandre, knowing which version of the "truth" he preferred to hear, chose to believe Maximin and not Brigitte.

As far as can be determined, there was no foundation for any of the allegations being made against Rose. Maximin later retracted all he had said, no incriminating love letters or tokens were ever produced, and even Alexandre, looking back on his months in Martinique later on, confessed that he had acted impetuously, in response to "the passions and anger of youth."[5] Soon after he completed his investigation, by now near the point of collapse from rapidly wors-

ening fever, Alexandre succumbed to his illness and was taken in by
acquaintances in Fort-Royal—the Taschers being understandably furious with him, especially after Brigitte told them everything Alexandre had said and done.

To add insult to injury, Alexandre sought shelter during his illness
with one Madame du Turon, one of the talebearers who spread the
damaging rumors about Rose—and once he was over the worst of
his disease, he seduced Madame du Turon during his convalescence
and caused more gossip to fly. Rose's Aunt Rosette wrote about the
goings-on to Edmée in Paris, telling her in detail all that Alexandre
was doing and saying, and adding that Alexandre had been upset with
her for not coming to see him while he was staying on the du Turon
estate. "I would have found myself very much out of place in such
society," Rosette told her sister icily, and there was no need to say
more.

By this time a countercurrent of outrage had arisen. Rose's friends
and relatives, filled with indignation over Alexandre and Laure's calculated mischief-making, and eager to defend Rose against their cal-
umnies, were forming a united front. Rose's uncle Baron Tascher
offered to make the journey to Paris to be with her and protect her
against her husband's verbal assaults. Joseph wanted Rose to return
home before things got any worse for her. Rose's morals— and Alexandre's slanders—continued to be the principal topic at many dinner tables and card parties, until over time, the sting of scandal lost
some of its bite.

Alexandre left Martinique under a cloud. He had brought much
discredit on himself. Instead of attaining military distinction, as he
had hoped, he had made his name memorable for dishonoring his
own wife (for in the end, few of the creoles of Martinique believed
his allegations against Rose) and for cuckolding Madame du Turon's
husband, who was livid and highly vocal in his dispraise of the young
major.

Wanting to avoid any appearance of being in the wrong, Alexandre
boldly presented himself at Trois-Ilets to say good-bye. Rose-Claire
noticed his unease.

"I saw that he was troubled and moved," she wrote afterward. "He
seemed to be anxious to get away from me as quickly as possible, to

avoid my presence. His heart was already reproaching him for such ill-advised behavior."[6]

Joseph shouted at him. "So this is the outcome of your illustrious military campaign against the enemy! You have done nothing but declare war on your wife's reputation and dishonor us all!"

The rebuke stung, but Alexandre, stony-faced, hiding his emotions, did not let himself be provoked. Besides, he had already made up his mind to rid himself of Rose and of all connection with her shabby relatives.

Over a month earlier he had sent Rose a scathing letter in which he ordered her to leave his house once and for all, and threatened her that if she did not obey him she would "find him a tyrant." At the time Alexandre made his last visit to Trois-Ilets this excoriating letter had not yet reached Paris; in fact it was on the high seas, being carried to France by Laure who had recently embarked on her homeward journey.

Once the letter arrived in Paris, however, the uproar in the family broke out afresh.

"If I had written to you in the first moment of my rage, my pen would have burned the paper and you would have thought from hearing all my invectives that I had seized a moment of temper or of jealousy to write to you," Alexandre began, bringing the full weight of his rhetoric to bear on his subject. "But I have known what I am going to say to you, at least in part, for more than three weeks. Despite, therefore, the despair of my soul, despite the fury which suffocates me, I shall know how to contain myself; I shall know how to tell you coldly that in my eyes you are the vilest of creatures, and that my stay in this country has revealed to me your abominable conduct."[7]

He proceeded to list all his accusations, citing two of Rose's alleged lovers in particular, and claiming to have in his possession a gift Rose made to one of her lovers. Certain "indiscreet people," he said, had told him all he needed to know, and there were incriminating letters, and the slaves had been talkative.

"There is, consequently, no more occasion to pretend, and since I am not ignorant of any details you have no other alternative than to be truthful."

Alexandre did not blame anyone but Rose herself—not her family, not even her lovers. She alone was responsible for her reprehensible behavior; she was "beneath all the sluts in the world."

"You alone have abused an entire family and carried disgrace and ignominy to another, distant family of which you are unworthy," Alexandre wrote. Rose's monumental betrayals dwarfed any minor peccadilloes of his own, or any tensions and difficulties that had arisen over the past three years. Her overriding sin was, of course, the adultery that had produced Hortense.

"What am I to think of this last infant," Alexandre said, "born eight months and several days after my return from Italy? I am forced to take her, but I swear by the heavens that she is by another, and that a stranger's blood flows in her veins.... She owes her life to an adulterer."[8]

Since it had become clear to Alexandre that he could never trust Rose again, he had decided to end their marriage. "Have the goodness to go to a convent as soon as you receive my letter," he insisted. "This is my last word, and nothing in the world is capable of making me change.... No tears, no protestations! I am already on guard against all your efforts, and my care will always be to arm myself further against vile promises which would be as contemptible as they are false."

The malignant letter had its effect. Until now no one had known to what lengths Alexandre would go to free himself from Rose; now he had revealed how selfish and vicious he could be, when goaded by wretchedness and influenced by others more hardened to human sympathy and more practiced in the refinements of marital politics.

Stunned as she was by all that had happened, Rose-Claire saw that Alexandre had been drawn into the worst of his cruel behavior by others—specifically, though she did not say so, by Laure de Girardin. "He has let himself be carried away," she wrote to the Marquis de Beauharnais, "without reflecting, without thinking what he has done."[9]

Rose-Claire was entirely too generous, of course. Alexandre knew full well what he had done, but he had no second thoughts about it. He was quite ruthless, and quite determined. When he returned from Martinique he did not go to live with his family but stayed in the Duc de la Rochefoucauld's establishment, resisting all efforts made by Edmée, the marquis and others to persuade him to reconcile with Rose.

Declaring that his terrible discoveries in Martinique had so trau-matized him that he would never be the same man again, and that his very soul was "ulcerated to the utmost," he fulminated angrily against Rose and continued to insist that she take refuge, as rejected, separated or abused wives often did, in a convent.

To Rose, finding herself at the center of an ugly contretemps, Alexandre's actions must have seemed diabolical, the doings of a madman. Not only was he doing his best to ruin her reputation, but he was ruining her children's future. For if he spread lies about Hor-tense's paternity, he would not be above lying about Eugene's pater-nity as well. Rose no longer cared about Alexandre—indeed she must by this time have hated him passionately—but she did love her chil-dren. She could not let Alexandre's venom destroy them.

Her mother wrote her from Martinique, urging her to return home and forget that Alexandre ever existed. "Oh, my poor daughter, all your sorrows are in my breast," Rose-Claire wrote. "They leave me without rest both night and day! Come, mingle your tears with those of a tender mother! All your friends do you justice, they love you always and will console you!"[10]

Though the wounded, angry Rose must have been comforted by her mother's assurances, she was not tempted to return to Martinique. A resolution of her wretched situation was now at hand, and lacer-ating as Alexandre's attack was, the fact that it brought her long-festering marital situation to a head must have come as something of a relief.

For three years she had lived with worsening tension, suffering under the coldness and mistreatment of a husband whose absence was more and more welcome. She had been progressively more miserable, more discontented, more irate. Now all that was at an end.

Besides, she had realized for some time that there was a livable, even a pleasant, alternative. She would seek a legal separation from Alexandre. She believed that, under the law, he would be obligated to provide for her, and for her children. She knew that his finances were in disarray; he had run up many debts, and had overspent his income. But surely his first obligation was to her, no matter what he might think of her or how he might have convinced himself of her unworthiness to be his wife.

At the end of November 1783, Rose gathered her courage and told Euphémie to pack her things and Eugene's. Entrusting baby Hortense to Edmée, she left the house on the rue Neuve-Saint-Charles for the last time and drove to the convent of Penthémont, determined to start a new life.

6

"The Little American"

A visitor to Paris in the winter of 1784, standing at the top of the Mont Ste-Geneviève to look out over the skyline of the city, would have beheld a lively panorama. Paris was a city of grey stone, with the imposing façades of tall mansions, sloping mansard roofs, church spires and the massive outlines of old, squat, thick-walled monasteries all faced in the same coolly elegant material. Tile roofs alternated with blue slate, stone chimneys with brick. Here and there a crenellated battlement, a remnant of a more beleaguered era, thrust itself up amid the peaceable structures, and in the distance, at the city's heart, was a dark mass of low, deeply weathered medieval buildings threaded by winding narrow streets, their crumbling clutter an offense to the more spacious districts at the city's perimeter.

That perimeter, as the visitor could plainly see, was widening. Large expanses of the old walls enclosing the city were being pulled down, and in the empty spaces and on waste ground, houses and villas were being erected, along with new roads and new bridges spanning the river. Along the wide boulevards, mansions rose, surrounded by wide gardens and deep paved courtyards. On the left bank, laborers were laying out the Cours, planting trees and erecting dwellings along its borders.

The visitor, looking out across the Seine, could still make out the outlines of houses centuries old on the bridges, the immense bulk of the Tuileries Palace, the Louvre with its span of colonnades, and the long avenue of the Champs-Elysées, along with the triumphal arches at the Porte St-Dénis and the Porte St-Martin. But there were almost as many new structures, it seemed, as there were old ones, and a new wall was rapidly being erected to enclose the expanding capital.

Angry Parisians were calling the new wall the "wall of captivity," because its tall mass made them feel hemmed in, hindering their view of the outlying countryside and preventing the fresh country air from sweeping through the congested, smoky city.

They blamed the tax collectors for the new wall; it was their exorbitant demands that made gates and barriers necessary. But it was not really the tax collectors who were at fault, it was the government's perpetual shortage of money—and for this they blamed the king and his ministers and especially the queen, whose extravagance was at the root of the problem. They complained, loudly and strenuously—and then they returned to the task of building afresh.

It could not have escaped an observant visitor's attention, there on Mont Ste-Geneviève, that despite the chill air and short days of winter, despite the frost that lingered on windowsills and rooftops, in muddy gutters and along the riverbanks, the sound of hammering and sawing, of heavily laden carts trundling along cobblestoned streets and workmen shouting, singing and conversing with one another never ceased. Night and day, in bitter cold and pallid sunshine, the labor continued. Great houses with dozens of rooms were erected in a matter of six or eight weeks, smaller buildings in even less time. The rush to build was inexorable, a mania as gripping as the mania for speculating on the bourse or wagering on racehorses.

Another mania held the city in its grip: the craze for all things American. Thanks in large part to French aid, the American colonists had defeated the British and declared themselves heroically, if vulnerably, independent. The French wholeheartedly applauded this remarkable achievement—and embraced, at least in theory, the principles on which the new republic was founded, principles of freedom and equality, liberty and simplicity, a turning aside from differences in rank and birth, from ceremony and privilege.

These newfound American values were heady, they created a euphoria and a sense of boundless possibilities. America was pointing the way: the French, their superior culture enlightened and leavened by the American ideals, would follow. To be sure, the Americans had gone further than the French were prepared to go; there were no aristocrats or kings in America, only honest, rough-hewn frontiersmen (some of whom, admittedly, owned vast tracts of land worked by hundreds of slaves). Some of these rough, democratic frontiersmen were hard to distinguish, in their wealth, from the great nobles of France with their feudal titles. Still, the American frontier was new, the vast estates were of recent acquisition. In their very newness lay their hope—and hope was what France very much needed in this noisy, frenetically active winter of 1784.

Everywhere the visitor looked, he was bound to see evidences of the American craze. Men ordered their tailors to replace the gold and jeweled buttons on their breeches and waistcoats with steel buttons, and put steel buckles on their shoes, for steel was a republican, egalitarian metal. Women abandoned their elaborate day-dresses of lace-trimmed silk and wore simpler, more informal muslin gowns in snowy white or pale pink, with rustic straw hats tied under the chin with ribbons. It was a charming affectation, sophisticated women dressing as milkmaids perched on gilded settees in sumptuous drawing rooms, but it was a pervasive one. Even the queen found refuge from the increasing stresses and sorrows of her life in her exquisite miniature dairy, where she milked her white cows and turned the handle of her butter churn herself.

Conversations were laced with republican language, republican attitudes were expressed at many dinner tables. Even those whose understanding of things American was imperfect marbled their speech with references to equality and freedom, and spoke airily and at times self-consciously of reforming the monarchy and expanding the liberties of Frenchmen.

Behind the grey stone walls of the spacious convent of Penthémont, where the conversation in the well-appointed salons ranged over many topics, the woman known as the "little American" was flourishing. Rose—Viscountess de Beauharnais—was prized by the other residents of the convent as a living representative of Americana, as indeed she was. She came from the New World, she wore her becoming, thin muslin gowns with a familiarity the others envied, she was (so it was said) "rich as a creole" but she had an attractive simplicity and warmth of manner that marked her as a product of a fresher and more natural world.

And it was not only her desirable, faintly exotic origins that set Rose apart. She was exotic herself, or so she seemed to the ladies of Penthémont. Of small stature but lithe and graceful, with a sway in her walk that she no doubt owed to the example of her nurse Marion and the other slaves she had grown up among, Rose was distinctive. No one walked like she did, and no one had her rich, melodious speaking voice, with its charming overtones of creole speech. Beyond this, she was lively and eager albeit soft in manner, and had an outgoing warmth and concern for others that contrasted with the brittle narcissism of so many upper-class women. People responded to her, forgave her her faults, and looked forward to her company.

Penthémont was one of several convents in Paris that offered inexpensive but elegant lodging to highborn women displaced through marital irregularities of various kinds or through bereavement or family upheaval. The capital was full of excess women of high rank: widows, spinsters, orphans, rejected wives, dowerless women over thirty who preferred to live apart from their relatives. Women who were embarrassments to their families—those with deformed faces or crippled limbs, the eccentric and the deranged, dwarves and oversize women so far outside the fashionable norms as to be considered grotesque—had for centuries been sent to convents where they could live comfortably amid the nuns (many of whom were also highborn) without taking holy orders themselves. In the late eighteenth century, some Parisian convents had all but ceased to be religious institutions but still took in aristocratic boarders.

Penthémont was a large complex of buildings set amid extensive gardens that gave the appearance of a college or exclusive finishing school in the country. The women who lived there had their own large, pleasant rooms or suites of rooms, and they came and went as they liked, the only constraint imposed on them the observing of prescribed hours for entering and leaving the grounds. Many of the women had children, most had servants. In the afternoons and evenings, when they were not otherwise occupied, they met in the convent's parlors to socialize, share their individual dramas, and, when appropriate, commiserate with one another.

For Rose, residence at Penthémont was her first taste of freedom.

She no longer had to answer to Alexandre, or to be confined with her aunt and the elderly marquis in what must have become an uncomfortable ménage. She could come and go very nearly as she pleased, drive out along the fashionable streets of the Faubourg St-Germain, cross the river to shop in the rue St-Honoré, visit cafés and restaurants and meet her expanding number of friends to socialize.

Penthémont was for Rose a window onto a larger world. Sitting in its comfortable salons, mingling with women who, whatever their present circumstances, were nonetheless at home in the highest circles of society and the royal court, women connected by blood or marriage to the great nobility, was an education in refined manners. The myriad subtle differences between these privileged ladies and the people she had met at the house on the rue Neuve-Saint-Charles were not lost on Rose, who took eager note of everything from the way the Penthémont ladies entered a room to the way they sat down to the unmistakable air of entitlement that clung to them and that was reflected in their every gesture and nuance of speech.

Grace, polish, ease of bearing, an aristocratic presence: Rose's companions at the convent exuded these qualities and, by sheer propinquity, Rose absorbed them. She absorbed as well a great deal of information about the ways of the world, how no one really expected husbands and wives to be faithful to one another, but entered marriage with a tacit understanding that, within a framework of civility and consideration, infidelity would be a pastime enthusiastically pursued by both parties, at least in youth. And how this was an amorality rooted in sophistication, not cruelty.

She began to understand that Alexandre, ruthless and self-regarding as he was, was a product of this set of attitudes; his behavior with Laure de Girardin was fairly conventional: only his tortuous, wilful tergiversations, his romantic extremes and exaggerated airs—in short, his style—were distinctive.

Rose had already sensed, before coming to Penthémont, that the life of a titled woman separated from her husband would offer her the greatest scope for contentment with the least sacrifice in respectability. Now she saw just how wide that scope could be. For here, along with the unfortunates and the marginalized, were truly splendid, thriving women, women in their prime, hardy amid apparent misfortune, sharing tales of their lovers and gossiping about the love lives of others—including the husbands from whom they were separated—making light of the game of sexual and marital politics. That such an approach to life was possible must have buoyed Rose's spirits as she went about the troublesome business of separating herself from Alexandre and arranging the legal formalities of her new life.

The first round of petitions and court judgments went swiftly and smoothly. Rose met with a representative of the court and told him in some detail the story of her failed marriage. She described how at first, Alexandre had seemed more than content with her, how pleased he had looked when they said their vows together, then his abrupt, inexplicable slide into dissipation, his long absences, his neglect of her and reproachful attitude. She described her young husband as having been so self-contained, so guarded that he never made his feelings known to her, and added that because of his detachment and formal manner he retained the upper hand in their relationship.

In effect, Rose told her interlocutor, she was an abandoned wife almost from the start of her marriage, for although four calendar years had passed since the wedding, Alexandre had spent less than a year under the same roof with her. Finally she came to the last ugly year during which Alexandre and Laure had stirred up scandal in Martinique and done such shameful damage to Rose, her children and her family. It was, Rose said, the cold, calculated nature of Alexandre's treachery that made her see that she must leave the marriage, to the extent that the law allowed her to leave it. She owed it to herself, she said, to free herself and her children from such a toxic yoke.

The official who took down Rose's declaration was more than sympathetic. To him she seemed a young woman "of excellent breeding, perfect manners," who was gracious and uncommonly fascinating. "One really cannot understand," another visitor to Penthémont commented, "when one sees and hears her, her husband's wicked behavior and the wrongs he has done her."[1]

While the legal separation was worked out—a process that took some time—the court granted Rose her temporary independence from her husband, and ordered that she should stay at Penthémont with Eugene, with Alexandre paying both Eugene's and Hortense's expenses. Edmée was at Penthémont too, at least some of the time, and no doubt it was Edmée who provided moral support for Rose, who was not yet twenty-one, in her efforts to extricate herself from her bond to Alexandre.

Edmée had gone through the legal process of separating from her husband Alexis Renaudin years earlier, though under quite different circumstances; because hers had been from the start a marriage of convenience, with Renaudin fully aware of Edmée's relationship with the Marquis de Beauharnais, the court had taken twelve years to reach a decision about granting the couple a separation. In the end Edmée had prevailed, and had been granted a portion of her husband's income.

Edmée may well have advanced Rose the money to pay the costs of her stay at Penthémont, for Rose had virtually nothing of her own. During the past year, while Alexandre had been in Martinique, she had been so hard pressed that she was forced to sell some of her jewelry. She had bought things on credit, as much as possible, expecting that Alexandre would eventually pay the bills, but he had not paid them, and the creditors were impatient. The small annual sum Rose's father had promised to send her under the terms of the wedding contract had not been forthcoming, and now she needed it badly. But the letters she received from Martinique contained no promises of money, only pleas for her to return home and live at Trois-Ilets.

Alexandre, living in Paris and reportedly "amusing himself greatly" while seeking to move up in the military world, was himself hard up for money. He was complaining to the authorities of wrongs and injustices concerning his finances. This time his complaints were directed against his elderly father, who, he claimed, had failed to pay Alexandre what was owed from his late mother's estate and was refusing to account for the money entrusted to him on Alexandre's behalf. The marquis, according to his son, had overspent the income from the estate by at least three hundred thousand livres, and owed much more than that in unpaid bills. Even the rent on the house in the Neuve-Saint-Charles had not been paid, and because of this fact, and in order to begin to put his own financial affairs in order, Alexandre was forced to sell all the furnishings.

This hostile gesture was as punitive as it was disruptive. Alexandre was angry at everyone, resentful of his father, furious at Rose, perhaps even, for the first time, in conflict with Edmée, who for so long had

been a surrogate mother to him. Alexandre's contemptible mistreatment of Rose had caused a major breach in the family, and had left
him isolated. Now he was taking his revenge.

In the spring of 1784, Edmée and the Marquis de Beauharnais
moved once again. They could not afford to live in Paris any longer,
and the house in Noisy-le-Grand that Edmée had given to Alexandre
and Rose as a wedding gift was being sold. They found lodgings in
Fontainebleau, a gathering place for aristocrats in financial difficulties.
Compared to Paris, Fontainebleau was inexpensive, yet it retained
some social cachet because the royal court visited Fontainebleau palace each fall and the king liked to hunt there.

Rose continued to live at the convent, and apart from her ongoing
financial difficulties, and occasional legal skirmishes with Alexandre,
the time passed quite pleasantly. She was just at the cusp of her
twenty-first birthday, admired and welcomed into the circle of
women, invited to dine in the mansions of the Faubourg St-Germain,
her name beginning to be repeated in fashionable drawing rooms. In
a sense, life was just beginning for her, or so it must have seemed as
she accepted the invitations that came to her and savored the elegance,
the studied nonchalance, the pleasure-centered pastimes of the new
social world she was discovering.

Rose's mental world was expanding as well. Paris was abuzz with
gossip, and in the convent salons, the topics of the day were aired—
the queen's continuing extravagance, the shameless opera by Beau-
marchais called *The Marriage of Figaro*, the details of the latest balloon
ascension. There were earnest discussions of the tender, candid au-
tobiography of Jean-Jacques Rousseau, which occasioned much favorable comment, and whispered mentions of *Les Liaisons Dangereuses*,
the novel everyone read but no one admitted to reading which laid
bare a sordid world of amorality, calculated seduction and the destruction of innocence—Alexandre's world, Rose must have thought
with a shudder as she listened to the whispered talk and took note
of the knowing glances that passed among the women.

Underlying much else that was talked of was the precariousness of
the financial system. Personal and national debt were increasing ex-
ponentially. Everyone was borrowing, no one was paying anything
back—except by borrowing more. The shortage of money faced by
Rose and her in-laws was symptomatic of a wider malaise, a spend-

thrift mentality, an uncontrolled acquisitiveness that disregarded limits and denied the inevitable coming of a day of reckoning.

Indeed there were ominous signs that the day of reckoning could not be far off. Bankruptcies were increasing in number, and among the bankrupts were titled courtiers close to the king and queen. Stories were told of prominent nobles who lived lavishly on credit, borrowing millions of livres from bankers, financiers and other courtiers, amassing vast quantities of paintings and fine china, tapestries and exquisite furnishings, magnificent jewels and grand wardrobes without paying out any cash at all. It was said, not entirely facetiously, that the measure of a nobleman's wealth was the value of his unpaid bills. By this measure, the entire noble class was becoming wealthier by the day.

As the months passed, and the lawyers argued the terms of the separation, Alexandre found himself to be more and more in want. His expenses had risen. In June of 1784—the month in which Rose turned twenty-one—Alexandre became captain of the Royal-Champagne cavalry regiment, a valued yet costly appointment, and aide-de-camp to the Duc de la Rochefoucauld, who had also risen in rank. In desperation Alexandre began to sell his possessions, including many which had been bought on credit and for which the bills were still outstanding. Some creditors he referred to Rose, others to his father. He demanded that Rose return to him jewelry he claimed to have bought her; according to Rose, she never received the jewels, and the likelihood is that Alexandre had in fact bought them as gifts for other women.

Unseemly wrangles arose, with Rose, far more knowing and self-confident now than she had ever been, standing her ground and Alexandre fuming impotently. If he had expected her to crumble under his threats and slanders, he discovered that he was mistaken.

Ever volatile, Alexandre's impatience and frustration now rose to dangerous heights. He had to contend with the ongoing nuisance and expense of lawyers and negotiations with his wife. His career was advancing rapidly, but it burdened him with higher expenses that he could not meet without taking on larger loans. His father owed him hundreds of thousands of livres, and it was becoming evident that he could never collect that debt. His personal life was a chaos of keen pleasures, inebriated celebrations and disordered relationships. Laure de Girardin had attached herself to another man whom she was soon to marry, and Alexandre too had moved on, enjoying fleeting liaisons with a number of women, at least one of whom was to present him with a second illegitimate child. He felt trapped, wronged, above all thwarted, and when Alexandre felt thwarted, he looked around for someone to punish.

In the cold February of 1785, he worked himself up into a fury. He went to Penthémont, climbed the stairs to Rose's third-floor rooms, and, entering unceremoniously, took three-year-old Eugene in his arms and carried him down to his waiting carriage. Before Rose could summon help, he was gone.

7

Liberation

$\mathcal{A}$lexandre was gone, and Eugene was gone with him. Her beloved son, her firstborn, had been snatched away, perhaps for good.

In the anxious hours that followed the kidnapping Rose endured what she later referred to as "the most terrible suffering." Shock, dread, tears of worry and rage kept her from sleeping and ate away at her peace of mind.

She had no idea where Alexandre might have taken Eugene. Alexandre himself had no permanent residence in Paris; he had been staying at the town house of the Duc de la Rochefoucauld, but he knew better than to take Eugene there. For all Rose knew, Alexandre had made arrangements for Eugene to be spirited away to Brest or Le Havre and shipped to Martinique. Anything was possible, given Alexandre's deviousness and vengeful nature.

In her hours of desperate concern Rose must have wondered whether Alexandre would try to kidnap baby Hortense as well. Although Alexandre continued to maintain that Hortense was another man's child, he had gone to visit her at least once at Noisy. And his revenge against Rose would be complete if he took both children from her.

Rose could not appeal to her relatives or in-laws for help; her father was thousands of miles away, her father-in-law lacked the strength to come to her aid. Besides, Alexandre was beyond the pale of family influence. He listened to no one, respected no one.

In desperation Rose went to the provost of Paris, and explained what had happened. She had undergone "the most painful disturbance," she said. Her husband had taken their son by main force, cruelly ignoring her distress in his need to dominate her and to possess the most precious result of the marriage, her "dearest pledge," Eugene. He could not be allowed to control Eugene's whereabouts and his future without regard for her; even if it meant seizing Alexandre's goods and income, Rose told the provost, he had to be made to return their son.

What happened next was testimony to Rose's widening influence—or at least the influence of her new acquaintances at Penthémont. Without that influence, her pleas could well have gone unheeded. Instead, within a month of the kidnapping, she and Alexandre were signing their separation agreement before a notary. Coercion had been applied, Eugene had been returned. And all the other outstanding issues had been resolved—at least on paper.

The separation agreement was a compromise, but at least it restored Rose's honor and went a long way to undoing the harm Alexandre had caused during his stay in Martinique. In it he admitted that he had slandered Rose, that, inspired by "the passions and anger of youth," he had accused her falsely of infidelity and of promiscuity before their marriage. He acknowledged that Rose had "just cause" in asking for a separation, and agreed to give her an annual income of five thousand livres, plus additional sums for the children, and to pay all legal costs.

One reason Eugene's abduction was so traumatic for Rose was that she knew the court might not let her keep her son with her once he left early childhood. When Alexandre took Eugene away with him, it was in a sense a foretaste of the future, and Rose knew it. Boys, particularly eldest sons, were considered to belong to their fathers. The court now ruled that Eugene would go to live with Alexandre on his fifth birthday. From then on he would stay with his mother only on holidays.

The agreement was signed in March of 1785. Within six months, Rose had moved in with her in-laws once again, in Fontainebleau. She could not stay at Penthémont indefinitely, and besides, Alexandre was proving to be unreliable in paying her the annual sum he had promised. Unless she wanted to return to Martinique, she had no choice but to live with her aunt and her father-in-law. She sent to Martinique for her furniture, had it shipped to the marquis's house, and, by the fall of 1785, had settled in herself.

The dark, decaying palace of Fontainebleau, built in the reign of Francis I and crumbling into ruin for the past two hundred years, was set in the midst of a wild vast forest, teeming with game. Each year in the fall, King Louis XVI came to Fontainebleau to hunt, and spent nearly every waking hour of the chill fall days pursuing stags, boar and other game from dawn until after sunset, driving himself to the point of exhaustion and then collapsing heavily into bed.

The king's pleasure was costly. Thousands of horses dragged hundreds of heavily loaded wagons through the forest to furnish and provision the palace during the king's stay, and the town of Fontainebleau was full of courtiers, servants and tradesmen seeking lodgings, running errands, creating an air of bustle and purpose. Many of the year-round residents of the town rented rooms to the personnel of the court during the fall, and Edmée and the marquis may have been among them.

Nor was fall the only busy season. For months before the king's arrival, laborers were at work readying the grounds of the palace, redecorating and renovating rooms, and huntsmen, pages and grooms were carrying out practice hunts in anticipation of the real thing to come.

It was all very exciting, the proximity of the royals, the comings and goings of important people, the plays put on at the palace by troupes of actors specially brought from Paris, the balls and suppers attended by the great nobles of the court, the whispers and rumors that ran swiftly through the town about goings-on among the courtiers and in the royal apartments.

It was the king's sport that brought the entire entourage from Paris, but it was the queen—graceful, charming, kindly disposed Marie Antoinette—who attracted most of the attention.

While she lived at Fontainebleau Rose must have seen the queen many times, riding in one of her carriages, attending public functions, appearing before crowds to receive their cheers—and boos. Although she had grown stout, and her tight corsets pinched her thick waist uncomfortably, Marie Antoinette retained the blonde, blue-eyed prettiness that had drawn so much admiration when she first came to France as a girl many years earlier. Scandal enveloped her, but she endured it stoically, and those who served her or observed her at close range saw a woman of rare poise and inner strength, her youthful frivolity laid aside, concerned for her children, tender toward her eccentric, obstreperous husband, greatly troubled about the future of her adopted country.

Most likely Rose saw King Louis less often than she saw the queen, for no one saw the king often during hunting season. He was as elusive as his quarry, hiding from his courtiers, disliking to show himself to his subjects, being by nature taciturn and timid. He was shortsighted, and could hardly tell one courtier from another without his spectacles, but as etiquette forbade the wearing of spectacles, he was often at a loss and public occasions were a torment for him.

Squat, ugly, obsessively fat with quadruple chins, the king was increasingly preoccupied with his hobbies, particularly his favorite pastime of making locks; when he came to Fontainebleau he brought with him his anvils and tools and the favorite servants who helped him at his forge. The queen objected, but he ignored her objections and shut himself away in a corner of the dingy palace, creating an oasis of privacy where he could lose himself in his adopted craft and where no one would reprimand him for wearing his spectacles.

Being so near the court for even part of the year brought Rose within the orbit of more influential people, and her acquaintance expanded. Edmée and the marquis entertained only modestly and infrequently, for their means were now limited. But Rose, thanks in part to friends and connections she had made at Penthémont, and thanks to Fanny de Beauharnais, who also lived at Fontainebleau and whose connection with Rose remained strong, was able to socialize more widely, and was even granted the privilege of following the royal hunt.

The exhilaration of that sport was unmatched. Rain or shine, she rode at breakneck pace across fields and meadows, fording streams and wading through bogs, tearing wildly along after the disappearing royal coach. Sometimes in a carriage, sometimes on horseback, occasionally on foot, she galloped along, heart pounding, now and then catching sight of the quarry herself but more often bringing up the rear of a long procession of riders and coaches. The raw cold air whipped at her face and ruined her coiffure, she often became soaked to the skin in her riding habit, but Rose loved these reckless gallops. They satisfied her streak of daring and gave her much needed physical release. They also gave her an excuse to be away all day from her aunt and the marquis, and she relished the escape.

Now in her early twenties, Rose was feeling the need to be on her own, established in her own household. Her difficult financial situation tethered her to her in-laws, but she was not at ease in the marquis's house any longer. Her legal separation from Alexandre created a certain distance, an awkwardness that could not be bridged. From time to time Alexandre visited his father, who was quite ill, and Rose had to accommodate herself to these encounters, and to Alexandre's varying moods. At least once Alexandre arrived on the day of a royal hunt. Rose had been invited to join, but no invitation was forthcoming for Alexandre. He requested to be allowed to follow the hunt at a distance, but even this was refused. His vexation was very great, and he made no effort to hide it. Cutting short his visit, he galloped off, seething with resentment, determined to find other amusements.

On Eugene's fifth birthday he went to live with his father in Paris, and Alexandre promptly entrusted Eugene to a tutor with a house on the rue de Seine. (Alexandre still had no fixed residence of his own, and was obligated to live with his regiment for at least six months of the year.) Though Rose and Alexandre were able to communicate civilly about their children from time to time, and although Alexandre seems not to have raised any further objections about Hortense's paternity, there was ongoing friction between the spouses. Alexandre's impatient creditors still came to Rose for payment, so that she lived amid constant harassment. Rose and Alexandre were at odds over unsettled property issues, and Rose, her patience long exhausted over the vital issue of Alexandre's default in paying her her legally stipulated allowance, was threatening to take her uncooperative husband to court once again.

It is not unlikely, though no evidence exists, that while living in Fontainebleau Rose began to have lovers.[1] It would have been the acceptable thing, in the worldly society in which she now found herself, for her to enter into an intimate relationship with an older man who could both protect and, to some extent, support her and pay her bills. The Duc de Lorge, a middle-aged peer whose wife was lady of honor at the court, was said to be her lover, and there may have been others.

By the start of Rose's second year at Fontainebleau a change was coming over the town. The royal finances were sinking further and further into disarray, and as an economy measure, the king's hunting season was shortened to a few days. The number of social events fell, far fewer courtiers and officials passed through town on their way to the palace, and instead of the usual bustle that bestirred the town in summer and fall, there was a distinct lull.

In the spring of 1787 Rose's uncle, Baron Robert Tascher, arrived from Martinique bearing some much needed funds. Edmée had been writing to him, telling him of her increasing hardship and urging him to collect whatever sums he could that were due her from property in Martinique and Sainte-Lucie. Beyond what Uncle Robert brought for Edmée, he gave Rose a letter of credit from her father for a little under three thousand livres—the first payment she had received from him in over eight years. And he said that more might well be on the way soon.

It was the first really good news Rose had had in a long time. She wrote to her father, urging him to send her more money as soon as he possibly could and to expedite payment to the marquis of the arrears of his rents from his estates. She waited in hope, her spirits buoyed by her uncle's visit. But month after month went by and no further sums were forthcoming. Joseph was at the nadir of his perpetual financial troubles. His mother-in-law Catherine des Sannois had recently died, leaving nothing to Rose-Claire. Joseph had counted on his wife's inheritance to pay off the mortgage on Trois-Ilets, and without it he was completely at the mercy of his creditors. Somehow he had managed to snatch from their grasp the few thousand livres he had sent to Rose, but there would be no more, despite the assurances of Rose's uncle.

By the spring of 1788, with her twenty-fifth birthday looming, Rose was realizing that her financial circumstances might never improve. Separated from Alexandre, she was even more in want than she had been while living with him—and she had the added nuisance of having to fend off his creditors, who were becoming more and more demanding. Her father would never be able to assist her, her aunt was generous but had little to offer. Her parents continued to urge her to return to Martinique, where her situation would be in every way easier; they had little money, but their home at Trois-Ilets was always open to Rose and Hortense.

Rose made up her mind to return to Martinique and began to make her preparations. Edmée lent her some of the money to make the journey, the rest she managed to scrape together by selling some of her possessions, including her harp. Whether she meant to return home for good or to stay only a matter of months is unknown, and possibly she was not sure herself.

With Euphémie and Hortense, Rose embarked on July 2, 1788 from Le Havre on the *Sultan*, a small mail ship, bound for the Windward Isles.

The voyage was relatively swift but not uneventful. Rough waters nearly capsized the ship before it could leave the harbor, and the passengers must have made the six-week ocean crossing in a state of dread. At last, however, they sailed into the turquoise waters of the Caribbean and smelled the sugar islands in the distance. The warm, languid air of the tropics enveloped them and soon the imposing peak of Mount Pelée came into view.

Rose was coming home to the land fondly called the Pays des Revenants, the "country of those who return," but she was returning greatly changed. She was now Viscountess de Beauharnais, her creole drawl had been sharpened by a Parisian crispness of speech, and everything about her—the style of her clothes, her manner and bearing, her tastes and preferences—bespoke a different and more sophisticated world. She could, and no doubt did, speak familiarly of the royal court, of the appearance and manner of the king and queen, of her headlong gallops following the royal hunt. And, of course, she was returning surrounded by scandal, for Alexandre's assault on her reputation still reverberated in Martinique, and his retraction before the magistrates of Paris counted for little in the drawing rooms of Fort-Royal.

Like it or not, Rose was a figure of controversy, with her family and friends defending her and Alexandre's sympathizers repeating his slanders. Laure de Girardin's family and friends had turned against Rose, and even her own old friends, well disposed toward her as they were, now saw her through new eyes. For she was no longer one of them, her years in France had altered her and had aroused secret envy in some. She had become a woman of the world, and as such she was an object of suspicion.

Apparently Rose reacted to the swirl of gossip her presence caused by ignoring it—and doing exactly as she pleased. Knowing that she could not win over her critics, she made no effort to ingratiate herself with them. She was simply herself, bright, appetitive, and full of ardor for life, effervescent, pleasure-loving, and warm. With her graceful figure, light brown hair and dark blue eyes with thick dark lashes, she was at this time at the height of her attractiveness and sexual allure. Men were drawn to her, and she basked in their attentions.

A naval officer who observed Rose in Martinique wrote that, "without being exactly pretty, [she was] nevertheless attractive because of her style, her gaiety and her good heart." "She defied public opinion rather openly," he added, and she spent money freely, expecting her more affluent admirers to pay her bills.

Rose took her five-year-old daughter to Trois-Ilets where Hortense met her aunt Manette, her grandmother and grandfather Tascher for the first time. It was a sad encounter, however, for Joseph Tascher had become a frail invalid and Manette, pale and bedridden, was gravely ill. Rose-Claire, bad-tempered and sharp, chastised Hortense for giving away coins to the slaves (who clung to her and kissed her feet in gratitude) and made her cry.

If Rose had changed in the nine years since she left Martinique, the island had changed as well. Fort-Royal was still provincial in many ways, but its citizens could now keep up with events in Europe through local newspapers and by attending the meetings of learned societies. The Circle of Philadelphians discussed and embraced the principles of the American Revolution; the Royal Society of the Arts and Sciences promoted the forward-thinking practice of inoculation and debated the merits of mesmerism in the treatment of disease.

Another topic of serious debate was abolitionism. The prevailing philosophical climate favored liberty for all, and found slavery abhorrent. In France, a Society of Friends of the Blacks advocated freeing the slaves, and there were some Creoles on Martinique who advocated this too, despite the alarmingly severe economic and social consequences it would be certain to bring. Four out of five people on Martinique were slaves, and there was a large population of freed slaves living in towns. The island had a history of slave rebellions, and there was reason to fear that, as the infectious ideal of liberty spread throughout the slave population, an uprising might well result.

By the spring of 1789 the chief topic of discussion had become the Estates General, the ancient representative body King Louis XVI had summoned to assent to the levying of new taxes. Among the twelve hundred delegates were Alexandre de Beauharnais and his brother François, the former bursting with liberal ideas, the latter a staunch conservative. It was said that the Estates General intended to draw up a constitution for France, inspired by the American Constitution but with the inclusion of the king, and optimists foresaw in this political experiment a way for France to overcome its financial and governmental crises and achieve far-reaching reform.

Bulletins from France were eagerly awaited, and each piece of news—already many weeks out of date, because of the long sea voyage—was eagerly, and nervously, examined and argued over. When, sometime in the late summer, it was learned that a new political body had emerged from the Estates General, the National Assembly, and that there was widespread unrest in Paris, with mutinies among the soldiers brought in to guard both the capital and Versailles, the islanders became alarmed.

Then arrived word that on July 14, with Paris full of rumors that the king had sent thousands of fresh troops into the city and that massacres of innocent citizens had begun on the rue St-Antoine, barricades were erected. A huge armed crowd of unemployed workmen, mutineers, and angry radicals marched to the medieval fortress of the Bastille, an antiquated and near-empty prison, expecting to find ammunition stored in its dungeons. When the commander of the Bastille's small garrison resisted the crowd's demands, shots were fired and eventually the fortress was captured. In the bloody aftermath the commander was butchered, his body mutilated, and many of the garrison soldiers were tortured and murdered by the crowd.

As they read the accounts of the events of July 14, 1789, the islanders could sense, even at a distance of thousands of miles, that an important turning point had been reached. It was not just that an ancient fortress had been captured by a mob in a moment of rebellious madness. This was an event of a different order, symbolic of a wider transformation. The invaders of the Bastille were being cele-brated by the Parisians as popular heroes, champions of liberty against the tyranny of the king. They had taken power into their own hands, acted on their own authority. The people, not the government, had acted swiftly, decisively, and with savage ferocity to defend themselves and their freedom, with consequences for the future that no one could as yet foresee.

8

Transformation

*I*t did not take long for the revolutionary climate in Paris to affect Martinique. A Colonial Assembly was appointed to match the new Constituent Assembly in the French capital. Delegates debated motions, discussed reforms, put forward declarations just as the delegates in Paris did, and representatives from the Windward Isles journeyed to France to make their voices heard in the new political forums that were undertaking to redesign the social order.

Under the increasingly weak sovereignty of the king, the National Assembly in Paris was exercising remarkable authority. On the night of August 4, 1789, three weeks after the capitulation of the Bastille, many of the noble delegates to the Assembly stood before their colleagues—and symbolically before the entire nation—and renounced their feudal privileges. These privileges, including the right to collect seigneurial taxes, exclusive hunting rights, the right to own serfs and to adjudicate disputes, had been exercised by noble families for centuries. Now, in the name of equality for all male citizens, they were offered up on the altar of liberty. Among the nobles who spoke eloquently on that historic night was Alexandre de Beauharnais, a warm advocate of equality.

Only a few weeks later, the National Assembly decreed the Declaration of the Rights of Man and the Citizen, a ringing pronouncement that disregarded the time-honored principle of the absolutism of the king and proclaimed, echoing the American Declaration of Independence, that government exists for the governed, not for the benefit of those who govern, that nature created all men free and equal, and that resistance to oppression is the right of every free citizen.

King Louis, well-meaning as ever but troubled by the Assembly's rebellious mood and too confused to perceive clearly that the entire political order had begun to unravel, tried to go along with the swift march of events. To show his good will he wore a tricolor cockade— the emblem of the political reformers—in his hat and welcomed delegations from the Assembly and from the city of Paris at the palace of Versailles.

"All Frenchmen are my children," he told his brother the Count of Artois when the latter urged him to take his family and leave the country while he still could. "I am the father of a big family entrusted to my care." There was unrest in the family, even hatred, but it was the duty of the patriarch to stand benignly by until harmony was restored.

Like the king, the provisional governor of the Windward Isles, the elderly Monsieur de Vioménil, wore the tricolor cockade in his hat, and it soon became unsafe to walk the streets of Fort-Royal without displaying the tricolor. Those who did not display it were suspected of harboring treasonous sentiments, or of disapproving of the work of the National Assembly, and were liable to be attacked. Women wore gowns of red, white and blue stripes in imitation of the patriotic Parisian fashion; red, white and blue ribbons were braided into horses' manes; red, white and blue streamers fluttered from the handles of parasols, walking sticks and carriage drivers' whips in a self-conscious parade of loyalty to the new governing bodies and their forward-looking principles.

But behind the patriotic façade there was widespread fear, for it was apparent that, with every daring political advance, forces of chaos were being unleashed. Crime was on the increase. Individuals, entire families were assaulted and killed, vehicles overturned, crops and manor houses burned to the ground. In the cities, hostile crowds roamed the streets, on the verge of riot.

For if the delegates to the new assemblies and conventions sought reform, the sansculottes of Paris, the peasants in the countryside and the slaves in the cane fields wanted revenge, and sought it with a feral savagery that made their social superiors shudder with dread. In panic, wellborn Parisians left France, fleeing the instability, the mounting disorder, the pervasive sense of fear.

The same atmosphere of panic, uncertainty and fear affected the colonial population of Martinique, especially the large landholders, called the "Grands Blancs," who felt themselves to be most affected by the advocates of political change and most vulnerable to the threat of a slave rebellion. But unlike the aristocrats of Paris and Versailles, they were unable to flee to safety; there were too few ships to carry them off the island, and by the summer of 1790, it looked as though what ships there were were about to be commandeered by the revolutionaries.

Battle lines had been drawn, between slave and free, black and white, citizen and soldier. There was no peace; in the long afternoons of sweltering heat, shots were fired, sporadic fighting broke out and gangs of toughs roamed in search of victims. Men were hanged in secret night raids, women were kidnapped and assaulted, and when the authorities ordered the soldiers to fire on the rioters or arrest the perpetrators of the night attacks, they did not always obey.

The Taschers remained at Trois-Ilets. Joseph was at the point of collapse, Manette very ill. Rose, fearful for her own safety and that of Hortense, decided to try to return to France, and her uncle Baron Tascher did what he could to protect her, sheltering her at Government House in Fort-Royal and attempting to arrange a passage for her and Hortense on one of the four warships riding at anchor in the inner harbor.

But the fate of the ships was in dispute. They were heavily armed, and as long as they remained under the control of Governor Vioménil and his officials, their guns could be used to prevent rebellion. Demands were made in the Colonial Assembly, echoed by the demands of the merchant seamen, that the warships be disarmed and put at the disposal of the Assembly delegates.

Meanwhile the weather threatened to disrupt all arrangements, for it was the season of the *ouracan* and if dangerous high winds arose, the ships would sink unless they could set sail quickly and escape the worst of the storm. (Shortly after Rose landed in Martinique in 1788 there had been a damaging hurricane, with crops destroyed and houses leveled; no one knew what effect another severe storm might have on the already unsettled state of affairs in Fort-Royal, let alone on the warships in the harbor.)

After several tense weeks, the situation took an alarming turn for the worse when the soldiers mutinied and delivered the forts on the heights above Fort-Royal into rebel hands. Rose's uncle was taken hostage. The governor fled into the interior of the island, knowing that, in the coming massacre—for the Grands Blancs feared nothing less than a bloodbath, with all the creoles slaughtered—he would be among the first targets of the rebels.

With her uncle unable to offer her any more help, Rose turned to two men—a naval officer named Scipion du Roure, who was serving aboard the frigate *Sensible*, and Baron Tascher's friend Durand du Braye, in command of all the warships in the harbor. She needed protection, for she and Hortense were in real danger at Government House, which had come under fire from the guns of Fort Bourbon. In a matter of hours, or at most days, all of Fort-Royal would be under the control of a politically inexperienced and vengeful group of townspeople, mulattoes, and slaves insisting that they were now free men and that they and they alone were the governing body in Martinique.

Early in September the new rebel government announced that Fort-Royal would come under general bombardment in twenty-four hours. The narrow, rutted tracks leading out of the town were soon clogged with people rushing to escape disaster. Carts and wagons piled high with possessions crawled along the muddy roads, some pulled by sweating, straining men for there were no horses or mules to be had. Civil war was imminent, with the guns of the four warships the only remaining line of defense for the duly constituted royal government.

Durand du Braye, unable to contact the governor and cut off from his superiors in France, decided to act on his own initiative. He lacked the forces to carry out a viable defense of the island—indeed he could not be certain that his sailors would obey his commands. He determined to make the attempt to sail to Bermuda to join a convoy en route to France. He managed to send a secret message to Rose, telling her to come to the harbor at once where a longboat would be waiting and urging her not to arouse the least suspicion, for if it became known that he intended to set sail the entire dangerous situation in Fort-Royal might explode, and no one would be able to escape it.

Rose had been vigilant, waiting in hope for just this message. Taking a small bundle of clothing and no trunks or bags (which would have betrayed her purpose as well as slowing her down), Rose hurried with Hortense and Euphémie away from Government House to the outskirts of Fort-Royal proper and then along its deserted streets to the Savane, the patch of open ground that lay between the town and the beach.

It was here, in this open area, that the greatest peril lay. Anyone crossing the Savane would be visible at once to the gunners in the forts, and would have no shelter or protection. Once Rose and her companions began their run toward the beach their intentions would be evident, and Durand du Braye's as well.

Rose grasped Hortense's hand and began to run. Soon they heard the crack of musket fire, and the booming of guns. Hortense remembered, many years later, that a cannonball hit the earth only a few feet away from them. Fortunately the shots went wild, and even before the runners reached the waiting longboat the rebels in the forts realized what was about to happen and began to aim at the ships rather than the trio escaping across the Savane. The ships were raising sail, drawing in their anchors and preparing to leave port. As Rose, Hortense and Euphémie were taken aboard the *Sensible*, they heard more cannonfire and began to fear that, having survived the flight across the town, they might well drown if a cannonball tore a hole in the frigate's hull.

For nearly an hour the guns pounded away, firing on the warships which hurriedly withdrew to the harbor mouth, out of range. There they remained, awaiting the promised bombardment of the town. For three days Durand du Braye kept his ships within sight of Fort-Royal, but then, with his supplies dwindling and still unsure of the loyalty of his sailors, he gave orders to sail for Bermuda. Once there, he took on fresh provisions and, in convoy with two other warships and a corvette, embarked for Toulon.

Rose, Hortense and Euphémie were aboard the *Sensible* for nearly eight weeks. Beyond the usual discomforts of the long voyage, there was the added inconvenience that the passengers had none of their possessions with them—no changes of clothing, no toilet articles, no smelling salts or headache powders, no nightgowns or warm cloaks or boots. Hortense's slippers soon wore out—she liked to dance on deck—and one of the sailors made her another pair from odds and ends of leather.

When she was not seasick, Rose kept company with Scipion du Roure, and may have shared his cabin. In any event her thoughts cannot have been happy ones, for she had left her father practically on his deathbed, and her sister incurably ill, and she had little hope of seeing either of them alive again. She must have been concerned to know whether Trois-Ilets was still safe, or whether the slaves had stormed the sugar mill and thrown the family out—or worse, stabbed or hanged them. She must have been worried about her uncle, about friends left behind, about the future of an entire way of life based on the inequality between master and slave.

The Martinique of her childhood was being destroyed, once and for all; only the lush tropical setting, the land itself with its green hills and bright flowers, its clear aquamarine waters and white beaches, would remain. But Rose's attachments were not only to the land, but to the people on it, black and white, the people who had formed her and with whom she still felt much affinity, despite her years in France. She was and would always be a creole, and it was creole culture that the rebels wanted to overturn.

Toward the end of October the *Sensible* sighted land, but it soon became apparent that the ship was off course. Driven in toward shore, the *Sensible* was in danger of running aground and breaking up on the rocky coastline. In desperation the captain ordered the anchor thrown out, and everyone on board, even Hortense, tugged at the tow line, trying to keep the frigate in deep water. Eventually, after a lengthy and exhausting struggle, the passengers and crew were relieved to feel the tow line begin to slacken slightly. The tide had begun to turn. Before long the ship was carried safely out into the channel again, and shortly afterward they landed at Toulon.

When after a few days' rest and a week's coach ride Rose at last glimpsed Paris she must have been astounded by the alteration in the mores and mood of the city. The people in the streets were plainly, even shabbily dressed. There were no more brocade jackets, silk breeches and lace ruffles to be seen, no elaborate high-piled wigs and jeweled hats, only suits of plain cloth and black tricorns, modest gowns and simple coiffures. Perfumes and pomades no longer masked the odors of sweat and dirt. Many people adopted the newest uniform of the revolution, the linen tunic and trousers called the "Carmagnole," in the patriotic colors of red, white and blue, and wore it day in and day out until the trousers were caked with the black mud of the streets and the tunic was stiff with dust and ash.

The tricolor was everywhere, worn on the bands of straw hats, on gloves, garters, parasols; children were small icons of the revolution in plainly cut suits of red, white and blue. Diamonds were nowhere in evidence, but people proudly wore pieces of polished grey stone made into necklaces or rings—slivers of the Bastille, whose hated building stones were crushed to make the highly valued trinkets.

People spoke to one another in simpler language, calling one another "Citizen" and "Citizeness" in acknowledgment of their new-found commonality, and there were no more deep bows and curtseys, no more doffing of hats or kissing of hands; instead, egalitarian manners prevailed. Even the king was expected to answer to "*tu*," the familiar form of "you" instead of the grander "*vous*."

The mood of the city had altered, and Rose must have been swift to notice the shift. An unaccustomed alertness was evident on many faces, an almost feral sniffing of the air, a quickening response to change. People listened apprehensively for the discharging of the alarm cannons on the Pont-Neuf and on the Arsénal, the signal for danger. Everyone was eager for news, and crowds congregated where news was to be found—in the new music-cafés where they drank coffee and listened to patriotic tunes while passing on the latest word from the National Assembly, in the place de Grève, where the troops of the national guard formed into parade order and discussed the rumors from the barracks, at the Palais-Royal, the nerve-center of political Paris, where speechifying, debate and agitation went on at all hours of the day and night, amid an atmosphere charged with excitement.

If the new Paris was wary and alert, it was also in search of diversion. Attendance was high at the circus, and also at Astley's Riding School in the Temple district, where the trick rider Antonio Franconi bestrode two handsome horses at once and made them pirouette on their forelegs. The shops and bookstalls were crowded, the theaters full; every night vaudeville, comic opera, classic plays and topical dramas drew large audiences. The new "Monsieur" theater, named for the king's brother, recently opened at the Tuileries at great expense, offered Italian opera with famous stars imported from Italy in the lead roles, and the opera lovers in attendance, though they wore their tricolor cockades and avoided offensive displays of wealth, nonetheless managed to add a hint of evening glamour to their egalitarian garb.

But there was an edginess to the festive spirit abroad in the capital, for everyone was concerned about the shortages of bread and coal, and it was said that farmers were expecting the new wheat crop to be scanty. Grain stores were declining rapidly, bread prices rising, and speculators were buying up much of the available grain and hoarding it, hoping to sell it in six months or a year at a great profit. Worried merchants raised their prices in anticipation of harsh financial times to come, uneasy Parisians hid their money and tightened their tricolor belts.

Only the rats, it seemed, were flourishing. They teemed in the thousands in every dark, crooked alleyway, haunted every courtyard, infested every attic and cellar. They ate through the sacks of stored grain in the riverside warehouses and swarmed over the provision ships bringing needed food into the capital. Nothing seemed to stop the rats, not baited traps, not firecrackers tossed into their midst, not vicious dogs or hungry cats. They were there, fat and sleek, their numbers growing hugely, gnawing away at the Parisians' foodstores even as the volatile political and financial situation gnawed away at their peace of mind.

Rose rented a house in the rue de l'Université and settled in there with Hortense, glad to be near Eugene, who had been enrolled by his father at the highly regarded Collège d'Harcourt. Eugene was nine years old, a dutiful if unimaginative boy with none of his father's erratic brilliance or verbal fluency. Because he suffered from a chronic eye disease, he had to miss many hours of instruction and fell behind in his studies, but he persisted, inspired in part by Alexandre's example and unwilling to bring discredit to the name of Beauharnais—a name that, in 1791, was becoming increasingly prominent in the political arena—by achieving only a mediocre performance in school.

Rose's return to France coincided with Alexandre's advancing celebrity. The revolution was turning out to be at once his proving ground and his field of glory. All his more positive gifts of mind and imagination were given full rein in the Assembly, and when he stood to speak, tall and fair and strikingly handsome, he was a compelling figure. Alexandre had been among the more prominent delegates from the beginning of the revolution, elected as one of the three secretaries to the Constituent Assembly and working tirelessly on issues of army and navy reform, problems of the sick and the elderly, constitutional questions and indeed any and all matters of public concern that came to his notice. In delivering his long speeches he did not so much forget himself as transcend himself, his vanity transmuted into a wide-ranging if abstract altruism, his proud intellect harnessed to the wider cause of Liberty for all—as the Assembly interpreted liberty.

Politically, Alexandre belonged to a group of liberal nobles called the "forty-seven," a group that included his mentor the Duc de la Rochefoucauld, the Marquis de Lafayette, the Duc d'Orléans and Alexandre's friend Charles de Lameth. Alexandre was perhaps the finest, or at least the most voluble, orator of the group, and extended his oratory to the Jacobin Club where he was chosen president. His celebrity extended far and wide; painters sought him out as a subject and when in August of 1791 the Salon of sculpture and painting was held, Alexandre de Beauharnais's portrait hung prominently in the crowded exhibition hall, along with that of another prominent delegate, Maximilien Robespierre.

By then Alexandre had become widely known as the man who had guided the destiny of France when for a brief time she found herself without a king.

Late in June, 1791, Alexandre had been elected to the rotating presidency of the Constituent Assembly for a term of two weeks. He had barely taken up his duties when word reached the Assembly that the king and his family had been secretly spirited away by persons unknown. Believing that King Louis had been kidnapped, most likely by a foreign power, the delegates feared that Paris would soon come under assault and all the advances made by the revolution would be reversed. Presiding over the hastily arranged meetings that were summoned in the wake of the crisis, Alexandre helped to calm the panic in the Assembly and in the capital at large, and prevented the most damaging of the rumors from causing riots. He ordered the arrest of the king and directed the search that resulted in his recapture at the town of Varennes near the Belgian border less than twenty-four hours after his escape began.

Once the errant king and his traveling party were back in Paris, Alexandre continued to direct affairs, and succeeded in holding together the conflict-ridden Assembly where the future of the monarchy was in bitter dispute.

Alexandre's distinction brought a certain distinction to Rose, who could not help but be associated with the party of the "forty-seven," if only because of the name she and her children bore. People pointed her out as the wife of Alexandre de Beauharnais, the lovely creole who lived apart from her husband yet was on civil terms with him and mingled familiarly with his friends and political associates and was said to be a gracious hostess.

At twenty-eight Rose could still appear young, but the strains under which she had lived had sharpened her features and drawn dark circles beneath her large dark eyes. Makeup helped to freshen her complexion, but all the unguents of Paris could not repair her blackened teeth (or ease the pain they must have given her) or sweeten her breath, and she had to be careful, when smiling her disarming smile, not to reveal the inside of her mouth. Her customary intensity was tempered by a new note of hesitation, a fear of making a false step, which added to her charm and kept her girlish.

Rose's lovely body drew much attention. "Her figure was perfect," the memoirist Madame de Rémusat remembered long afterward, "her limbs were supple and delicate, all her movements easy and elegant." Even her most fervent admirers admitted that Rose's attractiveness was rooted in the charming liveliness and "indescribable sweetness" of her expression rather than in perfection of feature, yet at social gatherings she often eclipsed beautiful women, though the precise source of her allure remained a mystery. Grace, warmth, the slow sway of her walk, her kindness and lack of artifice all contributed to the effect she created, and she still carried with her the seductive languor of the tropics and the lilt of creole speech.

Rose was captivating, and would have attracted attention even if she were not the wife of the Assembly's most celebrated orator. But as Alexandre's wife, she was perceived—correctly—to have influence, and so was sought out. Opportunities presented themselves; she was in a position to be helpful. She provided introductions, she wrote notes to government officials on behalf of friends and acquaintances and friends of acquaintances, she said a persuasive word at an appropriate time in an appropriate ear. She was good at these somewhat delicate maneuvers, which involved, if not exactly manipulating people, then guiding them to do what they were best at, directing their self-interest. Paris in 1791 was full of people with political, financial, and personal difficulties, all of which were made worse by the uncertain state of the government. Rose gained a reputation for helping to alleviate difficulties, for doing valuable favors. And if she began doing these favors out of kindness and a sincere desire to be helpful, she soon realized that her kind intentions and acts could bring her a profit.

Opportunities presented themselves in the sexual arena too, and Rose, who could no longer count on any reliable financial support from the debt-ridden Alexandre, from Edmée, or from her late father (Joseph Tascher had died, deeply in debt, soon after Rose left Martinique and had been unable to leave her anything in his will), now entered into liaisons that mixed passion, affection, hardheaded pragmatism and venality in varying proportions.

It was hardly unusual, of course, for Rose, as a married woman, to have affairs. But the liaisons she now formed had a decidedly utilitarian aspect; one suspects, though no definite evidence exists, that in choosing her lovers Rose followed her head first, then her heart. It was not that she was unfeeling, merely that, given her needs and her very limited means of filling them, she now took the seemingly unavoidable step of entering what would later be called the demi-monde, the shadow-world at the margin of respectability populated by women whose sexual arrangements and financial survival were intertwined.

It was perhaps a natural step for Rose, the earthy West Indian, to take, though in a disconcerting way it seemed to lend credibility to Alexandre's past slanders. For Rose to follow the lead of her sexual instincts, and to be largely unconcerned about the societal consequences of her behavior, was a course of action encouraged by the times, which loudly advocated liberty in all arenas of life, and by her own quivering vitality. Like other societal roles, the role of women in 1791 was in flux, with some people advocating that women ought to be as free in their personal lives as men, as well educated as men and able to divorce their husbands should they choose to do so. A few daring women became orators and organizers; others simply lived their philosophy, abandoning traditional roles and shaping their lives along fresh lines.

In joining the ranks of those who departed from convention Rose was taking a large risk, for if the revolution advocated liberty, the revolutionaries, by and large, wanted that liberty for men, not women. Utopians who gave public lectures on the value of advanced education for women were booed, female orators were denounced as dangerous radicals who were bent on destroying the family, and women who lived outside the bounds of acceptable morality were scorned and shunned as shameless libertines—or worse, denounced as unpatriotic.

Such was the rather perilous direction Rose's life now followed, a course not exactly political in nature (Rose confessed herself much too lazy to be committed to any particular political group or view) but near to the center of the political arena, amid the swirl and excitement and danger of Paris on the brink of ever more daring revolutionary change.

9

A Turn into Madness

*L*iving by her wits and with the generous support of lovers, Rose settled into her apartments in the splendid mansion at 46 rue St-Dominique, in the heart of the chic Faubourg St-Germain, and flourished there. Fine houses in fashionable neighborhoods could be rented very reasonably in the third year of the revolution, as many emigrés had left hurriedly and allowed their furnished mansions to be turned into elegant hotels. Rose had the friendship and further support of a woman she had known as a girl in Martinique, Desirée Hosten, a wealthy widow of radical political views with two daughters, one of whom was close in age to Hortense.[1] Rose also drew heavily on the good will and abundant resources of one Monsieur Emmery, a banker from Dunkirk who had once been a Tascher family friend and who now proved willing to make loans to her so that she could live well.

Amid a circle of friends—fellow creoles, Alexandre's colleagues from the Assembly and Charlotte Robespierre, sister of Maximilien, aristocrats who had not emigrated, such as the Marquise de Moulins, the Marquise d'Espinchal, Madame de Lameth and Madame de Genlis, literary characters such as Bitaubé and Aunt Fanny's lover Cubières-Palmézeaux, and a handful of foreigners, among whom the Prince de Salm and his sister Amalia de Hohenzollern were the most prominent—Rose entertained in her newly decorated blue and silver drawing room. At last she had the means, and the freedom, to make her house a gathering place, if not for the highest circles of society, at least for a respectable tier. She was known for having a wide and varied acquaintance, for having "many connections in the offices of the ministries" as well as old friends from Penthémont and Fontaine-bleau, monarchists and anti-monarchists, ardent revolutionaries and others indifferent to political affairs, insofar as indifference was conceivable in the Paris of the early 1790s.

Dressed stylishly in the bright yellows and purples then in fashion (tricolor gowns were temporarily abandoned in the winter of 1791 to 1792), wrapped in a costly shawl, a matching hat setting off her brown curls, Rose went to dinner parties at the magnificent Salm mansion or visited the salon of Alexandre's aunt Fanny de Beauharnais in the rue de Tournon, where, it was said, lights burned all night long and conversation never ceased.

There was much to talk about that winter. The creoles exchanged news from Santo Domingo, where thousands of rebellious slaves had burned many plantations to the ground and massacred their white owners. Monarchists speculated about the future of the royal family and whispered about emigré armies being formed just across the borders. Financiers talked of the rapidly falling value of the paper money, or assignats, which the government had put into circulation in lieu of coins, and of the frightening inflation of prices. Everyone talked worriedly about food shortages and food riots and about inflammatory rumors that the king, never a true friend of the revolution, was deeply involved in a conspiracy to starve the populace of Paris.

A subject of perennial concern was the revolution itself. Many people believed that, after several years of turmoil, social upheaval and constitutional change, France had at last achieved stability. There were celebrations to mark the end of the revolution. The outflow of emigrés slowed, briefly, and the taut, wary mood of the city seemed to slacken. Conversation in the salons and drawing rooms turned to gossip and more general topics—the novels of Rose's creole friend Madame de Hautpoul, the current fad for séances and the lore of the Cabala, and, Aunt Fanny's favorite subject, the "illuminist" teachings of the writer Saint Martin.

Rose visited Fontainebleau, and also spent time at Desirée Hosten's other home at Croissy, a small suburban village where she met, among others, Madame Campan, formerly the queen's principal bedchamber woman, the attractive, impassioned Jean Tallien, a connoisseur and collector of women who worked in the public prosecuting office, and the worldly Gascon Bertrand Barère de Vieuzac, a clever lawyer who, like Rose, was good at adapting himself to fit whatever circle he found himself in.

Along with the other members of the Constituent Assembly, Alexandre had left the political arena in September of 1791, to make way for the new governing body, the Legislative Assembly. The welfare of France continued to be his abiding passion, however, and before many months had passed he found a new niche in the revolutionary army. So immersed was Alexandre in public affairs that it was largely left to Rose to look after the children. Eugene was then eleven, Hortense nine; they were children of turmoil, never having known a settled life and in recent years caught up in the maelstrom of the revolution. Their birthright was aristocratic, yet Eugene, who was particularly close to his father and proud of him, was learning to be a good republican.

Hortense was still young enough to be more absorbed in friends and pastimes than in the upheavals of government. With her cousin Emilie and Desirée Hosten's daughter, also called Desirée, Hortense put on comedies in a small theater set up in her mother's rooms, attracting an indulgent audience from among her mother's friends. She was a thoughtful little girl, with a long face and a marked overbite. She had her mother's grace, and her father's pale blonde hair and blue eyes, but she did not promise to develop into a beauty— and in the Paris of the 1790s, beauty was still very much the measure of a woman's worth.

The apparent calm of the winter of 1791 to 1792 was abruptly shattered when late in April Parisians awoke to find themselves at war. Emigré armies, backed by the formidable professional troops of Austria and Prussia, were massing on the border, preparing to invade France and oust the revolutionary government. The Legislative Assembly voted to declare war and the National Guard, gathered on the Champ-de-Mars before the Altar of the Nation, announced to the citizens of the capital that "France is at war with tyrants!"

The stirring announcement unleashed furious activity. Parisians threw themselves into preparing for war with an avidity not seen since the enthusiastic destruction of the Bastille three years earlier. Spurred on by desperation—for it truly seemed, in the early weeks after war was declared, that France was about to be overwhelmed by superior force of arms—the citizens turned every square and marketplace into a workshop. The broad esplanade outside the Invalides became an open-air armaments factory, with two hundred and fifty forges operating nonstop, their orange flames glowing by night like some hideous vision of hell, their thick black smoke drifting across the river by day. Teams of grimy, sweat-drenched metalworkers labored to produce cannon at the rate of four a day, while out in the river itself, boats near the Tuileries gardens were turned into workshops where rifles were made. Women were enlisted to sew uniforms, children to scrape the saltpeter from city walls for use in making gunpowder. Heavy bells were lowered by rope from the towers of churches to be melted down to make lead bullets.

But the exhilaration brought on by all this communal effort soon turned to apprehension. For the revolutionary armies sent into the field were losing, and losing decisively. Alexandre de Beauharnais's prolix memos about the need for army reform had gone unheeded; the men in the hastily recruited regiments were poorly equipped, badly trained, inadequately provisioned. Prudent officers realized that to commit such troops to battle, given their shortages of arms and materiel, would mean sending them to certain death, with no chance of victory to redeem their sacrifice.

What was even more sobering was that the spirit of the revolution, which had brought about so much liberating social and political change, was having an unanticipated subversive effect on morale and discipline. Men accustomed since 1789 to asserting their individual rights against entrenched authority and privilege brought this same mentality to soldiering, with the result that groups of soldiers took it upon themselves to vote on whether or not to obey the commands of their officers. Widespread mutiny and desertion depleted the ranks; some officers were murdered by rebellious troops, others resigned in frustration. Still others, surveying the situation as coolly and professionally as they could, recommended that the government make peace before a cruel and humiliating surrender was forced upon it by invading armies.

By July the capital was in a state of near-panic. A crowd had overrun the Tuileries, shouting threats, breaking furniture, and insulting the king and queen; they had barely been restrained from harming the royal family. Responding to the worsening war news, volunteers were pouring into Paris from the provinces, eager to fight in defense of their homeland, but it was not enough merely to fill the depleted ranks; there had to be reorganization, rearmament, above all a transformation in attitude on the part of the men. Meanwhile, in the faubourgs where laborers predominated, there was an unsettling increase in crime and disorder. Gangs of toughs in red Phrygian caps—in ancient Greece, the symbol of the freed slave, now the symbol of the radical element in the Parisian population—ran through the streets waving thick cudgels, shouting that the Austrians were coming and assaulting anyone they suspected of being an "enemy of the revolution."

Day after day the Parisians suffered, besieged not only by the foreign armies but by the relentless soaring temperatures of the hottest July in memory, fearing that deserters from the army were about to invade the city, dreading further increases in the already high prices of bread and wine, avoiding the noisy demonstrations by red-capped revelers shouting "Death to the King! Kill the Queen! Tremble, tyrants! We are the sansculottes!"

Near the end of the month a stern challenge was issued by the commander in chief of the combined emigré and foreign armies, the Duke of Brunswick. Responding to the threats made against the royals by the menacing crowd in the Tuileries, the duke swore that if the palace was invaded again, or if disrespect was shown to the king and queen, Paris would be utterly destroyed. Any soldier who resisted the advancing armies would be shot immediately.

The duke's warning was taken as a challenge. Crying "Citizens to arms!" soldiers demonstrated, radical leaders shouted for an end to the monarchy that had betrayed the citizens and the revolution, and on August 6 a huge crowd gathered in the Champ de Mars to insist that the king abdicate.

All the forces unleashed by the revolution were building toward an explosive climax. Citizens were made to swear oaths "to be faithful to the Nation, to uphold Liberty and Equality, to die defending them." Streets were patrolled at night, and anyone out after ten o'clock was liable to be arrested. The radical leaders of Paris, not the Legislative Assembly, were in control of events, and events were moving quickly—too quickly for judgment to restrain emotion and the raw momentum of fury unbound.

After a night of confused alarms when all the bells of the city were rung to rouse the populace, an enormous crowd swept into the gardens of the Tuileries on the following afternoon, August 10, shouting "Treason! Treason! Death to the traitors!" Armed with knives, pikes, axes and sticks, the angry Parisians—craftsmen, shopkeepers, laborers, apprentices, women mingling with the men—stormed the palace, determined to complete the bloody work they had left undone two months earlier. The Swiss Guard, in charge of defending the palace, fired on the crowd until their ammunition ran out, after which they continued to stand their ground, fighting hand-to-hand in the gardens and on the palace steps until they were overwhelmed and murdered by the oncoming tide of axe-wielding citizens.

For three hours the crowd rampaged through the palace, stabbing and bludgeoning everyone they found there, from grooms to cooks to young page boys. They did not find the king or the queen. They had escaped to the hall where the Legislative Assembly was held. Frustrated at not being able to massacre the sovereign, the blood-crazed invaders began slashing the bodies of the slain guardsmen and palace servants, cutting off their heads, their hands, the men's penises—whatever would serve as a gruesome trophy. Finally, with the palace a shambles and a thousand corpses rotting in the heat, the Parisians left, but their bloodlust was not yet abated.

Three weeks later, in the first week of September, with the newly formed radical Insurrectionary Commune of Paris in effective charge of the government of France, another orgy of bloodletting began. Newspapers spread false rumors that counterrevolutionaries were at work, royalist conspirators plotting with the enemy to destroy the revolution. Priests and prisoners came under suspicion. One widely circulated pamphlet described a plot by the former King Louis— now deposed by the Assembly—to kill all the citizens of Paris on the night of September 2.

Some two hundred assassins in the pay of the Commune (so it was said) began their butchery on that day, September 2, and kept it up for the next five days. Priests were attacked and killed as they

rode through the streets in hackney coaches. Prisoners, male and female, were dragged from their cells and stabbed; even the prison
hospital at Bicêtre, which housed the invalid poor and insane, was
the scene of a brutal assault. The destruction spread to the town of
Gisors, where Alexandre's colleague and former patron the Duc de la
Rochefoucauld, always an active and high-minded supporter of the
revolution, was cut to pieces and his son murdered, his wife and aged
mother forced to watch in horror.

Each murderous act seemed to lead on to another, in a chain of
ever more ghastly massacres. Stupefied with drink, the assassins in
Paris emptied prison after prison, loading the piles of corpses into
carts bound for the quarries at Montrouge. No one attempted to
stop them; they claimed to have the sanction of the Commune, and
in some cases they carried out a brief and grotesque mock trial in
which the victims were questioned about their loyalty and condemned
before being dispatched.

Seminarians at St-Firmin were killed, and many priests at the abbey
of St-Germain, and at the Carmelite convent in the rue de Vaugirard,
where one hundred and sixty priests were being detained for refusing
to take an oath to uphold the constitution; a group of assassins
wearing red caps and butcher's aprons killed all but forty.

Slaughter on such a scale had not been seen in France since the
days of the religious wars two hundred years earlier. Victims num-
bered well over a thousand. Walls were covered in blood, courtyards
fouled with reeking innards. In the center of paved streets, gutters
ran red, and the stench of death was everywhere. It was as if a savage
delirium had settled over the city, a blood-frenzy that led the assassins
to dehumanize their victims even as they dismembered them and
desecrated their corpses. At the height of the savagery, the murderers
dined at tables made from their victims' naked bodies, drank their
blood, cut off their ears and pinned them to their tunics. A demon
of carnage had been loosed, a fiendish spirit that had nothing to do
with liberty, equality or fraternity. The revolution had taken a turn
into madness.

Terrified by the sudden escalation of violence, near enough to the
sites of slaughter that she could hear the cries of the dying, Rose
shut herself in the house in the rue St-Dominique and waited for

the chaos to end. Eugene and Hortense were with her, their schools having closed the previous month.

Rose was well aware, as were all Parisians, that her situation had changed. Nothing was as it had been, and no one knew what to expect. When on September 20 the Legislative Assembly was dissolved and a new body, the Convention, abolished the monarchy and began making sweeping changes in every area of public life, it was clear that anyone with ties to the old order was in great peril.

With foreign armies poised to cross the border at any time, a hostile government installed at the Tuileries, paid assassins at large in the city and winter coming on, many Parisians hastily abandoned their possessions and made every effort to leave the country. The Commune made it difficult to leave, ordering the city gates closed and sending patrols out to guard the roads. There were no horses to be had, the army had taken them all, and even carts and wagons were in short supply. Still, some would-be emigrés made it to safety, fleeing to the Normandy coast in hopes of finding a ship that would take them to England.

For the citizens unable to escape, Paris was a sober, even a somber place that fall. Social life ebbed, most of the great houses and salons were closed, though the theaters remained open. Efforts were made to wash away the bloodstains from the recent massacres, the walls were scoured with vinegar and the bloody remains dumped in the river or buried in shallow graves. But the streets were still dirty— much dirtier, people said, than in the days of the monarchy—and the new government was no more efficient than any of the earlier ones in keeping the gutters swept and the sewers unclogged. The muck gave rise to a new occupation, that of "gutter leaper." For a small sum a woman in a clean gown and unsoiled clogs could hire a gutter leaper to carry her on his back across a filthy open sewer, preserving her clothes and her dignity.

Rose determined that her children, at least, should escape the dangers of Paris, and she made arrangements with her friend the Prince de Salm, who was about to emigrate, to take Hortense and Eugene with him. But Alexandre, when he heard of the plan, intervened to prevent it, sending an army courier to intercept the traveling party and ordering Hortense back to Paris and Eugene to school in Strasbourg, where he himself was. Recent events had not shaken Alexandre's faith in the revolution, and if it became known that his children had been sent out of the country his own loyalty would be put in question. He was already suffering under the stigma of having an emigré relative; his brother François, an ardent royalist, had become an officer in the army of the Duc de Condé, bringing all the Beauharnais family under suspicion.

Alexandre's faith in the revolution was naive, and Rose knew it. She took no interest in politics, but she had become adept at the art of survival, and her instincts now told her that her very survival, and that of her children, would soon be at stake. She set about to broaden her circle of acquaintances, drawing on her own reputation as a broker of favors, on Alexandre's military rank and on the influence of her lovers. Calling herself "Citoyenne Beauharnais," and affirming her loyalty to the new government, Rose braced herself for the unknown perils to come.

10

Citizeness Beauharnais

The new government that swept into power late in September, 1792, began at once to dismantle the past. There was to be a fresh start. Not only was a new governing body, the Convention, installed, not only was the monarchy abolished, but time itself was revolutionized. Beginning on September 22, 1792, the Convention declared a new calendar to be in effect. That day became day one of Year One of the Republic One and Indivisible. Each year would have twelve months, but they were to be new months, with names derived from the cycle of nature— Nivôse, Snowy Month, Pluviôse, Rainy Month, Ventôse, Windy Month, and so on—rather than from Roman gods, rulers or numerals as in the past. Weeks were declared obsolete; instead each month was to be divided into three cycles of ten days each.

There were no more Sundays, no more religious observances or religious holidays; instead, revolutionary festivals were established, festivals of agriculture, liberty, marriage—and of the Supreme Being. Belief in an afterlife became anathema. Death, according to the Convention, was nothing more than an eternal sleep and all ideas of heaven and hell belonged to the oppressive, prerevolutionary past and ought to be discarded. Saints' names disappeared from roads, villages, public buildings. Babies, no longer christened in church with the names of saints, were now named Republic or Civilization or Equality instead of Jean or Marc or Marie.

Insofar as possible, old ways of thinking were being changed. And in January of 1793, the quintessential symbol of all that was being discarded, King Louis XVI himself, was led to the scaffold in Revolution Square and executed by the quintessential symbol of the new government, the guillotine.

Rose stayed on in Paris as long as she could, amid increasing difficulties and dangers. There were severe shortages of food and coal. Bread was so scarce that rioters broke into the bakeries and stole what few loaves they found there. Many shops were empty. Even when goods were to be had, they cost so much that no one could afford them—least of all Rose, who was struggling to get by on small loans from the ever faithful banker Monsieur Emmery.

Every time she left her house in the rue Dominique (no longer the rue St-Dominique) she risked encountering an angry throng from one of the Paris sections or a local Jacobin club, holding a demonstration to demand that the Convention dispense bread, restore order and punish the enemies of the revolution. Amid the general disruption, political factions fought for supremacy, leaders rose and fell and the Convention delegated more and more of its powers to the Committee of General Security, which carried on the urgent work of raising armies and keeping them (badly) equipped and supplied, and the Committee of Public Safety, the true executive of the revolutionary government, which had the nearly impossible task of preserving an independent France within a hostile Europe.

Rose was no stranger to the elegantly appointed headquarters of the Committee of Public Safety, whose salons were furnished with luxury goods confiscated from the mansions of the emigrés. Her friend Barère was secretary to the committee, and Rose, persisting in her part altruistic, part self-interested career of brokering her valuable contacts on behalf of those in need or in danger, was often present at Barère's early-morning receptions. No doubt Rose cultivated her friend Charlotte Robespierre as well, whose ascetic, austerely republican, chillingly ruthless brother Maximilien became head of the committee and its most feared member.

Another public body became increasingly visible in the spring of 1793, the revolutionary tribunal. Its task was to discover, bring to justice, and eliminate anyone held to be an enemy of the revolution. And in that anxious season, when the officials in Paris faced not only the armies of Prussia and Austria, Spain and Piedmont, but hordes of hostile peasants rising in counterrevolution in the west and south, nearly everyone came under suspicion as an enemy of the revolution. The tribunal sent its thousands of spies into every neighborhood, set neighbor against neighbor, even relative against relative. Scores of denunciations were made, victims were hounded down and taken from their houses, often in the middle of the night, and, after a hurried trial, were sent to their deaths.

"Vive la Sainte Guillotine!" The macabre cry rose from many throats as, eager to watch the ritual murder that was becoming Paris's daily spectacle, crowds gathered along the rue Honoré and the rue Antoine to watch cartloads of victims pass. They watched the former queen, now simply the Widow Capet, a shrunken, prematurely aged figure with grey hair and a sour expression, as she was led along on her way to execution, and jeered at her as she passed. They laughed and shrieked themselves hoarse at the antics of the crazed prisoners brought to the scaffold, their cries and moans, their fainting fits, their final despairing screams as the executioner, his purplish smock saturated with the blood of previous victims, took hold of them and laid them face down on the bloody plank beneath the triangular blade.

They relished the slurp and smack of boots sticking to the blood-drenched scaffold, the fearsome sound of the wooden neckpiece closing over the victim's thin white neck, the slight creak of the heavy, razor-sharp blade as it fell, then the leaden chopping sound, the strong spurt of blood, the head falling into the waiting basket, the lifeless corpse, still twitching, thrown into a waiting cart piled high with red bodies. Throughout the grisly spectacle they shouted and cheered, yelled encouragement, and showed their disappointment when the last of the victims had been dispatched and the last spectator had rushed forward to dip his or her handkerchief in the blood, a talisman against future harm.

Three thousand men and women died under the guillotine's swift, efficient blade in the latter half of 1793, so many that the cemeteries of the city could not hold them, and new ones had to be created in haste. Parisians living in the eastern part of the city, near the new graveyards, complained that the graves were too shallow and that they could not rid their houses and possessions of a perpetual "corpse stench" that hung over the entire vicinity. Such complaints did not deter the revolutionary tribunal, however, which felt hampered in carrying out its cleansing work by the limitations of the killing machines. Members of the tribunal investigated commissioning a larger guillotine, with four blades, which could despatch four times the number of victims in a day.

Citoyenne Beauharnais adapted herself to the times, staunchly proclaiming herself a loyal sansculotte and Jacobin, patriotic in her dress, cautious in her speech—for even the slightest word spoken against the government, however innocuous, could lead to arrest and death—outwardly supportive of the gory displays in the Place de la Revolution.

Behind closed doors, however, Rose no doubt gave in at times to her apprehensions, and became absorbed in trying to discover whether or not she was likely to fall prey to the revolutionary tribunal's insatiable appetite. All her childhood superstitions, her sense of fate and of the fragility of life, come to the fore. No doubt she laid out her fortune-telling cards often during the unnerving months of 1793, telling her own future and those of her friends, trying to see beyond the horrors of the present.

In September of 1793 the Convention issued the Law of Suspects, which identified as "suspect" all those who "by their conduct, their connections, their remarks, or their writings show themselves the partisans of tyranny." More specifically, it ordered the immediate arrest of all relatives of emigrés who "had not constantly demonstrated their devotion to the revolution." As the sister-in-law of François de Beauharnais (and as an aristocrat herself), Rose came under suspicion. Alexandre too, his father and Edmée, all his cousins, even his bastard children were in danger. Every citizen was required to obtain from his or her local municipal office a special certificate of citizenship, without which they were liable to arrest. Realizing that she would have a much easier time obtaining a certificate outside of radical Paris, Rose moved to Desirée Hosten's rented house in Croissy, six miles from the capital, and there Eugene joined her from Strasbourg.

A benign political atmosphere appeared to prevail at Croissy. The decrees from Paris were observed, but not strictly, and when an effort was made to find twelve villagers to serve on a local committee to investigate antirevolutionary activities, very few volunteers came forward, and the project was abandoned. There was a "national agent," elected by the villagers, whose task it was to keep the Committee of General Security informed about political attitudes and activities in the village, but he seems to have taken a tolerant rather than a suspicious view of the goings-on in the community. Certainly he did not oppose the awarding to Rose of her precious certificate of citizenship, and he even agreed to take twelve-year-old Eugene on as an apprentice, teaching him his own trade of cabinet-making. (Patriotic children all had to learn trades.) Hortense was apprenticed to a seamstress, and was an obedient learner, though the art of making gussets and darts interested her far less than finery and jewels.[1]

For a few brief months Rose seems to have evaded the menacing snare of the revolutionary tribunal, thanks in part, no doubt, to her friendship with Barère and with the public prosecutor of the tribunal, Pierre-François Réal, as well as the influential Convention deputy Jean-Lambert Tallien. The tally of her protectors was long, but the list of the proscribed connections was longer. Her friends from her Penthémont days and from her sojourn at Fontainebleau, her social contacts from the rue Dominique, her Beauharnais connections, all were drawn from the ranks of the aristocracy—and many had become emigrés. Try as she might to force herself into a republican, even a Jacobin, mold, Rose was ineradicably a member of the aristocratic elite, by birth, by long association, by marriage, probably also by sentiment, though she was not one to either speak or write about political philosophy. Had she not been married to Alexandre, and had Alexandre not forcibly prevented Rose from sending Hortense and Eugene out of the country, Rose herself would no doubt have been in Coblentz or Verona by the fall of 1793, living with her children among other emigrés and hoping for the return of the monarchy.

Once again, Alexandre was the problem. Alexandre, with his unswerving idealism, his gullibility, his naive denial of the revolution's increasingly retributive savagery. And his incompetence.

Alexandre had been promoted to a rank far above his actual capabilities. He had been given command of one of the newly formed armies of the republic, the Army of the Rhine, where he had soon shown his deficiencies as a commander. Largely because of his reluctance to commit his troops to battle (and because of his constant time-consuming pursuit of women and pleasure), the French-held city of Mainz, under siege from the Prussians, fell to the besiegers. In disgrace, he resigned his post, and by order of the Convention, retired to what he hoped would be obscurity on his family estate at La Ferté.

But Alexandre de Beauharnais bore a famous name. He had been too prominent throughout the course of the revolution to simply disappear. Though he made a characteristically flamboyant public confession of his inadequacy, admitting that he was "tainted" by aristocratic blood though "liberty and equality were engraved on his heart," from the time the Law of Suspects was issued he was a marked man.

Meanwhile Alexandre's sister-in-law Françoise de Beauharnais, wife of his emigré brother François, was arrested and imprisoned in Paris. Rose went to the offices of the Committee of General Security, hoping for an interview with an influential committee member, the elderly, vengeful lawyer Marc-Guillaume Vadier, so that she could plead for Françoise's release. The interview was refused—an ominous sign, not only for Françoise, but for all others associated with the Beauharnais name.

If she could not see Vadier, Rose could at least write to him. "I write to you frankly, as a genuine sansculotte," her letter read. "I am convinced that, on reading this memoir, your sense of humanity and justice will cause you to consider the situation of a woman who is utterly miserable." Françoise was innocent. Her only mistake was in marrying her husband, "an enemy of the republic," Rose insisted. She did not deserve punishment for that.

Rose was well aware that the arrest of Françoise was in all likelihood a prelude to the arrest of Alexandre. In her letter she tried to convince Vadier to spare him, and urged him to keep in mind the sharp divergence that had always existed between Alexandre's leftist opinions and his brother's staunch defense of the king.

"It would cause me chagrin, citizen-representative, if you were to confuse Alexandre in your mind with the elder Beauharnais [i.e., the elder Beauharnais brother, François]. I can understand your point of view; naturally you doubt the patriotism of former nobles, but perhaps there are those among them who are ardent friends of Liberty and Equality."

Alexandre, Rose insisted, had never departed from republican principles, his unswerving devotion to them was well known. "If he were not a republican he would have neither my respect nor my affection," she added. As an American—a label to which she clung more tenaciously than ever—she had always understood Alexandre's egalitarian ideals, even though the rest of the family misunderstood him.

"If I could have seen you, your doubts would have been dispelled," Rose told Vadier. "My household is a republican household. Before the revolution my children were indistinguishable from sansculottes, and I hope they will be worthy of the republic."[2]

Rose's letter was touching in its earnestness, but no one, least of all the shrewd Vadier, really believed that she was "a genuine sansculotte" or that her children had been raised as other than children of privilege. Rose herself was too well known, her social life too conspicuous, her associations with highborn lovers too notorious, for her Jacobin pose to be credible. She could not save her sister-in-law, or her husband, or herself. The most she could hope to do was to postpone for a few months the blow that must inevitably fall.

Early in March of 1794 officials in La Ferté were alerted that an arrest order had been issued for Alexandre de Beauharnais. When they went to apprehend him, he objected. Surely an error had been made. He was no enemy of the revolution; he belonged to the local Jacobin Club. But his arrogant bluster was ignored. He was taken to Paris, to the Luxembourg prison, and there informed that he had been formally charged with dereliction of duty in the defense of Mainz. After a few days he was transferred to a much more terrible prison, the former monastery of the Carmelite Friars, where prisoners awaiting execution were held.

When Rose learned what had happened to Alexandre she must have suffered fresh agonies of fear. Her husband's arrest put her under redoubled suspicion, and she knew that there were informers and spies in Croissy, that her house was being watched, her movements monitored and noted down, her every word reported. No doubt she worried about her children, and wished that she could send them away. Yet any effort she made to do so, the sending of a letter, a whispered discussion with a trusted friend, even an attempt to find horses and a cart, could give the revolutionary tribunal an excuse to arrest her.

So she stayed on in Croissy, living as quietly as possible, bearing up as best she could under the extreme uncertainty of her situation, throughout March and early April. The news from Paris was grim. Robespierre, head of the Committee of Public Safety and swiftly becoming the most powerful man in France, was stepping up his campaign to eliminate his enemies, and with the aid of his remorseless deputy Saint-Just, known as the "Angel of Death," was summoning more and more victims to the scaffold. There were those among Robespierre's colleagues in the Convention who urged moderation, and asked what had become of the spirit of fraternity, but there were many more who cringed in fear and did not dare speak out at all.

The last hope of the condemned, a Committee of Clemency that was established to scrutinize the list of imprisoned suspects and re-prieve those judged to be wrongfully seized, was lost when the Com-mittee was abruptly disbanded shortly after it was established. Purgation, not clemency, was the order of the day. Assassins were threatening Robespierre, plotters were said to be conspiring to murder the members of the revolutionary tribunal. With such clear threats to peace and order at hand and increasing, only one course of action made sense: to step up the process of eliminating the opposition.

Now the carts rumbling along the rue Honoré and the rue Antoine brought twenty, thirty, even forty or fifty victims to the scaffold at once. Old people, young girls, pregnant women—no one was spared. Lined up like dolls or toy soldiers, one by one they were handed up the steps to the waiting executioner, to be sent to their deaths with mechanical swiftness and precision. Many more women were being killed than in the past, wives, widows, sisters, mothers of emigrés and male suspects. Trembling with fear yet doing her best to keep her pretense of ardent patriotism intact, Rose must have appealed for leniency again and again to every influential friend she had, especially Barère, who was attempting in vain to unite the bitterly divided fac-tions in the Committee of Public Safety. If Rose appealed to Char-lotte Robespierre, her plea was in vain—or Charlotte's influence with her brother was not sufficiently strong to save Rose from peril.

For soon after Alexandre's arrest an anonymous message was sent to the Committee of General Security, informing them that Desirée Hosten's houses in the rue Dominique and at Croissy were "gathering places for suspected persons," and naming some of these. "Beware of the former viscountess, wife of Alexandre de Beauharnais," the informant went on, "who has many connections in the offices of the ministries."³ Rose and her friend Desirée Hosten were "dangerous," according to the letter-writer. They had to be eliminated.

On April 19, 1794, "as a measure of public safety," two deputies of the Committee of General Security, Citizens Lacombe and George, along with a member of the local committee, strode along the high street of Croissy bearing a warrant from the Committee for the arrest of Citizeness Beauharnais and Citizeness Hosten. Rose and Desirée Hosten were taken to Paris and detained there overnight in the convent of the English Ursulines while the house was searched. Quite possibly Rose had taken the precaution of removing or burning any incriminating papers in her possession; in any event, Lacombe and George found nothing to complain of among her effects, only "a multitude of patriotic letters which would serve only as praise for the citizeness." The house was sealed, a report was drawn up and signed by the deputies. All was in order.

No record exists of Rose's terrible hours in detention at the Ursulines convent. Probably she and Desirée Hosten were ordered to wait with other detainees in an overcrowded room. So many hundreds of arrests were being made, there was not enough space in the prisons of Paris to hold the accused, and the committee had to find temporary accommodations wherever it could. Even as she awaited word of her fate from the Committee of General Security, Rose may have hoped that one of her friends would manage to free her. By the second day of her detention, however, what hope she may have had must have dwindled. The worst had happened. Citizeness Beauharnais was officially committed to the prison at the former monastery of the Carmelite Friars, there to await death as an enemy of the revolution.

She had not been able to escape her fate. With the swiftness of a deadly *ouracan*, doom had fallen on Rose Tascher, Creole of Martinique, and no refuge was at hand.

11

The Days of the Red Mass

*S*trong-willed and stouthearted as she was, and clever at making and seizing opportunities, Rose was also high-strung and anxious, a creature of nerves. She was labile, full of apprehension, always a step away from losing courage and bursting into tears. So when she entered the dim interior of the Carmelite Prison, knowing that all who entered there were marked for death, her stomach sank and she grew pale with dread.

She found herself among walking specters, thin, dirty, unshaven men with kerchieves around their heads, their clothes ragged and unwashed, and gaunt, grief-stricken women, shorn of all adornment, some with their hair cut short, all plainly and meanly dressed. There was not enough room for them all; the sleeping rooms were filled to overflowing, and many inmates slept in the dank hallways where the air was thick with the stench of ordure and so humid that their clothes grew soaked overnight.

Every day more prisoners were brought in, and others left, taken off in carts to the Conciergerie to be tried and executed. No one knew, from day to day, when it would be his or her turn to be called to face the tribunal; each evening a list of names was read, and those whose names were not on the list felt the deliverance of a reprieve.

For Rose, already taut with worry, the constant cycle of dread and relief was in itself a torment. Beyond this, she had to accustom herself to sleeping on a straw mattress crawling with lice in a poorly lit dormitory with a dozen other women, to eating one scant meal a day, to dressing and undressing, washing, even relieving herself in public, for there was no privacy, and to being watched by taunting, foulmouthed guards who ransacked her few belongings frequently, looking for contraband.

It must have taken every bit of strength Rose possessed merely to cope with the shock of finding herself in such hellish circumstances, let alone to come to terms with the likelihood of execution. The darkness, the smells, the closeness of the atmosphere, the confinement must have depressed and disoriented her, while the indignities she faced from moment to moment must have eaten away at her veneer of composure and forced her to struggle for emotional equilibrium.

Her one consolation, in the early days of her confinement, were the visits of Hortense and Eugene. Hortense's governess Mademoiselle Lannoy brought them to the prison often, along with the family pet, a pug named Fortuné, and a basket of clean laundry. Seeing the children gave Rose something to look forward to, though their visits must have been deeply upsetting as well as joyful and each leave-taking must have been extremely painful, since neither Rose nor her children could be certain it would not be their last.

Rose saw Alexandre too, for while men and women were segregated from one another in their dormitories and at meals, at other times they were permitted to spend time in each other's company. No doubt Rose and Alexandre took some comfort from one another, for however bruising their relationship had been to Rose, and however uncomfortable and annoying it had been to Alexandre, their past was overshadowed by the enormity of their present peril. They were drawn together in a tender friendship in what they knew to be their last days, brought closer by their love and deep concern for their children and by what remained of family feeling.

Spiteful jailers soon intervened to prohibit the children's visits, but they came to the prison anyway, standing in front of the gates in the rue Vaugirard and looking up at the grey stone walls in hopes of catching sight of their parents. They were allowed to continue to bring clean linen to Rose, and they wrote out the lists of garments in their own handwriting, as a clue to their well-being. The guards took no notice of Fortuné, who wandered in and out of the prison at will; seeing this, and realizing that they could take advantage of Fortuné's proximity to their mother, the children wrote notes and concealed them under the dog's collar, where Rose found them.

Whether under Fortuné's collar or through some other subterfuge, Rose and Alexandre did manage to communicate with the world outside the prison. Alexandre found a way to send carefully prepared letters and petitions to the Convention, urging the members to reconsider his arrest and set him free. And when Hortense and Eugene were prohibited from entering the prison, their parents arranged for them to be taken to a structure in an adjacent garden from which two of the prison windows were visible. Rose and Alexandre appeared in the windows, and for a moment, the family was reunited, albeit at a distance. Making these arrangements required passing messages to the outside; presumably other messages, perhaps between Rose and her friends Barère, Réal, and Tallien, were also sent and received.

Gradually, as the early weeks passed, the gaunt, spectral figures around Rose took on names and identities. Some, such as the Prince de Salm (arrested when he returned Hortense and Eugene to Paris after Alexandre prevented their emigration) and Madame de Lameth, she knew already, others she came to know. Few of them were aristocrats, most were laborers, craftsmen or professional men caught up in the revolution's bloody undertow. An official list of the prisoners, preserved in the archives of the Paris police, includes clockmakers, tailors, domestic servants, soldiers, notaries and porters, along with a tobacco manufacturer, a painter, a lemonade-seller, and several jewelry-makers not yet out of their teens. There were a handful of former clergy—friars, priests, several abbots—and a number of military officers, along with farmers, fishmongers and day laborers.[1] In all, Rose's fellow-detainees at the Carmelite Prison were a cross-section of the population of Paris, the vast majority of them guilty of no crime save the unpardonable blunder of having offended the suspicions of those in power.

To keep up their spirits the prisoners adopted a tone of audacious bluster, a belligerent insolence in the face of death. Gallows humor prevailed: they joked about the guillotine and about the executioner, they held farcical mock trials and mimicked members of the government. One prisoner who survived the ordeal recalled later how he and his colleagues "laughed openly at the divinity of Marat, the priesthood of Robespierre, the magistracy of Fouquier [chief prosecutor of the revolutionary tribunal], and seemed to be saying to that bloodstained rabble, 'You may kill us when you please, but you will not prevent us from being pleasing!' "[2]

Above all, it was considered essential to be cheerful at all costs, and not to give in to melancholy or despair. Unhappiness was concealed beneath a mask of insolent frivolity. Every hopeful occurrence, however slight, was taken as an excuse for manic celebration; after the carts left each morning with their load of condemned prisoners, those remaining held a rapturous orgy of merrymaking.

In the shadow of the scaffold, the inmates gave in to an almost irresistible erotic impulse—a deep-seated natural response, no doubt, to the threat of extinction. The dark, fetid corridors were full of the sounds of lovemaking.[3] Romantic bonds were swiftly formed, rapidly consummated—and suddenly severed when the lovers' names were called by the jailers and their idyll abruptly ended by the guillotine. It was a frenzied time, a chaos of the emotions, when amid the muck and slime of the worst prison in Paris, and under the constant awareness of imminent death, it was nonetheless possible to taste the sublime.

Rose began a romantic liaison with the young and handsome General Lazare Hoche, a popular hero for his victories against the counterrevolutionary Vendéan rebels and former commander of the Army of the Moselle. The tall, curly-headed, ebullient Hoche, with his dashing manner and striking duelling scar, doubtless lifted her spirits; beyond this, Rose, always alert to opportunity, may have hoped that because of his popularity Hoche would in time be freed and that his freedom would guarantee hers. (Of the many men in the Carmelite prison at this time, Hoche was certainly among the best known and most likely to be rescued—if rescue was possible—by influential friends.)

That Hoche had only recently married a young wife whom he adored does not seem to have affected his liaison with Rose. Hoche wrote tender love letters to his wife, but she was not with him, and Rose was, and for all either of them knew, death could be only hours, or days, away.[4] Both Rose and her lover may have hoped that Rose would become pregnant, knowing that, with some exceptions, pregnant women were usually transferred to the much more pleasant environment of the Evêché hospice to await their delivery, and were not at risk of being brought to trial for many months.

Alexandre too formed a passionate liaison while in prison, and his lover, the beautiful blonde daughter of the recently executed General de Custine, was on terms of familiarity with Rose, whose dormitory room she shared. Rose was not like the other prisoners, Delphine de Custine was to write later. She could not seem to adopt the mask of bravado the others wore so bravely, her nerves were too taut; she was often in tears, her face puffy and her eyes red. She was visibly discouraged, to such a degree that the other prisoners were embarrassed by her emotional cowardice.

Yet they could not help but like her and feel protective of her, this small, sweet creole lady with the lovely smile and the tear-stained face. The charm of her manner, her unaffected appeal, her naturalness and the concern she showed for others won them over. She told their fortunes with her cards, she grieved openly when the day's quota of victims said their good-byes, her changing expressions and mercurial moods revealed openly what they were all feeling but did not allow themselves to display. They knew how much she dreaded the guillotine, and they hoped that she would be spared.

One night when Rose had been at the Carmelite Prison for about a month, Lazare Hoche's name was called by the guard reading the list of those to be removed to the Conciergerie the following morning.

It must have seemed, to Rose, as if a blow had been struck against her as well as against her lover. Even as she said her tearful good-byes, Rose must have been calculating, with dread, the implications of his summons to appear before the revolutionary tribunal. Hoche's popularity had not been able to save him—indeed it had seemingly worked against him. If he could not avoid the tribunal, then how could she? With Hoche's departure Rose's spirits sank lower, and she waited, disheartened and hopeless, for news of his death and for her own fatal summons.

The prison population was growing. There were more bodies jammed side by side in the corridors at night, more mouths at the refectory table for meals, more victims leaving each morning in the fearsome carts. The pace of the killing was speeding up, and still rumors spread that the public prosecutor was dissatisfied; he wanted swifter judgments, more efficient executions. Having large numbers of suspects detained in the prisons was a danger to the state, in the prosecutor's opinion. Such overcrowding bred conspiracies, rebellions, plots against the ruling committee. He wanted the prisons emptied, as rapidly as possible.

The last time there had been official pressure to empty the prisons, the September Massacres had resulted. Rose had heard horrifying stories of those days of butchery from an acquaintance at Croissy, Abbé Maynaud de Pancemont, who had been among the few clerics to survive the bloody attacks. Pancemont had told tales of brutal beatings and stabbings, of merciless killing sprees carried out by drunken assassins in a wild debauchery of violence. She knew that a similar onslaught of vengeful ferocity could be triggered suddenly, at any time, and when the guards began making sinister jokes about the good times they had in the September Days, and teasing one another about uncovering plots among the prisoners, her fears were redoubled.

Toward the end of May a young woman was arrested for attempting to stab Robespierre with a large kitchen knife she had concealed in her gown. She admitted that her aim had been to "kill the tyrant" and put an end to the glut of executions that had become a national calamity. The would-be assassin was arrested, yet there were many who secretly sympathized with her purpose, and were sorry that she failed. Some three hundred thousand people had been judicially murdered, and yet Robespierre had announced that an even more thorough cleansing of the body politic was needed. More deaths were necessary, he announced, to purge France of impure, corrupt elements that were impeding the progress of the revolution.

In response to the assassination attempt, and in an effort to find and eliminate still more "enemies of the people," a new law was passed, the Law of 22 Prairial, which inaugurated a bloodbath of unheard-of proportions.

Now there was no pretense of a trial for arrested suspects, only a routine sentence of death. The harried clerks of the revolutionary tribunal worked day and night, scrawling out the hastily written death warrants, and the prosecutor, Fouquier-Tinville, kept watch on their labors, it was said, around the clock. Now the deputies to the Convention feared to attend its sessions, dreading to attract the suspicious gaze of the all-powerful Robespierre, and feared equally to attend the killing sessions in the Place de la Révolution. The terrible click, slice, and leaden chop of the guillotine's blade went on, more rapidly than ever, but there were few onlookers to cheer and shout. Nearly everyone knew someone, or was related to someone, who had been executed. The entire country was in mourning, in confusion, in mounting panic. Where was the logic in this mad orgy of death?

Many whispered that Robespierre was himself the madness, that he was the high priest of this Red Mass, the holy guillotine his great altar. The whole bloody business was a product of his disordered mind, a mind unhinged by fanaticism and led into terrifying excesses unrestrained by humanity or sane reason.

Robespierre must be stopped. Yet how to stop him? Who had the power? The deputies cringed in fear, the prisons grew more crowded, and in the sweltering heat of July 1794, the Great Terror went on toward its gruesome climax.

On July 21 Alexandre de Beauharnais was suddenly summoned to appear before the revolutionary tribunal, charged, along with forty-eight others, with being an enemy of the people, accused of plotting a large-scale escape from prison. He was condemned to death.

There was no time to say good-bye to his children, or to Rose. On his way to take his seat in the waiting cart he handed Delphine de Custine a ring with an Arab talisman. Then he was gone. From his cell in the Conciergerie, where he waited to be taken to the guillotine, Alexandre wrote a last letter to Rose.

"I am the victim of the wicked lies of several so-called patriots," he wrote. "This devilish plot will hound me before the revolutionary tribunal; I have no hope of seeing you again, my dear friend, or of embracing my dear children."

Faithful to the last to the ideals of liberty, equality and fraternity, Alexandre could not see what so many others had come to realize: that the revolution itself was flawed, that in its search for earthly perfection it lost touch with humanity, just as Robespierre had, and that it was doomed to devour all its sons and daughters.

"During the storms of a revolution a great nation struggling to break its chains must wrap itself in a righteous suspicion," he wrote. "It must fear more to overlook the guilty than to harm the innocent." He was nothing more than an unfortunate victim of that "righteous suspicion." Alexandre was forgiving his enemies, striving, as ever, to take the larger view, to be the staunch patriot to the end.

"I regret my separation from a country which I love, for which I would have given my life a thousand times." "I shall die calmly, yet aware of the tenderest affections; I shall die with the courage of a truly free man, with a pure conscience, with an honorable spirit, whose most fervent prayers are for the welfare of the Republic."

For once Alexandre's exalted rhetoric matched the extremity of his circumstances, and his valor shone through. "Good-bye, my friend," he told Rose. "Find consolation in my children, console them by teaching them, above all by teaching them to overcome the memory of my fate by their virtue and excellence as citizens." "You know those whom I love," he wrote in closing. "Be their consoler and keep me alive in their hearts through your care. Good-bye—for the last time in my life I hold you and my dear children to my breast."

When a few days later Rose read Alexandre's name in the published list of those sent to the guillotine she fainted. She was weak and ill. For more than two months she had lived like an underfed animal in a dark and dirty cage, in daily dread of death. All around her people were sickening and dying, for the stifling heat bred infection in the airless prison rooms, and there was no clean water or nourishing food to restore health.[5] She had grown thin, there were dark circles under her eyes and her gaunt body was lost in the folds of the shapeless prison gown. A Polish doctor who examined her shook his head sadly and told the jailer that she could not live more than a week or two.

Rose knew that her hour had come. Her death would be ordered soon after Alexandre's, as it was customary for widows to be sent to the guillotine shortly after their husbands were executed. With the aid of Mademoiselle Lannoy, Eugene and Hortense had petitioned the Convention and the Committee of General Security for Rose's release, with no result. They had also appealed to Rose's friend Jean Tallien, and no doubt approached everyone else they could remember from among Rose's acquaintances who could possibly intervene to save their mother's life.

Guards came into Rose's dormitory and removed her straw mattress—a sure sign that a prisoner was about to be transferred to the Conciergerie to await execution. In her weakened state Rose could hardly protest this indignity, and in any case she had practically lost all hope. When the order for her transfer came, however, she was not taken away with the others. If, as the doctor said, she was dying, then there was no need to send her to the guillotine. Let her die in the prison, and spare the state the trouble and expense of dispatching her.

The prison itself was in any case in a state of turmoil. The chief jailer had himself been arrested, accused of permitting prisoners to correspond with friends on the outside. The guards, worried that they might be the next victims, resisted obeying the new jailer, who ordered all the prisoners locked in their rooms and waited nervously for fresh instructions from the Committee of Public Safety. In the Convention, a handful of deputies had at last begun to conspire against Robespierre. And as if to echo the rising swell of tumult in the city, the skies opened and a drenching rain flooded the streets of Paris.

It rained throughout the day on July 27, while in the Convention, a critical political battle was being fought. Robespierre had been calling for more punishments, denouncing his colleagues and threatening to arrogate more power to himself. Now his opponents, few in number at first, began to stand up to him. Slowly, over the course of the day, while the storm rattled the windows and the streets outside filled with mud, the political momentum turned. By the end of the day Robespierre stood accused of being an enemy of the people. He and his supporters were arrested.

Word came to the prison that the tyrant had been dethroned, and there was rejoicing. But no one felt safe, for Robespierre had strong support outside the Convention. The Paris Commune, the Jacobins, all those who put more faith in Robespierre's personal rule than in the wrangling deputies of the Convention, all these could be counted on to come to his defense.

Throughout the night of July 27, while the troops loyal to the Convention fought with the hastily summoned forces of the Commune, the prisoners in the Carmelite Prison prepared for the worst. Anticipating a massacre, the men constructed barricades from chests and beds, chairs and sticks of furniture. They had no weapons, but they armed themselves with boards and staves. No one slept, save those so far gone in illness that they lay in a permanent stupor. In the streets outside the prison, the rue de Vaugirard and the rue Cassette, the sound of boots splashing through the mud seemed never to stop. Orders were shouted, drums beat, the clatter of weapons alternated with the crashing of thunder and the pounding of the rain on the convent roof.

Sometime during the night, unknown to the prisoners, the decisive moment came. In the Place de Grève, in the pouring rain, the National Guard, mustered by Paul Barras, faced the ragged sansculottes of the Commune, and declared them to be outlaws—which meant that every Parisian had a duty to attack and kill them. Resistance melted away, Barras and the Guard were triumphant. The Convention prevailed, and it was Robespierre's turn to go to the guillotine.

On August 6 an official order was received by the jailor at the Carmelite Prison for the release of Citizeness Beauharnais. Rose, greatly revived in health and spirits by the lifting of the Terror and the better conditions instituted in the prison since the fall of Robespierre, gathered her few belongings and prepared to go home.

She knew how lucky she had been. Of the thousands of prisoners who had suffered with her during her hundred-odd days of captivity, all but a few hundred had died. She had been spared, thanks to her illness and the Polish doctor, thanks to the timing of the coup in the Convention, thanks above all to Jean Tallien who worked behind the scenes to bring about her release.[6]

What relief and joy Rose felt as she walked for the last time through the narrow corridors of the prison can only be known by those who have themselves passed close to the brink of death and been snatched back, at the last moment, into life and hope. Shaken and nervous, she made her way along, cheered on by the applause and acclaim of her fellow prisoners.[7] She had attracted much affection during her captivity, now her release was noisily welcomed. In her nervous state, the shouting and clapping became too much for her. Her tears flowed, she faltered, then came close to fainting and had to pause for a moment before going on. When she had recovered, she did her best to say her good-byes to all those who were wishing her well, receiving their blessings and thanking as many as she could before entering the waiting carriage. The uproar and applause were still audible as she drove away along the rue de Vaugirard, toward Croissy and freedom.

A New Life

*E*nervating though her prison ordeal had been, within a few days of her release Rose was able to be reunited with friends and to begin the process of rebuilding her life. Many of those she had known in prison had died, but toward those who survived she must have felt a strong—indeed a lifelong—affinity.

One observer saw Rose at a dinner party with her prison companion Santerre, the former brewer and revolutionary who had made a name for himself during the attacks on the Tuileries, and recorded that she talked about life and death, and told the story of how, as a girl in Martinique, she had been told by a fortune-teller that "she would one day be queen of France, but that she would not die a queen." It was a prophecy she must have pondered often during her captivity, as she dealt out the cards to tell her fortune and the fortunes of others.

"Robespierre nearly upset the prophecy," she told the dinner guests with a brittle laugh, making the others laugh as well, yet for Santerre at least it must have seemed an echo of the macabre laughter of the prison, not the easy laughter of a relaxed social occasion. Politically, the Terror had ended. Emotionally, however, it would linger for a very long time. Parisians could not rid their imaginations of the ghastly executions they had been forced to watch, the dread, confusion and revulsion they had been forced to feel. The shadow of the guillotine still fell across the Place de la Révolution, and the aftermath of its menace still made itself felt in many hearts.

Rose was aware that she owed her deliverance in large part to Jean Tallien, and she lost no time in expressing her thanks and obligation to him and to his young and extravagantly beautiful mistress Theresa Cabarrus, who was widely believed to have goaded Tallien into acting to oust Robespierre and end the glut of executions. Tallien's political fortunes had risen. With four or five others, he was among the leading figures in the Convention, and was serving as its president. Moreover, he was a celebrity. Tallien and Theresa Cabarrus were lionized by grateful Parisians; everywhere they went crowds gathered to cheer them and pay homage. Rose, ever quick to seek a place within the ambiance of the celebrated and powerful, attached herself to the Tallien circle, befriending Theresa who was rapidly becoming a cynosure of style.

She also revived her liaison with Lazare Hoche, who, like her, had somehow managed to survive, despite being condemned by the revolutionary tribunal. Now that she was a widow, Rose could, and did, contemplate remarriage—a socially desirable, indeed imperative, goal for a youngish widow of thirty-one with two children—and marriage to the handsome Hoche, a widely admired military figure likely to rise to greater eminence, would be much to her advantage. But to her dismay, Rose discovered that her lover had no intention of divorcing his wife to marry her.

Rose had come up against the limits of her own influence, or so it seemed. She could sway Hoche, she could draw him to her, but she could not persuade him to lend her his respectability. She was not, after all, the sort of woman an ambitious man would want to marry. She had a past, she was notorious for her many lovers, and even in the era of the revolution, with its exaltation of freedom of all kinds, its recent legalization of divorce, and its legacy, from the old regime, of sophisticated liaisons between married lovers, Rose's marketability as a wife was diminishing. She had no fortune—though she talked as though she had, and attempted to give the appearance of affluence. She had no powerful family connections. Unkind critics remarked that, now that she was past thirty, she had lost her freshness and was rapidly losing what remained of her looks, though they had to concede that her ingenuous charm, and her skill with cosmetics, combined to give her a continuing allure.

Had Rose been given to introspection, which she definitely was not, she might have had to admit to herself that in her relations with Hoche she had come up against the limits of her own character. Having never known romantic love, only liaisons motivated, on her part, by financial need and expedience, Rose had no real experience of loving, only of using. She thought, and acted, like a kept woman— only she had not, so far, found a man (or yielded to one) who would free her permanently from financial worries.

Financial worries had, in fact, been the principal recurring theme of Rose's life, as they had been of her father's, and in the tumultuous months of late 1794 and early 1795, Rose's anxieties about money paralleled the broader anxieties and convulsions of the French economy.

The assignat was losing value. Prices of goods in the shops had to be changed several times a day, so rapidly did the paper currency sink to new depths. People made a habit of doing their shopping as early in the morning as possible, certain that if they waited until afternoon, their bills would not stretch as far. In the climate of spiraling inflation, bankers and speculators flourished. No one wanted the rapidly deflating paper notes; value was to be found only in things—in coins or jewels or, for the lucky ones, buildings and land.

Auction halls sprang up in former mansions, churches, anywhere spacious; shrewd auctioneers drew throngs of eager onlookers to bid on the spoils of the Terror. Anything of value that belonged to guillotine victims—jewels, fine clothing, furnishings, linens, china, ornate mantelpieces, sculpture—now came under the gavel, usually at a fraction of what the former owner had paid for it. Relatives of victims, bypassing the auctioneers, heaped their goods on carts and sold them in the marketplace or in the courtyards of their houses, hawking their family heirlooms like shrill-voiced street vendors.

As the assignat continued to fall, barter replaced purchase, and suddenly everyone was a trader—not only businessmen and merchants, but chambermaids, grooms, former clergymen, returned emigrés, even highborn ladies. Enterprising traders went into the countryside to buy up butter, cheese and wine, and returned to Paris to sell their wares for two or three times what they had cost. Salons and drawing rooms were turned into bazaars, with displays of fabric and lace, tobacco and sugar, soap, salt, oil—whatever was scarce and therefore precious.

Larger-scale speculators swarmed in dozens in the stock exchange—the "Black Forest," in contemporary slang—buying and selling assignats and gold, bonds and shares, manipulating the market for their own profit, and in the process, weakening the entire economy and worsening the monetary crisis. There was rampant speculation in flour, coal, wood and wine, in provisions for the army, in guns and boots, tents and woolen cloth for uniforms.

Quality was compromised whenever possible: spoiled flour, sour wine, boots with shoddy soles and adulterated foodstuffs were passed off as genuine, all in the name of increased profits. Cunning dealers grew callous to the harm their maneuvers were doing; no one but the victims seemed to care that bad food made people ill, or that the ever-deteriorating cycle of rising prices and monetary deflation caused massive hardship and suffering, or that the soldiers in the field, given thin, poorly sewn uniforms and guns that malfunctioned, could not defend themselves and died of exposure.

But there was little time to ponder such ethical dilemmas. The pace of events, the panic into which all were thrown with each fresh wave of inflation, the general climate of anxiety made people desperate, and when desperate, they thought only of themselves, and of their own survival. Hence the mood of raw, impatient greed that made every transaction tense, every exchange crackling with venality, every conversation edgy with money-hunger and the lust for gain.

Besides, what were ethics when there were fortunes to be made! Amid the anxieties and the uncertainties, the worry that the mad pyramid of speculation would end in a swift and unexpected collapse, sudden opportunities loomed—opportunities which, if grasped at the right moment, could yield unimagined wealth. Everyone in Paris in the winter of 1794 to 1795 knew stories of men and women who had become wealthy overnight, and nearly everyone dreamed of attaining overnight riches himself. It was this dream, fueled by the frenzy of day-to-day commerce, that bred the raw appetitiveness, the coarsening stridor, the crass, frenetic money-lust that held Paris in its grip.

Alexandre's revenues and all his possessions from his estate at La Ferté had been confiscated by the government, but Rose, eager to sell his effects, petitioned the Convention to release them to her. (Her own, far less valuable possessions were still being held by the Committee of General Security.) Her expenses were high, as she had to pay tuition for Eugene at the Irish College and for Hortense at the National Institution, a school run by Madame Campan at St-Germain-en-Laye. She could not pay her maid, or the few other servants she employed, and had to borrow small sums from various friends just to get by from week to week. She owed the banker Emmery a great deal, and could not afford to make even token payments on that debt. Emmery had made his loans to Rose in the expectation of being reimbursed, at some point, from the income from her widowed mother's estate in Martinique. But Martinique was now in the hands of France's enemy, having been invaded early in 1794 by the British, and the likelihood that any funds would be forthcoming from that source seemed slim.

When the Convention refused to release Alexandre's possessions, Rose, in desperation, wrote to her mother. It was extremely difficult to send or receive letters from the Antilles because the British navy controlled all the sea-lanes, but Rose persisted until she found an obliging traveler bound for New England who agreed to hand on the letter to an American ship captain once they landed.

"Doubtless you have heard of my misfortune," Rose wrote to Rose-Claire Tascher. She said nothing of her months in prison, or of her remarkable escape from the guillotine, only that she had been a widow for four months. "For consolation I have only my children, and you, dear mama, for my support. My most eager wish is that someday we may all be united."[1]

It was the briefest and least revealing of letters. But then, Rose was not close to her mother, and in any case what counted was the number of letters she sent, and not their length. Knowing how slender the chances were that any of her letters would reach Trois-Ilets, Rose wrote her mother often.

"As for your poor daughter," she wrote in December of 1794, "she exists, as do her children, but they have the misfortune to have lost their father. . . . My children now have only me for their support, and I cling to life only to make them happy. Even as I do, they owe to M. Emmery of Dunkirk their means of subsistence."[2]

By January of 1795 Rose was using every stratagem she knew to stave off ruin—spurred on, no doubt, by the sight of ruin all around her. The deep snows, fierce storms and harsh killing frosts of the endless winter of 1795 were unendurable for many Parisians already weakened by disease and shortages of food. Every day dozens of dead bodies were found in the icy streets, the numbers of beggars rose and those lucky enough to have shelter and a little money spent hours waiting in line in the cold for a few overpriced pieces of bread or a candle. Most of the trees in the Bois de Boulogne had been chopped down for fuel. There was no drinking water; people broke icicles off roofs and let the pale wintry sun melt them.

The stock exchange had been closed the month before, amid worsening chaos. Speculators moved to an unofficial site in an alley off the rue Vivienne, and carried on their unsavory business there, but by now it took whole bags stuffed with assignats to buy only one gold coin, and it was tempting, in the freezing days of January, to burn the paper money to keep warm instead of attempting to find anything to buy with it.

"I know your tender concern far too well to have any doubt that you are urgently attempting to obtain for me the means I need to live on and to repay what is owed to Monsieur Emmery," Rose told her mother in yet another letter. She instructed Rose Claire to send what money she could to either Hamburg or London, to bankers who would be able to transfer the funds to Dunkirk.[3] Without knowing when, or whether, any funds would be forthcoming Rose traveled to Hamburg and attempted to raise a loan on the Martinique estate from bankers there, pledging her remaining jewelry as collateral should the income from the estate not be sufficient.

It was her last expedient. But then, as the terrible winter began to recede, there was a modest upturn in Rose's fortunes. The Committee of General Security at last returned her possessions to her, and she received a substantial sum as compensation for Alexandre's goods. Her recently widowed Aunt Edmée, having sold her house in Fontainebleau, was able to make Rose a small loan, and her friendship with the Talliens had begun to bring her very significant rewards.

A passionate, pleasure-loving woman, overflowing with sweetness and charm, with a girlishness that clung to her well into her fourth decade and a marked sense of style, Rose de Beauharnais came into her own in the frenzied, disorderly period following the end of the

Terror. Society was as chaotic as finance; there was no clearly defined social order, no hierarchy of rank. The social rhetoric was still republican—every house had a red liberty cap prominently displayed, every monument bore the inscription "Unity, Indivisibility of the French Republic; Liberty, Equality, Fraternity or Death"—yet with the titled emigrés beginning to return, and with the extreme republicans in disfavor, new gradations of distinction were forming.

One thing was clear: women were more important than ever. The striking, Amazonian Therese Cabarrus Tallien, tall and dark, with a crowd of admiring young men always following her purple carriage; the cool, remote, fascinatingly beautiful Juliette Récamier; the strident, coarse-featured Madame de Staël, mannish and neurotic but with a brilliant wit; the dark, ribald Fortunée Hamelin who brought manic gaiety into every gathering along with the strong scent of attar of roses—these stood out, in the spring of 1795, as social lions. And there were others, not quite as celebrated, but dazzling in their own way: the beautiful Madame Regnault who sculpted and sang, stylish, black-haired Madame Visconti whose teeth were the envy of other women, lovely Madame Hottinguer and charming Madame Jouberthon.

The women seemed to take over, to incarnate the sprawling, unconfined spirit of the times. They dominated every gathering. They dressed extravagantly, even outlandishly, with scant regard for former proprieties. Some dressed like men, others like women of the street, their near-nudity an insolent reminder to everyone who saw them that they had cast off all restraint and were answerable to no authority, no confining code of decorum. They invented, then discarded, fads in dress and adornment with bewildering rapidity. They drove fast cabriolets and English whiskys, or fragile phaetons painted with cupids and voluptuous nudes framed in gold leaf and pearls, whipping their horses onward in risky abandon.

These highly visible, brazen beauties were an affront to every civilized standard—and they were irresistible.

Rose took her place among them, elegant in her dress, outgoing without being aggressive, youthful and graceful. A woman who admired her wrote of her "young and charming face, surrounded by a profusion of light hair, with a pair of large dark-blue eyes, and exhibiting altogether the image of the most graceful of sylphs."[4] She danced well, her figure was enviably full, and she retained the fine manners of the old regime, the manners she had studied so carefully at Penthémont. From a short distance away, and with her mouth closed to hide her blackened teeth, Rose still looked quite young and pretty, often attracting more attention than younger and more striking women, her ingenuous sweetness disarming all who approached her.

In the late spring of 1795 Rose entered the louche, slightly sinister orbit of Paul Barras, a rich, disreputable but highly influential prof-iteer whose salon was a magnet for the low and the immoral. What drew her there, first and foremost, was her need for money. Barras lived grandly, and surrounded himself with other wealthy men, among whom Rose was sure to find some who would be prepared to be generous to her. She had become accustomed to solving her incessant financial problems by forming liaisons, sometimes sexual, sometimes merely social, with wealthy men. She had never been a courtesan, merely a compromised woman. Now, however, she entered fully into a disreputable, sordid world whose outskirts she had been exploring, in the company of Therese Tallien, for several months.

Contemporaries were unanimous in finding the goings-on in Bar-ras's several mansions repellent. All the vices converged there: the greed and dishonesty of corrupt business dealings, lust and sexual profligacy ("the most infamous debauchery was openly practiced in his house," one visitor wrote), homosexuality, then considered an unspeakable perversion, gluttony, all amid an atmosphere of overripe excess. Barras himself, who was fortyish, set the tone for this contin-ual orgy of self-indulgence, entertaining lavishly night after night, filling his crowded salons with debauchees and financial intriguers, scantily clad, voluptuous women and attractive young boys. He was a dark Pied Piper, vulgar and coarse, presiding with enthusiasm over scenes of uncouth revelry and unrestrained pleasure. Long, inebriated evenings gave way to unwelcome dawns, when the partygoers, di-sheveled and hung over, stumbled through rooms rank with stale odors out into the unflattering daylight.

Such was the world that Rose now entered, and over which she soon came to preside at Barras's side. For she became not only Bar-ras's mistress but his hostess, her name intimately associated with his, her fortunes aligned to his. In return he gave her money, and intro-duced her to his friends through whom she could make more money.

One of these friends, the banker Gabriel Ouvrard, was among the richest men in France, having earned his first enormous fortune in his early twenties. Ouvrard knew which army contracts could be bought and exploited for the most money, which commodities earned the most on the black market, which deals could be struck and which were best avoided. Rose cultivated Ouvrard and others, listened to their recommendations, and began to prosper.

Once again, Rose had found her way out of difficulties. With Therese Tallien and a few others, she reigned over an inglorious shadow-kingdom, the puppet of a villainous manipulator. She spent her nights in dissipation—relatively mild dissipation, for Rose did not drink to excess and does not seem to have had an inordinate appetite for sex—and her days following up on the profitable financial advice she was given by Barras, Ouvrard and others. She had herself driven to and from the stock exchange in an attractive carriage pulled by a pair of handsome black Hungarian horses—a gift from the Committee of Public Safety, which had at last begun to compensate Rose for the losses her late husband had suffered. She shopped, she socialized, she spent hours making herself attractive.

For the first time in a long time, Rose was genuinely content. She had found a truly congenial environment, one that suited her nature very well. She liked having plenty of money to spend, she liked the atmosphere of overripe abundance, the long undisciplined evenings, the louche pleasures; it all reminded her of home. The lushness of Barras's notorious establishment was not unlike the Caribbean atmosphere of laziness and decay that had nurtured her, and from which she had been alienated for far too long.

Especially, she liked Barras himself. He was complex, charismatic, ambitious. His power awed her and made her feel safe. It did not trouble her that his methods were unethical and his morals ruthless. Apart from her natural sweetness and kindness, Rose had scant moral sense, and found the moral rigidity of others baffling. Besides, her relationship with Barras was not exclusive, and he made few demands on her. His sexual tastes were varied and Rose was one among many pleasurable partners. The entire arrangement was loose, worldly, agreeably casual.

For Rose, this was life at its best. Indolence, abundance, a comfortable environment, pleasure. No pressures, no public performances.

A man to lean on, but one who was not possessive and who shared Rose's own relative indifference to morality. She had wanted a husband, she had wanted to marry Lazare Hoche. Instead, she had stumbled into an even better arrangement, one that allowed her, in the fashion of her far-off youth, to drift from day to day as if swinging in her hammock, admired, secure, her needs gratified to the point of surfeit, taking no thought for what unexpected storms or unregarded misfortunes might lie ahead.

13

"She Offered Her Entire Soul in Her Eyes"

In the summer of 1795, Paul Barras was shadowed wherever he went by a short, thin, gloomy little Italian with scraggly hair that fell well below his frayed collar. Nabuleone Buonaparte, a young Corsican artillery officer who had become a minor celebrity when he directed the defense of Toulon against the British fleet, had come to Paris in search of wealth and further advancement, and though his appearance was unprepossessing at best, he soon made himself welcome. He held forth in loud, brusque tones on many subjects. He was a passable reader of palms, and Parisians, in the aftermath of the Terror, were mad for fortune-telling of all kinds. He was lively and passionate, with arrestingly antique features, piercing grey-blue eyes, and a broad forehead that was often creased in anxious thought. When he allowed himself to relax and show pleasure, which was rarely, a smile of dazzling charm lit his entire face and made it youthful; his enchanting smile made him memorable, and helped people to forget, for a moment at least, his ragged clothes and self-conscious demeanor.

They made an odd couple, the tall, broad, black-haired Barras and his small, shabby companion, but everyone took note of Buonaparte, for he had been promoted to brigadier-general at the age of twenty-four, and was obviously Barras's protégé, and no one had more influence than Barras; clearly this was a young man worth watching.

People noticed that the young Corsican was particularly ill at ease with women. Having been raised in a society where women were generally held in low esteem—except when they were called upon to join in family vendettas—as servants to men, with little purpose in life beyond childbearing and cooking, he was overawed by the female-dominated social life of Paris, where magnificently underclad, confidently outspoken beauties flaunted their power and played commanding roles in politics, business and society. Women set the tone: men followed.

"Women are everywhere," Buonaparte wrote to his older brother Joseph in July of 1795, "applauding the plays, walking in the promenades, reading in the bookshops. You will find the lovely creatures even in the professor's study." They were not only ubiquitous, they were in control. "Here is the only place in the world where they deserve to steer the ship of state," the young officer observed, "the men are mad about them, think of nothing else, and live only for them. Give a woman six months in Paris, and she knows where her empire is and what is her due."[1]

Prominent among the women was Rose Tascher, the former Viscountess de Beauharnais, now at her most socially confident and gracious. Her youthful charm had lost none of its force, and the gentleness of her disposition, the warmth of her glance, her sympathetic, generous, welcoming manner must have seemed a balm to the wounded spirits of a raw, unsophisticated young man new to the ways of the capital and singularly unlucky in love.

Or rather, unlucky in his pursuit of a wife. For Buonaparte, consumed with ambition and temporarily short of funds, was intent on finding a rich woman to marry, and so far every woman he proposed to had refused him. There had been a number of them, most recently Desirée Clary, a plump, unattractive heiress whose sister was married to his brother Joseph and whose parents had intervened to oppose the match, and Laure Permon, a handsome, well-to-do widow of forty and a friend of his mother's, who had scoffed at the idea of marrying an inexperienced young man with nothing to offer.[2]

Buonaparte's lack of success in finding a wife, his dislike of Paris society, his revulsion at the dandified young men who frequented fashionable drawing rooms at that time, with their delicate whiskers and girlish "spaniel's ears" haircuts ("It is on such beings as these that Fortune confers her favors," he wrote. "Heavens! How contemptible is human nature!"), all increased his natural melancholy and made him morose. "I hardly care what happens to me," he told Joseph. "I watch life almost indifferently.... If this continues I shall end by not stepping out of the way of a passing carriage."[3] He felt himself to be prey to all manner of passing whims, from suicide to "a marrying madness."

Buonaparte's emotional torment was real, but his professional prospects were actually quite bright in the summer of 1795. He had been offered, and turned down, a military appointment to serve under Rose's lover Lazare Hoche in the Vendée, and he had good reason to expect that other such offers would be forthcoming, thanks to the notoriety he had achieved in Toulon. He had made a bold suggestion to his army superiors that he be sent to the Sultan of Turkey as artillery adviser, and arrangements were being made to send him. Meanwhile he had been given an appointment by the Committee of Public Safety to plan an invasion of northern Italy, and the careful drawing up of this plan engaged most of his free time when he was not making the social rounds with Barras, searching for wealthy widows.

Rose, for her part, was savoring her freedom, and her prestige. She cultivated her social role, continued to make money—it was perhaps at this time that Rose, for the first time in her life, envisioned becoming financially independent—and guarded her preeminence among the reigning beauties of Paris by spending hours at her dressing table, carefully applying the abundant makeup that helped to preserve her youthful appearance.

She was still involved with Hoche, but his military responsibilities kept him away from Paris much of the time; whether, in the summer of 1795, she still wanted to marry him, or whether she wanted to marry at all, is conjectural. She had at least one other wooer, the Duc de Caulaincourt, and there were certainly other admirers—indeed Rose Tascher was among the most admired women in Paris, second only to Therese Tallien and Juliette Récamier.

Barras, writing of her many years later in his splenetic old age, recalled with considerable bitterness that Rose was always able to divorce her heart from her head, that in conducting her liaisons she always put self-interest first. And if he was accurate in this, it would be quite understandable; given all that Rose had been through, her abandonment by a husband who failed to provide for her, her years of struggle to find the wherewithal to provide for her children, her nightmarish imprisonment during the Terror and her miraculous survival were bound to make her self-protective, and so deeply fearful of ever becoming financially vulnerable again that she could never put her emotions first.

But Barras, of course, was implying far more than this. He meant that Rose was venal, calculating, and so focused on gaining her own advantage that she had closed off her heart, and viewed men only as vehicles of pleasure and avenues to wealth. That she had become, in all but name, a hardened courtesan, beneath her carapace of creole languor and soft voiced, gentle warmth.

"The men who possessed her," Barras wrote of Rose, "may have flattered themselves on her apparently passionate abandon, but the lubricious creole never for a moment lost sight of business. Her heart played no part in her physical enjoyment."[4] It was a harsh indictment, and one warped by Barras's deep resentment, but it may have held an unpleasant truth—that Rose, because of the life she had led, and the extremes to which she had been forced, may, by 1795, have lost the capacity to love disinterestedly.

In October of that year Rose moved into a comfortable house in a rather disreputable neighborhood, at Number 6, rue Chantereine. The house's former occupant, Julie Carreau, had been a dancer notorious for her many lovers. She had been married to the actor François Talma, but like many marriages in this chaotic era of casual liaisons and easy divorce, it had soured and the partners had separated. The area around the rue Chantereine attracted women like Julie and Rose, older women of some means who met discreetly with their lovers in snug houses hidden behind tall hedges or at the end of winding lanes leading off the main road.

Rose paid a high price for this seclusion—four thousand francs a month—and in addition, she needed a larger staff of servants to run the house, including a gardener, a cook, several maids, a groom for the horses and a coachman to drive her carriage. At this time she hired a new servant, Louise Compoint, to be her personal maid and also brought in workmen to make renovations to the house and decorators to supply new furnishings. Altogether she spent quite a lot, and gave the impression that she had a good deal of money— an impression that was not lost on, among others, Brigadier-General Buonaparte. He knew that creoles were reputed to have large fortunes, even though, in wartime, it was difficult to obtain funds owed from rents on plantations in the Windward Isles. No doubt he took careful note of Rose, and of her apparent wealth, but before he could approach her he was caught up in swift-moving political events that provided him with an undreamed-of opportunity.

The beleaguered Parisians, impoverished by inflation and forced to endure the multiple evils of food shortages, unemployment and a widening gulf between the ostentatiously rich, privileged few and the wretched many, had been restive all summer. Minor outbreaks of violence had begun to increase in September when the Convention submitted a new constitution, one that offended the growing royalist sentiment and entrenched in power the worst and most hated politicians and power brokers. The Paris sections, ever volatile, raised the alarm on October 2 and for a day and a night the city was full of the sound of drums beating and bells ringing in warning. An opposition force many thousands strong was preparing to attack the government offices in the Tuileries.

At this point Barras, who had been given orders by the Convention to defend the capital against the threat of yet another seizure of power by extremist Parisians, turned to his protégé Buonaparte and gave him authority to mount a defense.

There was little time. By the time the Corsican was brought in, late in the stormy evening of October 4, thousands of insurrectionists were gathering in the vicinity of the palace, and a wave of popular feeling against the government was sweeping through the sections. Once again, it seemed, the course of the revolution was about to be determined by a confrontation between entrenched power and the angry, uncontrollable force of the Paris mob.

With hard rain lashing the city, churning the mud in the streets to a stinking black bog, Buonaparte gave swift orders to seize forty artillery pieces from the National Guard at Neuilly and bring them to the streets nearest the Tuileries. When, on the following day, the insurgents tried to rush the palace, they were met with a murderous cannonade that killed many hundreds and left hundreds more severely wounded.

Never before had government forces loosed such deadly firepower on their own citizens. Never before had the power of the Paris sections been broken so decisively. What happened on the fifth of October, 13 Vendémiaire by the revolutionary calendar, was unique and memorable, even though it infuriated many Parisians and left many army officers open-mouthed in astonishment.

Brigadier-General Buonaparte became Major-General Buonaparte, chief defender of the new government, the Directory, headed by Director Paul Barras.

Suddenly Buonaparte was among the most important men in France, the preserver of order, the irreplaceable right-hand man of the state. He became well-to-do overnight, and moved from his dingy lodgings to a fine house in the rue des Capucines. He drove a splendid carriage, had servants, improved his appearance. (Though not a great deal, for it was as much his philosophy as his limited means that had made Buonaparte careless of his dress; he disapproved of finery, thought that gloves were a "useless luxury," and ranted on angrily about men who spent too much money on their boots and too much time polishing them.)

His first thoughts, on attaining this new financial status, were of his relatives. Buonaparte was one of eight children in a tight-knit, fiercely clannish Corsican family, and he eagerly shared his newfound wealth with his brothers and sisters. His first impulse, on succeeding against the mutinous crowd, had been to write to his older brother Joseph and tell him everything that had happened.

Predictably, the social world seized eagerly on Buonaparte and lionized him; invitations by the dozen arrived at his door in the rue des Capucines. No longer Barras's shadow and protégé, he was now seen in the best drawing rooms on his own, holding forth in his customary manner on a wide range of subjects, attracting eager listeners of both sexes, reading palms, striving to appear composed and debonair when in fact he was perpetually ill at ease.

For in fact, his celebrated triumph did not bring him either gratification or contentment. He burned to advance himself further, and for this, he was convinced, he needed a rich wife. To find a rich wife he needed to make the rounds of the salons, the haunts of the well-to-do. Yet the social round was essentially alien to him, merely a means to an end. He was not, as he told a friend later on, "made for pleasure," and in the midst of socializing he was always preoccupied, his mind roving outward in a dozen directions, all of them linked to his career.

Rose, meanwhile, began to view General Buonaparte with new interest now that he had become the rising star of the Directory, the new government he had been so instrumental in rescuing from disaster.[5] She cultivated him, invited him to her home, took care to find out what his ambitions and goals were and to discuss them with him.

Toward the end of October 1795, Rose wrote to the general in a coyly petulant tone. "You never come to see a friend who loves you any more," she complained, "and you have entirely abandoned her. You are wrong to do so, for she is tenderly attached to you. Come tomorrow, septidi [the seventh day of the ten-day revolutionary "week"], and dine with me. I need to see you and to talk with you about what is advantageous to you." "Good night, my friend," the note ended. "I kiss you. Widow Beauharnais."[6]

Rose's note implied a friendship that had begun some time earlier, and there is no question that she had met Buonaparte, and become acquainted with him to a degree, several months before his stunning military success.[7] Now, however, she took him up with fresh urgency. Suddenly he was a Someone, and a someone who could be useful to her. And she may, like others, have thought him intriguing, his charming smile drawing her in and his restless, driving energy sexually exciting to her.

In any case, she now concentrated her interest on him, and he responded, and an alchemy of intimacy began to develop between them, of a kind that Rose, with her considerable experience of men, recognized and kept under her control.

"Madame de Beauharnais had always listened with interest to my plans," Buonaparte recalled while on St. Helena many years afterward. "One day when I was sitting next to her at table, she began to pay me all manner of compliments on my military qualities. Her praise intoxicated me. From that moment I confined my conversation to her and never left her side. I was passionately in love with her, and our friends were aware of this long before I ever dared to say a word about it."[8]

Hortense remembered how when she first met the general, at a dinner party, he ignored her and talked only to her mother. Hortense was sitting between the two of them, but gradually, as Buonaparte talked on and on, leaning farther and farther over toward Rose, Hortense was so squeezed out that she could not reach the table any longer.

That such a celebrated lady as Rose de Beauharnais, with her famous aristocratic name and elegant manners, should show such interest in him seemed to the raw young Corsican a stroke of amazing good luck. She flattered his vanity, she built him up. She almost made him forget, while he was with her, that he was shy and awkward with women. "Madame Bonaparte was the first to give me confidence," he said toward the end of his life, looking back. With her beautiful voice and expressive face, her brow surrounded by an enchanting halo of wayward curls, her smooth, radiant skin, her deep blue eyes and long lashes, her gaze that was fixed on him alone, Rose captivated Buonaparte, and made him expansive and optimistic. "She offered her entire soul in her eyes," a contemporary wrote of Rose in 1795.[9] It must have seemed, to young General Buonaparte, that she was offering it directly to him.

Never mind that Rose was past her prime, or that she had been and still was the mistress of Barras and of other men. Buonaparte was quite carried away—even more so when he realized that she could well be the wealthy widow he had been searching for. She lied shamelessly about her financial condition, telling the general that she had expectations of receiving several million francs from property she owned in Martinique and Santo Domingo. She may well have lied about other things, including her age, and so great was his fascination for her that he would have been inclined to believe her.

By December, the "marriage mania" Buonaparte had feared was taking him over. He had fallen in love with Rose "in all the full sense of the word, in the full force of its meaning," an acquaintance thought. Rose was his first love, and he gave his strong, energetic passion for her free rein. Just when they became lovers is not known for certain, but it was probably in November or December of 1795, and to judge from Buonaparte's rapturous love letters, he, at least, found their lovemaking to be deeply, voluptuously fulfilling and exquisitely pleasurable. He was erotically stirred as never before, awakened to ecstasy, led by Rose into dimensions of emotion and sensation he had not known existed.[10]

The winter of 1796 was so bitterly cold that Parisians, wrapped in layer upon layer of clothing, took their hatchets and went out into the old royal forests to find wood. They chopped down the dead frozen trees and dragged the heavy frost-covered branches back across icy meadows to the river, which was frozen solid, and then loaded them into horse-drawn sleds for the trip to the capital. Because food supplies were scarce, they wandered through the forests burrowing under the snow for acorns and mushrooms, even, in their extremity, stripping the bark off the cold trees and eating it.

The great cold brought silence to the city, for no vehicles could drive along the roads and the ordinary noise of commerce was stilled. There were occasional sleigh bells, the sound of footfalls on cracking ice, the snuffling of horses and the swearing of watchmen. Icy winds that swept down out of the north whistled and moaned through the narrow streets, along walls and up chimneys. In the long dark nights, packs of wolves, spreading southward from the great ancient forest of Ardennes, hunted in the outskirts of the city and howled to one another mournfully across the quiet empty wastes.

In this bleak season, the enraptured General Buonaparte asked Rose Beauharnais to marry him, and she did not at first give him an answer.

She struggled inwardly, torn between giving up the pleasant independent life she had made for herself and the return to respectability and security that marriage to a successful, well-connected military officer would offer her.[11] Buonaparte was not her only suitor. There was still Caulaincourt, though not Hoche: away from Paris much of the time, and with his wife pregnant with their first child, Hoche had apparently decided to give Rose up, at least for the time being. But Rose, who was avid for love, and who still was Barras's mistress, was ambivalent about marriage, and under no pressure to agree to any match. She was at the height of her unique attractiveness, greatly admired and in a position to attract new lovers, and new suitors; she felt no urgency about accepting any proposal.

Unlike Buonaparte, she was not in love. She looked at the thin Corsican, with his pallor and his sickly air, his threadbare uniform and ill-made, poorly blackened boots, his broad Italian accent making him seem out of place, and she saw a figure of ridicule. To be sure, he was passionate and lively, but, as she remembered later, he was "altogether strange in all his person." He had acquired a case of scabies in Toulon, and the odor of his skin disease, combined with his bad habit of bathing infrequently, kept people at a distance.

On the other hand, his features were delicate and not lacking in charm, and there was his bewitching smile. Like Rose, he had kind instincts; some months before he met Rose, while he was still an impoverished officer, he had devoted many hours to helping the Permon family, visiting the father who was dying, looking in every day to bring groceries, going out in the middle of the night to get the doctor, making certain that nothing was wanting in the household. The Permons, friends of his parents, had looked after his own father on his deathbed; it was the least the general could do to return the favor now.

Beyond this, Buonaparte had a mystical, dreamy side that harmonized well with Rose's natural languor. "When I first knew him," the memoirist Laure Permon Junot wrote, "he loved very much all that led into reverie: Ossian [the pseudo-antique poet], the twilight hour, melancholy music. I have seen him wax passionate at the murmur of the wind, speak with rapture about the soughing of the sea, and speculate that nocturnal apparitions were not entirely beyond belief—in short, he had a penchant for superstition." If Rose could not feel comfortable with the Buonaparte who moved and spoke awkwardly, who talked too much and overanalyzed everything, who spat out his words and even managed to make Italian, the most graceful of languages, seem graceless, she could find common ground with the Buonaparte who was all but hypnotized by slow, sweet music and who loved to sit in a darkened room and dream of ghosts.[12]

In the end it was the general's rapid, and increasing, political ascendancy that convinced Rose to accept his proposal—or so she said afterward. She knew that others would be shocked that she should ally her exalted name—in actuality her late husband's exalted name—to the name of an obscure Corsican family. She knew that she was taking a risk. But the revolutionary government had made it relatively easy to obtain a divorce, and with the church eviscerated of its moral suasion, and social relations in a general state of turmoil, no one held marriage in as much regard as in the past. Knowing that she could extricate herself if the marriage should prove to be a mistake, Rose agreed, in January of 1796, to become the wife of General Buonaparte.

By this time a sort of partnership had developed between Rose and her future husband. He had long since discovered how useful she could be to him. He made her his advocate, taking her along when he went to ask an important favor of anyone. Sometimes she actually spoke for him, socially adroit as she was, and with a wide acquaintance. Barras claimed, and it seems plausible, that it was Rose who came to him in the winter of 1795 and asked that General Buonaparte be given command of the army of Italy. Soon afterward, he obtained the command.[13]

They made good partners, the energetic little general and the graceful leader of society. Both were capable of nearly invincible singleness of purpose. Both were focused on their own advancement, singly and, after January of 1796, together. Both were outsiders to traditional French society, he Italian, she a creole from the provinces. Both were inclined to shade the truth when it was advantageous to do so.

They were alike in many ways. That they were unalike in passion did not deter the enamored Buonaparte from plunging ahead with his exciting plans. He made his preparations for the invasion of Italy, reading every book he could find and studying every available atlas and chart. And he told his bride-to-be to order her wedding dress and invite her witnesses, for before he left on his campaign he intended to marry his living reverie, his dream of perfect passion, the woman he now insisted upon calling Josephine.

14

"The Lubricious Creole"

The witnesses arrived at the city hall at seven o'clock on a chilly March night, having been summoned in haste and told that their presence would be required. Paul Barras, Therese and Jean Tallien, and a young officer, Captain LeMarois, were ushered into a cold room by a perplexed underling who brought in a tin lantern and set about making a fire in the fireplace.

They quickly surmised what was happening: General Buonaparte, who was due to leave Paris in two days' time to take command of the army of Italy, had decided to marry his fiancée before he left, and required their presence as witnesses to his wedding. How he would manage to squeeze in a wedding, not to mention a honeymoon, before his departure when he was so pressed for time and so overwhelmed with preparations, no one could imagine. And no one was surprised that he was late.

The bride arrived—no longer Rose Tascher de Beauharnais, but Josephine, soon to become Josephine Buonaparte—with her witness, Jérôme Calmelet, who for some time had helped to handle her business affairs. No member of the groom's large family had been invited, not even Buonaparte's brother Joseph. The general knew that they would be dismayed by his choice of a bride and he preferred to postpone facing them. Neither Eugene nor Hortense was present either. Josephine knew that Eugene, who had come to venerate his late father as a sainted hero of the revolution, would consider any second marriage his mother might make as a profanation of his father's memory.[1] And Hortense, normally mild and accepting of everyone, had taken a dislike to the Corsican whose talkativeness, awkward jollity and domineering manner offended her. Josephine's Aunt Edmée, who was looking forward to her own wedding to the elderly marquis, was not among the wedding party; when and how Josephine told her about her wedding plans, and what her reaction was, is unknown.

At least one of the witnesses, Barras, may have been aware of how remarkable it was, given the recent serious quarrel between the bride and groom, that there was going to be a wedding at all. Shortly after the banns were published, on February 19, Buonaparte had decided to investigate Josephine's finances. Without telling her of his intent, he contacted the banker Emmery, who had been acting as the conduit of funds from Martinique to Paris. Emmery told Buonaparte that the Tascher plantation and other properties currently brought in some fifty thousand francs a year, and that he was able to advance Josephine about half of that sum—a very small amount, considering the eroded buying power of the assignat.[2]

Buonaparte now knew for certain Josephine had lied about her finances, and that whatever money she had came not from her family property but from her lovers and from her own investments. She was not wealthy. She was not honest. But he was so enamored of her that he wanted to marry her anyway. And besides, as Barras had pointed out to him, her aristocratic connections, her current position as a leader of Directory society, and her distinguished name would lend him a decidedly superior social air, and make him less conspicuous as a foreigner lacking in distinguished breeding.

Josephine was furious when she found out that Buonaparte had been asking questions about her finances. They quarreled, there was conflict—and eventually Buonaparte asked his fiancée to forgive him.

Now all was forgiven, apparently, but as the evening wore on and neither the bridegroom nor the official who would perform the ceremony, Citizen Leclercq, appeared, it began to look as though the hastily arranged wedding might not happen after all.

After what seemed a very long delay, Leclercq arrived, along with his underling Collin-Lacombe, a former deputy with a wooden leg. Now the ceremony could go forward—but where was Buonaparte? The room had warmed up, the bride no longer shivered in her white satin gown as she paced before the fire. The wick of the candle in its tin lantern grew longer and longer, and no one took the trouble to trim it. Finally Leclercq, tiring of the long wait, became sleepy and went off to bed, leaving Collin-Lacombe to cope with General Buonaparte, if and when he ever arrived.

Whatever excitement or pleasure Josephine may have felt when the evening began must by this time have been extinguished. She knew that she was marrying a man who poured nearly all of his remarkable energy and drive into his profession. Now she was discovering, perhaps not for the first time, that she would always have to take second place to the demands of that profession, even on her wedding day.

At last, sometime between nine and ten o'clock, a carriage was heard outside in the rue d'Antin and Buonaparte made his entrance. Ignoring the protests of Collin-Lacombe, who did not have the authority to sign the official documents making the marriage legal, Buonaparte insisted that the ceremony take place. There had been no time to obtain the birth certificates of the bride and groom; the general used his brother's, which advanced his age to twenty-eight. Josephine gave her age as twenty-nine, though she was in fact thirty-two.[3]

The brief civil ceremony was quickly performed. The witnesses signed their names, and Collin-Lacombe, presumably, presented the certificate to Leclercq the following day for his signature. All was in order. General Buonaparte was able to depart for Italy a married man.[4]

Josephine stayed on in Paris, and her life went on much as before, except that her husband was not there to control or govern her. She saw the same friends, frequented the same theaters and cafés, overspent at familiar shops and, at night, was drawn as ever to Barras's notorious establishment where, almost certainly, she continued to enjoy her role as his mistress.[5]

She was now pointed out, not only as one of the leading hostesses of the capital, but as the wife of the remarkable General Buonaparte, and this gave extra dash and sparkle to her adventures with Therese Tallien and the flamboyant Fortunée Hamelin.

Parisians were caught up in an endless mania for dancing, a craze so "sudden, impetuous and terrible," a contemporary said, that it seemed almost a disease. People danced on the tombstones at the cemetery of Saint-Sulpice, and at the Prostitutes' Ball at the Hotel de la Chine, at the dance hall set up amid the ruins of the Bastille, even at the Carmelite convent which held such grim memories for the former Rose de Beauharnais.

Dancing became a kind of exorcism in which the horrors of the recent past were conjured away. At the Victim's Balls, relatives of guillotine victims scoffed at death, wearing red ribbons around their necks as reminders of the bloody chop of the blade, bowing their heads jerkily in imitation of the falling heads, clothing themselves in bloody scarlet. Their feverish derision, their macabre humor were infectious; to laugh at death and loss became a hallmark of the frenetic age of the Directory.

Since her girlhood Josephine had been known as a remarkably light and graceful dancer, and she now joined in the general dancing with enthusiasm. Her friend Therese, who had a predilection for shedding her clothes and revealing her voluptuous Amazonian figure, occasionally danced in the nude. Fortunée, the youngest, least inhibited and most spontaneous of the trio, flirted brazenly as she twirled in her thin, revealing gowns, her black eyes flashing with unmistakable invitation.

Josephine and her lewd friends were highly visible in the spring of 1796, bare armed, bare shouldered, bare legged and at times all but bare breasted, attending receptions and parties in their clinging Grecian-style gowns of sheer gauze, their trailing skirts raised and tucked away into their belts, glittering diamonds at their throats and wrists, girlish circlets of fresh pink roses crowning their antique coiffures. Sometimes they wore gowns with immensely long trains, sometimes wide witchy hats with exaggerated brims. From time to time they were attended by fawning young men, "handkerchief bearers," who fetched and carried for them and provided a tawdry sort of entourage.

They followed every fad, shopping at Nancy's or Caille's or Rose Bertin's for the newest classical fashions—Vestal dresses, Aurora gowns, Minerva tunics—at the shoemakers for pointed shoes to go with their blue and white striped stockings, or for Roman sandals, to be worn with gold rings on each toe and diamond bracelets hugging the ankle. They shopped for the blonde and brunette and even purple wigs that every fashionable woman had to have; Josephine and Therese were said to own sixty wigs between them.

Adorned in their showy finery, gilded lilies from the hothouse, these fantastic creatures displayed themselves at the theater, at grisly dinner parties where a coffin was placed behind every chair, and at exclusive balls at Wenzell's assembly hall, whose vast rotunda featured an Altar of Love around which they danced until the early hours of the morning. Or they went to Frascati, the pleasure garden where under festive pink and blue lights one could wander through an artificial landscape complete with pasteboard grottoes and imitation Greek temples, miniature torrents and fountains running red with wine punch. Lovers eager to escape the brightness of the fireworks could linger in the recesses of dark paths overgrown with trees, or find excitement in the gambling halls where under branching chandeliers and smiling cupids, fortune hunters played at dice and cards.

Always curious to know the future, Josephine frequented the establishments of the fortune-tellers who set up booths along the boulevards, offering to predict one's destiny from crystals or cards.[6] In the aftermath of the Terror, Parisians were mad for the occult, their eager credulity piqued by reading cheap novels full of charms and curses, spectral figures and messages from the beyond.

Madame Villeneuve in the rue de l'Antéchrist had a large following, as did the Italian Monsieur Martin, a palm reader whose legless body was encased in a box, and who summoned his clients into a chamber of horrors full of skeletons and books of black magic bound in human skin. The line of carriages outside Monsieur Martin's ghoulish consulting rooms was nearly as long as that outside Corcelet's, the gourmet shop where the elite gathered to buy truffles in champagne, or Garchy's, the premier manufacturer of ices.

For a number of years Josephine had been an avid patron of Madame Lenormand, known as "The Sorceress," a psychic who had given advice to all the notables of the revolution, from Robespierre to Barras. No doubt she consulted Madame Lenormand when she was weighing her decision about marrying Buonaparte, and now that he had embarked for Italy, she must have questioned the psychic about how he and his army would fare. Would he survive? Would he be wounded, and come home a helpless cripple, minus an arm or a leg, like the hundreds of crippled beggars, many of them ex-soldiers, who were to be seen along the boulevards?

The Sorceress practiced several forms of divination, sometimes breaking a mirror and reading the meaning in the pattern of its shattered fragments, sometimes conjuring with the white of an egg or taking a scoop of ashes from the fire and throwing them into the wind. She also read tarot cards, with their vaguely menacing arcana of occult transformations, death and rebirth, strokes of fortune and malevolent influences. What she saw ahead for Josephine we do not know, but her advice must have weighed heavily with her client as she considered whether or not to join her husband in Italy.

As the weeks went by, the new bride's memory of the hastily arranged wedding in the city hall, and the two-day honeymoon that followed it, must have begun to seem more dream than fact. To be sure, Buonaparte sent Josephine passionate love letters, filled with expressions of a rare ardor. She could hardly put him out of her thoughts, his letters arrived so frequently and were full of pleading for her to write in return.

But marriage itself seemed a quaint, even archaic institution in the Paris of 1796, a relic of another time. Before the revolution, the social rules governing upper-class marriage had been well established: husbands and wives were courteous to one another, produced children together, and led separate romantic lives. This decorous social pattern had long since given way to the erotic free-for-all that was the Directory, with its enthusiastic disregard for rules of all kinds, its light-hearted libertinage and its proclivity for divorce.

Permanence in relationships had become a thing of the past. Transient pleasures, fleeting unions were the desired norm; even when an association was of long standing, as in the case of Josephine's with Barras, there were no formal ties or obligations involved. Josephine's friend Therese would divorce Jean Tallien in 1797, and would ultimately have a number of children by a variety of lovers.

Along with the dissolving of domestic ties went a fad for sordid adventurism, a craze for reckless and brazen behavior that led women to drink too much, flaunt their sexuality too openly, provoke and stalk potential lovers and generally act contrary to what was presumed to be the natural order of things, with men in the lead. The shift in women's behavior, combined with the vulgarity on display throughout the capital—painted phalluses and priapic pictures on walls and doors, printed pornography widespread and easily available, actual scenes of debauchery and free love on view in many public places— had the result of undermining whatever stability marriage represented. Josephine could hardly have entered upon married life at a time less favorable for honoring and keeping her conjugal vows.[7]

Toward the end of April, 1796, less than two months after her wedding, Josephine entertained two officers at her house in the rue Chantereine. One, Colonel Leclerc of the Army of Italy, was stocky and solemn, an undistinguished young man with little to say. But the other, Lieutenant Hippolyte Charles, was not only handsome but highly entertaining.

As warmhearted and likable as Josephine herself was, Lieutenant Charles made her laugh until she cried with his jokes and puns. He was witty but not brittle or malicious; his constant good humor and even disposition were as restful as they were delightful. Unlike the intense, passionate Buonaparte, Hippolyte Charles was blithe and carefree, undemanding, with an easy social grace that lightened the mood of everyone around him. What was more, he was very dashing in his sky-blue hussar uniform with scarlet belt and red leather Hungarian boots, black shako hat and fur-lined coat.

Before long all the women were in love with Hippolyte, or so Josephine told Talleyrand. Therese Tallien, Fortunée Hamelin, even the cool Juliette Récamier were quite enamored of him. He was the beau ideal of the fashionable drawing rooms in May and June, his dark beauty a foil for the pallor of the women, who were just then following a fad for wearing blonde wigs. Hippolyte was elegant— "no one before him has ever known how to tie a cravat," Josephine said—and with his fine features, olive skin, black hair and merry blue eyes he was quite irresistible.

To be sure, there was more to Lieutenant Charles than puns and buffoonery. Although he was only twenty-four, he was already an experienced soldier, toughened by combat and sobered, despite his frivolous demeanor, by the shocks and sorrows of battle. It may have been his war experience, in fact, that made him "play the punchinello," as a contemporary said, using humor, as an intelligent, warmhearted man might well use it, to keep the harsh realities of the military life at bay.

Whatever his attitudes, Hippolyte Charles was extremely attractive to Josephine, and the attraction was mutual; they soon became lovers. At first she may have thought of him as only a fleeting amour, hardly more to her than one of the decorative "handkerchief-bearers" who followed her from one social event to another. But before long she was so filled with desire, so unable to control her feelings for the handsome lieutenant that the thought of leaving Paris, and Hippolyte, made her weep with anxiety and dread.[8]

Buonaparte—or rather Bonaparte, as he now chose to be called, altering the spelling of his name and giving it a French rather than an Italian pronunciation—was writing to Josephine nearly every day, imploring her to join him in Milan. His letters became more agitated as hers to him decreased in frequency, and especially after she wrote to tell him, in May, that she was ill, with several doctors in attendance.

"Your letter is short, sad, and in a trembling hand," he wrote in mid-May. "What is it, my adorable one? . . . Try to amuse yourself, and realize that there is no torment more real for my soul than to think that you are suffering and unhappy." "Rather than know you to be melancholy I almost think that I would myself find a lover for you," he added, knowing nothing of Hippolyte Charles but sensing, even as he teased her, that something was very wrong.[9]

The vain, boastful General Joachim Murat bragged that he had seduced both Josephine and Therese on a visit to Paris, and while Bonaparte knew perfectly well that this story was in all likelihood nothing more than a barracks exaggeration, he was so beside himself with worry that he allowed his fears to control him. Always superstitious, he grew pale with apprehension when the glass on his portrait miniature of his wife was shattered. "Either my wife is very ill or she is unfaithful," he muttered to one of his officers, certain that doom had fallen.

Briefly elated by the possibility that Josephine's illness might be a pregnancy, Bonaparte's hope soon gave way to despair. "My life is a constant nightmare," he wrote to her. "A deadly presentiment prevents me from breathing. I no longer live. I have lost more than life, more than happiness, more than repose. . . . My forebodings are so deadly that I think of nothing except seeing you, to press you for two hours against my breast, and we die together."[10]

Written in fevered haste, in scrawled, barely legible handwriting, his letters betrayed his disordered emotions and his anguish. Again and again he told her that his love for her was beyond any imaginable love, and that it would endure as long as he lived. Every moment of his life was hers. She dominated his thoughts, sleeping and waking. His strength, his arms, his spirit were all hers. "My soul is in your body," he swore fervently, "and the day that you change or cease to be will be the day of my death."

By mid-June Bonaparte's letters were half deranged. He could neither eat nor sleep. In his wretchedness he scratched agonized, all but incoherent messages—and then tore them up or stuffed them into his pockets, fearing to send them. Josephine's failure to join him in Italy had convinced him that she no longer loved him. If she had a lover, he swore, he would "tear his heart out." "All the serpents of the Furies are in my breast," he told her, "and I am only half alive! ...I detest Paris, women, and love....My condition is terrible."[11]

The letters to Josephine were sincere yet melodramatic in their rhetoric. To Barras Bonaparte was more direct. "I am desperate. My wife does not come. Some lover keeps her in Paris. I curse all women."[12]

Josephine's growing preoccupation with Hippolyte Charles was, indeed, keeping her in Paris, but there is reason to think that her claim of illness was a valid one. From 1796 on, and quite possibly earlier, Josephine suffered from migraine headaches that incapacitated her and confined her to bed in a darkened room. The excitement of her intense new love affair, her worries over Bonaparte's jealousy, combined with the stressful demands of her new public role   for now that she was Madame Bonaparte, Josephine was expected to appear at ceremonial gatherings, to represent her husband on formal occasions—must have put her under considerable strain. The attacks of migraine may have been one result.

And she had other preoccupations. She had to help arrange the wedding of her elderly Aunt Edmée, and there were legal affairs to attend to, in her ongoing effort to recover the remainder of her first husband's estate for their children. Someone had to be found who would represent her legal interests when she left for Italy—and by June it had begun to seem imperative that she go.

It was with the deepest reluctance that she made her preparations.

Travel meant expense, and she was, as usual, out of money. What if she became ill along the way? Would there be places where she could stop and rest, if necessary for a day or more? She hated the jolts and shocks of riding in a coach, even on the smoothest road in the best weather; it frightened her, sometimes so much that she insisted on stopping the coach and getting out—something that might not be possible on this journey. The long and perilous trek over the Alps must have loomed as a purgatory.

But at least Hippolyte would be with her. It was agreed: Hippolyte and his senior officer Junot would be her official escorts.

On June 24 passports were issued for Josephine Bonaparte, her maid Louise Compoint, and the rest of her party. Two days later, with the last of the numerous trunks and boxes loaded aboard, fresh food stored away, along with warm blankets and loaded pistols to repel bandits, the three large traveling carriages rolled away along the rue Chantereine, bound toward Lyon and the south.

15

Italian Sojourn

*T*he air grew warmer and drier, the towns smaller and the landscape starker and more bright as Josephine's large, unwieldy traveling coach lumbered along the rutted roads toward Chambéry. In the distance were brown foothills, and beyond them, the looming snowcapped crags of the Alps, rising tier upon tier in forbidding masses. She rode with her tawny pug Fortuné on her lap, his growls and barks an irritant and a warning to her companions. He had received a new leather collar for the trip, hung with bells and inscribed, on a silver plate, "I belong to Madame Bonaparte."

Fortuné tolerated Hippolyte, having no doubt spent a good deal of time in his company and gotten used to him. But he bared his teeth at the other two occupants of Josephine's carriage, Junot and Joseph Bonaparte, the latter ill-tempered and out of sorts because of a painful venereal complaint.

Josephine could hardly have made her brother-in-law's acquaintance under more awkward circumstances. Not only was he in pain, irascible and uncomfortable, but he was in the awkward position of observing (and pretending not to observe) the intimacy between his sister-in-law and her lover. Even if Josephine made some effort to be discreet about her relationship to Hippolyte, there was no disguising the fact that, when the travelers stopped for the night, she and Hippolyte were together, as were Junot and Josephine's maid Louise.

To Joseph, at twenty-eight, oldest of Napoleon's siblings and, since his father's death, the head of the family, Josephine was nothing short of a disaster. Not only was she much too old to be a suitable wife for his brother Nabuleone (who now wanted to be known as Napoleon), but she was a widow with two children, stigmatized by her revolutionary past, notorious for her many liaisons, and far too free and brazenly independent to fit the Corsican model of wifely behavior. (As Bonaparte wrote to Josephine a few weeks before she began her journey, "In well mannered countries,...a wife writes to her husband, she thinks of him, she lives for him."[1])

Joseph disapproved of everything about his new sister-in-law, from her indolence (Corsican wives were diligent, hardworking and self-sacrificing) to her extravagance (Corsican wives were frugal) to her easygoing disposition (Corsican wives were passionate and vehement) to her apparent indifference to family (to Corsicans, family was everything). He frowned on her shockingly revealing clothes, her girlish garlands of flowers, her immodest speech, her disgraceful friends, even her pampering of the growling Fortuné. She could hardly have done anything to lower his opinion of her, and as their days of enforced companionship passed, Joseph's near-perpetual scowl must have caused much strain.

Beyond Chambéry the road narrowed and became much rougher, leading up into the hills. Here groves of olives, their silver leaves shimmering, gave way to acres of vines and then to thick woods of oaks and sycamores. The military escort, riding alongside the carriages, became alert, for the hills were full of outlaw bands—former soldiers, escaped felons, bandits—which preyed on passing vehicles. Villages became rare, then disappeared entirely, replaced by small wayside inns built of chunks of rough-hewn stone.

As they began to ascend the slopes of the high mountains, the air turned cool, even at midday, and drifts of mist and fog arose from time to time to obscure the narrowing path. The entire party now had to put on their warmest cloaks, hoods and muffs to defend against the wintry climate, and still they shivered, and passed around flasks of brandy to warm their blood.

This was no-man's-land, wild, untamed country outside the jurisdiction of even the most diligent local magistrate; crimes committed here went unpunished, and for the most part, unnoted. Swift streams rushed alongside the upward path, churning into foaming cascades; thickets of spruce and fir clung to the steep rock faces, and huge boulders strewn at intervals beside the road and hanging precariously over it were reminders that the danger of avalanches was everpresent.

Soon the road narrowed to a path, then to a mule track. At the last remote posthouse the carriages and horses were sent back, their contents laboriously loaded onto mules led by local guides. Now the going was arduous, for a sharp wind blew nearly constantly and icy rain drove the travelers to seek shelter and warmth at frequent intervals in wayside huts. The mules plodded upward along zigzag switchbacks, clinging to the sheer mountainsides, their riders averting their eyes from the cliff edges they skirted, dropping away thousands of feet below them.

On they went, over rocky ledges, across dazzling snow fields, through sun-dappled meadows where expanses of lavender crocus and white saxifrage grew in lavish abundance. Above and all around them loomed the tall conical peaks of the high mountains, often wreathed in clouds, their slopes gleaming with ice, their ridges glowing faintly pink in the afternoon light. Broad-winged lammergeiers floated silently over the frozen expanse, gliding on the updrafts of the incessant sharp wind. Beneath the towering summit of Mt. Charbonel, the long line of mules crossed through the Mt. Cenis pass, then began the steep, dizzying, zigzag descent into the Italian foothills.

Josephine found the going very difficult and tiring. The constant jostling made her head ache, and she was warm with fever. Apart from her physical weariness, she was in a state of stress, upset by the public demands her new life as Madame Bonaparte was making on her. Although she had spent less than three days with her husband since the wedding, much had been asked of her in the months of his absence. For he had achieved spectacular successes in Italy, and Parisians, eager to celebrate his triumphs, had made her his surrogate in their ceremonies of congratulation.

"Long live Citizeness Bonaparte!" they shouted when she left the Luxembourg Palace on the arm of Junot after presiding at a formal presentation. "Long Live Our Lady of Victories!"

The list of Bonaparte's victories in Italy was nothing short of remarkable, and all the more remarkable for having been achieved against terrible odds. His army, poorly clothed and shod, ill-equipped and inadequately provisioned, had again and again triumphed over far larger enemy forces. Within weeks of beginning his campaign he had seized Milan from the Austrians and was advancing through Lombardy, sending back to Paris curt dispatches giving news of success after success, along with captured battle flags.

The key to the general's amazing good fortune lay in his ability to invigorate and inspire his troops—and maneuver them rapidly and secretly over rough terrain. He appealed to their patriotism, to their determination—and to their greed, for he promised them that if they achieved victory, rich spoils would be theirs. He won their loyalty by his own fierce bravery and apparent indifference to his own safety; he rushed headlong into danger, leading charges, facing enemy fire, urging his men on to follow his fervid example.

It seemed certain there would soon be more ceremonies for "Our Lady of Victories" to attend, more plaudits for her to receive on behalf of her husband. That meant more pressure to fill a role, to adopt a pose—to be, in short, not herself but who others expected her to be. She had not anticipated this when she married Bonaparte; she had known then that in marrying an important man she would be obligated to be his hostess, but that was something she had done for Barras—and done exceptionally well. Carrying out a formal public role was an unexpected drawback, and one that caused her considerable tension.

When at last the trail widened and the travelers were able to transfer to coaches for the rest of their journey, they found themselves in a sunny region of vines and corn, fertile hills where a hot sun beat down on golden grasses. Another day brought them to Turin, where Josephine was received royally, and where she rested for a few days before continuing on to Milan.

They must have been poignant days, for Josephine knew that once she reached Milan, she would only be able to see Hippolyte briefly and furtively. Her infatuation was strong, her preoccupation with her lover obsessive. She may have been drawn to Hippolyte in part because she needed an emotional refuge from the devouring passion and need of her husband (a passion and need that his increasingly distraught letters made only too plain), and from the obligations her marriage was creating. With the jokey, fun-loving Hippolyte there were no strenuous demands, only languid, pleasure-filled hours, the pleasure heightened by the fear of discovery. Only now the pleasure was fleeting, and bittersweet.

Yet Josephine's involvement with Hippolyte had another dimension. Almost from the start, they had been in business together, and with others, deeply involved in the lucrative, corrupt enterprise of army contracting. Now that Bonaparte's victories were creating more demand for everything from boots to horses to canvas to rice and butter, opportunities in the highly profitable enterprise of supplying these growing needs were expanding—and waiting to be exploited. With Josephine on her journey into Italy was Antoine Hamelin, husband of her friend Fortunée Hamelin, who was hoping to become an army contractor with Josephine's help. Bonaparte's brother Joseph too had become an army supplier, and there were many others eager to enter the high-paying trade. The interests of the Bodin Company, the firm through which Josephine and Hippolyte had their financial dealings, were certain to unite them from time to time, even if their romantic trysts had to be curtailed.[2]

When at last the carriages and outriders of Josephine's party arrived in the courtyard of the Serbelloni Palace in Milan, a large crowd was waiting to greet the new arrivals—but General Bonaparte was not among them. The needs of his troops had called him away, and, much to his chagrin, his separation from his wife had to be prolonged for a few more days. Josephine was left to discover the wonders of the imposing palace on her own, with the Duc de Serbelloni, newly appointed President of the Directorate of the Cisalpine Republic, as her guide.

It was a monumental structure, quite the grandest dwelling Josephine had ever occupied. Ionic columns decorated the classic façade, built of rose-red granite embedded with sparkling crystal particles. Inside, the walls of the vast reception halls were faced with marble, inlaid in intricate patterns; life-size statues, bronzes, fine paintings adorned the walls and recesses. In anticipation of his wife's arrival Bonaparte had ordered art works from all over northern Italy brought to the palace and displayed there, and had instructed the servants to fill the rooms with fresh flowers from the extensive palace gardens.

A parade of Italian notables arrived to be presented to Madame

Bonaparte. Though the general had made Lombardy a republic titles had not been outlawed, and the array of elegant counts and countesses, dukes and marquises, dressed in the elaborate gowns, knee-breeches and swords of the old regime, who bowed and curtseyed to Citizeness Bonaparte was imposing indeed. And they brought her gifts—bolts of Milanese silk, gossamer-light and shimmering with iridescence, strings of luminous pearls, lengths of finely wrought lace, antique vases and cameos. The gifts, Josephine soon discovered, were bribes. Bonaparte was imposing heavy taxes on the conquered population, and was stripping palaces and mansions of priceless works of art; the highborn visitors were hoping that Madame Bonaparte could be persuaded to use her influence to moderate her husband's exactions.

The petitioners who presented their gifts and made their obeisances to Josephine were struck by her charm and graciousness, but shocked by her attire. Catholic Italy had never before seen the revealing fashions of the French Directory, and both women and men looked askance at the semi-transparent fabrics of her gowns, the bare-armed, open tunics she wore over flesh-colored tights, her hair worn loose around her face and garlanded with flowers. Such antique naturalness of dress seemed pagan, immoral, an invitation to lechery. The clergy protested, articles appeared in the newspapers denouncing the shameless habits of French women, and there were whispers—perhaps begun by Josephine's spiteful maid Louise Compoint, with whom she had quarreled upon arriving in Milan—that Citizeness Bonaparte was as free with her affections as she was unrestrained in her garments. Before long her affair with Hippolyte Charles was all but common knowledge.[3]

Yet Bonaparte, when at last he rejoined his wife, seemed to be oblivious to the gossip and criticism. He embraced, stroked and fondled Josephine passionately, constantly, and publicly, "playing with her like a child, teasing her, making her cry, and lavishing on her hearty, coarse caresses." Discreet onlookers, embarrassed by his erotic excesses, backed out of the room or looked out the window.

"You are the one thought of my life," he had written her during their separation. "If I am wearied with the turmoil of affairs, if I fear the outcome, I put my hand upon my heart and feel your portrait there; I gaze upon it, love fills me with absolute happiness." He was, observers agreed, entirely besotted with his lovely underdressed wife, and it was with the deepest regret that he forced himself to leave her again after only two days in her company.

In the letters he wrote her from his camp at Castiglione, he teased her about her having found a lover, and when she sent someone (possibly either Antoine Hamelin or Hippolyte) to see him about becoming a supplier of provisions for his troops he chided her for "having known for a long time and known WELL this gentleman whom you recommend to me for a business contract."[4]

Bonaparte swore to his wife that he was not jealous ("I have too high an opinion of my adorable sweetheart for that"), yet he gave orders that all her letters be brought to him at his headquarters so that he could open them and read them.

He loved her to distraction, but he knew her history; clearly, he sensed that, being left alone so much, she might be tempted to stray. He had heard the sordid rumors spread by Murat, and indeed for most of the past several months he had been tormented by jealousy. There was only one way to assure her fidelity. She must accompany him in the field, while he was on campaign.

"A few days ago I thought I loved you," he wrote to her after leaving her in Milan, "but now that I have seen you again I love you a thousand times more." He asked her to meet him in Brescia, and she came, toward the end of July, bringing her maid and Antoine Hamelin with her and a coach-load of trunks.

The roads were full of soldiers, some marching rapidly in column, others straggling along at a slower pace. Carts carrying wounded men and provisions trundled by, and swift couriers, riding as fast as their superb mounts could take them, sped past on their way from one camp to another. Looking out across the broad green plain from the carriage window, Josephine could see columns of smoke rising, and could hear, in the distance, the booming of artillery.

Her reunion with Bonaparte in Brescia was brief but eventful. Once again he overwhelmed her with attention, caresses, practically making love to her before the eyes of his military staff and others. But he was preoccupied, brusque, distracted by the frequent bulletins he received and orders he sent, his mind full of plans and responses to the unfolding situation as it developed. For there was an Austrian army nearby, marching on Mantua, and more enemy troops might soon be sent in across the Alps.

Years later Josephine told a confidant, the Comte de Ségur, that while they were in Brescia, a town that had formed part of the independent Venetian Republic, the town governor, hating the new French conquerors more than he resented the encroaching Austrians, determined to deliver General Bonaparte to his enemies. Knowing that the Austrians were very near, he made contact with them secretly and promised to keep Bonaparte within the precincts of the town until his capture could be carried out.

On the day that the general and his wife planned to leave Brescia, the governor tried to persuade them to stay, inviting them to an evening party and no doubt hoping that they would spend the night. But Josephine demurred, bored by formal fêtes—as she later told her Aunt Edmée in a letter—and eager to be off. Bonaparte wanted to stay, Josephine insisted upon going. They could not agree until finally, Josephine refused absolutely, digging in her heels obstinately and virtually forcing her husband to give in. Give in he did—only to discover, when they were less than three miles outside the town, that the Austrian army had begun to pour in. Had they left any later, Bonaparte would have been captured for certain.

Not for the first time, Josephine had been lucky for her husband. He was by now convinced that his good fortune in battle, in politics, in all the important arenas of life was linked to his finding and falling in love with her. She was his charm, his talisman; from the time he met her, he had had nothing but opportunity and success. She would bring him greater glory in his present campaign, of that he felt sure.

But when they reached Verona, there were still more Austrians in view, long forbidding columns of men and equipment that had come down from the north through the Brenner Pass. Bonaparte quickly sent his wife and her maid Louise to Peschiera, sixteen miles away on the shore of Lake Garda, with Antoine Hamelin to escort them. But here too she was at risk, for the enemy was encamped so near the town that at night the flares from their bivouac fires could plainly be seen.

Now Josephine was very frightened. The French commander of the town of Peschiera had no confidence in his ability to protect her.

She would be a valuable hostage, should the Austrians sweep in and take over the town and discover her identity. All that night she lay on her bed fully clothed, sleeping only fitfully, waiting to be told that it was time to flee once again.

On the following morning, Junot appeared, with an escort of dragoons. Bonaparte had sent him with orders to take Josephine, Louise and Hamelin to Castelnuovo. But by the time Junot arrived in Peschiera, the presence of the Austrians made that impossible, so they set out westward, along the shore of Lake Garda, hoping to reach the camp at Castiglione in safety.

Amid the crackle of musketry the coach started out, Josephine with her nerves on edge and her head pounding, the air filled with the acrid smell of burnt cartridges and gunpowder. No longer an adventure, her presence on campaign with her husband had become a terrifying nightmare. The wild swaying of the coach, the sharp cries of the outriders when an Austrian gunboat bore down on them, the shrieks of the weeping Louise unnerved her, making her short of breath and overcome with dread.

Sharpshooters in the gunboat began firing on the coach. The driver cracked his whip, urging the horses on, and Junot ordered his dragoons to return the fire. Soon, however, the passengers felt a violent wrench and the coach swayed, then came to a sudden halt. One of the horses had been hit, and an outrider killed. They could not go on, exposed as they were to the murderous fire. Obeying Junot's shouts the women and Hamelin got out of the coach and were handed down into a deep ditch beside the road—fortunately empty of water now, at the height of midsummer.

Cautiously the travelers walked the length of the ditch, hidden from view of the enemy on the lake, Josephine and Louise making their way along in their flimsy shoes, their skirts over their arms. Swiftly Junot gave orders for the dead horse to be unhitched so that the coach could go forward. At last, having reached a point along the road where they would no longer be vulnerable to enemy fire, the passengers got back into the coach and resumed their journey, shaken and agitated.

Continuing on to Desenzano, they paused, unable to go ahead because of the congestion they encountered. A battle had been fought here the night before, with both armies trying to seize the road. On either side the fields, waist-high with ripening grain, were filled with bodies of the dead and dying, fallen horses, abandoned guns. Salvage parties were just beginning to walk through the area, giving water to the survivors, stripping the enemy dead, taking prisoners. A great stench rose into the afternoon air, sickening the passengers and forcing them to hold their scented handkerchieves to their noses.

The stink of the battleground, the sight of the broken men, their proud uniforms dusty and bloody, waiting beside the road for the hospital carts to arrive, made the tenderhearted Josephine weep afresh, and she was still weeping, distraught and exhausted, when at last the coach reached Castiglione and she fell into Bonaparte's outstretched arms.

This sketch of Josephine by Pierre Prud'hon comes closer than any other representation to revealing her complex inner self.
© Corbis-Bettmann

Josephine at her most captivating. Painting by Pierre Prud'hon in 1805.
© *Corbis-Bettmann*

Rose Tascher's first husband Alexandre de Beauharnais.
© *Corbis-Bettmann*

Nabuleone Buonaparte as a boy of sixteen in military school, a portrait drawn from life by a friend. The sketch is inscribed, "My Dear Friend Buonaparte."
© *Corbis-Bettmann*

"The Morning of the 18th Brumaire." Engraving from a painting by Schopin. The artist's imaginary composite portrait includes, from left to right, Joseph Bonaparte, Hortense, Josephine, Eugene, Lucien Bonaparte, Berthier, General Joachim Murat, Napoleon Bonaparte, Cambacérès, Talleyrand, Charles Victor Leclerc (husband of Paulette Bonaparte), Kellerman, Moreau and Bessières.

A sketch by Prud'hon of Empress Josephine in her gardens at Malmaison.
© Corbis-Bettmann

Josephine as empress in court dress and wearing a fortune in pearls and gems.
© *Corbis-Bettmann*

Hortense Beauharnais as Queen of Holland.
© *Corbis-Bettmann*

This engraving of
Josephine as empress
captures something
of her wistful,
worried state.
Engraving after
a painting by
J. E. Laurent.
© *Corbis-Bettmann*

Wash drawing of
Josephine as empress in
a regal but stiff formal
pose, as many of her
subjects saw her.
© *Corbis-Bettmann*

Prince Eugene de Beauharnais,
Josephine's dutiful son and
Bonaparte's most loyal deputy,
in the uniform of the Imperial
Guard.
© *Corbis-Bettmann*

Emperor Napoleon in his
middle years, stout and
paunchy, but with his
penetrating eyes
and look of fierce
determination
unaltered.
© *Corbis-Bettmann*

16

"I Don't Like the Honors of This Country, and I Am Often Bored"

ourage, my dearest," Bonaparte said as he consoled his over-wrought wife. "I shall make Würmser"—the Austrian commander—"pay dearly for the tears he has caused you."

He took her into his temporary headquarters, a stone peasant cottage, where she was able to lie down and collect herself, however briefly. Bonaparte could not offer Josephine more than a few hours of illusory safety. The Austrian army was approaching rapidly. If she did not leave soon, she might be trapped in the fighting that was sure to erupt.

Bonaparte gave Antoine Hamelin fifteen hundred louis and placed his wife in his care, telling Hamelin to take her as rapidly as possible into Tuscany. He had signed a treaty with the Tuscan grand duke; provided the French were able to hold Castiglione, and protect the surrounding region, there should be no Austrian incursion into Tuscan territory.

Hamelin bundled the still shaken Josephine back into the coach and they started out again, southward this time, across the low-lying plain toward the Apennines.

For the next several weeks, through the hottest part of the hot Italian summer, Josephine and her companion wandered from town to town, anxious for news of the French army, never entirely certain, when they stopped for the night, whether they would be among friends or foes. The countryside was full of rumors: that the Austrians had overrun Lombardy and expelled the French; that Würmser was about to exact a terrible revenge on all of Italy; that General Bonaparte was dead and his widow was carrying his body, encased in a coffin, with her on her travels. When Josephine and Hamelin were staying in Florence, curious Florentines broke into the mansion where they were in order to see for themselves the corpse of the famous French general.

They were staying on the coast, at Livorno, when they received the welcome news that Bonaparte had defeated the Austrians at Castiglione and that many thousands of the enemy had been taken prisoner. But they had hardly had time to fully absorb this good news, and relax in consequence, when more bulletins arrived. Bonaparte's army had been badly beaten at Rovereto and again at Bassano; his scattered forces had fled.

Shock and dread now plagued the harried Josephine. Without Bonaparte and his army to protect her, she was surely doomed. Depressed and deeply troubled, her head pounding, she imagined the worst.[1] Yet afflicted as she was, and seemingly cut off from all avenues of safety, she somehow managed to communicate with Hippolyte. They arranged to meet at Brescia. There, in the headquarters of the absent Bonaparte, Josephine, Hamelin and Hippolyte dined together and afterward Josephine and her lover spent the night in the general's bedroom, guarded by a protective chambermaid and an acquiescent grenadier posted outside the bedroom door.

Shortly after she returned to Milan early in September of 1796 Josephine wrote a letter to her Aunt Edmée. She was once again feeling relatively safe, for Bonaparte's defeats were transient and he was currently prospering on campaign. But she had been through a harrowing few weeks. Indeed, after all that she had endured, from fearing death and coming under enemy fire to punishing attacks of illness to the minor but wearying inconveniences of inadequate sleep, uncomfortable lodgings and a near-constant state of uncertainty and worry, the weeks must have seemed like months. A young cavalry officer, Baron Carrion-Nisas, who saw her at this time, noted that Madame Bonaparte wept often, several times a day, and that the smallest incident could trigger her tears.

She was overwrought, her nerves in shreds. She was ready to give up the grand life, the receptions and honors, the constant tributes (while in Lucca, she had had the honor of being presented with the chrism, or sacred coronation oil with which kings were once anointed). "I would prefer to be an ordinary person in France," she told her aunt. "I don't like the honors of this country, and I am often bored."

"It is true that the state of my health renders me melancholy," she added, "for I have much discomfort. If happiness could ensure health, then I should be doing well. I have the best husband in the world." She went on to tell Edmée how good Bonaparte was to her, how he adored her, "as if she were a goddess," how he never let her want for anything. He was good to her children too, sending them gifts—an enamel watch set with pearls to Hortense, a gold watch to Eugene. She and her children were much loved, that was certain.[2]

And yet, had she written the whole truth to Edmée, she would have been forced to add that Bonaparte was in essence an absent husband. She had seen him for only two days in July and three in August. In September he had been in Milan for a week and a half, but much of that time had been occupied with formal events and long meetings with his officers. Even when they were alone he was preoccupied, either lost in sensual adoration or with his mind on military affairs. In fact she had spent much less time with her second husband during the first six months of their marriage than she had with the wayward Alexandre Beauharnais.

Once again, late in the fall, Bonaparte believed that Josephine might be pregnant, and wrote to her from the field, asking for "news of your little belly." In actuality they had spent so little time together that the likelihood of a pregnancy was small. Although Bonaparte waxed rapturous about Josephine's "little Black Forest," which he loved to visit and to kiss (the name was a somewhat complicated pun; the "Black Forest," Parisian slang for the stock market, was a reference to the commodity value of Josephine's sex), his visits were infrequent. Still, he hoped and expected that she would give him a child before long, and she may have felt the same.[3]

In truth Josephine did not yet know her husband very well, although she was becoming better acquainted with him on each of their brief periods of companionship. His increasing fame had not changed him much. Though he had become widely celebrated and admired in the past year he had not altered his appearance; his dress, while less shabby than when Josephine first saw him, was understated—a single-breasted suit buttoned to the neck, with a band of narrow gold embroidery, a tricolored plume in his hat—and his bearing modest. Physically he was still extremely thin, slightly below average height (the best estimates of Bonaparte's height suggest that he was about 5'6"; Josephine was about five feet tall). He continued to wear his sparse powdered hair longer than was fashionable, falling to his shoulders. His small face, with its narrow lips and long nose, was striking and odd, almost grotesque, the broad forehead creased with worry lines, the restless, hungry, watchful outsize eyes alive with intelligence and, when he was in good humor, playfulness. His gestures were rapid and lively, his heavily accented speech clipped and sharp.

Though his speaking voice was loud and resonant, Bonaparte's singing voice—and he liked to sing—was a raucous squall that made his companions long to overcome their deference to him and put their fingers in ears. "No, no there could never be/A sweeter child, dearer to me!" his favorite song began, and he sang it lustily and often.

He had such a superabundance of energy that he frequently paced back and forth, or was overcome by an urge to go walking or riding. He rode headlong, dashing wildly across every sort of terrain, refusing to be daunted by obstacles, no matter how formidable. To suggest that he might want to backtrack in order to avoid a thicket, or a fallen tree, or a swollen stream was to earn one of his thunderous dark looks. He was an audacious rider, but not a skillful one. He often fell, though he never seemed to hurt himself much; after each fall he would simply cry out "Broke my neck!," pick himself up, and remount his horse. No one dared remark on his frequent accidents, fearing his wrath, but privately those around him worried that at any time, a single thoughtless leap or daring gallop might put an end to his career, or even his life.

What was worse, Bonaparte forced others to share his fearless races across country. Driving a calèche or other light vehicle, he would insist that his wife and other companions join him as he tore across ploughed fields and bounded over expanses of waste ground, sending mud or dust flying as the light wheels of the carriage bounced dangerously from rut to rut. The passengers suffered with each juddering bump, clutching at handholds when the carriage went around corners on two wheels, nearly tipping over. Even the hardiest survivor of these perilous excursions arrived home with his stomach clenched in fear.

Josephine was discovering that Bonaparte enjoyed the discomfiture of others. Not only did he like putting them at risk, he enjoyed teasing them to the point of embarrassment and beyond, badgering them with preposterous name-calling, pinching and pulling their noses and ears painfully. Such familiarities were no doubt meant in jest, but there was an edge to the playfulness, for Bonaparte was socially gauche and the clumsy physicality and awkward verbal sparring were his substitutes for normal communication, and he was irritably aware of his inadequacies.

Throughout the fall of 1796, with Bonaparte away most of the time, Josephine pursued her twin passions, for Hippolyte Charles (who was himself away much of the time, distinguishing himself for bravery at the Battle of St-Georges in mid-September) and for pursuing army contracts. For distraction she now had her friend from Paris, the coarse, manic, always entertaining Fortunée Hamelin, to keep her company. With Fortunée came a number of Paris dressmakers, wigmakers, milliners and jewelers, all eager for commissions, not only from Madame Bonaparte and her fashionable friends, but from the minority of brave Milanese ladies who had begun to emulate the Parisians' style.

For Josephine had a following, albeit a relatively small one; when she wore a revealing rose-pink tunic with a black-fringed train and black gauze sleeves, some of the Italian countesses ordered tunics like it—and also long nut-colored gloves, and shoes of yellow Moroccan leather, and white stockings with green coins—whatever was currently in favor with the general's lady. A few of them even imitated the "dragoons' coiffure" the Parisians affected—a small imitation military helmet crowning a mop of disorderly curls—and copied Fortunée Hamelin's showy practice of scattering gems all across the torsos of her gowns, so that she sparkled like "a river of diamonds" in the candlelight.

Not surprisingly, traditionalists and the clergy reacted strongly to what they saw as the corruption of Milanese women. Once again denunciations rang out from pulpits, pamphlets appeared condemning the scandalously underclad Madame Bonaparte and stern husbands warned their wives and daughters about the evils of behaving the way the French women did, with their immodest speech and frank, unwomanly gaze. Factions formed within the crowd of sycophants at the Serbelloni palace, with some favoring the French and their bold republican mores and others secretly hating the invaders; people grumbled that Josephine Bonaparte ought to go back to Paris where she belonged.

The grumbling of the disaffected Milanese became open muttering, then outright complaining in November when Bonaparte's armies once again began losing battles and, with tens of thousands more Austrian troops swarming in over the Alps, he dreaded losing everything he had gained since the spring. Then in the marshes near Arcole he turned the tide and achieved a great victory. Once again he set an example by his own bravery, crossing a bridge under enemy fire, urging his men on, as reckless in the midst of battle as he was when dashing across country in his calèche.

"At last, my adorable Josephine, I am reborn," he wrote exultantly after the battle. "Death is no longer before my eyes, and glory and honor are again in my heart." Six thousand of the enemy lay dead on the battlefield, and another five thousand had been taken prisoner. Bonaparte's life had been saved, not once but twice: first by his adjutant, who threw himself heroically between his commander and the bullets that would certainly have killed him, and again when his young brother Louis, who was serving as his aide-de-camp, pulled him out of a ditch in which he would otherwise have drowned.

Buoyed up by his victory, and by his everpresent conviction of his own invulnerability, the general turned his thoughts to his wife. "Good God! How happy I should be if I could see you at your pretty toilet, little shoulder, little white breast, elastic and so firm, above it a pretty face with a creole headscarf, good enough to eat." He lingered over her every appealing part, especially the "little Black Forest." "I kiss it a thousand times and I await impatiently the moment of being inside."

"To live in Josephine," he wrote, "is to live in Elysium. A kiss on your mouth, your eyes, your shoulder, your breast, everywhere, everywhere!"

In December Josephine welcomed to Milan her sister-in-law Pauline Bonaparte, Napoleon's vivacious, ill-disciplined, strikingly beautiful sixteen-year-old sister. Pauline, called in the family "Pretty Paulette," was irrepressible, and irrepressibly sensual. At thirteen, she had fallen in love with a thoroughly unsavory seducer of forty, a friend of Barras, Stanislas Fréron. Bonaparte's efforts to detach Paulette from her debauched lover had only made her more determined to marry him, and when she was fifteen she and Fréron became secretly engaged.

As headstrong as she was flighty and emotional, Paulette announced that Fréron was the only man she would ever love, and resented her family's opposition to him as her future husband. She resented even more the opposition of the sister-in-law she had never met, Josephine, with her reputation for sexual wantonness.

When Paulette came to Milan, escorted by her Uncle Fesch, a hearty, ruddy-faced priest who was profiting from (what else?) army provisioning, she was strongly prejudiced against Josephine, and nothing in their new acquaintanceship dispelled her aversion. Her dislike for her sister-in-law grew as, day by day, she witnessed Josephine's obvious allure—her sweet face and graceful, supple figure, her natural elegance, her overwhelming kindness and charm. Envy compounded Paulette's dislike, envy not only of her sister-in-law's social adroitness but of her large and growing wardrobe, her jewels and pearls, her position as a leader of fashion. Apart from being admired for her undeniable beauty, what Paulette wanted most was to be a leader of fashion herself—Bonaparte would later on call her the "Queen of Fripperies" for her shallow preoccupation with adornments of all kinds—and to see Josephine occupying the role she coveted filled her with envenomed adolescent spite.

Ignoring Josephine's warm efforts at friendliness, Paulette was coldly malicious to her sister-in-law, nursing her grievance over Fréron, begrudging Josephine's full wardrobes, showing jealousy when Bonaparte displayed his usual lavish affection for his wife. A one-sided rivalry developed between the two women, a rivalry grounded, in no small part, in Paulette's precocious awareness that, at sixteen, she was far more lovely than Josephine, at thirty-three, had ever been.

When early in the new year of 1797 Josephine and Paulette went to Bologna, to be near Bonaparte on the next phase of his campaign, the rivalry curdled into open malice. The irrepressible Paulette began mimicking Josephine, making faces at her behind her back, plaguing her with ridicule, making hateful and vindictive remarks. Forgetting her grand passion for Fréron, she flirted extravagantly with the many officers at Bologna, including Hippolyte Charles, knowing—for she eagerly collected gossip—that the most effective way to wound her sister-in-law was to steal the attentions of her lover.

Continuing to suffer from ill health, assailed by imaginings that Bonaparte was dead, afflicted by the daily slurs, snubs and machinations of her young sister-in-law, Josephine began to long to return to Paris, where she could once again live in comfort among friends.[4] She sent gifts to those she missed—a Livorno straw hat for Therese Tallien, sausages and cheese for Jean Tallien, a necklace of coral beads for their daughter Thermidor, Italian liqueurs for Barras.

"I cannot accustom myself to being separated so long from my dear children," she wrote to Hortense. "I want to press them to my heart. I have every reason, however, to hope that this moment is not very far distant, and this helps me to recover from the indisposition from which I have been suffering." Bonaparte, having finally taken the key fortress of Mantua, was successfully pressing on with his campaign against the papal states. By the end of February, 1797, the pope had turned over to him Bologna, Ferrara, Ravenna and Ancona; most of Italy was now in French hands. When the fighting ended, they could all go home—or so Josephine anxiously hoped.

"Write to me often," she told Hortense. "It is very long since I have had news from you. Love your mama as she loves you, and you will adore her. Good-bye, my good little Hortense. Your mama embraces you and loves you with all her heart."[5]

Josephine longed to go home—but for the time being, Bonaparte had other plans. He would enjoy his conquests for a while. He rented the Villa Crivelli ten miles from Milan at Mombello, and invited his relatives to spend the summer there with him and his wife.

So it was to be a summer of family, only not Josephine's family but Bonaparte's. Paulette and Joseph she already knew; the former was hateful, the latter sour and disapproving. Elisa, Caroline, Louis and Jerome she would soon meet, along with her mother-in-law Letizia. Bonaparte's remaining brother Lucien had not been invited to

Mombello; the general had not forgiven him for marrying an un-suitable wife, and would not receive him.

Family matters were much on Josephine's mind in April as she prepared for the move to the Villa Crivelli. Bonaparte was eager for Paulette to marry, and was considering which of his officers to give her as a husband. There would be a wedding to arrange, beyond the complicated tasks of entertaining and accommodating her in-laws and the other guests Bonaparte was sure to invite. The villa needed repair, there was furniture to be bought and the household staff to supervise.

And, as always, there would be Hippolyte, her heart's desire, her constant distraction, her torment. How, in the midst of so many people, so much activity, would she manage to be with him?

17

"Our Family Shall Want for Nothing"

All the roses in the gardens of the Villa Crivelli were in luxuriant bloom in early June of 1797 when Madame Letizia Bonaparte, with her two youngest children Caroline and Jerome, stepped out of her carriage and surveyed the grandeur of the elegant mansion before her. Wearing, as she always did, the sober, long-sleeved black gown, black shoes and veiled black bonnet of a Corsican widow, she was in contrast with the richness of color around her, the vivid reds and pinks of the flowers, the golden sunlight pouring down over the lush green countryside, the blues and greens of the liveried servants who stood around the carriage waiting to attend her and her children.

Madame Bonaparte, a much admired beauty as a girl, was still good-looking in her late forties, though her shrewd black eyes were ringed with wrinkles and her once abundant dark hair had thinned and grown grey. Fiercely proud, dignified, outspokenly critical of all that was light and frivolous, she bore on her sharp features a grim integrity that came from viewing life as a series of hostile combats against a bitter fate. She was a survivor.

As a girl Letizia had overcome the dangers of fighting in the Corsican revolution, wearing a dagger in her belt and tasting the hardships of combat. She had come through the perils of childbirth twelve times, delivering at least one of her babies herself. She had struggled with the adversities attendant upon early widowhood, and had raised her eight surviving children with meager resources. And she had surmounted the tribulations of being expelled from Corsica and thrust into the maelstrom of the revolution, with all its hazards and uncertainties, and come out virtually unscathed.

Given all that she had faced and overcome, Letizia was unfazed by her second son's remarkable success. To be sure, she had put to good use the generous sums of money he had sent her over the past eighteen months, ever since his sudden eruption into prominence, and she felt considerable satisfaction at the honor her Poleone was bringing to the Buonaparte name. But the palatial expanse of the Villa Crivelli, its princely grounds and extensive staff of servants, now assembled in greeting, left her unaffected. She felt, if anything, a certain contempt for the villa's evident luxuries and undoubted comforts. Luxury and comfort bred weakness and vice; she much preferred austerity and frugality.

Letizia knew whom to blame, of course, for the opulent environment: her newest daughter-in-law Josephine Beauharnais. It was no secret that the notorious Viscountess de Beauharnais had a taste for extravagance and wasted money on such things as rented villas and large staffs of servants; she thought only of pleasure and self-indulgence. Everything Letizia had ever heard about her daughter-in-law predisposed her to despise her—and to condemn her harshly for seducing and corrupting the dutiful, naive Poleone.

And when Letizia met Josephine, nothing in the younger woman's sweetly welcoming manner dispelled her preconceptions. Letizia was and always had been a respectable woman of the lower Corsican nobility. Viscountess de Beauharnais—she could hardly bring herself to think of Josephine as Madame Bonaparte—was a whore, as she had been heard to say out of Josephine's hearing. Letizia would behave toward her daughter-in-law with cold correctness, but she would never accept or include her as a genuine member of the Bonaparte clan.

If Letizia was cold but correct, her oldest daughter Elisa was bluntly hostile. Plump and shapeless, with an unattractive round face and a perpetually cross expression, Elisa was as homely as her sister Paulette was pretty, and she took no pains to improve her appearance. Vain of her intelligence, she lashed out with her sharp tongue at everyone who came her way, and was particularly malicious toward Josephine.

Accompanying Elisa to Mombello was her new husband Felix Bacciochi, a Corsican officer fifteen years her senior, whom she detested; she had married him, over her brother Napoleon's strong objections, because at twenty she was an old maid and he was the only man who had ever asked for her hand. Felix was a feeble character, fat, bovine and ineffectual, and mildly absurd because of his name Bacciochi, which meant "Kiss-Eyes." Inoffensive but dull, he took little interest in anything beyond playing the violin, at which he showed a mediocre talent. Knowing that Elisa's celebrated brother was opposed to his marriage must have made Felix very uncomfortable at Mombello.

Of the other members of the Bonaparte family, nineteen-year-old Louis, aide-de-camp to his brother and hero of the Italian campaign, stood out for his mildness—rare in that family—and his easygoing nature. Napoleon cherished Louis. He had tutored him, cooked for him, groomed him for the military life, practically raised him as he might have raised a son. And Louis in turn had made his brother and the rest of the family proud. He had shown exceptional bravery, passing again and again under enemy fire in order to deliver messages. Most important, when his brother was in danger in the marshes near Arcole, Louis had saved his life.

Of the remaining members of the clan, fifteen-year-old Caroline was a fresh-faced, bright girl, too stout and square to be attractive, and Jerome, now thirteen, distinguished himself only by resembling his brother the general and playing jokes on the others. Uncle Fesch, Letizia's stepbrother who had come to Italy with Paulette six months earlier, stayed contentedly in the background of family life, more than pleased with the commissariat assignment Bonaparte had given him. Joseph's wife Julie, the heiress who had brought him her fortune, also remained quietly in the background, obedient to her husband and tractable with the others, her demure behavior a constant reproach to the gentle but graciously prominent Josephine, who presided at Mombello like one born to royalty.

All Josephine's social talents now came to the fore. Bonaparte wanted Mombello to be more than just a military headquarters located in a splendid aristocratic mansion; he wanted a court, and she saw to it that a court was created. No business was conducted inside the villa. Instead, those officers and visitors with dispatches or petitions were moved outside into the gardens, where a large tent was erected to shelter them. The ornate salons and reception rooms inside the villa were left free for special receptions and dinners, where a select list of guests, including artists and musicians, statesmen and intellectuals, were admitted to pay homage to General Bonaparte and to mingle with his semi-literate relations at the long formal dining table.

Among Josephine's pleasures at Mombello were the vast gardens and greenhouses. Here, escaping from her unpleasant relatives and from the constant activity under the huge tent, she could walk along poplar-lined paths and rest under the shade of mulberries and ilex. The warm air was full of the scents of honeysuckle and jasmine and lilac. There were beds of purple cyclamen and blue forget-me-nots, and late anemones still blooming by old stone walls. Songbirds clustered in the woods and shrubs at the edges of small blue ponds, and waterbirds—ducks, swans, egrets and diving birds of all sorts—floated serenely along the gleaming surface of the water, under the hot sun.

Josephine was beginning to sense a special affinity for swans. There were swans in abundance at Mombello, elegant and unruffled, their calm restful to her edgy unease. Had Josephine been of a more reflective nature, she might have seen herself in the swan: emerging from an awkward provincial youth, like the gawky adolescent swan; undergoing a transformation to resplendent sophisticated womanhood, like the maturing swan, its beauty and grace emerging as it aged.

For like the swans of Mombello, Josephine, in the summer of 1797, had entered into her full glory. Her first youth was long gone, but it had left in its wake an elusive resplendence, a sort of vaporous aspect that set her apart and made her seem a creature out of a fairytale. Her tender expression, its sweetness and delicacy set off by her shining chestnut hair falling in spiraling curls from a golden net, held an indefinable attraction. Her melting blue eyes under long lashes, her dazzling complexion and ideal figure were, as Bonaparte liked to say, "incomparable." Younger, more brilliantly beautiful women such as Paulette Bonaparte, seemed almost too obvious, too fleshly by comparison to Josephine's tremulous, wispy, altogether mysterious charm.

Soon after the Bonaparte clan gathered at Mombello, the general announced that his sister Paulette would be marrying Brigadier-General Victor Leclercq, a brave though markedly prosaic and physically unprepossessing officer on his staff. No doubt Bonaparte thought that Leclercq would be a steadying influence on the flighty Paulette; what the bride thought has not been recorded, though undoubtedly she was pleased to be the object of much attention and admiration. Her old lover Fréron, it seems, was forgotten—or at least pushed into the margins of her thoughts.

With Letizia looking on, her hands always busy with the knitting in her lap, Josephine made the wedding arrangements. Many things were needed, an expensive new dress for Paulette, flowers, food for the guests, decorations for the villa's chapel. Couriers were sent to Milan a dozen times a day, and cartloads of goods came up the dusty road to the villa.

Amid all the preparations Elisa and her husband were not forgotten. Elisa appealed tearfully to her stony brother for forgiveness for going against his wishes in marrying Felix. After a scene, Bonaparte yielded to family feeling and pardoned her trespass, and agreed to permit the marriage to be blessed in the chapel. So on the appointed day the two couples stood before the altar, Paulette stunningly lovely, Elisa plain but triumphant, and repeated their vows.

Celebrating continued for weeks following the weddings. Josephine arranged receptions and parties at which Paulette and Victor Leclercq, Elisa and Felix Bacciochi were the guests of honor—along with Letizia, who sat, a remote, dignified figure in her black widow's weeds, and accepted the bows and compliments of the guests with tolerant equanimity.

The highlight of the wedding festivities was an elaborate excursion to Villa Villani on Lake Como, where family and guests feasted while watching displays of fireworks and a flotilla of boats, each one brilliantly illuminated, was set adrift on the lake. All manner of honors were paid to the newlyweds: they rode in gilded carriages fit for royalty, escorted by squadrons of smart red-jacketed cavalry officers; they received the admiring plaudits of villagers; for two days they were made to feel as if they, and not General Bonaparte and his wife, were the true celebrities of the family.

It was Josephine who designed and arranged all the grand enter-tainments for Paulette and Elisa and their husbands, but instead of appreciating her efforts and the good will they represented, the Bon-apartes grew increasingly hardened against her. Joseph in particular was cold and rudely contemptuous, Elisa markedly unpleasant, Letizia icy. Paulette, by far the worst behaved of the family, called Josephine "the old lady" and stuck her tongue out at her behind her back; she spied on her, soaked up gossip about her and laughed at the way she dressed—the laughter concealing a good deal of envy.

According to her in-laws, the list of Josephine's faults was long indeed. She had a notorious past. She had enticed Bonaparte into marriage (how else could his marriage to such an old and undesirable bride be explained?). She was barren. She was a spendthrift. She was vulgar, displaying her many jewels and bracelets with a lack of re-straint that was almost as shameful as her lack of modesty in dress. She kept immoral company. (Here the Bonapartes pointed their col-lective finger at Josephine's friend and companion, General Berthier's mistress Marchesa Visconti, whose independence, free morals and scanty attire made General Bonaparte himself exclaim "Good God! What women! What morals!")

The weight of all the enmity directed against her made Josephine weary and ill, and she was glad when toward the end of July the Bonapartes went their separate ways, Joseph to Rome, Elisa to Cor-sica, taking Letizia with her, Jerome to Paris to return to school. Paulette, unfortunately, remained; Leclercq's military duties were in Italy, at Bonaparte's side, and she had to be where he was, which meant that she would go on annoying her sister-in-law at every op-portunity.

Though well aware of the envenomed attacks his relatives were making against his beloved wife, Bonaparte had not come to her defense. He may have despaired of being able to create harmony between them, or, more likely, he yielded to his admitted weakness in dealing with his relatives. (He called himself a "milksop" when it came to his relations.[¹]) He was powerless to reprimand them; the most he could bring himself to do was glare at Paulette when she was at her most egregious, and she effectively ignored him.

"Our family shall want for nothing," he had declared to Joseph early in his triumphant career. Since then he had spared no effort in furthering the wellbeing of every family member, even the "ill-balanced" Lucien. He had lavished funds, promotions, honors and opportunities on them all, and would continue to do so. At bottom, his loyalty and devotion to his blood relations ran deeper than his impulse to guard his wife against their assaults.

Josephine observed this, understood it—and despaired. Her every instinct told her that in marrying Bonaparte she had unwittingly acquired a clutch of new enemies—grave enemies, Corsican enemies, the sort who practiced the vendetta and who would never, ever leave her in peace. But she did not allow herself to dwell on such morbid imaginings for long.[2] They brought on migraines, and migraines kept her in her room, suffering and in low spirits, for days.

With the fall came a temporary change of scene. Bonaparte went to Passeriano in the Venetian Republic to negotiate with the Austrians, and in September he sent for Josephine to join him. For six tense weeks the talks between Bonaparte and the Austrian diplomats, chiefly the exuberant, rotund Austrian Count Cobenzl—an amateur actor with a commanding presence—went on, interspersed with official dinners and receptions. Arriving at a definitive peace settlement was extremely difficult, and Bonaparte, made irritable and edgy by the long negotiating sessions, at times behaved like a sullen child. He glowered, he pinched and slapped and teased, he even threw bits of bread across the table at Josephine, who gave him reprovingly maternal looks.

But neither she nor the Austrians could cope with his monumental childishness. At times he raged at the Austrian diplomats, shouting insults, making threats, even breaking dishes to punctuate his tantrums.

"Your empire is nothing more than an old hag of a servant whom everyone in the house rapes!" he shouted at Cobenzl, his fury breaking through the veneer of politeness at the negotiating table. Gesticulating wildly, red in the face, he roared and ranted, knocking over furniture and walking out of the discussions with a final cry of "You can have your war!" Nonplussed, the Austrians thought he had gone mad.

It was left to Josephine to soothe her enraged husband—whose wrath may at times have been nothing more than a powerful negotiating ploy—and at the same time, placate the unsettled Austrians. Count Cobenzl in particular, who remembered well the days of Louis XVI and the Austrian archduchess Marie Antoinette, found Josephine's gentle presence an eye of calm in the hurricane of Bonaparte's turbulent ravings.

She could provide calm for others, but her own inner turmoil remained unstilled. Letters from Milan had informed her that Hippolyte had been involved with another woman, an Italian, who looked much like her. Whether or not the woman was younger, closer to Hippolyte's own age, is unknown. Weeping, Josephine clutched her little pug dog—not Fortuné, but the new dog Hippolyte had given her when Fortuné was killed—and mourned. She was grieving for Fortuné, for the loss of Hippolyte's exclusive affection, for her own lonely state, in exile far from Paris.

To compensate for her low spirits, and as a reminder that before too long she hoped to be home again, Josephine turned her thoughts to the house on the rue Chantereine and ordered it redecorated from top to bottom. Bonaparte had already sent home many art works, and there were his military trophies, and the abundance of gifts she had been given during her time in Italy. At least some of these could be incorporated into the new designs for the rooms.

She wrote to a friend, the architect Vautier, and gave him free rein in making the house over according to the best prevailing taste— walls in strong dark colors, decorated with white stucco or carved wood embellishments, draperies in violet and black, hand-painted wallpapers in antique designs, rich mahogany tables and chairs modeled after Roman or Etruscan styles. It was all to be done quickly, and with no compromise in price or execution. She wanted her house ready when Bonaparte returned to Paris.[3]

For by November he was traveling again, having successfully concluded the first phase of the Austrian negotiations. He was on his way to attend the second phase, at Rastatt near Stuttgart, intending to go on to Paris as soon as these talks were concluded. At last Josephine was free to go home.

Before leaving, however, she had a final obligation. She agreed to accept the invitation of the erstwhile Republic of Venice—now, under the newly negotiated treaty terms, a client state of Austria—and enjoy a four-day visit to the sublime city of the canals.

No record exists of Josephine's reaction to her first sight of Venice, but it is hard to imagine, despite her weariness with public fêtes and celebrations, that she was not enchanted with the old, rich, mellow pink-brick city swimming in the silvery light of its lagoons. Here was Italy at its most bewitching, a unique blend of faded grandeur, light-drenched color and exotic, reeking, weather-stained quaintness and decay.

When she was rowed at night along the Grand Canal, past the stately palazzos with their ornate balconies, colonnaded gothic windows and crenellated rooflines illuminated with torches and wax-lights, thousands of gondolas crowded the waterways, each carrying a lantern; the water shimmered with a thousand golden reflections. When she went to picnic on the Lido, the panorama of sand, sea and sky merged into one seamless, horizonless vista. All the glories of the city were presented to Madame Bonaparte: the splendors of St. Mark's, the magnificence of the doge's palace, where a great ball was held in her honor, the pageant of a regatta and boat parade. And everywhere she went, Josephine was cheered and applauded, her loveliness admired, her elegance in dress remarked on.

After four days, her senses filled with lasting impressions, she took her leave. Now at last she was on her way home, to Paris, to her newly redecorated house, her old friends. But it would not be an unclouded homecoming, of that she was now certain. She had had news from Milan, where dark rumors about Hippolyte—who had just been promoted to captain in the First Hussars—were flying. It was being said that Bonaparte had ordered Hippolyte's arrest and that he intended to have him executed.

Even if the rumors were false, and she could not be certain either way, she had reason to worry. She could be certain that Bonaparte had been warned, not once but many times, that Hippolyte represented a danger to his marriage—by Paulette, by the cold, hostile Joseph, by Josephine's spiteful former maid Louise Compoint, perhaps by Antoine Hamelin who, like Louise, had reason to know from experience that she and Hippolyte were lovers. And she knew that all Bonaparte's relations would be pressuring him to rid himself of her, as quickly as possible.

Wrapped in furs, her hands buried in a warm muff and her pug dog on her lap, Josephine made her way slowly toward Paris, in dismal December weather. Crossing the Alps was perilous and time-consuming in winter, the deep snow was hazardous and many travelers became snowbound or lost their lives in spectacular avalanches. She was fortunate, and arrived safely in drizzly, rainy France to find organized welcomes in every town she passed through.

In Lyon the residents turned out in the December cold to cheer her and watch her symbolic coronation with a crown of roses; the civic authorities gave parties and dinners where she met the leading citizens. In other towns she was called upon to speak, and told the waiting throngs what they wanted to hear—that General Bonaparte was eager and willing to sacrifice himself for their benefit, for the benefit of the republic. She was shrewd. She knew that Bonaparte's celebrity had made him political enemies who wanted to frighten his supporters by saying he was ambitious for power. She said the right things, made the right impression to counteract these fears. Gently disarming, elegant and graceful, with her warm smile and melodious voice, she made herself loved.

"Companion of the hero admired by every nation,/ In thee our hearts acclaim his source of inspiration," sang a chorus in the town of Moulins. The townspeople shouted themselves hoarse when Josephine's carriage made its way along the main thoroughfare, cheering loudly for "Our Lady of Victories," for "Our Savior Bonaparte," and crying "Long Live the French Republic!" Not until she was a mile beyond the town, and the last of the cries of "Godspeed!" faded into silence, did the tired Josephine allow herself to sink back into the soft cushions of the carriage, close her eyes, and rest.

18

"The Most Unfortunate of Women"

When Bonaparte returned to Paris early in December of 1797, he was greeted with an unprecedented outpouring of adoration. He was, Laure Junot recalled, "a colossus of great and pure glory," a deliverer of heroic proportions, acclaimed wherever he went and subjected to an unending series of celebratory events.

Given a command of secondary importance in 1796—the Directors had intended that his Italian army create a diversion to draw Austrian troops away from the more important defense of Vienna—he had astounded everyone by making Italy the central theater of war, and then by threatening Vienna himself. He had ended by bringing mighty Austria low. Under the terms of the treaty of Campo Formio, Austria made peace and turned over to France Belgium and the west bank of the Rhine. France was becoming the leading power in Europe, and Bonaparte, as military commander, as statesman, as creator of new political entities such as the Cisalpine Republic, was rapidly becoming the leading figure in France.

He held no political office, yet he seemed to command all the political loyalties of the French—or at least of the Parisians. They followed his carriage through the streets, shouting "Long Live Bonaparte!" They held parades in his honor. The municipal council changed the name of the street he lived on from rue Chantereine to rue de la Victoire. Parisians placed Bonaparte's flower-wreathed picture in their drawing rooms, in shop windows, wherever it could be widely observed as a symbol of their allegiance. "May God preserve him for our glory," they called out when they heard his name spoken, "and deliver us from the yoke of the Directors!"[1]

The extraordinary public enthusiasm for Bonaparte was as much a sign of the profound weariness of the French with republican rule as it was a mark of genuine respect for the victorious general. Nearly nine years of revolution had worn the French down; they longed for an end to the constant turmoil. They had known fear, uncertainty, economic chaos, crime, corruption and war. They had lived under the constant threat of violence. They had endured, and become all but inured to, the daily spectacle of heads being severed and blood flowing freely over the cobblestones. At first secretly, then in conspiratorial whispers, and finally openly, sometimes clamorously, they had begun to long for the return of the monarchy.

Or if not for the old monarchy of the Bourbons, then for the idea of a monarchy, of a single strong leader who could put an end to the republican wrangling and restore stability and order. Bonaparte had done it once before, when Paris was erupting into chaos in the fall of 1795. He had done it in Italy. Many had begun to hope that he could do it again.

For the Directory was tottering. Barras, always a staunch republican, was still in office but several of his colleagues had been changed by a dissatisfied electorate, and a strong monarchist faction threatened to oust the Directors and set up yet another weak, experimental government that would be vulnerable to the tugs and pulls of faction. A purge was under way; for the moment, the left-leaning republicans were in control, and those who disagreed with them were being exiled in large numbers to Guiana.

It was in this unsettled yet hopeful atmosphere that on December 10, 1797, the Directors formally received Bonaparte in a ceremony held in the courtyard of the Luxembourg Palace. The crowd of spectators was so large that it spilled out onto the surrounding streets. Every rooftop had its cluster of onlookers, every window its row of eager faces.

An Altar of the Nation had been erected atop the palace steps. Beside it stood the five Directors, looking both pompous and silly in their wide red capes with gold facings, ornamental swords and tricorn hats with red, white and blue plumes. The members of the Council of Five Hundred were also present, robed in toga-like swathes of russet velvet with tall blue hats, and with them, an array of dignitaries, all in the faintly outlandish finery, inspired by the antique, that Directory taste demanded.

An orchestra of two hundred struck up a familiar tune: it was the "Song of Return," composed especially in honor of General Bonaparte and played throughout the city in the days since his arrival. Suddenly, from the midst of the swirling crowd, the general himself appeared on the steps before the altar, his unadorned uniform simple and stark amid the flamboyance of the others. He was escorted by his aides-de-camp, among them his handsome sixteen-year-old stepson Eugene. At once thunderous applause filled the courtyard, and did not stop for many minutes. The general, conspicuously shorter than his escorting officers, nobly simple in his elegant uniform, accepted the accolade without noticeable change of affect. He was neither aloof nor ingratiating, merely, authentically, himself.

In that moment, recalled Madame de Staël in her memoirs, "he was the hope of every man, republican or royalist; all saw the present and the future as held in his strong hands."[2]

It was a remarkable moment, a moment to be savored, a culmination. Bonaparte had believed for some time that he was a man set apart. For several years he had felt the groundswell of a special destiny. And he had always, until recently, associated the fulfillment of that special destiny with Josephine. She had brought him luck.

On this day, however, she was not at his side to share his triumph. He felt her absence even more keenly than usual. She was on her way to join him, he knew, but she was taking a long time to reach Paris. And it was rumored—so his eager relatives told him—that she was not traveling alone, but with her lover Hippolyte Charles.

When at last Josephine's carriage arrived in the rue de la Victoire, and she stepped out onto the snow-covered ground, she was tired and strained. The trip, her ongoing battle with migraines, the apprehension she felt about meeting her husband combined to age her; to observers she appeared to be, not a lithe, girlish thirty-four but a careworn forty.

So many worries assailed her: worries about Bonaparte's reaction to the rumors about her involvement with Hippolyte; worries about her in-laws, especially Joseph, and what they had been telling her husband in her absence; worries about when and how she would see Hippolyte now that she and Bonaparte would be living under the same roof day after day; worries about Hippolyte's fidelity to her. One worry Hippolyte had relieved her of. He had helped her to obtain the love letters she had written to the late General Hoche (who had recently died of pneumonia), ensuring that Bonaparte would never see them and become enraged.

A more immediate worry was that she was late. A great ball had been scheduled in her honor, given by the Foreign Minister Talleyrand, but because she had not arrived in time to attend, the ball had been postponed—not once but twice. She was aware that Bonaparte would consider her delinquency inexcusable, and that her in-laws would add it to their list of her transgressions.

Still, she had to attend, fatigued or not. It was not merely a ball, it was practically a state occasion. Late on the night of January 3, 1798, General Bonaparte and Madame Bonaparte alighted from their carriage at the Hôtel Galiffet, Talleyrand's mansion, and, passing through the spacious entrance hall and up the wide staircase with its marble balustrade, entered the densely crowded, grandly decorated main ballroom.

Four thousand guests mingled in the huge room, all waiting for the entrance of the guest of honor. When they saw the Bonapartes they burst into polite applause, though those closest to Josephine noted that her face looked drawn and pale. Although the ball was being given for Josephine, it was Bonaparte, the hero of the hour, who was assailed by admirers. The attention he attracted helped to avert notice from her, and from the evident tension between the two of them. Onlookers assumed, seeing how he remained by her side all evening, that his attentiveness was a sign of devotion; in actuality it may have been evidence of jealousy and insecurity, or an effort to counteract the rumors, circulating among the more shrewd guests, that the general's wife was in love with another man.

In the lavishness of the gilded walls, the expensive art works and reproductions prominently displayed, the overabundance of fine food and drink, the magnificent silver and china, Talleyrand's ball was a reminder of the opulence of the ancien régime. Republican simplicity had been abandoned completely. Though the ball was being held in the depth of winter, the house was full of the springtime scent of fresh jasmine; the host had ordered hundreds of blooming jasmine bushes brought north from Provence especially for this one night, at great expense.

The Bonapartes stayed for supper, which was served in the pre-revolutionary style, with the women seated and the men standing behind them, serving them (Talleyrand served Josephine), but left before the dancing resumed, soon after the last sumptuous course was taken away. Unlike his wife, Bonaparte was a poor dancer; no doubt vanity forbade him to display his lack of expertise in the complex dances then in fashion. Besides, he had much on his mind.

Beyond his painful concern over the stories he was hearing about Josephine, and his annoyance over her extravagance in the redecoration of their house, he was preoccupied with his future. He was casting about for a new challenge, and at the same time avoiding giving the appearance of posing a political threat to the Directors. The Directors, for their part, were eager to exploit his remarkable military skills while not wanting to exalt him any further in the public eye. Deciding what course to adopt would require a good deal of careful thought, and much diplomacy.

By February Bonaparte was fretting, restless from a lack of focused activity and pacing like a tiger in a cage. Declaring that Paris "weighed him down like a cloak of lead," he set off on a fruitless visit to the Channel ports, leaving Josephine to see old friends and settle in to the newly refurbished house.

She had wasted no time in resuming her former ties—with Therese Tallien, with Madame Campi and Fortunée Hamelin, with her Aunt Edmée and her aged husband, now living at Saint-Germain where Hortense was in school, with Barras, to whom she was closest, and above all with Hippolyte.

She was reckless. She saw Hippolyte, who was on leave from the army and living in the house of the senior partner of the Bodin Company in the Faubourg St-Honoré, nearly every day. Her visits were prompted to some extent by her business interests, which were becoming increasingly meshed with those of the merchant house. But it was no secret that Hippolyte had moved into quarters in the Bodin mansion, and because Madame Bonaparte's movements were watched now as never before, it soon became a topic of gossip that she spent much time each day in the house where Hippolyte lived.

She knew this—and yet she persisted. She had reached a point of wretchedness in her life with Bonaparte where she no longer concerned herself with what was being observed, what was being said about her. As Barras wrote later, Josephine "committed every folly" for Hippolyte's sake, giving him enormous sums of money, even jewels, as she might have to a daughter.[3]

She was lavishing herself, her time, her possessions, on her lover— but there was a logic to her actions, a logic born of desperation.

For by the winter of 1798 Josephine had become desperately unhappy. She was miserable as Bonaparte's wife, unsatisfied, overly regimented, worn down by his quixotic behavior and endless emotional demands. The pressures of her inescapable public life made her nervous and kept her on edge. All this might have been just bearable had her in-laws not harassed her. But they were a constant goad, worsening her unhappiness and increasing her insecurity. A friend told her that Joseph had been overheard to say that he would not rest until he had created a breach between his brother the general and his wife, and Joseph, she knew, was an implacable enemy.

Sensing that it was only a matter of time before her marriage ended, Josephine was risking everything on her lover—and on the business in which both had invested. Her desperate plan seems to have been to make as much money as possible through the Bodin Company, then to extricate herself from her regrettable marriage and marry Hippolyte.

"I am going to the country, my dear Hippolyte," Josephine wrote her lover. "I'll be back at five-thirty or six o'clock at Bodin's, looking for you. Yes, my Hippolyte, my existence is a continual agony. You alone can bring me happiness. Tell me that you love me and that you will love no one else. I'll be the happiest of women." The note told all: she was suffering, she was escaping, she needed reassurance. And she needed money. "Send me fifty thousand livres through Bodin," she added. "Adieu, I send you tender kisses. All to you."[4]

Sometimes she saw both Hippolyte and Barras in the same day, before going home to her husband.

"I am in bed for three days, my dear Barras, with a bad cold and fever," she told her friend toward the end of February. "It frustrates me, because it deprives me of the pleasure of seeing you a moment this evening. Good day, excellent dear one; I kiss you and I love you tenderly."[5]

Whether Barras, or other friends, tried to dissuade Josephine from her rash course is unknown; certainly she was acting imprudently, taking a grave risk. She was making several bold assumptions: that the Bodin Company was sound, and that she could continue to ensure, through her influence, that it received vital government contracts; that she—and Hippolyte—could profit sufficiently from those contracts to build themselves a fortune to live on; most important, that Hippolyte was willing to cooperate with her in her rash venture, and that he loved her enough to marry her.

He had resigned his army commission in March, and was devoting himself to business. And business had never been better. For Bonaparte, having decided, after his tour of the Channel ports, against considering an invasion of England, was caught up in a new and much more ambitious venture, and it was already generating much new commerce.

Bonaparte had made up his mind to attempt to undercut the power of Britain by attacking her empire abroad. In the greatest secrecy, he and Talleyrand had devised a plan under which, after France secured the cooperation of the Ottoman Empire—nominal ruler of Egypt— Bonaparte would invade Egypt, conquer it, and then proceed to cut off Britain's trade routes to India.

Throughout the latter part of February and into March, the new expedition was equipped and provisioned. Once again, contracts were available for uniforms, boots, guns, horses, foodstuffs of every sort in huge quantities. There were nearly two hundred ships to be loaded, more than fifty thousand troops and sailors to be outfitted. And because Bonaparte planned to take along a number of scientists and scholars, each of whom required a staff of assistants and special supplies, still more goods of all kinds would be needed.

All the provisioners of Paris were flourishing, including Bodin and Company, by mid-March. Bonaparte, his spirits buoyed by the prospect of his grand eastern adventure, was preoccupied with making his preparations and with consulting the mathematicians, botanists, linguists and other specialists he had persuaded to accompany him. He did not trouble himself unduly with his wife's comings and goings. But Joseph did. In fact, Joseph had been keeping careful track of Josephine's movements over the past several months, gathering information from others, keeping his ear to the ground. One afternoon in mid-March he told his brother what he had learned.

Their conversation went on for a long time—long enough, no doubt, to make Josephine very nervous. Joseph explained the disturbing, incriminating facts as he had uncovered them: that for some time Josephine had been using her influence illegally to procure purveyance contracts for Bodin; that she herself had been profiting from the provision of inferior merchandise to the army; that, through Bodin, she had been speculating in currency exchanges (a lucrative sideline of the provisioning business), and profiting at government expense; and finally, that she had been seeing her lover Hippolyte Charles daily at the Bodin headquarters in the Faubourg St. Honoré.

Bonaparte trusted Joseph more than he trusted anyone. He listened, increasingly dismayed, to the case against his wife. When Joseph finished, Bonaparte called Josephine into the room.

"At the end of their conversation," Josephine wrote to Hippolyte the following day, "I was asked if I knew Citizen Bodin, if it was I who procured for him the furnishings of the army of Italy, . . . [if it was true that] Hippolyte lived at Citizen Bodin's house at Number 100 Faubourg St-Honoré, and that I went there every day?"[6]

She denied everything, down to the last detail. She had never met Citizen Bodin. She knew nothing about army contracts. She had never been near the house in the Faubourg St-Honoré. It was all a monstrous lie.

She went on the attack. She told Bonaparte that if he wanted to divorce her he did not need to resort to such accusations. He only had to tell her, plainly, that he wanted to end the marriage.

"I am the most unfortunate of women," she told Bonaparte, in tears, "and the unhappiest." Her tears flowed freely—and they were no doubt unforced, for her unhappiness was genuine.

The following day she managed to find enough privacy to relate what had happened in a letter to Hippolyte. By this time her emotions were in a state of extreme turmoil.

"Yes, my Hippolyte, they all have my hatred. You alone have my tenderness, my love. They must see how I abhor them from the frightful state I've been in.... They see my regrets, my hopelessness at being deprived of seeing you as often as I desire to."

"Hippolyte," she went on, "I'll kill myself. Yes! I want to end a life which from now on can only be burdensome to me if it cannot be consecrated to you."[7]

Her histrionics subsiding, she wrote in a more practical vein, begging her lover to help her cover up the truth of her activities. She urged him to persuade Bodin to lie for her, to deny that he knew her and that she had secured business for him.

"Ah! They torment me in vain," she wrote in conclusion. "They will never detach me from my Hippolyte. My last breath shall be for him." She arranged a rendezvous with him for the following day, then closed with "a thousand burning kisses, like my heart, and as loving."[8]

Somehow, the crisis passed. By daring Bonaparte to divorce her—an unthinkable course of action for him, despite his growing disillusionment—Josephine managed to keep him off balance. He loved her, yet he trusted his brother, and could not dismiss the accusations his brother had made. Nor could he spare the time to focus, for long, on domestic disaster. The Egyptian expedition was gaining momentum. There were dozens of orders, requests, letters to be sent out, troops to assemble, plans to make and equipment to organize.

In haste, much harassed with business, Bonaparte did what was most expedient. He decided to take Josephine with him on his campaign. That would keep her away from her lover, and out of trouble. He told her to pack her things for a brief sojourn in Egypt—and to tell no one where she was going.

Early in May, after having spent only four months in Paris, Josephine once again got into a large traveling carriage bound for the south. Her reckless plan had backfired. Her investments had not brought her wealth, she had not been able to break free from her marriage, and Hippolyte had not come to her rescue. She discovered, much to her discouragement, that she lacked the means, the strength, the will to break away.

Not only had she been unable to escape from her wretched situation, she was enmired in it more deeply than ever. For now Joseph, her enemy, had more power over her than ever. Bonaparte had put

Joseph in charge of all his business and personal affairs for the duration of the Egyptian venture. She would be answerable to him for all that she spent, and no doubt for where she went and whom she saw as well.

One again she was leaving Paris for an indeterminate period of time, to be stranded in a foreign place, surrounded by strangers, and at risk of harm. She had no idea when she would see Hippolyte again, or whether, while they were apart, he would be faithful.

Her thirty-fifth birthday was approaching: by common reckoning, the midpoint of life. Assuming she was spared to live out a long lifespan, what would her next thirty-five years bring? Would she ever succeed in freeing herself from the regrettable bond to Bonaparte? Of course, he might very well divorce her, submitting to family pressure. But that would almost certainly mean poverty, given her precarious financial state. No, she would simply have to endure for the time being, awaiting another opportunity to create a new life for herself.

After several days of hard traveling they reached Aix, en route to Toulon. From Aix the best road went through Marseille, but Bonaparte was eager to avoid being seen in Marseille, knowing that there were British spies everywhere and wanting to keep his movements secret from the British until the last possible moment. He gave orders to the coachman to find another route, along country roads through the hills to the coast.

They set off at dusk, the heavy carriage jolting uncomfortably along the narrow rutted road. Recent spring rains made the going muddy, and the dim lamps of the carriage barely illumined the way. After several hours the passengers attempted to sleep, while the coach climbed higher into the hills. Nearing the town of Roquevaire they began to descend, the road dipping down the side of a steep hill toward a river, turbulent and swollen with the recent rains. A bridge had spanned the river until the day before, when it had suddenly collapsed, carried away by the onrushing flow of water. In the dark, however, the driver could not discern much of anything, not the collapsed bridge, not the river, barely even the muddy road. And the horses were going faster and faster as the coach descended the hill.

Suddenly the galloping horses plunged and reared in confusion, shaking the carriage violently and waking the occupants. For a sickening moment it seemed as though the heavy vehicle would overturn, but it managed to right itself, and once the frightened horses had been brought under control the dazed passengers descended to see what had happened. A large tree branch had fallen across the road, blocking it completely. On the other side of the branch, at a point only a few feet from where they had halted, was a steep cliff dropping away to the swift torrent. Had the branch not barred their path, they would all have fallen to their deaths.

Bonaparte was no doubt reassured by the miraculous stroke of good fortune. Providence always defended him; his luck still held. But Josephine, tearful and anxious, may have experienced something closer to a reprieve. Yet again, as when she had survived the horrors of the Carmelite prison, and as when, on the shores of Lake Garda, she had fled safely from the Austrian sharpshooters, she had come close to death, but had been spared.

In the following days, as her nerves quietened, she may well have recalled the prophesy of the fortune-teller in Martinique, who had foretold that she would one day be queen of France. The thought would surely have brought a fleeting smile to her face, and yet there was something comforting about it. For deep down, she believed herself to be a favored creature of fortune. Just beneath her elegant exterior, Josephine Bonaparte was still Rose Tascher, survivor of the great hurricane, grasper of opportunities, risk taker. She needed no glib fortune-teller to reveal this truth about herself, a truth that, if it often led her into folly, invariably saved her from despair.

19

"All I Do Is Cry"

Hundreds of ships rode at anchor in Toulon harbor, their masts rising in thick clusters from the sparkling blue water. The armada extended for several miles, with each ship attended by long-boats coming and going from the quays, ferrying men and provisions, horses and sea-chests aboard. On shore, boxes and barrels were stacked awaiting loading, and carts came and went with still more cargo, all of it destined for Egypt.

It took thousands of sailors and laborers many weeks to assemble all the components of the great armada: the artillery and ammunition, the tons of hay and oats and the huge casks of beer and brandy, the sacks of grain and barrels of oil, the live cattle and fowl to be slaughtered en route. The nearly forty thousand soldiers and civilians who were to accompany Bonaparte on his Egyptian expedition had been arriving in Toulon since April, making their own last-minute preparations for a journey so exotic its requirements could hardly be foreseen.

Josephine had thought that she too would soon be en route to Egypt, but in recent days Bonaparte had changed his mind and decided that she ought to delay her departure temporarily. She should go to the spa at Plombières in the foothills of the Vosges mountains, he said, and take the waters there, which were known to promote fertility. "He will come and look for me in two months," Josephine told her correspondents.¹ Within two months, she thought, Bonaparte would have subdued the country and arranged comfortable accommodations for her. At Plombières she would be far from Paris—and Hippolyte—and yet she would be spared the initial rigors of the military campaign. Besides, she might, if all went well, become pregnant later through the benefits of the spa waters. Bonaparte may have reasoned that motherhood would cure Josephine of her foolish infatuation with Hippolyte Charles, not suspecting the depth of her passion for her lover nor the degree of her unhappiness in their marriage.

Secretly Josephine must have been pleased that Bonaparte was to sail without her. True, Plombières was far from Hippolyte and Paris, but it was also far from her suspicious husband and her hostile in-laws. Staying at the spa would give her a respite from her difficulties, and perhaps allow her to think of a new way of escaping from them.

On May 19 Josephine went aboard Bonaparte's flagship, *L'Orient*, to say her good-byes. It must have been a tearful parting, for she was taking leave not only of her husband but of her son, Eugene, now seventeen and quite changed from the plain-featured, squarely built boy he had been only a few years earlier.

Eugene had inherited none of his late father's arrogance—nor his intellect. He was very much his mother's son, with Josephine's easy-going manner and welcoming smile, her charm of address, her warmth and geniality. Good-looking and svelte, he excelled at games and physical exercises of all kinds, and was a good dancer; he was also very fond of girls, and during the long summer at Mombello had delighted in flirting and playing with Bonaparte's younger sisters. He would be traveling to Egypt as one of Bonaparte's aides-de-camp, and Josephine, knowing what hazards might lie ahead for the soldiers and officers alike, realized that he was very much at risk.

With a group of officers' wives she watched the fleet depart from a balcony on shore, stirred by the pageantry in the harbor as cannon in the fortress roared salute after salute and martial music floated up from military bands on the quays. There were many popular songs about Bonaparte and his exploits, and these, along with patriotic republican tunes, were played again and again as the long lines of vessels moved slowly seaward.

In the far distance, at the mouth of the harbor, the flagship suddenly struck a sandbar and was grounded. Smaller ships rushed in to tow Bonaparte's vessel to safety, but the accident spoiled the grand spectacle, and reminded observers of the risks inherent in the venture. Who was to say what treacherous shoals might lie ahead?

Such musings may have preoccupied Josephine as she traveled northward to the mountain spa. Distasteful as her marriage was to her, she knew that she would be in a far worse position if Bonaparte were to die while away on campaign. Already his business affairs were in Joseph's hands; if his estate were to pass into Joseph's governance she would be in danger of losing everything—except her stake in the Bodin Company.

But the company was in serious trouble. The nature and extent of the its dealings in poor-quality goods was becoming widely known, and causing a scandal. Even before she reached Plombières Josephine learned that an effort at reform was under way, to limit the number of accredited contractors doing business with the government. The Bodin Company, its reputation compromised, its members known to be reaping unwarranted profits, was among those likely to lose accreditation, which would almost certainly assure its financial ruin. In distress, Josephine wrote to Barras.

"I learn, my dear Barras, that General Bruce does what he can to ruin the Bodin Company's business. I beg you, write General Bruce on their behalf. We owe all our profit to them, and I hope you will counteract the scandal."[2]

Josephine had a great deal at risk, for not only had she invested in the company but she had made a place there for Hippolyte, who had no other source of income. If the Bodin company were to lose its contracts, then Hippolyte would be ruined—and their love affair too might unravel. From the start, the attraction between Josephine and Hippolyte had mixed pleasure with mutual profit; Josephine may have realized, in her heart of hearts, that if the profit ended, the pleasure might not be sufficient to keep him with her.

The elite of Paris gathered in the charming spa-town of Plombières-les-Bains early in the summer, escaping the heat of the capital amid the cool greenery of the pine forest. Former emigrés mingled with government officials, bankers and the everpresent wealthy speculators to drink the health-giving waters and bathe in them, while at the same time socializing and passing on news and gossip. A feature of spa life was the promenade, a daily ritual during which greetings were exchanged and finery and possessions displayed.

From the balcony of her rented house, the Maison Martinet across from the Hôtel des Dames, Josephine could watch the parade of spa guests as they passed to and fro along the street. One day she joined three friends who were standing on the balcony, watching the street scene below. The weight of four people was too great for the aging structure to bear. Suddenly the entire balcony collapsed, sending the four people hurtling twenty feet downward to the street.

Fortunately no one was killed, but Josephine, in agony from pain in her back, legs and arms, was unable to walk and was immediately put to bed. Doctors brought from all the nearby towns examined her, shook their heads, and muttered that she might not recover the use of her legs.

For the second time in as many months she had suffered a serious, near-fatal accident, and the coincidence must have given the superstitious Josephine a severe fright. She was lucky to be alive.

The entire town, it seemed, was concerned about her. She was their most celebrated guest, even though one of the Directors, Rewbell, was also in residence taking the waters. People busied themselves providing food and medicine, sending fresh flowers to her house every day and musicians to play under her window. Daily bulletins on her condition were dispatched to Paris every afternoon. What Josephine needed most, however, was family. A messenger was sent to Hortense in St-Germain with news of her mother's accident, and she soon arrived, along with the aged Euphémie, Josephine's former slave from Martinique.

Hortense was fifteen, fair and plump and outgoing, though more plain than pretty, her features marred by an overly long nose and full cheeks. She had been a favorite student at Madame Campan's school, singled out from the field of privileged pupils—which included Bonaparte's sister Caroline, many daughters of titled emigrés and Elisa Monroe, whose father would later become the American president— and rewarded for her talents at drawing and dramatics. (Neither of Josephine's children excelled at intellectual pursuits, though of the two, Hortense was the more thoughtful.) In coming to Plombières

Hortense missed her school prize-giving; Aunt Edmée collected her prize for her.[3]

For two weeks Josephine stayed in bed, in constant pain and unable to dress or feed herself because of the weakness in her arms. Doctors drew blood from her veins and applied leeches to her wrists, prescribed medicinal drinks, ordered compresses made from boiled potatoes strapped to her limbs. Adopting a remedy centuries old, they ordered a sheep killed and wrapped Josephine in its fleecy skin.

"All I do is cry," the patient confessed in a note to Barras, dictated to an amanuensis. Bonaparte, informed via courier of her debility, urged her to travel to Naples and embark from there for Egypt. But travel was impossible, for the time being. The slightest jolt brought on terrible pain in her lower back. "My dear Barras," she wrote, "you have no idea how much I am suffering!"

Her worst fear, that she might not be able to walk, receded when by mid-July she was able to take a few steps, yet her pain and soreness went on. She confessed to Barras that she did not yet envision a complete recovery. In fact it was a full two months before she made plans to return to Paris, and even then she had to travel slowly, for fear of risking further injury. Bonaparte had made arrangements for her to meet a companion in Paris and then travel on to Naples. But the thought of making yet another long journey, going over the mountain passes on muleback in the chill of fall, must have seemed beyond her strength. When she finally reached Paris late in September, and learned that because of a British blockade, no ship traffic was possible in the Mediterranean, the news must have come as a relief.

Bonaparte's Egyptian campaign had reached a sudden stunning impasse. After landing in Alexandria, overwhelming the local garrison and advancing inland to Cairo, the French had defeated the defending Turkish army at the evocatively named Battle of the Pyramids. But ten days later, the British Admiral Nelson destroyed the French fleet, effectively trapping Bonaparte and his men in northern Egypt and preventing them from communicating with the continent. Bonaparte's romance with the East turned sour. Though he made himself master of the Nile delta, he could not return home to savor his triumph, and it would be only a matter of time before his supplies ran out.

But Bonaparte was suffering from an even worse affliction. While in Egypt he was informed, yet again, of Josephine's infidelity with Hippolyte Charles—and this time he believed what he heard.

"I have much domestic grief," he wrote to his brother Joseph, "for the veil is completely lifted . . . You alone remain to me on this earth; your friendship is very dear to me. All that remains, for me to become a misanthrope, is to lose you and see you betray me." He had made the mistake of concentrating all his emotions—adoration, anguish, anger and resentment—on one person, his wife; now that he saw clearly that she had betrayed him, he felt drained and empty, bereft of feeling, "bored with human nature." "I have nothing to live for," he told Joseph, sincerely crushed and disillusioned. "At twenty-nine I have exhausted everything."[4]

Because of the British blockade this letter never reached its intended recipient. The courier who carried it was captured, and this and other letters fell into enemy hands. Josephine, far away and in ignorance of Bonaparte's sad realization about her, could not counteract the effects of his disillusionment, either in person or by letter. Bonaparte, heartbroken despite his assertions of emotional numbness, was left on his own to try to assuage his grief.

And a profound grief it was. Bonaparte's adoring love for Josephine had been more the love of a boy than a grown man, absolute and trusting, naive and utterly deluded about her ultimate loyalty. She had once vowed to give him a "tender and constant" love, and he had returned it with a much greater intensity. "There has never been a love like mine," he once told Josephine, "it will last as long as my life."[5]

Now that deep and lasting love underwent an irreversible change. It did not wither away, but it became corroded by bitterness and resentment. Night after night, Bonaparte sought out Eugene and talked to him at length about his mother's behavior. He went over and over the damning evidence of her infidelity, as though by repeating all that he had heard he could force himself to come to grips with it.

He tried by other means to adapt himself to the changed terms of his marriage. He was well aware that husbands routinely managed to live with unfaithful wives—by being unfaithful themselves.

Several months after the onset of his heartbreak, in September of

1798, he had six Egyptian women brought to him at his Cairo head-quarters. He looked them over, and found them to be far too plump and graceless to be sexually pleasing. He had them taken away again.

But another woman, the young wife of one of his junior officers, pleased him very much, and he made her his mistress. Pauline Bellisle Fourès, or "Bellilotte," as he called her, was ten years younger than he was, blonde and girlish, with a liking for wearing men's uniforms. He rented a house for her near his headquarters, and visited her there often. They rode together in the general's carriage, with Eugene, thoroughly chagrined, as their mounted escort. Bonaparte tried to send Bellilotte's inconvenient husband back to France, but the British blockade made that impossible; Lieutenant Fourès was soon in Cairo again, angry and violent, and his frightened wife sued for divorce.

Bonaparte and his army were trapped in Egypt, yet that captivity had an oddly liberating effect on the general. His dalliance with Bellilotte was only one symptom of that liberation.

"In Egypt," he told the memoirist Madame de Rémusat several years later, "I was relieved of the restraints of an annoying civilization. I dreamed all things and saw the means of carrying out all that I dreamed. . . . That time I spent in Egypt was the most beautiful of my life, for it was the most ideal."[6]

Deluding himself into thinking that he was truly in another realm, free of restraints, Bonaparte indulged himself, allowing his reveries to carry him away. "I saw myself on the road to Asia," he told Rémusat, "riding on an elephant, a turban on my head, and in my hand a new Koran which I wrote according to my desire." Endeavoring to escape his emotional pain, he fantasized that he was an Oriental sensualist of the sort imagined by romantic writers, a voluptuary heeding no laws but those of pleasure. He doused himself in musky cologne, he surrounded himself with servants in exotic livery. He became—or tried to convince himself he had become—another man. [7]

Meanwhile Josephine, in Paris, was working on a less grandiose transformation of another sort. She had long wanted to buy the château of Malmaison, adjacent to St-Germain on the banks of the Seine. It was a fairly small, rather plainly designed house, with three stories and a slate roof, a modest residence as country houses went, but surrounding it were three hundred acres of fertile land, kept fresh and green by their closeness to the river, beautifully landscaped in the English style. Vineyards were planted on the sloping terrain, and fields of wheat adjoined the extensive gardens. Edmée and her husband lived nearby, and Hortense's school was close as well.

With the forty thousand francs Joseph allotted her once a year, Josephine was not in a position to buy Malmaison, which cost over three hundred thousand and was badly in need of expensive renovation. But she had always been able to secure loans when she needed them, and she found a way now to arrive at terms with the owner of the property. By the spring of 1799, she was installed at Malmaison, hugely in debt and worried about her future, as always, but worried amid gracious surroundings.

Her situation was not unlike what it had been fifteen years earlier, when she was separated from Alexandre de Beauharnais and attempting to build a new life on her own. Then she had been seeking independence, now she felt independence was being thrust upon her by circumstances.

For she, and all of France, had learned of Bonaparte's disillusionment and anger toward her. His correspondence, captured by the British, was published in the London newspapers; not only all of France but all of Europe, even America, knew that the general was determined to break off relations with his erring wife and was thinking of divorcing her.

A woman less resilient than Josephine, less adept at responding to the rigors of an inconstant destiny, might have panicked. Here she was, nearly thirty-six years old, facing the failure of a second marriage and more deeply in debt than ever. Her recent efforts to build a fortune were collapsing as the Bodin Company sank deeper and deeper toward bankruptcy, its head, Louis Bodin, in prison. Her love affair, the one saving grace in an emotionally beleaguered life, was disintegrating; although Hippolyte stayed with Josephine, sometimes for weeks at a time, during the winter of 1798 to 1799, he complained that she was too demanding, and was clearly in retreat from what, for him, had become a burdensome entanglement.[8]

Frightened by her own vulnerability, yet choosing to live at a distance from the political and social ferment of Paris, unwilling to subject herself to either the scorn or the sympathy of her friends and acquaintances in her time of embarrassment and distress, Josephine isolated herself at Malmaison. There she could soothe herself by walking in the gardens, there she could take refuge from the importunate creditors who came to her door, insisting that she pay her bills. At first she saw only Hortense and Edmée, and Madame Campan and her two nieces. She invited Bonaparte's brothers and sisters to dine, well aware that they would probably refuse her invitations—which they did. Her mother-in-law Letizia, however, kept up an outwardly correct semblance of good relations.[9]

Josephine told Barras, with whom she maintained a close intimacy, that since moving to Malmaison she had become "such a savage" that the social world terrified her. "Moreover," she added, "I am so unhappy that I don't like to be an object of pity for others."[10]

But object of pity or not, she was far from inactive socially. She wrote letters to influential people. She cultivated old contacts such as Joseph Fouché, minister of police, and made new ones, among them Jérôme Gohier, president of the Directory, and Madame Gohier. Josephine's overtures to Fouché resulted in at least a modest increase in income; according to Fouché's memoirs, he paid her as a police informant. Her ties to the Gohiers were even more important. Jérôme Gohier, a worldly politician and debauchee, visited Josephine frequently and kept her abreast of events in Paris, where, in Bonaparte's absence, the political climate had gone from bad to worse.

Ridiculed and reviled by the public, wary of appearing outside the Luxembourg Palace lest they be pelted with dirt clods, the five Directors quarreled among themselves and carried on ceaseless intrigues—to the detriment of the government. While public order crumbled, public finance deteriorated and Parisians were once again suffering from severe food shortages, inept bureaucrats wrangled over trifles, unable to prevent the breakdown at all levels of administration or the alarming increase in crime. Once again France was at war, and her armies, unable to defend the territories Bonaparte had won, were suffering defeat after defeat.

As if to underscore the melancholy state of affairs, the sun rarely shone throughout the summer of 1799. Rain fell ceaselessly from grey skies, pouring down on the slate roofs of the capital, collecting in the muddy streets, turning the unrepaired country roads into quagmires. Crops were ruined in the fields, disease spread among both humans and animals, and people murmured that the bad weather was an omen, a sign from heaven that the times were out of joint and a new dispensation must surely be at hand.

By June of 1799 Bonaparte had been gone for over a year, and his sojourn in the Near East had affected him deeply. Five months earlier he had launched a fateful campaign eastward into Syria—modern Israel—across the Sinai desert. It was as if he and his army had entered a nightmare. Sandstorms choked them, the burning, remorseless heat pounded them relentlessly. Those who did not succumb to thirst or hunger were laid low by plague, and thousands died.

In the midst of it all, Bonaparte, who had fancied himself a romantic desert warrior, gave up his fantasies and took on a hardened persona, ruthless and coldly brutal. After seizing Jaffa, he ordered his troops to kill everyone in the garrison, even the women and children, and over the course of the campaign thousands of unarmed Turkish prisoners were slaughtered—many bayoneted in order to save ammunition. Following the failed siege of Acre, the turning point of the entire venture, there were fresh horrors, as bubonic plague swept through the French army and the stricken men were once more forced to march across the burning desert; those too ill to march had to be left behind to die.

When after being cut off from all news for many months, Bonaparte learned for the first time that France's government was in turmoil and that foreign armies were making inroads into the territories he had conquered, he decided to abandon his Near Eastern experiment and gamble all on a sudden return to Paris.

The news was dire. Italy had been lost. The fortress of Mantua, which Bonaparte had besieged so arduously and for so long, was back in Austrian hands once again. Tens of thousands of Russian troops were massed on the borders of the Alps and on the Danube.

Browned by the sun, coarsened by the suffering he had endured and inflicted, Bonaparte took a few companions and secretly embarked aboard a frigate, the *Muiron*, for France. The scimitar he wore in his belt was a token of his changed persona, the strong young Arab slave Roustan, his new bodyguard, standing at his side was a reminder of the experience that had seared his soul. He did not take Bellilotte with him, but he told her to follow him soon. They would be together in Paris, he told her. He would divorce Josephine and marry her.

Slipping out of the Nile delta, the *Muiron* entered the Mediterranean where Admiral Nelson's fleet, remarkably, failed to detect it. Helped by shrouding fogs, the frigate sailed to Corsica, where the party rested for eight days, and took on supplies, then on to the Côte d'Azur, landing at St-Raphael on October 9.

News of Bonaparte's arrival in France ran like wildfire along the south coast, then northward, via telegraphic post, toward Paris. People responded with overwhelming joy.

"Long live Bonaparte! Long live our father!" was the cry as townspeople and villagers waved torches to light the travelers' route to Aix. Spontaneous demonstrations were held, speeches of welcome made. A new song was quickly learned, with the refrain, "He's come back, all is well." Ignoring the possible threat of plague—for Bonaparte and his soldiers had all been exposed to plague carriers—the people thronged to greet their deliverer. "Hail the name which we adore, / That man beloved by France, / 'Tis he will save us evermore," they sang, confident that as soon as the general arrived in Paris, all the chaos and ill fortune would end.

All Paris was jubilant, but Josephine, who learned of her husband's unexpected return while dining at the Luxembourg Palace with the Gohiers, was immediately apprehensive. She knew that Bonaparte's relatives would be only too eager to greet him in order to relay to him all the latest gossip about her. She would be lost unless she reached him before they did. She hurried home, ordered a few things packed, and, taking Hortense, set off early in the morning along the Burgundy road, the road that led through Dijon to Lyon, hoping against hope that hers would be the first familiar face he would see.

20

A Fissured Marriage

*J*osephine had made the wrong decision, taken the wrong road. While she traveled in the post chaise along the Burgundy road, cursing every hill and rut and obstacle that slowed the horses, Bonaparte was traveling northward toward Nevers, taking the more westerly route to Paris. His brothers Joseph and Lucien caught up with him along the way, and after an emotional reunion they began to tell him everything that had been happening in the capital in his absence.

The government, they told him, was about to fall. The Directors were hopelessly at odds, the people were clamoring for a popular hero—and their overwhelming choice was Bonaparte. Joseph and Lucien had been in close contact with a growing political faction that would gladly back their brother in a coup.

All looked favorable, if Bonaparte acted quickly. There was only one impediment: he would have to rid himself of Josephine, who had become an embarrassing encumbrance given her brazen liaison with Hippolyte Charles and her close association with corrupt provisioners. Her long intimacy with Barras would also create difficulties, they pointed out—and she was on familiar terms with Gohier, who would have to be ousted in the coming coup.

All that he learned from his brothers hardened his determination, long nurtured, never to resume his former relationship with his wife.

When he reached the rue de la Victoire and discovered—perhaps, despite all, with a touch of dismay, perhaps only with relief—that she was not there waiting for him, he proceeded to remove all trace of her from the house, ordering the servants to take her possessions away. His sisters added their accusations to those he had already heard, further depressing his spirits, which were already very low.

Angry and full of chagrin, Bonaparte told everyone he saw that his marriage was over, ignoring the mildly surprised response that greeted his announcement, and the reminders he was given that by playing the outraged, cuckolded husband he risked making himself look ridiculous. He didn't care. He would never forgive her. As he told one companion, "If I were not sure of myself I would tear out my heart and throw it into the fire!"

When Josephine finally arrived at the rue de la Victoire, exhausted from her days of anxious travel and terribly worried about the damage her in-laws had most likely already done, she was refused admittance. The porter told her that she would not be allowed into the house. Undaunted by this cold greeting, she pushed her way past the porter's lodge, past the frightened servants who had been ordered not to let her in, and rushed up the spiral staircase to the door of Bonaparte's private sanctum. It was locked.

According to Josephine's own account of what happened next, she cried out to her husband to let her in, and when he answered in stony anger that his door would never again be open to her, she crumpled in a heap on the staircase, weeping.[1]

She stayed there for hours, while on the far side of the thick door, there was nothing but icy silence. She wept, she begged him, in the name of her children—who were disconcerted witnesses to the dramatic, almost operatic, scene—to open the door. But in his newfound flintiness Bonaparte was adamant. It was a battle of wills, hers against his. And in any sort of battle, Bonaparte expected to win.

The contest went on until the middle of the night, by which time Josephine, who had no doubt slept little for the past several days, was beside herself with wretchedness. Her emotions wrung to the core, she thrashed about on the staircase, striking her head on the unyielding door, abject to the point of despair.

All her courage had left her, she was reduced to quivering terror. Never before, not when on shipboard in the stormy Atlantic, not when in fear of stark poverty, not even in the face of imminent death under the blade of the guillotine, had she been so frightened or so vulnerable. Her entreaties were pitiful. Yet they met with no response.

At around four in the morning, Eugene and Hortense mounted the stairs and knocked at their stepfather's door. Hearing their voices, he unlocked it and stood in the doorway, a severe expression on his face, yet with traces of tears on his cheeks. His stepchildren knelt at his feet, seizing his hands and weeping piteously. They urged him not to send their mother away, and not to abandon them.

Seeing them there, the fresh-faced young Hortense and Eugene, who had been at his side throughout his long sojourn in the desert, brave and faithful and uncomplaining, very much a veteran of the wars now, having been wounded in the head at the siege of Acre, Bonaparte's heart was softened. Could he really bring himself to punish them as well as Josephine by divorcing her?

He told Hortense to fetch Josephine, who was no longer sprawled on the stairs but had gone down to the main floor of the house.

When she entered his room he began to criticize her sharply. All the resentment he had built up over the course of their months apart came spewing out in a venomous cascade. She had betrayed him. She had behaved shamefully, entirely forgetting her marital vows and her obligations to him and to his family. She had disgraced herself, her children, and her in-laws. She was low, shameful, utterly undeserving of forgiveness. He would never live with her again, Bonaparte told Josephine. They would live apart from now on, for the rest of their lives.

"As for you," Bonaparte said, turning to Eugene, "you will not be burdened with your mother's wrongs. You will always be my son. I will keep you near me."[2]

"No, my general," came the reply. "I must share the sad fate of my mother, and, from this moment, I bid you adieu."

The pride and loyalty in Eugene's words broke through Bonaparte's hardened exterior; he opened his arms to the young man and began to weep. Josephine and Hortense joined in the embrace; shortly afterward all were reconciled, with Josephine promising never to see Hippolyte Charles again.

As Bonaparte told an acquaintance the following day, "I have not the kind of heart which can bear to see tears flowing. Eugene was with me in Egypt and I have been accustomed to look on him as my adopted son. He is a brave and good boy. Hortense is just about to come out into the world. All who know her speak well of her to me. I confess ... that I was deeply moved. ... One can't be a man without being weak."[3]

By this time the reconciliation was well under way. Josephine had learned all that Joseph and Lucien had said about her, and had had a chance to justify herself, though the most damaging accusations— that she had had an intimate and indiscreet involvement with Hippolyte, and that she had done business with a company that swindled the government—could hardly be refuted. Bonaparte, as he himself acknowledged, had yielded to his own weakness for his wife and her children; he had seen all, known all—and despite all, he had forgiven.

The domestic turmoil on the rue de la Victoire was only a skirmish within the larger political ferment. Ever since his return from Egypt, Bonaparte and his brothers had been gathering support for a change of regime. Collaborating with two of the five Directors, Abbé Siéyès and Roger Ducos, Bonaparte counted on the personal loyalty of nearly two dozen of his generals, plus significant financial aid from prominent bankers. He gambled that in any confrontation with elected officials, his immense popularity would sway the public to his side. Even so, he was careful to stage the principal events of his coup outside of Paris, respecting the volatility of the fickle crowds of the capital.

The times were exhilarant; the prospect of a better future seemed to shimmer just beyond the horizon. All centered on Bonaparte. He had, as one shrewd observer wrote, "calmed all inquietudes, dissipated all alarms, and revived all hopes."[4] A new song, "The Bonaparte," was heard throughout the capital, whistled in the streets, sung in wine cellars, performed in theaters.

So strong was the public's urge to rid themselves of the dulling, alienating deadweight of the Directory that they would have welcomed almost any solution to the political crisis. They knew with utter clarity whom they wanted to lead them—what they could not see was what form his leadership ought to take. They were reluctant to abandon the hard-won liberties of the past ten years for any form of one-man rule, yet they wanted a strong central figure to govern their destinies, as the monarchy once had.

Always careful to present himself as an ardent republican, Bonaparte incarnated the revolution in his political rhetoric. But at the same time he offered the charisma, the almost mystical power, of an anointed ruler bearing a transcendent mandate. His remarkable military victories (his recent defeats were overlooked), the admirable simplicity of his personal life, his powerful sense of mission all made him seem, to an agitated people burdened with an incompetent executive, the savior they had long awaited.

On November 9, the members of the upper house of France's parliament, the relatively conservative Council of Elders, were alerted to the existence of a "Jacobin plot" to overthrow the government. They responded by turning over command of the Paris troops to Bonaparte, who announced his intention to rescue the republic from its danger. Meanwhile Bonaparte's allies were working behind the scenes. Of the five Directors, Barras was coerced into resigning, Moulin and Gohier were imprisoned in the Luxembourg Palace, and Siéyès and Ducos awaited the outcome of events.

On the following day, the two parliamentary bodies met at St-Cloud to decide the future—and discovered that Bonaparte's soldiers had arrived at the château before them and occupied it as they might have occupied a fortress. In this embattled environment, the members of the Council of Elders became restive and the more combative members of the lower house, the Council of Five Hundred, actually turned on Bonaparte when he appeared among them. ("Twenty assassins threw themselves upon me and sought out my breast," he later wrote.) Amid shouts of "Death to the traitor!" and "Outlaw him!" Bonaparte fell to the floor, unconscious.

Lucien Bonaparte, president of the Council of Five Hundred and one of the principal architects of the coup, rushed outside, rallied the assembled troops, and led an attack on the "assassins" who had assaulted his brother. The deputies were routed. Late that evening a handful of them returned, under threat from the soldiers, and voted to turn over supreme power in the state to a consulate, with Bonaparte, Siéyès and Ducos as the three consuls. In effect, Bonaparte, as first consul, controlled all.

The new first consul moved into the dilapidated Tuileries Palace in the snowy February of 1800. It was an auspicious beginning to the new century.

Much of the old palace was still a shambles, neglected since it was ransacked by crowds of angry Parisians in the first years of the revolution. Bullet holes pockmarked the walls. Bloodstains darkened the ornate staircases and torn draperies, their rich fabrics slashed by knives, hung askew from their rods over the broken windows.

The words "the Tenth of August" were scrawled in large black letters on many walls, reminders of the infamous—to revolutionaries, the glorious—day when the Parisians had overrun the palace, mowing down the Swiss Guards, in an effort to capture the king.

Bonaparte ordered the damage repaired, but the work went slowly, hampered by loud protesters who insisted that the defaced walls were a monument to liberty and a reminder that France must never again submit to the yoke of a tyrant. Gradually the graffiti were painted over, windows replaced, new furnishings brought in. Josephine was given the apartments of the late Queen Marie Antoinette on the ground floor, with a large reception room, the yellow salon, redecorated to her taste. Adjoining her dressing room was a small apartment for Hortense, who filled it with furniture and with the accoutrements and odors of her oil painting.

Compared with the splendor of the ancien régime, the new decor of the Tuileries was relatively modest. For Josephine, however, the adjustment to living in a palace, even a modestly appointed one, was very great. A uniformed hussar and several valets in livery stood before the door of her apartments at all hours of the day and night, to guard her person and carry out her orders. A chamberlain oversaw the running of the household with its large staff of servants. An exotically dressed mameluke, Ali, brought from Egypt along with Bonaparte's mameluke Roustan, glared fiercely at all who presented themselves at the entrance to Josephine's private rooms, a scowl on his ugly features.

Though she was still plain Citizeness Bonaparte, wife of the first consul, Josephine felt much more exalted than that, and according to the memoirist Laure Junot, a member of her official entourage, she stepped with ease into her new role. Bonaparte's recently acquired valet, Constant Wairy, was struck by her light, airy step and the "rare perfection" of her limbs and figure. The charming sweetness of her expressive features was compelling, Constant thought; whatever her mood—and she seemed incapable of disguising her feelings—she was always lovely to look at.

Constant recalled her simple elegance as she entered a roomful of people, with Talleyrand escorting her. In her white muslin gown with short sleeves and her pearl necklace, her plaited hair confined by a tortoiseshell comb, she was so striking that an audible murmur of admiration passed from one. end of the room to the other.[5] Some observers with less gallantry than Constant noted that she was "nearing forty," and quite looked it. And her teeth, which she tried her best to hide, were the blackened, ruined stumps of an old woman.

Following Bonaparte's elevation his wife was on view, subjected to public scrutiny, as never before. She was judged, criticized, and not infrequently condemned for her shallowness.

"A head without a brain" was the terse assessment of one courtier, who found her to be thoughtless and indiscreet about everything: her husband's political plans, the identities of her old lovers, her blatant maneuvering to obtain posts and perquisites for those who came to her with requests. Empty-headed and labile, "she occupied her day," this acerb observer wrote, "between futile and gallant conversations and tears which the harshness of Bonaparte drew from her." Anxious, "prompt to laugh and cry," Josephine was torn by loss. Those who knew of her long intimacy with Hippolyte Charles (and the whole of the fashionable world knew) saw how difficult was her inner struggle to renounce him finally.[6]

In her ill-advised candor Josephine spoke thoughtlessly of the old days, of her happy life before her marriage, when she was "the little Beauharnais" and "the little American," courted by many admirers. It was clear to those listening that she was somewhat dismayed, even embarrassed, to be living so grandly. And while this may have done credit to her character, it seemed a backhanded insult to Bonaparte, whose abilities and remarkable affinity for his compatriots had brought her to her present eminence.

He had brought her there, but in another sense she had been born to her role, for it was Josephine, born Rose Tascher de la Pagerie, who bore noble French blood, and not Nabuleone Buonaparte of Ajaccio. In reconstituting the court and society of the Tuileries, Josephine took the natural lead. She still had many friends and acquaintances among the gradually returning emigrés. She had known well the salons of the old regime, she had lived on the margins of the court at Fontainebleau. She had suffered, been stigmatized, nearly been executed for bearing the title Viscountess de Beauharnais.

It was with the aura of that former title haloing her that she presided as mistress of the Tuileries, and moved in the new social circles that formed in the early days of the Consulate.

Social life was reviving rapidly, and taking on a new tone. Gone was the madcap energy of the Directory, the macabre "Victim's Balls" and the frenetic mania for wild dancing. Now the dancing proceeded at a more stately pace, the guests sleek and elegant in black gowns and black coats and trousers, the sexes tending to remain separate from one another except when dancing. The old republican roughness of dress and rawness of manners were giving way to a greater degree of gentility; it was no longer risky, either socially or politically, to display taste, refined grooming or politeness. Here and there, at a ball or evening entertainment, one caught sight of a powdered head or even, among the elderly, an old-fashioned powdered wig.

The transformed social atmosphere was on display at the twice-weekly receptions of Jean Cambacérès, who as the newly appointed second consul* kept open house for his colleagues and underlings. Cambacérès himself, a slow-moving, slow-talking lawyer with unhealthy yellow skin and a severe myopia that gave him a permanent squint, bored his guests with endless accounts of his current illnesses. His solemnity invited ridicule, though his magnificent displays of food and wine, and the eminent company he attracted, ensured the success of his gatherings.

Bonaparte reigned over Parisian society with a paternal air, watchful for breaches of decorum. "I want nothing disorderly in my house!" he exclaimed. "No scandal!" He meant his court to set an example, and indeed it was remarked that, with the beginning of the new century, "society wore an appearance of morality and domestic virtue which it had never before displayed in France."[7] Louche morals, adultery, libertinage were to be outlawed. Therese Tallien, with her five bastard children and several assorted husbands and dozens of lovers, was no longer welcome in the drawing rooms of the Tuileries.

---

*The provisional triumvirate of Bonaparte, Ducos and Siéyès had given way to the newly constituted trio of Bonaparte, Cambacérès and Lebrun.

Women's dress, always symptomatic of the state of public morals—
or so the moralists declared—came under the first consul's particular
scrutiny. He frowned on the prevailing modes, which continued to
imitate antique styles; thin, clinging fabrics, revealing and seductive,
were favored by fashionable women, along with cashmere shawls, lace
bodices and tunics in the stylish shades of "Charlotte Corday" green
and "fly's bottom" violet. Fripperies such as heron's feathers, plumed
turbans and blue wigs annoyed him, but when women adopted English "spensers"—short jackets—and velvet Admiral Nelson bonnets
he grew red in the face and told the offenders bluntly that, dressed
as they were in the styles of France's enemy, they were not fit to join
civilized republican company.

Like other women, Josephine dreaded her husband's frequent brutal assessments of her appearance. Once, soon after they moved into
the Tuileries, she wore a gown that drew Bonaparte's wrath. He lifted
an inkwell from his desk and flung it at her, the dark ink staining
the gown and ruining it, the shock and humiliation of the episode
marking a new stage in what had become a fissured marriage.

There had been a reconciliation, but full harmony was not restored.
Bonaparte would never recover the uncritical, unquestioning adoration
he had once felt for his wife; the most he could manage was an
enduring and sentimental fondness. It was as if, in deciding not to
put her aside, he had to find a rationale that allowed him to feel
magnanimous—and superior. She had erred, he told himself; he, out
of an undeservedly generous love, had forgiven her—but only because
he accepted the fact that she could not help herself. She was a flawed
being, childlike in her undisciplined desires, and like a child, in need
of guidance and chastisement, and punishment. He could never again
trust her, of course, but then, only a fool would put his trust in a
wayward child.

Beneath this working rationale, which formed the new psycholog-
ical ground of Bonaparte's relationship to his wife, darker and subtler
undercurrents flowed. For if the first consul was capable of a wide
range of benign attitudes toward Josephine—affection, playful teasing, loyalty, protectiveness, ongoing sexual attraction—all his emotions were corroded by a lingering bitterness. He nursed his grievances
and, in Corsican fashion, began an attenuated vendetta against Josephine that often led him into cruelty.

He patronized her. He neglected her. He was unfaithful to her, chronically and at times ostentatiously. The price of his going on with their marriage was, for Josephine, to become a partner in a new, irrevocably altered union that was toxic at its core.

21

A Ride Through the Forest

One morning in the second year of the Consulate, Josephine was lying in her darkened bedroom at Malmaison, stricken with an excruciating headache. She lay still, for the least movement caused her more pain, and tried to sleep, despite the sounds of the stirring household in the corridor outside.

Bonaparte, restless and eager to be out of the house, paced irritably, upset with his wife for falling victim to one of her headaches and spoiling his plans. For several years he had felt restricted when riding or hunting in the rather small park adjoining the château, but until very recently, his efforts to enlarge it by buying surrounding acreage had not been successful. Now, however, he had concluded an arrangement to buy the woods of Bûtard, which would add significantly to the size of the property and also provide a pavilion where the hunters could eat and rest. He was bursting to show off his new acquisition. He wanted to take Josephine into the woods and spend the day with her and others exploring them.

Finally his impatience got the better of him and he burst into her room.

The sudden noise, the sudden eruption of light must have made Josephine cry out.

"Come, come, go with us," Bonaparte urged over her protests. "The air will do you good. It is the sovereign remedy for all pains."[1]

Josephine knew from experience that to be out in the sun made her head pound more fiercely, and that to be forced to ride in a carriage along rough country roads would be torture. She demurred, only to encounter her husband's stubborn insistence. He required her presence. She had no right to be sick when he needed her!

She knew better than to try to resist when he was in a peremptory mood. Moving slowly, her pain evident on her face, she forced herself to get out of bed and sent for a hat and shawl. With two companions, her niece Emilie Lavalette (daughter of Alexandre Beauharnais's brother François) and the newly married, pregnant Laure Junot she got into an open carriage and resigned herself to mollifying her impetuous husband.

"No words can describe the terrors of Madame Bonaparte in a carriage," Laure Junot wrote, recalling this excursion, "and it is as difficult to express my own impatience, when I see a want of compassion for such weaknesses; they are troublesome, it is true, but are fruits of education, and no fault on the part of their victims, on whom they inflict a sort of martyrdom." Laure felt compassion for Josephine, suffering the dual agonies of her migraine and her phobia. "Napoleon was not of my mind," she noted dryly. "He had no pity for his wife, and made no allowance for her."[2]

Josephine had suffered from an excessive dread of carriage rides for years, but her fears had escalated after the coach in which she and Hortense were riding had been all but blown apart by a bomb on the previous Christmas Eve. The bomb had been meant for Bonaparte, who was riding in another carriage well ahead of hers; it was fortuitous that, having delayed her departure by a few moments in order to adjust her shawl, her carriage was not immediately behind his. Had she been any closer, hers would have been among the dozens of bodies strewn in gruesome heaps along the rue St-Nicaise, or buried under the rubble of collapsed houses. The shock to her nerves on that dangerous night had been profound. Afterward, she had been unable to stop trembling, and she wept, pale and shivering, for days.[3] Too nervous and keyed up to sleep, she lay awake at night, startled by every sound; even in the most familiar surroundings, the sight of a stranger's face could alarm her and make her cry.[4]

They started off through the trees, the three women in the carriage, and Bonaparte and his secretary Bourrienne riding ahead on their own mounts. Bonaparte was buoyant, boyishly playful. He galloped on ahead, then came back to seize Josephine's hand, then galloped off again. The wood became more and more dense, the road narrowing and the trees, with their thick curtain of leaves, obscuring all but the tortuous path ahead.

Suddenly the foliage parted to reveal a small stream at the bottom of a steep ravine. The road had ended. There was no way to go but straight down the steep bank.

Josephine cried out to the driver to stop.

"See there!" she shouted to him. "I will not go to Bûtard this way. Go on ahead," she told the bewildered postilion, who was lost, "and tell the first consul that I am returning to the château, unless he knows some other road."

With some difficulty the carriage was turned around, and they started back along the road the way they had come. Almost immediately, however, they heard hoofbeats behind them. It was Bonaparte, and when he drew level with them they could see how displeased he was.

"What is the matter? What is this new whim about? Return the way you came," he told the driver, laying his whip on the postilion's shoulders.

Against Josephine's objections, the carriage was turned once again and went back to the bank of the stream, which Josephine called "this precipice." Bonaparte was waiting for them there.

"Come!" he said to the driver, "a good plunge, then draw in the reins, and you are over!"

Josephine's scream could be heard, Laure Junot remembered afterward, from one end of the forest to the other.

"You shall never keep me in the carriage. Let me out! Bonaparte! I entreat your mercy! Let me out!"

Her terror was extreme, and pitiable. She wrung her hands and wept.

Bonaparte looked at her, shrugged, and in harsh tones told her to be quiet.

"This is utter childishness. You shall go ahead, and in the carriage." He swore, and looked angrily toward the postilion.

"Did you hear me?" he asked, his voice level and threatening. He had dismounted by this time, and approached the carriage. Laure Junot intervened to ease the situation, urging Bonaparte to be reasonable—for as any reasonable person could see, they truly would be in danger if they attempted to go over the steep bank.

"General," she said, "I am responsible for another life. I cannot stay here. The jerk will be violent, and may not only injure but kill me in my present condition." She smiled at him, counting on his good will, and knowing that he was fond of her. "You do not wish that, do you, General?"

At once Bonaparte's gallantry overcame his churlishness.

"I, do you the smallest harm? You? Get down at once. You are right; a jolt might injure you severely." He came up to the carriage steps and, holding out his hand to the young Madame Junot, began helping her out of the carriage—pointedly ignoring the distressed Josephine and the silent, no doubt frightened, Emilie.

As she prepared to step down Laure Junot added, with well-intentioned kindness, "And a jolt may be very injurious to Madame Bonaparte, General, for if she were as I am—"

She stopped in mid-sentence. Bonaparte was looking at her with a dumbfounded expression that would have been amusing had it not signaled a dangerous shift of mood. The suggestion was not an unreasonable one, or so it seemed to the rather naive, seventeen year old Laure. Wives were often pregnant, after all; why should Josephine be an exception? She did not realize that, since becoming first consul, Bonaparte had been concerned about founding a dynasty, and increasingly annoyed and chagrined that Josephine had not become pregnant. (Of course, his mistress Bellilotte had not given him a child either, so he knew the fault might rest with him. No doubt the realization of this possibility added to his irritation.)

So Laure had brought up an uncomfortable subject. But beyond that, Bonaparte seems to have ignored not only Josephine's terrible migraine but the severe injuries she had suffered in her fall at Plombières, with their long and painful aftermath, not to mention the bone-jolting shock of the exploding bomb, when she and Hortense were knocked to the ground by the force of the blast. Even though the chances of Josephine's being pregnant might be small, she was nonetheless at exceptional risk of injury, and Bonaparte knew it.

They looked at one another, Laure Junot and the general, for a long moment. Then Laure began to laugh at the odd look on his face, making him laugh in return, a harsh barking laugh that was so loud and so sudden—and so bitter in its clear message—that it was almost assaultive.

Laure jumped down from the carriage, aided by Bonaparte, who then addressed the driver.

"Put up the step," he said, "and let the carriage proceed."

Once again Laure Junot objected.

"General, you appear cruel," she said bravely, "and yet you are not so. Madame Bonaparte is ill. She has a fever. I implore you, let her get out!"

Bonaparte was suddenly livid. He gave her a look, she recalled, "that curdled her blood."

"Madame Junot," he said icily, "I never liked defiance, not even when I was a child; ask Signora Letizia and Madame Permon [Laure's mother], and consider whether I am likely to be tamed since." His expression and tone were menacing. Laure was silent. It was clear that further challenges to his will would be futile.

The moment passed, and he held out his hand to the young woman.

"Well, come, let me help you over this *formidable torrent*, this *frightful precipice*." His heavy sarcasm was intended to lighten the mood, but it only made Josephine cry afresh.

She cried, Laure thought, "as if she was about to be led to her execution." The weight of all her physical and mental anguish bore down on her, her husband's cruel indifference to it even more crushing. She cried out to the postilion to wait another moment, to put off the inevitable. The carriage stood still.

Striking the poor postilion roughly with his riding crop, Bonaparte shouted at him.

"Sir, do you intend to obey my orders?"

At once the whip was applied to the horses, which leapt down the embankment and across the stream, shaking the carriage so roughly that one of the springs was broken and a pin loosened. Josephine and Emilie, holding on for dear life, shrieked and gasped, their hearts pounding, until the ordeal was over.

"Madame Bonaparte's whole body was disordered with pain, fear, and rage," Laure Junot remembered. She was beside herself with fury, yet she dared not confront her bullying husband. She feared him too much. He knew too well how to hurt her, and his repertoire of tortures was broad and effective. Besides, she knew that in her angry, terror-stricken state, she was unlovely to look at, and when she was unattractive she drew more caustic barbs from Bonaparte, and these she found especially wounding. Sobbing loudly, she hid her face behind her muslin veil. The sound of her gasps and sniffs could be heard all the rest of the way to Bûtard.

When at last the carriage, rattling and swaying more than usual in its broken condition, arrived at the pavilion, Bonaparte dismounted and strode angrily toward the vehicle. He reached in and virtually pulled the weeping Josephine out, manhandling her roughly, and dragged her off into the woods away from the others.

Both were furious, Josephine because of her pain and humiliation, Bonaparte because his pleasurable excursion had been ruined. They began arguing, and although they were too far away for Laure Junot to hear every word they said, the gist of their quarrel was evident.

In response to Bonaparte's scalding insults, Josephine became accusatory. She reproached her husband with mistreating her, with neglecting her and causing her injury—and with infidelity. His voice rose in reply. Now Laure heard all, and remembered the words.

"You are a fool," he shouted. "If you repeat such things I will call you a wicked fool, because you do not think what you are saying. You know how much I hate your jealousy! It is all in your mind! If you keep it up you will only give me ideas. Come! Kiss me and be still. You are so ugly when you cry. I've often told you so."[5]

Eventually a bitter truce was arrived at, and the couple emerged from the woods, Josephine pale and shaken, Bonaparte sullen and lowering. The rest of the day went badly, and Josephine, unable to vent her anger on her husband, spoke spitefully to Laure instead.

Mistreatment, quarrels, injured feelings had become the common stuff of Josephine's marriage to the man she now addressed as "Sir," the man who had become the most powerful person in France. He was king in all but name, able to govern the destinies of private citizens as he did the lives of his soldiers. No one, least of all his wife, could escape the stranglehold of his control.

Nor, in her demoralized state, did Josephine try to escape. Bonaparte's coercive power was too great, her own will to liberate herself too feeble. Besides, she no longer had anywhere to go, or anyone to turn to. She had not seen Hippolyte in a long time, their love affair was long over.[6] Barras, ousted from his directorship, had been sent away, and was living far from Paris, no longer willing or able to offer Josephine either friendship or solace. Ever more isolated, despite the large numbers of people she encountered as wife of the first consul, Josephine wrote one of her rare letters to her mother in Martinique.

"Dear mama, I am sending this letter on the frigate which is coming to Guadeloupe to announce the peace with England," she began. Martinique was being returned to French control. "Well disposed, upright people" were being put in charge of colonial affairs.

"I have not heard news of you in a very long time, my dear mama," she went on, "but I think of you often nevertheless. I hope you are well and content and that you love your Yeyette." She sent news of Eugene, of his military command, and of Hortense, who was, as she composed her letter, occupied in painting a portrait of Bonaparte walking in his hunting park. She promised to send the painting to Martinique.

"Bonaparte would like it very much if you came to France, if you were able to accustom yourself to living in a climate so unlike your own. If you decide to do as we wish, you must plan to leave in time to arrive here in June." Rose-Claire Tascher was sixty-five, too old, as Josephine knew, to undertake the sea voyage to France, much less to consider exchanging the oppressive heat of the tropics for the cold of northern Europe.

The letter said little, and concealed much. Josephine had never been close to her mother, and had not seen her in twenty-three years. She did not tell her—possibly because Bonaparte still opened all her letters and read them, as he had begun to do five years earlier, in Italy—the truth about her present state. She did not say that she was often ill, that she had tried and failed to begin a new life with another man, that she lived amid the grandeur of a palace, yet with much inner disappointment and suffering. Possibly Rose-Claire would not have understood, or, had she understood, would not have been sympathetic. Yeyette had always been high-spirited, thoughtless and impulsive; whatever her present situation, she had undoubtedly put herself there.

"You would like Bonaparte very much," Josephine went on, "he makes your daughter very happy. He is good, lovable, in every way a charming man; he loves your Yeyette very much. Farewell, my dear mama," she concluded. "I kiss you and love you with all my heart. Your grandchildren join with me in kissing you. Remember me to family and friends. I kiss my nurse."[7]

She sealed the letter and sent it off by courier, knowing it would not reach the plantation at Trois-Ilets for several months. The reply, if there was one, has been lost. But Rose-Claire did not come to the Tuileries, and Josephine did not write to her again for a long time. If, in her worst moments with her domineering husband, Josephine thought fleetingly of escaping to Martinique, returning to that lush green world with its aura of overripe decay and its everpresent scent of sugar, she soon dismissed the thought from her mind. Bonaparte would never let her go. She had obligations to carry out, duties to perform as his consort. He held her, as he held France, in an ever tightening grip.

22

"Luxury Had Grown Abundantly"

*O*n the crowded gardens of the Tuileries and along the bustling new boulevards, Paris was coming back to life. Signs of returning prosperity, of renewed enterprise were everywhere: in the many new restaurants and cafés opening for business on every street, in the activity in the commercial quarters of the city, where merchants spread their wares behind broad panes of decorated glass, in the streets themselves, where for the first time in years, throngs of vehicles sped past. Fast cabriolets, with high-stepping spirited horses and young "jockeys" on the drivers' seats, whiskys, fiacres, demi-fortunes dashed over the cobblestones at a pace that frightened pedestrians and sprayed peddlers and street-sellers with stinking mud.

Gone was the frenzied, avid excitement of the Directory, with its brittle gaiety and air of desperation. The activity of the new regime was less dizzying, more stable, for the prosperity that flowed to the capital on Bonaparte's assumption of the title of first consul was spread widely among Parisians of all classes, and not confined to speculators and bankers. Not that there was an end to speculation; the lines were long in front of the lottery office in the rue du Faubourg-Montmartre, and vendors of "infallible" lists of winning lottery numbers did a thriving business.

Paris in the Consulate was awash in handbills. Walls and corridors were plastered with brightly colored papers advertising fencing lessons, concerts, cures for venereal disease, stage shows and vaudeville acts. Entertainments proliferated. For a few sous one could observe educated fleas, battling flies, or Coco the mounted deer, who paced and trotted like a thoroughbred at the Circus Franconi. There were blind street musicians performing on the boulevards, bearded ladies being exhibited, rope-dancers and—one of the wonders of Paris— the Incombustible Spaniard, who drank boiling oil and sulfuric acid, put a red-hot knife in his mouth, then walked barefoot across a white-hot cast-iron plate without raising a blister.

Visitors to the city were soon aware that the scars of the revolution—grass growing up through the cobblestones, signs of neglect on many formerly grand buildings, leaking ceilings, damp walls, dirty staircases—were slow to heal, and could not help but notice the mounds of garbage accumulated at streetcorners, reeking and infested with rats. But they also took note of the beautiful new landscaping in the city's gardens, the new bridges over the Seine, the leveling of many rundown old structures to make way for new. Streets named for Bonaparte's victories (rue de Rivoli, rue de Castiglione) were created, theaters built, the old Palais Royal, still raffish and sordid, rejuvenated with the addition of additional courts and walks.

Walking around the circumference of the city, something a healthy visitor could do in the course of an afternoon, one could discern significant changes. There were many more police in evidence, alert for disturbances or suspicious characters, than in the past. There were fewer newspapers available for sale (the majority of Parisian papers had been suppressed by the ministry of police, as potentially subversive). Tricolor cockades, once the ubiquitous mark of loyalty to the republic, were few and far between, but powdered heads were a common sight. "Monsieur" and "Madame" were heard far more often than the revolutionary terms "Citizen" and "Citizeness." And here and there, amid the throngs in the boulevards, at the theaters and in the public gardens, one could make out the noisy, exigent voice of a well-educated, well-dressed emigré, newly returned to the capital, demanding service or special favor in a tone that verged on insolence.

It was said that the cost of living in Paris had risen by nearly a third since Bonaparte came to power, and no wonder, for the pace and splendor of social life had increased greatly. In the winter season of 1802, it was estimated, some ten thousand balls were held, and at least six thousand formal dinners. Dressmakers worked long into the night sewing gowns for these occasions, and hairdressers could not keep up with the demand of their clients. Thousands of yards of satin and velvet, crepe and tulle were ordered from the silk mercers, and fragile satin dancing slippers, so delicate and perishable they lasted only a night or two, were used up and discarded at a tremendous rate. The women at these social gatherings were "generally covered in jewels," a traveler from England wrote; at all levels of the social scale, this visitor thought, "luxury had grown abundantly."

At the long, crowded dining tables of the wealthy, dozens of servants labored over meals of twenty-five courses. When the banker Ouvrard held a magnificent banquet in the orangerie of his mansion, vine branches with bunches of lush ripe grapes hung from the walls and fountains overflowed with wine punch. A marble basin of colorful live fish formed the centerpiece of the massive table, and around it in profusion were exotic fruits, some real, some made of spun sugar.

If the feasts were grand, the ornamented rooms in which they were held were even grander, with gilded walls, glittering gold-framed mirrors, fine soft carpets and paintings by Italian and Dutch masters. The minister of police, Fouché, was said to possess the most beautiful room in Paris, at his house on the Quai Malaquais.

Moving among the guests and waiting in the antechambers of the great houses, like ghostly souvenirs of the old court and the old ways, were valets in bag wigs and short velvet culottes, their neckcloths and sleeves trimmed in a froth of gold lace. Valets had not been seen in elite drawing rooms for more than a decade; now they made their reappearance. Returning emigrés sought out their former valets and hired them once more. New valets were trained. And the government, alert to opportunities for profit, imposed a "valet tax" on wealthy households. Two valets were permissible, but every additional valet cost one hundred francs extra in taxes.[1]

Try as he might to set an example of simplicity and understatement in dress, the first consul could not restrain the taste for superfluity and excess, the snobbish insistence on the finest, that overtook society with his accession to power. Men sought out the perfect bootmaker (Astchey), the perfect tailor (Catel), the perfect maker of culottes

(Henri). In their wide, overflowing cravats, blue frock coats with gold buttons and scarlet vests, their broad whiskers and moustaches trimmed to the ideal length and not a millimeter longer, they walked or rode self-consciously along the boulevards where they were sure to be glimpsed, appraised and admired by others. The women, in flowing gowns and tunics of Turkish blue or amaranth from Leroy, their hair in soft ringlets around the face or crowned with diadems of flowers, gathered to see and be seen, wary of rivals yet eager for compliments.

Bonaparte's sister Paulette was in the forefront of this ceaseless emulation, and her aim was to outshine all other women, especially her sister-in-law Josephine. Along with the rest of her family, Paulette was mortified when Bonaparte became reconciled to his wife, and it was a source of constant resentment to her that Josephine should preside over the yellow drawing room of the Tuileries, at the apex of consular society.

When Josephine drew all eyes in her gowns of clinging white crepe or muslin or shimmering silver lamé, the women remarking on her sweetly enchanting appearance, Paulette fumed. On one occasion she planned a toilette which, she announced, "she expected would immortalize her." The talents of two expensive dressmakers were employed to create a memorable—if predictably vulgar—costume crowned by a tigerskin fur headdress.

The effect, when Paulette entered the room, was immediate and electric. All eyes were on her at once, and soon all mouths were talking. "Such an impudent display of extravagance is very unbecoming in a woman," one guest was overheard to say. Others sneered at her heavy gold jewelry, the clusters of gold grapes in her hair that clashed with the tigerskin, above all, at her misshapen ears, thin and pale and undeveloped, odd knobby earlets rather than true ears.

"What a pity!" a rival beauty remarked with a smirk. "She would be so pretty but for that! . . . Look at those ears. Such a pretty head to have ears like that! If I had ears like those I'd have them cut off."

Mortified to the point of tears, her grand triumph in ruins, Paulette claimed to be indisposed and left the party early.[2]

In the new social world that was taking shape, with its refinement of taste and its renewed emphasis on polish and cultivation, Paulette was quite out of her depth. All of the first consul's relatives, with the possible exception of Joseph, could not disguise the fact that they were parvenus who only a few years earlier had been penniless exiles from Corsica. They had wealth, fine estates, influential acquaintances, and they could rely on the power of their brother to advance them even further. But they lacked elegance of style, taste, graciousness and aristocratic ease of manner—the very qualities that their despised sister-in-law, despite her tarnished reputation during the early years of the Directory, possessed.

Bonaparte himself had acquired the cachet of aristocracy by marrying the Viscountess de Beauharnais. The entire Bonaparte family could raise their social standing in the same way, through an advantageous marriage.

At a dance at Malmaison in September of 1801, Louis Bonaparte proposed to Hortense, and despite her misgivings, she accepted him. The bonds between Bonaparte and Beauharnais were about to be strengthened.

Both the bride and the groom had doubts. Louis, who was in love with a bridge inspector's daughter he had met while walking in the Tuileries gardens, claimed some years after the event that he had been forced to propose to Hortense by his brother.[3]

And Hortense, who confided to Madame de Rémusat that she felt a "pang of sorrow" when the betrothal was concluded, had an instinctive mistrust of Louis and would not have agreed to become his wife had she not believed that it would please her mother and help to heal the festering discord between Josephine and the Bonapartes. Hortense also believed that by marrying a brother of the first consul she would be in a position to advance her own brother's career, and to Hortense, at eighteen, Eugene was the most important person in the world.[4]

Young as she was, Hortense had already known disappointment in love. One of Bonaparte's aides-de-camp, Christophe Duroc, had wanted to marry her and she had been willing. Bonaparte had not made any objections, but Josephine had. She wanted a more impressive match for her daughter. Josephine had suggested an older man, a former lover of Madame de Staël; when Hortense learned that she might be wed to someone who had been intimate with such a "bizarre monster" as Germaine de Staël she refused to consider the match.[5]

That the two young people who were about to wed in the interest of family harmony were ill suited to one another seems to have bothered no one, except Louis and Hortense themselves. Hortense was cheery and good humored, likable and affectionate; people were attracted to her for her warmth and sparkle. She lacked depth but possessed a decency that Bonaparte admired. "Hortense forces me to believe in virtue," he once remarked.[6]

Louis, on the other hand, was morose and inward-turned, handsome in a fleshy way but with large troubled eyes that betrayed an unstable mind. The early promise he had shown as a young officer at his brother's side in Italy had been blighted. He had become ill, probably with syphilis, and the disease had begun to afflict him with severe pains in his joints. It had also, sadly, begun to affect his personality. He became misanthropic and withdrawn, brooding on his physical ailment and constantly taking leave from his military command—Bonaparte had promoted him to the rank of general—claiming ill health.

The family had sent Louis on a Grand Tour of northern Europe in hopes that a year of travel would draw him out and make him forget both his pains and his ill advised romantic attachments. But he returned to Paris after only a few months, complaining of arthritis and shutting himself away in a country house where he saw no one. Bonaparte, with his usual dismissive contempt for physical infirmities, shrugged off Louis's complaint as trivial and continued to have high hopes for him. Assuming that he had no children with Josephine, Bonaparte intended to make Louis his successor. Louis's marriage to Hortense would be only fitting, so that the next generation of the Bonaparte dynasty would also have Josephine's blood.

The wedding of Louis Bonaparte and Hortense de Beauharnais was to be held on January 4, 1802, but in the last days of the old year a very severe frost brought nearly all activity in Paris to a halt and soon thereafter the Seine rose to flood levels and many of the riverbank houses in the city were half under water. The Bonapartes, in particular, took the disaster to be an ill omen. When they stood, overdressed and angry, watching the wedding ceremony their extreme displeasure must have been evident on their faces.

Paulette, always the most visible and the most vocal member of the family, was not present; her husband had been sent to serve in Santo Domingo and she had gone with him—escorted by dozens of frigates and gunships loaded with her wardrobe and household goods.

The other members of the family, however, were on hand to observe the ill-advised joining of Louis and Hortense: Letizia, courteous but cold, Joseph, urbane and scornful, Elisa, red-faced with indignation, and Lucien, tall, dark and bespectacled, hostile and on the edge of contentiousness with everyone involved.

Lucien, always the most contrary member of the family, had been nothing but trouble for Bonaparte, who had had to relieve him of his duties as interior minister. Sent as ambassador to Spain, he had made a fortune there and had returned to Paris, no longer part of the government but still the family gadfly. Irked at Bonaparte for no longer seeking his advice, and vexed that Josephine was still Madame First Consul (Lucien had recommended that Bonaparte divorce her and marry the daughter of the King of Spain), Lucien had become malicious. He had told his unhappy brother Louis that the wedding was part of an elaborate plot to provide Bonaparte with an heir. Hortense, he said, was pregnant with Bonaparte's child; Louis was only needed to make the child legitimate and give it his name.

The wedding guests, shivering in their thin gowns and culottes in the intense cold, noticed that Hortense was sad-eyed and pale as she took her place before the papal legate who was to conduct the ceremony. Her eyes were red, and she had evidently been weeping. Josephine wept throughout the proceedings, as was her custom on solemn occasions.

After Louis and Hortense were pronounced husband and wife, Caroline Bonaparte stepped forward with her husband Joachim Murat. They had been married for two years, and had a child, but their marriage had not been blessed by the church—religious wedding ceremonies having been banned early in the revolution—and they wanted to repeat their vows before the legate.

"These double vows made me very uncomfortable," Hortense recalled later. "The other couple, so deeply in love with each other, were so content together." The happiness of Caroline and Murat was in sharp contrast to the edgy accommodation between the new bride and groom. And to make matters worse, Caroline, who had disliked Hortense ever since they were pupils together at Madame Campan's academy, was openly contemptuous of her newest sister-in-law.

Nothing could make up for the melancholy wedding held amid the disastrous floods and cold—not the generous dowry Bonaparte

and Josephine each provided for Hortense, not the dozens of peignoirs, camisoles, cashmere shawls, and lace-trimmed nightcaps that
made up her extravagant trousseau, not even the imposing mansion
off the rue St-Lazare that Bonaparte bought and presented to the
couple with its immense garden full of antique statuary. From the
first Louis was distant, hard and despising. He distrusted Hortense
and was suspicious of her efforts to be affectionate. Hortense was
Josephine's daughter: therefore she must be, like her mother, wanton
and promiscuous by nature, unfit to belong to a respectable family.

"You are now a Bonaparte," Louis told his wife soon after the
wedding. "Our interests must become yours, those of your own
family do not concern you any longer." He told her candidly that he
despised most women, and that he meant to govern her so absolutely that she would never bring him shame or dishonor, the "common fate of all husbands." His primary command was that she stay
away from her mother, so that Josephine's bad influence could not
corrupt her.[7]

The wedding of the first consul's stepdaughter sent delicious trem-
ors through Paris society. The doyenne of ancien régime hostesses,
the Marquise de Montesson, was giving a ball in celebration of Hortense's marriage, and invitations were valued beyond measure.

Madame de Montesson, who had been the morganatic wife of the
late Duc d'Orléans, hero of the republicans in the early days of the
revolution, presided like a fairy godmother over a ball of fairy-tale
splendor.

It was almost as if the old, prerevolutionary world had come back
again for one night. The elegance of the guests, sparkling with jewels,
colorful plumes and heron feathers nodding in the heated, still air,
the perfume of the masses of flowers, brought at great expense from
the warmer south, the spirited dance music, the entire panorama of
refinement and grace, bathed in the flattering light of a thousand
candles, reminded the older guests of the lost era of Marie Antoinette,
with all its enchantment and beauty.

Now that they had recovered some of their political and economic
balance, now that the forces of extremism seemed for a time to have
receded with the advent of Bonaparte's rule, it was safe to look back
across the chasm of a decade and more of revolution toward a vanished past, and to idealize it.

Madame de Montesson herself, in her old-style lace and satin gown, her ornate high-piled wig, seemed to incarnate that vanished past. She was sixty-five, but looked barely forty, still lovely and violet-eyed, the white of her wig echoed in the pale cream of her cashmere shawl. The many emigrés who flocked to the ball that night looked to her as their lodestar, their beacon of gentility. But Bonaparte too, like other republicans, turned to her as his guide and model in his search for gentler manners and lost courtesies, and he urged Josephine to go to Madame de Montesson for tutelage.

Every other dance was a waltz that night, the best of the dancers as light and graceful as professionals. The most celebrated dancers of the season, Monsieur de Trénis and Monsieur Dupaty, were present, and the others made way for them and watched them leap and spin and twirl their partners to the intoxicating triple rhythm.[8] Hour after hour the dancing went on, until after midnight, when Madame de Montesson's fine Saxony linen tablecloths were spread over the banquet tables and the guests dined on her plates of Sèvres porcelain with the escutcheon of the house of Orléans.

None of the guests seems to have recorded what Louis Bonaparte did or said on the night of his grand wedding ball, but Hortense left a lasting impression. In a loose-fitting gown copied from a statuette from Herculaneum, her hair crowned with flowers, she danced time and again. She was the celebrity of the evening, the First Stepdaughter, the happy bride. If a few of the guests remembered her sorrow and pallor on her wedding day, they searched in vain for evidence of that dejection now. As she danced her favorite gavotte with the blond, charming Charles de Gontaut, their fair heads dipping and nodding together in the exertions of the dance, she was luminous, with no shadow of disappointment on her pleasing features. Both the first consul, whose shrewd small eyes missed nothing, and the aged marquise, watching contentedly from her chair, nodded with satisfaction.

Ten months after the grand ball, Hortense gave birth to a son, whom she named Napoleon-Louis-Charles. If Louis had doubts about the child's paternity, he kept them to himself, although he had warned Hortense throughout her pregnancy that if she gave birth one day earlier than the normal term he would abandon her and never see her again. The new mother's relief after the birth must have been great, but the first consul's delight was even greater. Now there was a child whom he could designate as his successor, a true heir to the Bonaparte succession. If he were to die, his line would not be extinguished. He no longer needed to hope for a child from Josephine; from a dynastic point of view at least, she was expendable.

Now the first consul sang his favorite song with particular relish. "No, no there could never be/A sweeter child, dearer to me!" he sang, bawling out the refrain off-key. The grating sound caused everyone around him to wince, as usual, but so immense was his pleasure in his tiny namesake that no one, not even Hortense, dared try to restrain him.

23

"A Violent and Murderous Ambition"

Toward the end of the year 1803, two days before Christmas, Parisians noted a stillness in the chill air and a gradual darkening of the sky at midday. A storm was coming, but not a snowstorm, for the air was not cold enough, and the dark clouds massing on the horizon were streaked with lightning. Horses pawed the ground and tried to break free of their traces, and dogs and cats hid wherever shelter could be found. Even the rats that swarmed over the refuse heaps and infested old buildings were suddenly nowhere to be seen, hidden in walls and under bridges, heaped together instinctively for protection against the fierce onslaught they knew was about to come.

There were no balls or parties on that terrifying night; all were canceled. The hard rain began falling in mid-afternoon and within hours a fearsome wind was clawing at the leafless trees in the Tuileries gardens and whipping the river into foaming peaks. No vehicles could make headway against the strong blast; carts were overturned and wagons swept off the roads, while along the riverbank, fishing boats and barges were swamped or flung on shore by the force of the onrushing wind.

Hour after hour the gusts strengthened, with slate tiles torn from roofs, chimneys blown down and windows shattered. So loud was the moaning and howling of the storm that it made even shouted conversation impossible. Sleep too was impossible, for the violent blasts made walls and floors shake and quiver, and no one knew when the ceiling above them might collapse and the entire building come crashing to the ground.

When on the following morning the wind dropped and the city began to come back to life under grey skies, the full extent of the storm's havoc was revealed. Houses were torn apart, gardens savaged. Uprooted trees blocked the boulevards, and in the low-lying quarters near the river, streets and courtyards were fouled with black mud. Paris had been swept by a hurricane, and the religious services held that Christmas Eve were filled with worshipers thankful to be alive, glad that the capital had been spared far worse destruction.

The fearful storm frightened Josephine, and brought back memories of the devastating hurricanes of her childhood. All her superstitious instincts were aroused, for an event so rare and so overawing had to carry a deeper portent. She would have liked to consult her favorite fortune-teller, The Sorceress, to find out what the omen meant, but Madame Lenormand had been put in prison by Bonaparte, along with a number of others he found vexing, and she had to be content with telling her own fortune with cards instead.

Connections between the events of her own life and the churning violence of the great storm were not hard to make, for earlier in the year 1803, she had celebrated her fortieth birthday and entered the bleak season of middle age. Try as she might to hide the signs of advancing age—dyeing her hair, wearing thick white makeup and an abundance of rouge, sleeping with a slab of raw meat on her face to freshen her complexion, applying unguents to her gums to sweeten her breath—the imprint of the years was indelible, as Bonaparte was swift to remind her. Ageing faces, he remarked, are only pleasing when they smile; melancholy or anxiety, or especially anger, make them grotesque. But then, he had often stated a preference for "good, gentle, and conciliatory" women, whose faces showed only sweetness and simplicity.[1]

As she crossed the threshold of her forties, Josephine's basic sweetness of temper was often altered. She became shrill, accusatory, argumentative. She complained at length, to anyone who would listen, about Bonaparte's mistreatment of her. Her attempts to lash out at her overbearing, all-powerful husband were impotent; in actuality she was as feeble as a child when she attempted to confront him, arousing his contempt and hardening him further. Bonaparte's coarse, brusque exterior was like sandpaper to Josephine's tender feelings, he rubbed her raw. And too often, in her bruised and bleeding state, she forgot that beneath his hard rind he was often close to tears, easily moved by sentiment, vulnerable to the sight of others' distress; when she remembered this, she knew how to soften him—by gentle deference, by offering him soothing, nurturing peace when he was suffering from insomnia or from the convulsive stomach spasms that were the bane of his late nights.

She knew how to manage him, but very often her resentment overcame her common sense, and she did not keep her anger in check. To soothe and caress the man who injured her severely cost her too much stress and pain. Ineffectual as it was, it felt better to Josephine to complain, confront and accuse—which triggered the cycle of injury once again.[2]

What caused Josephine's smoldering anger to flare into flame were Bonaparte's infidelities, and the high-handed manner in which he flaunted them. To provoke her jealousy and wound her, he announced, from time to time, that like a dog, he had "gone into heat," and spoke at length and in detail about his newest mistress, "showing," Madame de Rémusat thought, "an almost savage surprise if [Josephine] did not approve." He spared her no particulars: the shape, physical anomalies, and anatomical attractions of each woman, down to each mole and cleft and pant, were enlarged upon with savor, to Josephine's humiliation. He knew that she paid household servants and others to spy on him and report on his assignations. It gave him special pleasure to inform her of other amorous meetings of which the spies were unaware, so that she could be in no doubt as to his full slate of adulteries.

It was noticed by the women in Josephine's entourage and others that when Bonaparte took a new mistress, he became even more harsh and violent toward his wife, and pitiless in his brutal silencing of her complaints. He asserted his need for the erotic distractions other women provided, indeed his right to enjoy them.

"I am not a man like others," he said, drawing himself up to his full five-foot-six-inch height, "and moral laws or the laws that govern conventional behavior do not apply to me."[3] Whereupon, as a rule,

Josephine burst into tears of pain and vexation and launched a tirade of complaints. Bonaparte, more than a match for this onslaught, erupted into fury, breaking furniture and abusing Josephine both verbally and physically.[4] Members of the consular household knew better than to attempt to intervene. They witnessed, in some embarrassment, the full tempest of the first consul's rage, relieved when at last it subsided, but always apprehensive in anticipation of its return.

Josephine, buffeted and injured, nursed her grievances and retreated to lick her wounds. She came to expect that there would be at least a short season of calm—the eye of the hurricane—between Bonaparte's destructive gusts, during which he would treat her with less severity and even show her a condescending tenderness. But she could never allow that lull in the tempest to blind her to the true state of affairs between them, for new storm clouds were always gathering, new mistresses appearing, and for Josephine, the skies were permanently dark.

She struck out blindly against the oppressive darkness, making her situation known to all those who served her, to visitors to the palace, even to tradespeople who came to sell her jewelry and hats and objets d'art. She ordered her waiting women to write venomous letters, full of reproaches, to her husband's mistresses, and then to send these unsigned denunciations via courier. She wrung her hands and wept over the wrongs done to her by her new nemesis Caroline Murat, who took an active role in encouraging the first consul's love life, introducing him to pleasing and available young women, arranging assignations, reminding him of Josephine's inadequacies and of her inability to bear children.

With tearful anguish Josephine poured into the astonished ears of her ladies stories of Bonaparte's base nature, how he was unrestrained by any moral scruples in fulfilling his vicious desires, how, if the eyes of the world were not on him at all times, providing a check on his worst excesses, he would give free rein to gross and unspeakable vice. Had he not seduced his sisters, one by one? she asked rhetorically. Did he not believe himself to be so far above ordinary humankind that he deserved to act out all his erotic fantasies, no matter how vile?[5]

Passing from suggestive slander to an active search for proof of Bonaparte's infidelities (proof hardly being needed, since he boasted of them), Josephine began hounding her husband and his mistresses in hopes of catching them in bed together. One night she woke Claire de Rémusat long after midnight in an animated state.

"I can't put up with this any longer," she whispered. She was certain that Bonaparte was in the small apartment off his upstairs study with one of his current lovers, the celebrated actress Mademoiselle George from the Comédie-Française. "I want to surprise them," she told the younger woman, preparing to climb the stairs to Bonaparte's study. Madame de Rémusat protested, but Josephine was almost obsessively determined to carry out her plan.

"Follow me," she said. "We'll go up together." She started up the narrow winding stairs, driven by her own excessive energy, with her companion behind her. Suddenly they heard a noise. Her nerves on edge, Josephine started, then drew back.

"Perhaps that is Roustan, guarding the door," she whispered. "That wretch is capable of slitting both our throats." Roustan, Bonaparte's massive mameluke, slept on a mat in front of Bonaparte's door, armed and forbidding.

Now Madame de Rémusat went back down the winding stair, as fast as she could in her long skirts, the clatter she made no doubt audible to the occupants of the upstairs rooms. Josephine, left in the dark (for her companion had the only candle), followed shortly afterward, laughing at the frightened look on her waiting lady's face, and the project was abandoned.[6]

On another occasion, however, Josephine's compulsion to discover Bonaparte with another woman led to a crippling contretemps. The court was at St-Cloud, where a staircase led from Bonaparte's private apartments to a hidden upstairs room that he used for erotic rendezvous. One night Josephine became suspicious when she saw Adèle Duchâtel, a tempting twenty-year-old brought to court by the Murats, slip away from the group gathered in the salon. Certain that Adèle was on her way to join Bonaparte, Josephine left her guests, beside herself with jealous passion, and made her way to the private apartment at the top of the stairs. The door was closed, but she could hear, through the keyhole, the sound of Bonaparte's voice and Adèle's. She knocked loudly.

"It is I, Josephine," she announced.

"You will imagine the trouble I caused them!" Josephine told

Claire de Rémusat, describing the scene. "They took a long time opening the door, and when they did, the state they were both in, their disorder, left no possible doubt. I knew I ought to restrain myself, but I couldn't. I scolded them."[7]

Adèle burst into tears, and Bonaparte, as furious as Josephine had ever seen him, became so violently angry that Josephine fled to her own apartments, trembling and so upset that she could hardly contain herself.

"All is lost!" she told her waiting woman. "What I anticipated is only too true.... I don't know what he'll do. He'll come, I'm sure of that, and I dread a terrible scene."

The terrible scene was not long in arriving. Bonaparte came crashing through Josephine's rooms, breaking furniture, shouting threats, and "insulting her in every possible way," according to the story as she told it later. No doubt there were slaps, hard pinches, rough shaking and quite possibly more, along with foul oaths and threats. The contempt in his voice was nearly as harsh as a blow. He shouted at her to pack her things and go. Her constant spying was intolerable. From now on, he said, he would listen to those who told him to get another wife, one who wasn't barren and old. He would abandon her, he said. She would be penniless.

Josephine was shattered, and sent for Hortense, who was often able to mollify her stepfather. But Hortense was not able to intervene. Her husband ordered her to keep her distance from the quarrel; like his siblings, Louis Bonaparte hoped for a definitive rupture between the first consul and his wife.

Bonaparte summoned Eugene, and told him—now somewhat calmer, but no less resolute—that he had made up his mind to divorce Josephine. Eugene, who was astute enough to understand that there was much more to the situation than a damaging domestic quarrel, did not try to dissuade his stepfather. He merely said that he would follow his mother wherever she decided to go, even back to Martinique.

For two days a tense and unsettled mood pervaded the palace. Servants tiptoed in and out of rooms, household officials attempted to maintain a discreet obliviousness to the strained atmosphere, though it was evident to everyone that the marriage had come to a critical point. Josephine, responding to the emergency by abandoning her reckless combativeness, and using her skills of seduction, submission and tears, gradually managed to bring Bonaparte back from the brink of dismissing her once and for all.

When at last a fragile reconciliation had been achieved, Josephine saw that she was on uncertain ground. Bonaparte told her candidly, laying aside his harsh façade and revealing his tender side, that he faced an irresolvable dilemma. His political interests were pushing him toward divorce, yet he confessed that he lacked the strength to renounce her. As long as she was obedient, and did not pursue or vex him about his liaisons with other women, he would not abandon her. Yet he asked her to do for him what he could not do for himself: to take on the responsibility of sacrificing her position as his wife when the appropriate political moment arrived.

"I want you to resign yourself to serving my political advantage," he said. "Of yourself, you can spare me the embarrassment of this painful separation."[8]

He expected her to step aside, of her own volition, when he felt that the time was right. Knowing this, she could never feel secure again. And in the meantime, while she waited for the signal that she must sacrifice herself, she did not dare object to his love affairs.

A momentous political realignment was in fact underway. By an act of the subservient Senate, in May of 1804 Bonaparte was elevated to the rank of Emperor of the French. A popular plebiscite confirmed his new status, and seemed to crown all his remarkable achievements with this ultimate accolade. Some republicans objected to the monarchical flavor of this new honor, but the vast majority of the emperor's subjects were carried along on a tidal wave of delighted approval. Emperor Napoleon I was, in their eyes, the symbol of a victorious France, splendid and unconquerable in battle, astute in governance, the arbiter of Europe's destiny. He both aroused and satisfied their patriotism, their battle lust, their thirst for military glory. A few months after his elevation to imperial rank, the French began officially celebrating "Saint Napoleon's Day," the emperor's birthday, August 15.

The new emperor underwent a personal transformation to accompany his advancement. Observers noted that he appeared more serious and severe, his gaze more lordly, his voice more stern and commanding. He developed a nervous tic at the corner of his mouth—a sign of his struggle for greater self-mastery—and he abandoned the simple uniform he had always worn for clothes that gleamed with rich ornamentation. His manner, always focused and preoccupied, now became lofty, the manner, one contemporary thought, of "a man who nourishes vast projects." His features "betrayed a violent and murderous ambition," revealing the passionate, driven, unsettled private man behind the imperial façade.

The emperor's self-image kept pace with his increased dominance. He surrounded himself with portrait busts of great men—Hannibal, Caesar, Scipio—and paintings of such heroes as King Charles XII of Sweden, reminders that he now belonged to an elite inner circle of eminence. He read aloud from the plays of Corneille—never quite getting the hang of the alexandrines, Claire de Rémusat thought—with their solemn, weighty pronouncements on fateful ends and noble destinies.

"I would like," he told his brother Joseph, "to be my posterity, to know the opinion men hold of me. I would like to hear the blazing verses a great poet, such as Corneille, will write about my deeds."[9]

Radiating an awareness of his own numinous luster, reeking of the musky cologne with which he showered himself daily, the emperor moved among his courtiers with a fixed smile on his lips, nodding to the right and to the left and swaying slightly (for he had been informed by old servants of Louis XVI that the late king had walked with a swaying gait). In his presence all conversation immediately ceased, all eyes were turned to him, and people hastened to form themselves into orderly rows between which their ruler walked, conspicuous and self-conscious, followed at a considerable distance by his wife and other members of his entourage.

Just before his elevation Bonaparte had displayed his ruthlessness by an act of regicide that shocked and intimidated a people in the process of re-embracing monarchical ideals. In response to an attempt on his life by rightist conspirators, the first consul ordered the most promising of the young royal princes in exile, the Duc d'Enghien, seized and executed by a firing squad. To many of the French, this act of cold-blooded vengeance seemed brutal and unjustified; a shiver of fear ran down their spines and they murmured to one another wonderingly about what sort of man this Bonaparte could be, that he shed the sacred royal blood of France with such unfeeling dispatch.

Of course, the revolutionaries of 1793 had sent their king to the guillotine with an almost ghoulish exuberance, but then, Louis XVI had been guilty not only of misgoverning his people but of abandoning them, while the young Duc d'Enghien was blameless.

The judicial murder of the young prince, the imprisonment of Bonaparte's political enemies, the exiling of suspected conspirators to the distant Seychelles Islands in the Indian Ocean, all combined to create what some called a "little terror" around the emperor. This atmosphere of awe and dread prevailed at St-Cloud, the grand, formal palace to which the imperial court now gravitated.

Surrounded by stylized gardens in the classical mode of Versailles, the palace of St. Cloud had spacious courtyards where military reviews were held, an orangery, and long walkways between manicured expanses of grass and shrubbery. Nothing wild, nothing asymmetrical was allowed to flourish here; even Josephine's swans, floating in the large pond opposite the terrace, were regulated as to size and number, their breeding controlled and their liberty restricted.

Bonaparte spent a great deal on renovating St-Cloud in order to make it a fit setting for his honored position. Immense heroic portraits of the emperor adorned the spacious rooms. A gilded chair, not unlike a throne, was set aside for the emperor at one end of the vast audience chamber. When the emperor dined, he dined in state, in a royal dining hall, with others looking on, glad for the privilege of being able to observe him. Access to the palace was allowed to only an elite few, carefully screened for suitability. There were no old soldiers wandering in the grounds at St-Cloud, hoping for a chance meeting with their commander, as there once had been at Malmaison; now even the emperor's most valued comrades in arms were stopped at the gate, their identities verified and their business asked, before they were permitted to cross the threshold.

The emperor was distancing himself from everyone, including his wife. Although Josephine was present, smiling and gracious and elegantly dressed, at the palace receptions, and although she presided as hostess at the formal dinners for fifty or a hundred guests held in the huge, magnificently appointed state dining room of St-Cloud, she was no longer a central figure in Bonaparte's household. She was addressed as "Your Imperial Majesty" and she wore a queenly diadem of diamonds, but she was rarely by the emperor's side anymore; she walked, escorted by one of the palace prefects, many steps behind her husband, and they usually occupied opposite ends of whatever large room they found themselves in. Declaring that he would never again undergo the "subjection" of sharing his wife's bedroom, Bonaparte slept in his own bedroom, which was some distance from Josephine's. When he wanted to be with her at night he made the long trip from his room to hers, dressed in his robe, slippers and madras kerchief, and he made the journey infrequently enough so that the servants took note and Josephine boasted of their intimacy throughout the course of the following day.

She was eager, given her highly precarious position, to bask in his reflected glory, however fleetingly. Like everyone else at court, she was both afraid of Bonaparte and eager to clutch him to her, to claim whatever portion of his loyalty and affection still remained to her. She was still his wife; as he often said, he was in her debt for the help she had given him in reaching his present eminence.

Since Bonaparte was emperor, Josephine had no choice but to be the emperor's wife, though neither the gilded immensity of St-Cloud nor the coldly ceremonious atmosphere that prevailed there was congenial to her.

"I feel that I am not made for so much grandeur," Josephine wrote to Hortense. "I would be happier in some retreat, surrounded by the objects of my affections."[10] In the spring of 1804, Hortense was expecting her second child, and for Josephine, the pull of family must often have conflicted with the obligations of her high rank. She enjoyed her little grandson Napoleon very much, and must have looked forward to the arrival of a brother or sister to join him in the nursery.

The hope she had once cherished, that Hortense's son would take the place of the child she could not have, and become Bonaparte's heir, had faded. She knew now that, barring some unforeseen change of heart on her husband's part, her time as his wife would end in the not too distant future. He would command her to step aside, and as his subject, she would obey. She awaited his pleasure, submissive to her fate.

Though some part of her continued to protest, however impotently, against the humiliations and indignities to which he subjected her, her better judgment told her that resistance was futile. Like the great hurricane, Emperor Napoleon had gusted through her life, sweeping all before him, and her few remaining hopes lay devastated in his wake.

"May the Emperor Live Forever!"

The guns began firing at six o'clock on the evening of December 1, 1804, and went on at regular intervals until after midnight. The city was ablaze with light, sputtering lanterns glowing along the streets, house and shop windows illuminated, hilltops crowned with fires and gleaming braziers. Soldiers in new uniforms milled along the boulevards, waiting for the signal to take up their posts on the coronation route. In the cathedral of Notre Dame, workmen labored by torchlight long into the night, completing the high raised platform where the emperor would sit on his coronation day, and placing thousands of wax candles in the twenty-four crystal chandeliers hung from the ceiling.

For months Paris had been preparing for the coronation of Emperor Napoleon, and the flurry of excitement the coming event generated reached its peak in the last weeks of November. People rushed to secure rented rooms or rooftops on the streets where the emperor's coach would pass, or hurried to dressmakers and tailors for fittings for their new clothes. Many dinners and fêtes were to be held in the weeks following the coronation day, and well-to-do Parisians had to have fresh garments for each one. Their tasks accomplished, the shoppers stopped at the embroidery workshop where the emperor's sumptuous velvet mantle was being covered in bees sewn with gold thread, and at the jeweler's where his crown was on display, along with his diamond-studded sword.

The empress too was to be crowned, but this decision had been made only recently, and with much ambivalence, by Bonaparte. All his relatives were bitterly opposed to Josephine's exaltation to the rank of empress. She had been entirely unsuitable as his consort when he was first consul, they argued; now that he was emperor, she was infinitely more unsuitable.

The approach of the coronation brought their collective anger to the boiling point. Joseph and Louis flatly refused the role offered them in the coronation ceremony, that of "Grand Dignitary of the Empire." They would be princes or nothing, they declared; what was more, their virtuous wives could not possibly be expected to take a subordinate position to the notorious Josephine de Beauharnais. Elisa and Caroline were given the rank of "Imperial Highness," with lands and titles, but they were not satisfied. They insisted upon being princesses, as Paulette was; Paulette's husband Leclercq having died, she had married Prince Borghese a few months earlier. Letizia, Bonaparte's mother, was so offended at being accorded only the rank of "Madame, Mother of His Majesty the Emperor," that she retired to Rome and ignored the coronation entirely.

Harassed by his plangent relations, tired of their incessant scheming and resentful of their airs and hauteur toward Josephine, Bonaparte impulsively went to his wife's bedroom one night a few weeks before the coronation and, taking her in his arms, relieved her anxiety by telling her that she would be crowned along with him in Notre Dame.

"The pope will be here at the end of the month," he told her. "He will crown us both. Start to prepare for the ceremony."[1]

There had been little enough time to prepare, and a great deal to do. Rehearsals of the complex ritual were ongoing, with Jacques-Louis David, the court painter, leading everyone through the carefully choreographed service. Predictably, the rehearsals were tense, and interrupted frequently by quarrels over precedence and rank; though the emperor had forced his three sisters and two brothers (Lucien and Jerome being excluded from the proceedings) to participate, and to observe at least a semblance of correct behavior toward his wife, they were seething with hatred and took every excuse to object to their subordinate roles.

Led by Caroline, who was pregnant, the three sisters and Joseph's wife Julie refused absolutely to carry the immensely long train of Josephine's purple velvet mantle. The furor grew, Bonaparte intervened. But even his most imperious command could not break the deadlock, and the conflict threatened to become so bitter that all the Bonapartes might walk out. Everything came to a halt. Day after day anxious intermediaries attempted to resolve the dilemma, while Bonaparte endured the persistent clamor of family complaints.

It may have been during this seemingly irresolvable impasse that the emperor came to Josephine and asked her whether, in the interest of putting an end to the contentious question of the succession and silencing his relatives' objections, she would agree to take part in an elaborate deception. Would she be willing to say that she was pregnant, and maintain the ruse for a normal term, then undergo a fictive childbirth? If so, he would find another woman—indeed he may have thought he had found her already—who would carry his child and, at the appropriate time, give birth to it in secret, allowing him to say that it was Josephine's baby?

Josephine agreed. If she had any reservations, they are not recorded, and indeed Claire de Rémusat thought that she was only too eager to encourage her husband's schemes for parenthood, provided they allowed her to maintain her status as his wife. The idea was presented to the emperor's principal doctor, Corvisart, whose cooperation would be essential to its success. But Corvisart objected, on ethical grounds. He could not, he said, participate in such trickery, especially when the succession of the imperial throne was at stake. Thwarted, the emperor did not lash out at Corvisart, but accepted his judgment, and the project was dropped.[2]

The entire court was holding its breath, hoping for a resolution of the controversy over who would carry the empress's train. Nearly a week passed, and Bonaparte, worried and losing sleep, was becoming more and more harassed. It irked him that he could not bring himself to coerce his ill-humored sisters into cooperating, but the claims of family were strong, and he was captive to their demands. Fortunately a way was found to solve the problem without any loss of dignity on either side. Someone remembered that, in the wording of the coronation ritual a distinction was made between "holding the robe"—a task for inferiors to perform—and "supporting the mantle"—an honorary office performed by persons of consequence. Elisa, Caroline, Paulette and Julie, along with Hortense, agreed to "support the mantle" of the empress, provided each had a special chamberlain to carry her own trailing train.

But hardly was this difficulty resolved than another cropped up. Joseph and Louis, chafing over their precise prerogatives as brothers of the emperor, insisted on being allowed to wear ermine-trimmed grand mantles, ermine being the symbol of sacred royalty. Josephine's mantle was to be trimmed with ermine, they argued, and she had no true imperial blood. The emperor's brothers, who shared his blood as well as his name, ought to share his ermine.

This time all the officials of the court in charge of protocol became embroiled in the disagreement. Heated words flew among the archchancellor, the treasurer, the interior minister, the grand chamberlain, the grand ecuyer and the grand marshal of the court. Tense and sleepless, the emperor too no doubt erupted in rage, and Joseph, who as the oldest brother still considered himself to be head of the Bonaparte family, fumed over the insult to his patriarchal rights. It was bad enough that his younger brother the emperor would not follow his advice and divorce his wife; now he was being asked to forgo the symbol of royalty while Josephine was being allowed to flaunt it.

In the end, with the weight of official opinion against them, Joseph and Louis gave way. They would wear princely mantles, but not ermine-trimmed royal ones. They would ride in the coach with the emperor and empress, but they would not sit beside them on the raised dais inside the cathedral. On these and other points of privilege the Bonapartes were defeated, and the defeats rankled, so that on the morning of the coronation day, their stony anger was evident on their disgruntled faces.

A visitor to Josephine a few days before the coronation found her in tears. She was nervous and anxious, under siege from outfitters and dressmakers, court officers and the usual array of petitioners entreating her favors. Her in-laws sneered at her and insulted her at every opportunity, and she dreaded the solemn, highly public ceremony at which she would have to perform. And she had another source of grief. Her husband had once again "gone into heat," and was exhibiting his usual unpleasant symptoms.

With the ladies of the palace he was unusually sprightly and animated, playful and flirtatious—"a real sultan," Claire de Rémusat thought. With Josephine he was harsh and reproachful, silencing her and keeping her at arm's length while he surrounded himself with many women, though in fact attracted by one in particular. What made this intrigue complex was that the object of his passion, the blonde, blue-eyed Elizabeth de Vaudey, was involved with Eugene, who was in love with her, and when she dropped Eugene for the emperor, the latter treated his stepson coldly for a time. Caroline, seeing that her brother was seriously infatuated with Elizabeth de Vaudey, and hoping that this infatuation might prompt him at last to divorce Josephine, stirred up conflict between the empress and Elizabeth, while at the same time attempting to fool Josephine by creating the impression that Murat and Elizabeth were lovers.[3]

Eventually Josephine realized the truth. Hurt and angry, she sent her servants to spy on Elizabeth, but nothing she did could dampen Bonaparte's infatuation, which only seemed to grow stronger with the approach of coronation day.

There was one more concern troubling Josephine. Pope Pius could not crown an emperor and empress who had been united only by a civil ceremony; there had to be a religious marriage. Bonaparte exerted his influence over his uncle, Cardinal Fesch, who at the last minute presided at a nuptial mass in the chapel of the Tuileries, with only two of the emperor's junior officers as witnesses. Because no parish priest was present, the legality of the ceremony was open to challenge under canon law, but Josephine obtained a written attestation that it had been performed, and afterward treated this document as one of her most precious possessions. Although Bonaparte had made it clear that one day she would have to give up her status as his wife, she continued to hope that her written proof of having undergone a religious marriage, along with her consecration as empress, might act as a brake on his divorce plans.[4]

Coronation day dawned overcast and bitterly cold. The freshly swept streets bore a rime of hoar frost, and from time to time there was a light fall of snow. Rows of soldiers were in place along the coronation route, standing in long ranks three deep. Behind them, squeezed up against houses and storefronts, Parisians waited for a glimpse of the emperor and empress and their retinue. They were more curious than eager, one observer thought; there had not been a coronation in Paris in nearly thirty years, and most people in the crowd had no memory of the last one.

At first light guests began arriving at the cathedral, shivering in their thin gowns and dress uniforms. There was no heat in the vast, high-ceilinged church; the air was so cold that the court officials, arriving after having walked in procession from the Palais de Justice, could see their breath freeze in front of their faces.

Presently the clatter of hooves on the icy cobblestones announced the coming of the pope, riding in a state carriage and escorted by dragoons, the apostolic cross carried before him. That the head of the Catholic Church, wearing his tiara and accompanied by six red-robed cardinals and a hundred bishops, could come to Notre Dame to say mass would have been inconceivable only a few years earlier. To those raised during the revolutionary years, when only the worship of Reason was permitted and churches were converted to taverns or stables or dance halls, the sight of the ascetic old man raising his hand to bless the onlookers must have seemed both exotic and some-how out of place.

Toward mid-morning there was a stir of anticipation in the crowd. The roaring of cannon from the Place du Carrousel heralded the departure of the imperial party. At the head of the long, slow-moving parade was Murat, governor of Paris, followed by hundreds of hussars in silver and gold and chasseurs in scarlet. Mounted officers escorted carriages carrying the state dignitaries, the masters of ceremonies and the emperor's sisters. Conspicuous among the mounted riders was the emperor's Egyptian bodyguard Roustan, arrayed in all his mameluke finery in a new pearl-studded dolman of green velvet.

Frenzied shouts arose from the spectators when the great gilded imperial coach rolled into view, drawn by eight cream-colored Spanish horses and surrounded on all sides by twenty cavalry squadrons. Nothing like it had been seen since the days of the old regime: the huge berline, topped by a golden crown, its painted panels covered with laurel wreaths, stars, bees (the new imperial symbol) and the letter *N*, gleamed in the wintry light, its immense wheels grinding noisily over the uneven surface of the narrow streets. Through the wide glass windows the emperor could be seen clearly, wearing a purple mantle and a white-plumed velvet hat, and beside him the empress, all in shining white, a brilliant bandeau of diamonds covering her brow.

It was nearly noon when the imperial coach drew up in the crowded square before the cathedral and the occupants proceeded to a nearby structure to put on their ceremonial robes. Inside the cathedral, sellers of lemonade and warm rolls and "bonbons à la Bonaparte" moved among the waiting guests, who by this time had been sitting, cramped and uncomfortable, for five hours.

Their tedium was forgotten, however, when the four hundred musicians of the orchestra began to play and Josephine, in a long white satin gown that sparkled with diamonds and gold and silver embroidery, began her stately procession toward the altar. Many were struck by her extraordinary grace and youthful beauty on that day. Despite the cares that burdened her, the stress of recent weeks and the sheer physical labor of walking in extremely heavy garments, the empress walked along the aisle as one transfigured, looking, Madame de Rémusat thought, like a girl of twenty-five.

Moving at a stately pace through the vaulted cavern of the ancient cathedral, her solitary figure dwarfed by its scale, Josephine must have been overpowered by strong sensate impressions. The volume of sound from the orchestra, the lingering scent of incense combined with the mingled colognes of the guests and the smell of candle wax, the richness of color, from the crimson cloths covering the walls to the vivid green carpet to the bright violets and blues and scarlets of the uniforms and liveries, all combined to drench her in sensations. And when, after the pope had anointed and blessed both the emperor and empress, Josephine knelt before her husband to receive her imperial circlet from his hands, she could not contain herself; her tears flowed freely as he took his time adjusting the crown over her tight curls, his manner almost playful.

She wore her circlet, the guests thought, with far more grace than many who were born to royalty, and throughout the three-hour ceremony she performed her intricate sequence of movements flawlessly. But her sisters-in-law, fuming and chafing, could not resist their impulse to malice. As the empress left the altar to approach the twenty-four steps that led to her throne and her husband's, her malevolent trainbearers suddenly dropped her eighty-pound mantle, leaving her to support its full weight. She could not move forward. The ceremony could not proceed.

"The emperor, seeing this, addressed a few dry and firm words to his sisters," it was noticed, and to the surprise of all, they obeyed him, hoisting the heavy train once again and following Josephine to the bottom of the steps. How she managed to ascend them unaided, pulling the heavy mantle along, was a mystery much commented on after the long ritual was over, but ascend she did, until both she and the emperor took their seats on their tall gilded thrones.

It was a glorious and memorable moment. The pope cried out in a loud voice, "Vivat imperator in aeternum!"—"May the emperor live forever!"—and the orchestra burst into rapturous peals of sound that echoed and re-echoed between the tall pillars and up toward the soaring stone vaulting. Josephine, both resplendent and appealing, was visibly moved, while Bonaparte, who had crowned himself with a golden crown of laurel leaves, was pale, his mouth set in a severe line and his face tense.[5] He was never truly happy unless he was active; after several hours of overdressed passivity, he itched to escape into busyness once again.

Josephine, in the first few months of her reign as empress, could hardly have been busier. The sweet indolence she had once enjoyed was completely gone, and her time was regulated according to a carefully constructed schedule. There were no more long undisciplined evenings, no more indulgence, no more languor; her once leisurely pace, her slow, fluid movements gave way to a tempo of hurry and agitation.

She had a great deal to do. The emperor expected his wife to supervise the observance of palace etiquette, and to ensure that the expanding corpus of regulations prescribed in the official etiquette book be carried out without default. It was her responsibility to invite the young wives of the court to breakfast and introduce them to the subtleties of the recently installed social code. She was to implement the emperor's specific requests, as when he ordered that ladies be taught to curtsey to him in the deep, sweeping manner once common at the Bourbon court, before the revolution. Josephine became, in one aspect at least, a kind of imperial housemother, expected to be alert to any and all breaches of decorum—an exhausting task, as there seemed to be no end to the protocols of the palace.

It was not just that there were rules in place excluding many unsuitable people from the imperial precincts. Each of the hundreds of household servants and officials, from the five bedchamber women to the footmen, equerries and pages had specific duties and privileges, and each was restricted as to where he or she was allowed to sit or stand, which rooms he or she was allowed to enter and how he or she was to dress, speak and approach superiors and inferiors. The rank of each household member in the hierarchy of status, the rules governing precedence—who was to enter a doorway first, who was allowed to speak directly to the empress (practically no one), which of her ladies, having the oldest and noblest prerevolutionary name, ought to occupy the senior position among her peers. The etiquette book governed nearly everything: the proper serving of meals, their number of courses, the correct way to eat; the rituals of the empress's morning levée and the emperor's bath, the stipulations concerning mourning, weddings, baptisms and other rituals; the codes of dress; even the placement of furnishings in the empress's "interior apartments," her private rooms to which only a few dozen servants and ladies of her suite had access.

When the etiquette book was silent, there were speaking oracles to be consulted, Madame Campan, Madame de la Tour du Pin, who had been a young girl at the court of Marie Antoinette, and the Marquise de Montesson, Josephine's primary teacher and guide, who was frequently at hand to remind her "never to forget that she was the wife of a great man."

In her role as hostess, Josephine was kept constantly in a state of preparing for, or presiding over, official events. There were dreary suppers for aging generals and balls for five hundred guests, civic and military festivals held in the open air over which the empress had to preside, looking serene and amiable, for hours while her limbs grew stiff and her ears and nose became red from the cold. There were nights at the opera and theatrical evenings at the palace where the emperor's sisters Caroline and Elisa, who fancied themselves gifted thespians, made the assembled audience titter and yawn. There were small "teas" at three in the afternoon, and late suppers, and concerts at the palace by celebrated Italian singers. At her morning receptions, the empress received a wide range of people, from arrogant or unctuous ambassadors to elderly former emigrés to military men who stood out awkwardly and had to be drawn into conversation by their tactful hostess.

Occasionally Josephine invited men of letters to the palace to read from their works. While they recited, she sat at her tapestry frame, working designs in wool. She made them feel welcome, and charmed them with her warmth and pleasant, even-tempered personality; they even forgave the frequent barking of Fortuné, who sat beside his mistress and growled, and on one occasion, bit Josephine's favorite writer, Antoine Arnault, on the calf.[6]

These literary gatherings were from time to time marred by the absurd presence of Elisa, costumed as a muse in outlandish multicolored veils and a laurel leaf crown, holding forth on the merits of the poems and plays as they were read. She had long since tired of the company of her dull Corsican husband and was accompanied everywhere by her poet-lover Fontanes, a vulgarian of modest literary attainments who looked to Elisa for his inspiration.

Josephine appeared to surmount the nuisance of Elisa's presence as she surmounted every other social inconvenience—by smoothing over any awkwardness with her kind solicitude and by setting the tone of every social event with her elegant yet approachable manner. She remembered people's names, and had the gift of making each one feel singled out and welcomed. She was genuinely concerned whenever she heard of someone in distress or undergoing hardship. She had long been known for her benevolence and good deeds; stories of her aid had spread through Paris time and again, with the result that her old reputation for frivolity and loose living had been overtaken by a reputation for goodness. Parisians who had no direct contact with her loved her nonetheless for her many kind acts, and for her lack of hauteur. Although, as empress, she was surrounded by considerable pomp and state she was never aloof or inaccessible. Her humility was as much admired as her beautiful gowns and lustrous pearls.

"I win battles," Bonaparte remarked, "but Josephine wins hearts." Her social abilities had always been valuable to him, though they were no longer essential. He did not really need her, and she knew it. By making herself useful to him, by doing well the job he had set her to do, she hoped to prolong their marriage. There was no question, however, that she had become completely dependent on him, and was almost pathetically grateful to him for delaying the moment when he would cast her aside.

With her accession as empress Josephine conceded what was left of her independence. In effect she made a bargain with Bonaparte. She would fulfill her demanding role, and enjoy its perquisites, as long as he would put off the divorce which he had told her was inevitable. But she would not resist him any longer. Her capitulation was final, and complete. Her spirit was broken.

"I wish to be always in your eyes the good, the tender Josephine, concerned only with your happiness," she wrote him. "My wish is ... to please you, to love you—rather, to adore you!"⁷ The adoration she promised was that of a worshipful subject, not that of a wife. The mixed emotions Josephine felt as Bonaparte's wife no longer mattered. They had been subsumed by stronger, larger loyalties, the unambivalent loyalties of inferior to superior, servant to master, vassal to lord. And just as a servant derived dignity from his or her place in a noble household, Empress Josephine, having laid aside her old persona with its resentments, grudges and rebellions, found dignity— or at least a measure of relief—in her new role.

Yet her insecurities and fear remained, and deepened.

Her manner, though ever gracious, had a constant undertone of diffidence. Her insecurity lent her charm, and brought her the affection of others. But it made her continuously vulnerable to Bonaparte, who played on it incessantly. When she overspent, as she did more and more, he demanded to see the bills and she trembled and wept, terrified to face his rage. When her throbbing headaches kept her in bed, she feared his displeasure, and knew that at any moment he might appear in her darkened room and yank her roughly out of bed, commanding her to get up and dress and carry out some public function, steeling herself to bear the increased pain brought on by any activity. She lived in a state of dread, and her headaches increased in frequency and worsened.

To be sure, Josephine's overly controlled, highly regimented life as empress brought with it many benefits. She was able to write to her mother, who throughout her adult life had never known what it was to be debt free, and tell her that she, Josephine, was personally taking on all her outstanding debt and paying it off—at the cost of increasing her own financial obligations, of course. In addition, she was able to arrange to have the treasury send her mother a pension of a hundred thousand francs a year. She gave houses, pensions, and court positions to her cousins and their in-laws. All six of her Uncle Robert's children came to Paris from Martinique with their father and were grandly housed on the rue de la Victoire, at the empress's expense.

The number and value of the many gifts she received as empress far exceeded what had come to her as wife of the first consul. Jewels, fine paintings, lengths of costly fabric, beautiful furnishings arrived at St-Cloud and the Tuileries, until there was no more room in Josephine's private apartments for them. Special rooms were set aside to receive her gifts, and they increased month by month until, in the end, they simply remained in the crates and trunks in which they were sent, unopened.[8]

Because she was unable to live within the limits of her allotted income, the financial security she had sought in earlier years still eluded Josephine, but she had the satisfaction of surrounding herself with signs of abundance. Her wardrobes were heaped with gowns, slippers, fans, and lingerie—much of it unworn. Ignoring Bonaparte's explicit orders to the contrary, merchants crowded in to her salon each morning to offer her tempting new modes, bonnets, furs and fabrics. She bought lavishly, and gave much away. She was able to fill all her rooms with sweet-smelling flowers. She wanted for nothing material, even though her apparent prosperity rested on a growing heap of unpaid bills.

Her precarious life as empress went on as, heavily rouged and draped with the jewels Bonaparte ordered the finance minister to send her from the treasury, Josephine appeared before the emperor's subjects, smiling graciously and speaking the words he had given her to memorize, knowing that if she misspoke them, his spies would be sure to let their master know.

25

"Josephine Empress of the French"

The warm sun of Italy beat down on the imperial carriage as it made its way along between rows of smartly uniformed cavalry officers, its speed decreasing as it reached the outskirts of Milan. Josephine, sitting beside her husband on the upholstered seat, fanned herself rapidly and closed her eyes, giving in to the weariness she felt. They had been traveling for a month, making the long and at times perilous journey southward from Paris through Burgundy and the Dauphiné and over the high passes of the Alps into the Lombard plain. Bonaparte was to be crowned King of Italy in Milan, and the Milanese, full of excitement and a spirit of celebration, had turned out in large numbers to greet them.

Seen in the harsh glare of noon, Josephine looked much older than her husband. Her thick white makeup and rouged cheeks gave her the appearance of a painted doll, and though her costume was splendid, it could not disguise the careworn look she wore, or the lines of pain on her drawn features. On the emperor's coronation day in Paris five months earlier, in the dim, flattering candlelight of Notre Dame, Josephine had looked youthful, but in the full light of day she looked older than her forty-two years, frail and dispirited.

The weeks of journeying had drained her, the long bouts of travel on poor roads, the nights of scant sleep in unfamiliar beds, the succession of formal receptions, parties and entertainments at each town that required her to be on display and maintain her queenly persona through hours of tedious socializing. Having missed much sleep, she was fatigued, and fatigue inevitably brought on the daggers of pain in her head that seemed to make her skin, her hair, even her eyes throb in misery, bringing dizziness and nausea and a longing for oblivion.

The carriage passed deeper into the city and the shouting, whistling and cheering of the Milanese became louder, all but drowning out the hoofbeats of the mounted escort, and a clangor of bells rang out from dozens of churches. The noise seemed to intensify the heat, and the empress, always on edge when riding in a carriage, began to feel trapped and craved air.

As the jubilation in the street grew more intense and guns began firing in salute, Josephine was able, from time to time, to catch a glimpse of her son, riding alongside the imperial coach, tall and imperturbable, in command of the cavalry squadron. Eugene was twenty-three, a good soldier with many years of experience despite his youth, physically adept and personable. He resembled his handsome father, whose memory he continued to revere. Bonaparte loved and trusted Eugene, and called him his "fearless, blameless knight"— the phrase associated with the great medieval hero of the Italian wars, the knight Bayard. Only recently he had given his stepson the title His Highness Prince Eugene, Arch-Chancellor of State and of the Empire.

Josephine fixed her gaze on her son, and the sight of him helped to steady her, and prevent her from becoming dizzy, as she often did when in distress. Keeping her attention on him, she was able to regain some measure of composure, so that when they reached the center of the city and made their way to the cathedral, she was calmer. She walked behind her husband into the church and knelt beside him to pray.

It was cool under the great dome, and quiet, save for the sound of workmen preparing for the coronation. Though the noise of the crowd outside could be heard, it was muffled, absorbed by the spacious interior and the thick old walls. As she knelt in the dimness, Josephine began to feel restored. Later, having recovered at least some of her balance and calm, she was able to go outside again and follow

Bonaparte as he met with the archbishop and other civic dignitaries in the first of what would be many receptions.

Bonaparte's coronation as King of Italy was the climax of an Italian sojourn that was to last for several months. The coronation itself, a theatrical affair with much pomp and splendor, put Josephine under little stress, for she was not crowned Queen of Italy; she merely sat, with the sour, cantankerous Elisa Bacciochi beside her, on a platform while the ceremony proceeded.

There were no difficulties over precedence this time, for Josephine wore no train, and Elisa was not called upon to support it. There was, however, much bad feeling, as Elisa was discontented with the title her brother had given her, Princess of Lucca and Piombino. Lucca and Piombino, she pointed out, were sorry little principalities, hardly worthy of her. When, shortly after the coronation, Eugene was created viceroy of Italy Elisa was mortified, and was pointedly rude to Josephine and her son every time they shared a banquet table or a salon.

Subdued and fatigued as she was, Josephine let Elisa's rudeness flow over her and did not react to it. Elisa and her siblings, Josephine told Eugene, "all are mistaken in failing to like us. If they were willing to be decent people, they would find no better friends than we."[1] She did her best to return good for evil, showing at times a marked benevolence toward her in-laws—not on principle, or for her own gain, but because it came naturally to her. She had never been vindictive. Had she been able to adopt other tactics toward the Bonapartes, such as confronting them angrily, or using her remaining influence with her husband to turn him against them, she might have been surprised to find that she could intimidate them, for they respected force and passion, and showed wariness in the face of a declared enemy. But she never stooped to their level, and the result was that their combined animosity and their continual machinations preyed on her fragile peace of mind.

For six weeks the newly crowned King of Italy toured the cities of the Romagna, while his uncrowned queen visited Lake Como and Lake Maggiore, in search of ease and rest. Bonaparte inspected fortresses and reviewed troops, instructing his deputy Eugene and passing on to him the news brought several times a day by couriers from Paris.

The news was ominous. William Pitt, the British prime minister, was gathering allies against France. Russia and Sweden had pledged to send troops against Bonaparte, and soon after his Italian coronation the emperor learned that Francis II of Austria had been added to the enemy coalition. There was little time to waste. Soon a campaign would have to be launched, for Russian and Austrian troops were being massed in large numbers for an assault against the newly created French Empire.

The Italian sojourn, which Bonaparte had hoped to prolong, was cut short: word reached the emperor at Turin, where he and Josephine were staying, that three separate foreign armies were forming, and would soon be on the march. Bonaparte announced that he would be leaving at once—and Josephine, her insecurities and fears of abandonment quickened, asked to be allowed to leave with him.

She could go with him, he said, but only—and the point was given stern emphasis—if she agreed not to suffer any migraines for the duration of the journey. He could not afford any delays. If she became ill they would not be able to stop to allow her to rest.

She agreed.

They set off, a cortege of some half-dozen carriages, with the emperor and empress riding together and their servants following, along with several carriages full of trunks. Bonaparte, his agile mind engaged with a thousand plans to be put into effect once he arrived at his headquarters, was impatient. He ordered the driver to make the fastest time possible, and soon the imperial carriage had begun to outpace the slower vehicles. The horses were driven to the limit of their endurance, and the carriage, bouncing roughly along on its slender wheels, shuddered and shook and seemed destined to break an axle, if not to overturn.

Shutting her eyes and holding on, Josephine endured the jolts and vibrations of the rocking vehicle, willing herself to overcome her fears. She had never before traveled so far in such haste, or in such inconvenience—for Bonaparte refused to stop except to change horses—and by the end of the second day they were far ahead of their servants and baggage, so that at night no lodgings were prepared for them, no food cooked, no beds made up or fires laid. Josephine had never been without a maid, or hardly ever; now there was no one to help her dress or arrange her hair, and she did not even have a change of clothes.

After the better part of a week they arrived, travelworn and tired, at Fontainebleau, where the palace servants, who were not expecting them for several days, were unprepared to receive them. Amid much scurrying and improvising a meal was thrown together, rooms warmed and beds made up. Almost immediately, however, Bonaparte went on to Boulogne, by himself, to supervise the French forces that had long been assembled there in anticipation of an invasion of England—an invasion whose present likelihood was small. Josephine, before long, left for Plombières, where she planned to spend the remainder of the summer.

The spa town of Plombières was decorated as never before to receive the empress. Flowers and greenery lined the streets, and the Capuchin convent, where the source of the healthful mineral waters flowed forth, was decorated with colorful hangings and banners. All the pine trees on both sides of the road into the town were outlined in lights of colored glass, which twinkled in the evening breeze. A large crowd had assembled in the afternoon to acclaim the empress on her arrival, and hundreds of people were still waiting, drowsy and cold, late in the evening when her carriage at last appeared on the torchlit road and fireworks burst forth to announce her presence.

Josephine had stayed at the spa many times before, but never as empress. Now the town officials, self-consciously aware of having royalty in their midst, insisted that she accept a large military escort to be on guard wherever she went, despite her protestations that the thirty soldiers she already had were more than adequate to keep her from harm. There was no escaping the marks of respect shown her throughout her stay at the spa. The soldiers were always on duty, the townspeople held periodic social events in her honor and expected to be entertained in return, and there were always small crowds on hand to call out or cheer when the empress came in sight. While taking the waters or making short trips in the hills around the town she was pursued by onlookers eager for a glimpse of her.

True relaxation was impossible. Even her leisure hours were occupied with arranging concerts and suppers, or having her portrait painted, or playing with her infant grandchild Napoleon-Louis, Hortense's second son, who joined her for a short time.

"He is very good-looking," Josephine wrote to Eugene in Italy, telling him about the baby. She had hopes that before long Eugene would have children of his own, for Bonaparte had been working to arrange a marriage for him with Princess Augusta of Bavaria, a sixteen-year-old beauty. "I have seen her portrait," Josephine told Eugene. "Nothing could be more lovely." If, as hoped, Eugene married into the old and respected house of Wittelsbach then both of Josephine's children would have exalted rank, and their futures—and hers—would be made more secure. When the time came for Bonaparte to divorce Josephine, she could take refuge with her children.

"I am ceaselessly occupied with you," she wrote to Eugene early in August, "with what you are doing, with your pleasures, but above all with your difficulties." She worried about the onset of war, about what would happen to her "tenderest of sons" when the fighting began. He had promised to come and visit her in the winter, when the campaigning season was over. In the meantime, she wrote, she missed him terribly.

"I groan always to be separated from you, my eyes are always full of tears, when I think of you or speak of you."[2]

She assured Eugene that her own life continued to be calmer. She no longer made jealous scenes, she accepted with resignation her husband's inevitable amours. "No more jealousy," she told her son. "He is happier and I am too." While they were in Italy she had discovered that Bonaparte was involved with a young woman in her entourage, but she hadn't spoken out accusingly about it. She had merely sent the young woman away, knowing that before long there would be another to take her place in the emperor's bed. She realized that it was useless for her to try to intervene, or to prevent his adulteries. Besides, it was often hard for her to summon the strength required for indignation. Acceptance was less taxing.

Late in September Bonaparte took Josephine with him when he rode eastward to begin his campaign against the continental armies. He left her in Strasbourg, in a suite of her own in the episcopal palace, while he went on through the German states, his armies moving with such remarkable speed that within weeks the vanguard of the Austrian army was cornered at Ulm and starved into surrender. Marching through pouring rain, sleeping in muddy fields despite bone-chilling cold, the imperial soldiers went on, after taking Vienna, to face the Russians in Moravia.

"I am on top of the world," Josephine wrote to Eugene after receiving news of the victory at Ulm. She told him of the thousands of prisoners captured, the battle flags and cannon taken, the good news Bonaparte had sent her, that "everything speaks to me of the most favorable campaign, the shortest and most brilliant ever carried out."[3] Her presentiments of defeat had turned out to be wrong. Bonaparte and his armies were prevailing over superior numbers, with relatively few casualties of their own.

"My health is very good," Josephine told her son. "I often go walking in the town and another part of the day I spend reading. That is what I am able to do best, far from the emperor and far from you." At the many receptions and balls over which she presided, she received the loud applause and hearty congratulations of the German princes and dignitaries present. Praise intended for the French armies and their extraordinary commander was showered on her, as her husband's surrogate. When she went to the theater, the entire audience stood and applauded enthusiastically. When her carriage passed along the street, Strasbourgers rushed up beside it and called out to her, expressing their admiration and loyalty.

She waited, excited and expectant, for Bonaparte to summon her to join him on campaign. Meanwhile she gave a grand fête for the ladies of Strasbourg, arranged for the presentation of a French opera, *La Vestale*, and received visitors in her suite of rooms, making sure each one was given a souvenir of his or her visit—a snuffbox with her portrait on it, or a small piece of jewelry.

Amid the freezing November sleet, marching at times in snow that drifted nearly waist-high, the Grande Armée went to face the Russians. Shrunken in numbers to seventy-three thousand men, and precariously far from its bases on the Rhine, where supplies and ammunition were stored, the army faced a crisis point. The Russians had eighty-five thousand men and twice as much artillery as the French, and reinforcements on the way.

On the night of December 1, camped near the Moravian village of Austerlitz, the emperor walked among his men, heartening them and assuring them of victory. Ragged cries broke from thousands of throats as he passed, the men formed a long procession and, by the light of torches, led him in honor to his tent.

The following morning the French skirmishers started forward against the Russian ranks, followed by columns of shouting infantry, bugles blowing and flags flying. Disorganized by French artillery fire, and unable to use their own guns to advantage, the Russians fell back, their lines breached. The French cavalry rushed in, and within hours the fighting was over. Twenty thousand Russian prisoners were taken, and many guns. Thirty thousand of the enemy lay dead and dying on the field of battle. Tsar Alexander, who had been in command, fled to safety in Hungary.

The continental armies lay in ruins. Emperor Napoleon, his forces strengthened by small numbers of German troops, had defeated the combined forces of Britain, Austria, Prussia and Russia, their armies far larger and their resources far greater—and defeated them so decisively that he was master of Europe. More lands were added to the French Empire, along with a substantial indemnity paid by the defeated nations to the French treasury.

Josephine was on her way to Munich, where her husband had promised to meet her and where, it was hoped, an agreement would be reached with Princess Augusta's father Maximilien Joseph, Elector of Bavaria, to marry the princess to Eugene.

Bonaparte instructed Josephine to conduct herself with greater detachment and regal majesty than ever, now that she was the wife of the conqueror of Europe. Greater honor ought now to be paid to her, to reflect the supremacy of France among the continental states.

"Be civil," he wrote to her, "but receive absolute homage. They owe everything to you, and you owe nothing in return except civility."

She was civil indeed, and, from a distance, youthful and lovely as she went from town to town across the principalities of southern Germany. The wooded, hilly countryside was pleasing, wrapped in its thick mantle of snow, and the towns, gabled and turreted and full of Gothic charm, were turned by their eager citizenry into stage sets for theatrical pageantry.

Triumphal arches were erected for the empress's carriage to pass under. Buildings were illuminated, decorated, beribboned and hung with tapestries and banners. Military parades were held with guns firing and bands playing. At Carlsruhe, a stone column one hundred feet high bore a carved dedication to "Josephine, Empress of the French."

Elegantly dressed and adorned with many jewels, as pale as an alabaster statue except for the spots of rouge on her cheeks, the empress admired the decorations, listened to the bands and the speeches, and made gracious responses. She was more than civil; she was good-humored and good-natured, tactful and benevolent. Her visits were remembered long afterward by those who saw her.

But the late nights and early departure times tired her, and it was no wonder that, when she arrived in Munich, she took to her bed and stayed there a long time.

She had one more task to perform, a most crucial one. Bonaparte had done what he could to persuade Elector Maximilian Joseph to give his consent to his daughter's marriage to Eugene, but the elector was resistant. It was up to Josephine to change his mind.

Her assignment was made awkward by two things: Princess Augusta was in love with her former fiancé, the Prince of Baden, and the elector wanted Emperor Napoleon himself to marry Augusta—after he divorced Josephine.

For nearly a month the empress made Maximilian Joseph and his wife Caroline the principal focus of her considerable personal charm. She quickly discovered that the elector, who was unpretentious and popular with his subjects, had a vain streak, while his much younger wife hated the French (especially Emperor Napoleon) but adored French literature, and liked to read poetry aloud. Josephine stroked the elector's vanity while doing her best to convince the electress, through her warmth and kindness, that at least some of the French, especially the creole French, were likable and that their culture had not been created out of thin air but out of the depths of their poetic souls.

While performing her diplomatic task, Josephine was at the same time becoming acquainted with the young woman who would, if all went well, become her daughter-in-law. Fortunately, she liked Augusta, who was not only attractive but intelligent and good-hearted.

"Her appearance is agreeable," she wrote to Eugene, "she might even be considered beautiful, but I pay much less attention to her external qualities than to those of her mind and heart, since it is on the latter that your happiness depends. You know, my dear, how your mother's heart is concerned with this, but in this respect I think you will have nothing to wish for."

The weeks of persuasion were a positive influence, but not the decisive one; in the game of dynastic politics, the final appeal was to naked self-interest. In the end, what was required to win Maximilian Joseph's consent to the marriage was a bribe. Bonaparte offered to make him King of Bavaria, and in return the elector offered to marry Augusta to Eugene. As for Augusta herself, if at first she clung to her feelings for the Prince of Baden, they soon melted away and she became enamored of her handsome bridegroom in his imposing cavalry uniform.

The wedding was held in the palace chapel, with both families present. The bride was fresh-faced and attractive, the dark-haired, dark-eyed groom a romantic figure, the "fearless, blameless knight" of legend. The emperor, standing off to the side, looked on benevolently, his usual intensity moderated, while the empress, overcome by emotion, wept and clung to him.

Josephine had confessed to Hortense in a letter that she was "a little tired" though she had been spared the pain of migraines during her stay in Munich. She was bearing up fairly well, happy about Eugene's marriage, and about the emperor's declaration that he intended to adopt Eugene, so that he would no longer be known as Eugene de Beauharnais but as Eugene-Napoleon of France.

No doubt Josephine hoped that her son's marriage would be more successful than Hortense's, which had started out badly and gotten progressively worse. Determined to "escape the common fate of all husbands," as he said with an edge of contempt, Louis Bonaparte kept Hortense in a state of miserable submission by having her spied on, forbidding her to form any friendships or other attachments, and making continual violent scenes that wore her down and harmed her health. Louis was jealous of Hortense's love for Eugene, and cruelly forbade her to attend Eugene's wedding. It was, as Hortense later wrote, one of the great disappointments of her life.[4]

Josephine sympathized with her unhappy daughter, both of them married to capricious, demanding husbands, both living under considerable strain. But unlike Hortense, Josephine had, to a large extent, made her peace with her condition. To be sure, her continual attacks of nerves made her agitated and took a heavy toll on her reserves of energy. But at a deeper level, she no longer suffered torment. She had accepted the shape of her future, she knew what to expect, and she was doing her best to adapt.

And she had adjusted, as well as physically possible, to her new regimen as empress, and to spending more and more time away from her husband. Increasingly it seemed as if they lived separate lives, he preoccupied with war and statecraft and the multiple tasks of imperial rule and she, with her heavily scheduled days, occupied with obligatory formal events and with the preparation of her elaborate toilette. Maintaining her impeccable image cost her a great deal of time and effort, more time and more effort, it seemed, with each passing year.

They were together infrequently, and even when under the same roof their companionship was fleeting and at times almost impersonal. Once in a while Bonaparte would tease Josephine and pinch her cheeks, or call her by a pet name from the past, or even, on rare occasions, spend a few minutes walking with her in a garden or romping with her and Hortense's two boys on the lawn. For the most part, however, he shut her out of his life, and saw to it that she was so hemmed in with responsibilities that she had little room for him in hers.

Emperor Napoleon now bestrode Europe like a colossus, but Empress Josephine, she to whom tall obelisks were built and triumphal arches dedicated, to whom flowery speeches were made and flattering tributes paid, was becoming more and more detached and incurious about the march of European affairs. To be sure, she read the letters Bonaparte sent her while on campaign, and rejoiced at his victories. But she did not inquire into their deeper meaning for the future, and she did not really comprehend how far he had risen in power and majesty.

As public affairs grew more momentous, Claire de Rémusat noticed, Josephine became more estranged from them. "The fate of the European world left her unconcerned; the circle of her ideas did not include grand speculations."[5] Her son's advancement, and the security it represented for her, helped to assuage the worst of her fears; for the rest, she "lived peacefully and disengaged [from events]; she showed equal affability to all, with little or no friendship for any individual, but great goodwill for each. Not seeking any pleasure, not dreading any nuisance, always sweet, gracious, serene, and, at bottom, indifferent to nearly everything, her attachment to Bonaparte had grown much colder, and she did not display the jealous upsets which had troubled her life so much in recent years."[6]

In her isolation, she cultivated equanimity, so that when she was with Bonaparte she could offer him the solace of her underlying calmness. It had been that calmness, which was in such contrast to his own constant disquiet, that had at first drawn him to her; it was its opposite, her angry, overemotional, quarrelsome side, that alienated him most.

After a little over a year as empress, she was learning to stand alone, both outwardly, as a gilded icon appearing on a decorated stage, and inwardly, where she was beginning to rediscover that primal insouciance she had once known in Martinique. Part of her was withdrawn, but with another part of herself she reached out as never before to her children, especially to her son, for help and support.

She danced with Eugene at his wedding ball, and accepted the congratulations of the many guests who came to pay their respects. The evening was splendid, the grand salon brilliantly lit, the music lilting, the waltzes and quadrilles performed with grace and precision. She watched for a time, seated in state, aware that many admiring eyes were on her. But before long weariness overcame her, and she asked Bonaparte's permission to leave. The ball went on until dawn, long after Josephine, overwhelmed and yearning for rest, had gone to sleep.

26

"I Will Behave Like the Victim I Am"

*I*n the vast, high-ceilinged Hall of the Marshals at the Tuileries, the members of the imperial court sat in their assigned places, dressed in their prescribed gowns, liveries and uniforms, listening to the music of Spontini.

Few in the audience of four hundred took genuine pleasure in the rather somber, ponderous score, and as aria after aria was sung, the courtiers began to droop visibly, their interest fading and their eyelids sagging. The tone of such formal occasions, one contemporary thought, was one of resigned boredom; night after night members of the household put on their opulent court garb, took their places in the salon or concert hall, then sat, rank on rank, for hours, oppressed by an increasing ennui and longing for escape.

Observers remarked that Emperor Napoleon's court was utterly stunning to look at, but utterly stultifying to participate in. And it was becoming even more stultifying, for the emperor, surrounded as he was by worshipful flatterers dazzled by the success of Austerlitz, had decreed that new refinements of etiquette be observed and new ceremonies conducted, so that nearly everyone in the palace was constantly afraid of committing some faux pas and earning Bonaparte's wrath.[1]

And his wrath, as the courtiers had good reason to know, could be bruising. He struck his servants when they displeased him, threw sharp objects at them, shoved them against walls and furniture. Wound like a tight spring, he uncoiled suddenly and unpredictably, pinching and slapping those nearest him so hard that he injured them, shouting and swearing, his eyes blazing, until his face turned brick red.[2] Even in repose his pent-up energy, itching to get out, caused him to cut and hack at the arms of any chair he sat in, until the upholstery hung in shreds or the wood was notched and spoiled.

While the music played in the Hall of the Marshals, a tense silence prevailed among the spectators, who were aware that they were being closely observed by the emperor himself. He sat on a gilded chair at the back of the huge room, surrounded by his relatives, foreign princes, and court dignitaries. On his right, returned from her self-imposed exile in Rome, was his mother, Madame Mère—or "Mother Joy" as the Parisians called her because in Latin her name Letizia, or *laetitia*, means joy. Toothless, conspicuous, still suspicious of everything French, and far from joyful, Madame Mère looked out across the room with cold hauteur. On the emperor's left was Josephine, her dark curls crowned with flowers, her expression alternating between its customary remote sweetness and anxious concern when she happened to catch a glimpse of Hortense, seated nearby.

Of the other Bonapartes, Joseph was away from court, Lucien permanently banished, Jerome, now a naval officer, away at sea, and Elisa in Italy, presiding over her unsatisfactory principalities of Lucca and Piombino. Only Paulette, Princess Borghese, and Caroline Murat, who now bore the title Grand Duchess of Berg, sat beside their mother in the imperial row of honor.

Eugene and Augusta, looking sleek and contented, sat side by side, near the emperor because of Eugene's newly conferred standing as his adopted son. They were visiting Paris for a time before returning to Italy. Predictably, Paulette and especially Caroline were offended at Eugene's adoption into the imperial family; it was bad enough that their brother forced them to buy expensive wedding presents for Eugene and Augusta, now they had to endure their being seated in a place of honor as well. Josephine, who knew how Eugene valued his father's sword, had recently sent him, as a wedding present, another treasure: the saber Bonaparte had carried at Marengo. It was "the gift of glory and of friendship," she told him, an heirloom from his adoptive father to place beside that of the late Alexandre de Beauharnais.[3]

Another of Josephine's relatives had been adopted by Bonaparte, her niece Stephanie de Beauharnais. Having taken the attractive, good-natured Stephanie under her wing when the latter was only fourteen, paying for her education at Madame Campan's school and looking out for her interests, Josephine was now gratified to have Stephanie enter the imperial family. A husband had been found for her, none other than Augusta's old love the Prince of Baden, and with Stephanie's marriage another link was forged between the Beauharnais family and royalty—much to the chagrin of the Bonapartes.

But of all those present at the grand concert, it was Hortense who drew Josephine's attention most. She had lost weight, her customary sparkle was eclipsed and her face wore a mask of sorrow. Her deeply unhappy marriage was growing worse, her Bonaparte in-laws treated her with open contempt, and she confided to Madame de Rémusat that she felt powerless to defend herself against the terrible widespread rumors that the emperor had been her lover, and that her older son was his.[4]

The boy, Napoleon-Charles, now three and a half, was an outgoing, charming child and his mother's favorite. He and his baby brother were Hortense's sole consolations in the midst of her troubles, and she clung to them, as she clung to her adored brother Eugene, with pathetic affection. Her husband Louis, on the other hand, drove her further and further away.

Splenetic and sharp-tongued, goaded to irascibility by constant rheumatic pain, Louis expected Hortense to obey his every whim, no matter how offensive. When the emperor's physician Corvisart suggested that it might relieve Louis's rheumatism if he slept wearing the stinking nightshirt of a patient with weeping sores, he tried the experiment—and insisted that Hortense sleep in the same room, in order not to alert the household to what he was doing. Loathsome as it was to her, she complied, uncomplaining.

The concert in the Hall of the Marshals was nearing its end. Dancers from the Paris Opera had succeeded the singers, and while they performed their ballet, the candles burned low, and the emperor, much as he had enjoyed the evening, was scratching at the arms of his chair, impatient to leave. When at last he stood, the entire audience rose with him, and remained standing, respectfully silent, while he and his family filed out of the room.

By the summer of 1806 the French Empire had expanded to include Belgium, Holland, most of Italy, and an amalgam of fifteen German states called the Confederation of the Rhine which sought French protection rather than face being absorbed directly into Bonaparte's domains. In return, the Confederation provided a large contingent of soldiers for the Grande Armée. Emperor Napoleon dominated Western Europe; apart from England and Spain, only Prussia and Russia had not been brought under his sway. Not since the time of Charlemagne had one sovereignty governed so much of the continent. The French engine of conquest was formidable indeed—and seemingly all but unstoppable.

Nonetheless, the Prussian king, Frederick William III, having received assurances of Russian support and British money, moved his armies into position to invade the newly formed German Confederation in August, 1806, and the Emperor prepared to lead the Grande Armée against him.

Bonaparte agreed, at the last minute, to take Josephine with him as far as Mainz, where he planned to leave her while on campaign. Toward the end of September they set off together, the emperor preoccupied, Josephine tense.

It was not only the coming campaign that preoccupied the emperor. He left behind in Paris a mistress, Eleonore Denuelle, who was pregnant with his child.

Her pregnancy was of great significance, for until it occurred he had not been certain he could father a child.[5] Now that he had proof that Josephine's barrenness was her fault and not his, his marital ambitions expanded. For some time he had known that he would eventually remarry, and that his bride would be a young princess from a great royal house. But now he was able to add to that expectation the strong probability of children, and this both energized and accelerated his aspirations.

Josephine too was preoccupied, and not merely by her customary worries about the continuity of her situation as empress. Some of the members of her household noticed that she felt a "tender sentiment" for her young equerry Corbineau, and they remarked on it in subdued tones.[6]

In Mainz the empress moved into the Teutonic Palace, knowing that she would be there for several months but hoping that, as Bonaparte promised, she could join him once he settled into his winter quarters farther east.

Bonaparte's leavetaking from Josephine had about it all the anguish of a definitive separation. He had worked himself up into a nervous state, possibly because of his active imaginings about finding a new wife, possibly because he feared that a separation from Josephine would end the good luck that she had brought him. Whatever the cause, by the time he summoned the weeping Josephine and embraced her, he too was in tears, and clung to her fiercely, as he did to Talleyrand.

"It is very hard to leave the two persons one loves best," he said as he released them. The words caught in his throat, and he sobbed so violently that his entire body began to convulse and his stomach churned, causing him to vomit.

The fit of emotion was slow to pass, but eventually, with the aid of a fortifying drink of orange-flower water, Bonaparte recovered and, calling for his carriage, abruptly took his leave.

Josephine, however, did not recover. The trepidation she felt at their parting continued long after he left, and his continued assurances that he would soon send for her failed to calm her anxieties. They had been growing more distant for a long time, but now it seemed as though a chasm had opened between them, and Josephine feared that the moment she dreaded most, the moment when he would ask her to sacrifice her position as his wife for the sake of his political advantage, might soon be at hand. Meanwhile the Bonapartes, principally Caroline and Joseph, were working harder than ever to wrench their imperial brother from his wife, and Caroline and Paulette were attempting to take on more prominent social roles at court. Left in her isolation in Mainz, Josephine feared that she would be eclipsed by her sisters-in-law in Paris, and injured by their intrigues; unless her husband summoned her to his side quickly, she might be eclipsed by some foreign princess he met and decided to marry.

And in fact, though he was still sentimentally attached to Josephine, Bonaparte was growing weary of her. He had made her empress, he confided to his secretary Roederer, "out of justice." She had been at his side during his early years, when his future was far from assured; she had lent him her aristocratic status to assist his ambitions; he felt it was appropriate that she should enjoy his years of fame and wealth. "If I had been thrown into prison instead of ascending a throne," he told Roederer, "she would have shared my misfortune. It is right for her to share my grandeur."[7]

Now that she had been empress for nearly two years, however, circumstances had changed. Justice had been served. She had shared his grandeur, and his wealth, for quite some time. Besides, she was beginning to make absurd accusations that were harmful to the reputation of the Bonaparte family.

"Josephine is decidedly old," Bonaparte told his brother Lucien, "and as she cannot now have any children she is very melancholy about it and tiresome. She fears divorce or even worse." Because Lucien was living far from Paris and was no longer involved in family politics, the emperor could speak freely to him. "Just imagine," he added, "the woman cries every time she has indigestion, because she says she believes she has been poisoned by those who want me to marry someone else. It is detestable."[8]

While in Mainz Josephine began imagining—or saying that she imagined—that the Bonapartes wanted her dead. Fretting and brooding, occupying her time playing endless games of patience and billiards in the company of Hortense and her two children, she could not prevent her fears from leading her into dark illusions. And when, in January of 1807, it became apparent that Bonaparte was not going to allow her to join him in his eastern camp after all, she broke into bitter recriminations.

Bonaparte was an ingrate, she cried out in Claire de Rémusat's hearing. When he married her, she had lowered herself to his level; it was not fair for him to put her aside now that he was the master of Europe. She sensed that his dismissal would not be long in coming. When it came, she intended to defy it.

"I will never give in to him," she insisted angrily. "I will behave like the victim I am—but, if I thwart him too much, who knows what he is capable of? Who knows whether he would resist the urge to despatch me?"[9] This "sinister suspicion" obsessed the empress for a time, driving away the resignation she had been able to arrive at during the previous year and bringing on her headaches once again.

On the emperor's orders she returned to Paris late in January, and soon succumbed to a series of migraines and to a deep depression that lasted for several months. Much of the time she kept to her bed, attended by doctors who could do nothing for her; they tried to raise blisters on the back of her neck in an effort to relieve her pain and fever, but the treatment was ineffective.[10]

She sought relief at Malmaison, where workmen were engaged in renovations. Watching their progress distracted her and gave her some ease, and when the weather was not too cold she walked in the gardens, watching the black swans float on the lake, feeding the peacocks, visiting her menagerie where zebras, seals, kangaroos and seventeen tortoises were kept in cages. In the greenhouses, rare tulips and double hyacinths from Holland bloomed alongside jasmine, mimosa, heliotrope, rhododendrons and a unique purple-flowering magnolia, the only one in France.

She sent some of the many Malmaison flowers to the Tuileries to decorate the walls of a ballroom. Outside it was still winter, but inside, there was an illusion of spring, with grass-green carpet spread over the dance floor, the balconies and staircases, and greenery and fresh moss framing the mirrors and windows. Dancers whirled and bobbed amid the sweet-smelling blooms, and formed a long chain that snaked in and out of one room after another while the empress and her ladies watched from her loge.[11]

Guests at the ball had traveled long distances to witness the splendor of the French imperial court. In addition to many Germans, Russians, Italians and Swiss, there were a number of Americans present, and even representatives of the Grand Turk in lavishly embroidered robes, turbans and jeweled scimitars. Paris was becoming the mecca of the world, the capital of the great Emperor Napoleon who in his victories at Jena and Auerstädt in the previous October had soundly defeated the Prussian army and proved yet again the astonishing superiority of French arms. Most of the guests did not yet know the outcome of a more recent battle, in the muddy marshes at Eylau in East Prussia, where the French narrowly escaped defeat at the hands of the Russians and lost fifteen thousand men.

Josephine knew, for she received frequent letters from Bonaparte—sometimes several in a single day—and he had not spared her the tragic details. He had been deeply troubled by how close his army came to losing; had the Russians not withdrawn at the last minute they would surely have overwhelmed his forces.

On the night of the Tuileries ball, she was mourning, as she told Eugene in a letter, "the loss of so many brave men" at Eylau, among them her favorite Corbineau. "All this is so sad," she told Eugene, "and what is even more terrible is the manner in which the emperor exposed himself to danger." Her heart was heavy, her head ached, and, apart from her children, she had nowhere to turn for sympathy and comfort.[12]

In his letters Bonaparte chided her for losing heart. "They tell me that you cry constantly," he wrote. "Fie on you! How ugly that seems! Your letter of January 7 grieves me. Be worthy of me, and show more character. Carry out your necessary social duties at Paris and, above all, be happy.... I don't like faint-hearted people; an empress must have courage!"[13]

But it was difficult to muster any courage when she was so often ill, and beleaguered by her grief, her fears, and the growing enmity of those around her. Josephine's principal lady of honor, the former Duchesse de la Rochefoucauld, a haughty relic of the old regime, had turned against her and, in the emperor's absence, showed her open contempt. Though many in Josephine's very large household were loyal, and felt strong affection for their mistress, many others followed the lead of the lady of honor and, in subtle but unmistakable ways, ceased to show the empress respect. Every day, sometimes every hour she encountered looks of disdain or coldness, and even overheard insolent remarks murmured just loudly enough for her to hear. She was too kindhearted to dismiss the offending servants, and in any case there were too many of them. Besides, she may have felt that it would be futile to attempt to hold on to her dignity by wholesale dismissals when it was becoming more and more clear that she might soon be dismissed herself.

After all, she could not blame her attendants for trying to protect themselves from the change their instincts—and widespread gossip—told them was near. They were only being sensible; court politics dictated that unless they distanced themselves from the present empress they would not be offered places in the household of her successor.

Week in and week out, Josephine's in-laws found ways to goad her with their animosity. She dreaded the awkward family dinners over which she was forced to preside, where the Bonapartes ate in conspiratorial silence amid an atmosphere of ceaseless petty conflict. On her name day, the feast of Saint Josephine, she had to endure watching Pauline and Caroline act, with ill grace, in two plays given in her honor at Malmaison. Joseph, she knew, was continuing to urge his brother to dethrone her and give her a small principality to reign over, as Empress of Nothing. And Letizia, dour and dissatisfied, was counting the days until her famous son Poleone would end his stubborn attachment to the old whore he married and find a young wife.

Josephine's greatest worry, however, in the winter and spring months of 1807 concerned the beautiful young Polish lady Marie Walewska, her husband's most recent and most ardent love.

Polish noblewomen visiting Paris brought the news from Warsaw: Emperor Napoleon was infatuated with Marie, a virtuous, sweet-natured blonde noblewomen of eighteen who was married to a husband of seventy. The emperor pursued her, they said, with the passion of a young man caught up in his first rapturous adoration. And she, though at first she refused his wooing, in the end yielded to his pressure and to the urgent pleas of Polish patriots who begged her, for the sake of the fatherland, to obtain a separation from her husband and become the emperor's mistress.

For Marie and her compatriots, it seemed, nothing short of Poland's liberation was at stake. In the last generation the Polish kingdom had been devoured by Prussia, Austria and above all Russia, until nothing was left but the memory of the former sovereign realm and the eager desire of the Poles to regain their homeland for themselves. Bonaparte, the sworn enemy of the three devouring powers, represented a hope that Polish sovereignty might be restored. Poland, Marie told the emperor when she first met him, "waits for you so that it may raise itself."

For Bonaparte, much affected by Marie's gentle, unaffected nature, her angelic face and evident vulnerability—all of which reminded him of Josephine in former days—what was at stake was his heart. Until now, his adulterous liaisons had been unromantic. He had used them to assuage his lust, to offer himself novelty and adventure, to stroke his vanity, to prove his power. But Marie had a youthful purity, an idealism, an inner quietness that stirred something far deeper in him, a longing for peace and soothing comfort, for the drift into reverie that he had valued as a younger man. Josephine had once offered him these same satisfactions, but his bond with Josephine had become corroded, he was disappointed in her—and besides she was far past her prime, tiresome in her querulousness and a grotesque nuisance with her wild accusations of murder and poison.

Bonaparte was in love—and his love for Marie exaggerated his dissatisfactions with his wife, who was in any case far away. He continued to write to her often, his brief, rather perfunctory letters peppered with affectionate phrases that, in the light of what she knew of his dalliance with Marie Walewska, were unconvincing. When Josephine wrote back, alluding to her fears that he had fallen in love with another woman, he sent airy, patronizing denials to his "little Josephine, good, sulky and capricious," and added "thousands of kisses."

"Put no trust in all the evil reports which may be circulated," he told her. "Never doubt my feelings, and have no worries." His dismissive reference to "all the evil reports" must have made her worry still more. Clearly he knew that word of his liaison with Marie was spreading, yet Marie was so important to him that he did not care. He was so enamored of her that he was even neglecting vital matters of governance, and failing to cultivate his all-important popularity with his subjects.

During his long months of absence from Paris in the fall of 1806 and the spring of 1807, an unsettled mood had spread through the city. News of the hard-won victory of the Grande Armée at Eylau, and of the large number of French casualties suffered in the battle, made Parisians uneasy. For the first time in years Bonaparte had not been overwhelmingly dominant on the battlefield; his famed immunity to injury or defeat seemed under threat. From his headquarters at the castle of Finkenstein in Poland he had issued a call for tens of thousands of recruits for his next campaign; there were grumbles, and some men were reluctant to come forward. Public confidence had dipped, not drastically, but noticeably; the stock market fell, and ceremonies marking important commemorations drew decorous applause rather than feverish ovations. Signs of emperor-worship, heretofore omnipresent, were subdued, and throughout the capital, people waited for word of the next engagement by the Grande Armée, hoping, albeit guardedly, for a decisive victory.

In the midst of these trials and uncertainties, Josephine had one thing to look forward to: the birth of Eugene's first child. She hoped for a grandson, and sent the most celebrated midwife in Paris, Madame Frangeau, to Italy to attend Augusta at her delivery.

"I await impatiently the news of your wife and of my new child," she told Eugene. She regretted not being able to be present at the birth, but trusted that Augusta would follow the midwife's advice exactly. She had sent a number of gifts for the new baby—an elaborate layette with embroidered, lace-trimmed gowns, caps, bibs and blankets, and some lengths of beautiful lace for the mother-to-be— along with a copy of the baptism ceremony used for Hortense's second child. On the all-important issue of the baby's name, she urged Eugene to write to the emperor to ask his advice.

When the baby was born, three weeks late, Eugene informed his mother that it was a girl, and that he and Augusta wanted to name her Joséphine-Maximilienne-Eugénie-Napoléone. The empress was overjoyed. A grandson would have been a delight, but a granddaughter—and a namesake—was almost equally thrilling.

"I congratulate you with all my heart, my dear Eugene," she wrote. "I am enchanted to have a granddaughter." The good news was much needed, she added, for she had been ill for several days and in low spirits. When a few weeks later a lock of the tiny Josephine's hair arrived from Italy, she treasured it, and sent Augusta a letter of motherly advice and a beautiful gift.[14]

But in the midst of the rejoicing an ominous message arrived from Hortense: her older son Napoleon was ill, and slow to recover. She was worried. He was her favorite, her firstborn; though his brother Louis was the one who inherited the Bonaparte good looks, Napoleon had his grandmother's warmth and charm and his mother's cheery vitality. Now all his usual energy was dampened as he lay coughing, his cheeks red and his eyes bright from fever, in his small bed in a royal residence at The Hague.

Young Napoleon was, for the time being, heir to the empire, and for nearly a year he had been heir to the Kingdom of Holland as well, for his father had been given the Dutch crown. King Louis and Queen Hortense officially resided at Laeken near Brussels, but Hortense was unhappy there; she fretted over her children's health, and was convinced that the cold and perpetual damp and fog of Holland were harmful to them. Sadly, her son's grave illness was confirming her fears.

By the time Josephine received Hortense's letter from The Hague telling her of little Napoleon's illness he had been in decline for several days. More bulletins arrived—hasty notes, most likely, revealing both the little boy's worsening condition and Hortense's rising alarm. No doubt Josephine wished that she could be at his bedside. But she did not dare go anywhere without her husband's permission, and he was in Poland, with his mistress, unaware that any danger threatened.

Powerless to act, made more apprehensive by every successive letter from Holland, Josephine suffered and worried from a distance as her grandson's life ebbed. The cough became croup, the child's larynx swelled until he could barely breathe, and he lay in a feverish stupor, his blonde hair tangled on the pillow, his brokenhearted mother at his side.

After six days he died, and Hortense, so beside herself with grief and exhaustion that for several hours she was in a kind of trance, collapsed into inconsolable despair. Now Josephine was permitted to join her daughter and mourn with her, and she did so, bringing Hortense and her younger son back with her to Malmaison.

"Poor Hortense!" Josephine wrote to Eugene. "What a sweet child she has lost. Since this sad event, I seem not to live; I only suffer and cry." She was concerned about Hortense, who was so shattered by her loss that she withdrew into a state of numbness. "Her health will come back," she told Eugene, "but her heart will never be consoled, I sense this through all that I suffer."[15]

On the advice of the imperial physician Corvisart, Hortense left for the spa at Bagnères, and baby Louis, two and a half years old, remained with his grandmother.

"The little one becomes stronger and more lovable every day," Josephine told Eugene. "He resembles his poor brother very much; he has his manner and his voice but the pleasure I have in seeing him near me does not console me for the loss we have had."[16]

A cruel reckoning was at work: Bonaparte's son by Eléonore Denuelle was thriving, while young Napoleon, once Bonaparte's heir, lay in the chapel at Notre Dame awaiting his official funeral. His death weakened Josephine's already precarious position, and moved closer the day she dreaded—the day she would be asked, for the sake of France, to renounce her husband and her crown.

27

"They Are Inveterate Against Me"

In the deep, cool green forest of Fontainebleau the colors of autumn were beginning to blaze out among the darker evergreens. Patches of bright orange and bronze and gold leaves were lit by the early-morning sun, and the low shrubs that lined the narrow paths taken by huntsmen in pursuit of game had clumps of red mingled with their green. Few in the nearby town could remember so fine a season as this autumn of 1807, the air crisp and chill, the sun warm, the fine old trees with their thick dark trunks rich with color, the animals plentiful and fat.

Nearly every morning that November the quiet of the forest was shattered by the blast of hunting horns, as the horses and carriages of the imperial hunting party thundered swiftly along the twisting alleys between the trees, the men darting past to follow a fleeing stag, hounds at their horses' heels, the women in open carriages speeding along behind them, the delicate vehicles rocking and swaying dangerously with each sudden turn.

Emperor Napoleon had summoned a vast court to the old palace in the forest, some twelve hundred people in all, and had spent lavishly from his full treasury to renovate and refurnish the rooms, repair the park, and clean out the lake; Josephine noted with pleasure that swans had been brought in to keep the lake free of weeds.

On fine mornings the emperor was up before dawn, decreeing that the entire court should follow him into the forest. The men put on their hunting uniforms of green and maroon, the women their gowns of green and yellow and their black velvet hats with sweeping white plumes and took their places in open carriages. After an hour or so of sport, they met at a summerhouse where servants had prepared breakfast. They ate in the open air, exhilarant, their senses sharpened and their appetites keen from all the riding and driving.

The emperor was noticeably preoccupied. Some mornings he rode into the forest accompanied only by his favorite equerry, looking thoughtful and abstracted, wearing the splendid sable-lined coat Tsar Alexander had given him three months earlier at their momentous meeting at Tilsit on the Niemen River.

Since the Tilsit conference his sense of his own importance, already strongly developed, had expanded; together he and the tsar had determined Europe's future, speaking as equals, while the Prussian king Frederick William rode up and down nervously nearby, awaiting the outcome of their discussions. Tsar Alexander, his armies defeated by Bonaparte at the battle of Friedland in June, had turned from enemy to friend—even admirer. He admired Bonaparte as he might have admired an elder brother. Indeed Bonaparte had been convinced that the tsar would welcome him into his own family, as a brother-in-law, if he indicated a desire to marry Alexander's nineteen-year-old sister Catharina Pavlovna.

For several months he had been perusing a list of eligible princesses from the great ruling houses, mulling over the advantages of each from both a dynastic and a political standpoint. His new wife had to be young and fertile, of course, and if possible, attractive. She also had to be of the very highest rank, to complement his own. His alliance with her had to improve his standing among the European powers—if such improvement were possible.

Now in the fall of 1807 the emperor realized as never before how inappropriate it was for him to be married to a member of the lower French aristocracy. Josephine's lack of royal status demeaned his imperial crown. She was an embarrassment, an inconvenience, a hindrance. His French subjects were fond of her, but outside of France, she did not reflect well on him.

Since returning to France from his grand conference with Tsar

Alexander the emperor had made a significant adjustment in his relations with his wife. He no longer visited Josephine's bedroom, and when they met in the course of the day, his manner toward her seemed to others cold or perplexed. He seemed at a loss to know how to behave toward her, she made him uncomfortable. She was like an obstruction in the middle of his path, in his way, forcing him into inconvenient detours. That he still felt an underlying affection for her only added to his discomfort and constraint.

He had told her that he expected her to lay aside her rank as his wife whenever he asked, and she had said, more than once, that she would obey his command—though her expressed compliance was at odds with the defiance she continued to display to others when he was not present. Her private behavior, and the court controversies to which it gave rise, with one faction among her entourage encouraging her to believe that the emperor would never find the courage to divorce her and the other attempting to prepare her for the inevitable final separation, were disruptive and, in Bonaparte's view, regrettable. One of his preoccupations, as he rode by himself in the forest, was how to move his wife closer to accepting the step that he knew he must take.

Everyone at Fontainebleau that autumn knew, or thought they knew, what the emperor was thinking about when he made his private forays into the woods. He was planning his divorce and remarriage, going over his tactics for each. In their cramped apartments, knots of guests discussed the matter of the emperor's present and future marriage endlessly, remarking on the large numbers of couriers coming and going between Fontainebleau and the Russian court (which could only mean one thing—that Emperor Napoleon was wooing one of the tsar's female relatives), on the coldness and distance between the emperor and his present wife, on the urgent need for an heir now that Hortense's son, who had been the designated heir, was dead.

To be sure, they told one another, the emperor was not allowing his preoccupation to interfere with his amours. He was said to visit the room of the beautiful Genoese opera singer Madame Gazzani at midnight, gliding quietly across the dark garden that separated his bedroom from hers. And he was pursuing another beauty, Madame de Barrar, one of Paulette's ladies in waiting, who was said to be immune to his advances. His recent affair with Marie Walewska too was common knowledge, and there were whispers of other fleeting liaisons, significant only because he was who he was, the most powerful man in Europe, perhaps in the world.

Encouraged by some in her household to show herself as much as possible, to contradict the rumors of her imminent fall, Josephine attended the plays and concerts, balls and hunts that punctuated the autumn season, and invited large numbers of people to her private rooms for morning receptions, luncheons, and evening card games and conversation. Among them was the handsome young Prince Frederick of Mecklenburg-Strelitz, the brother of the Prussian queen, who was decades younger than the empress but was clearly attracted to her. He was handsome, attentive, admiring; now forty-four and constantly reminded that she was aging, Josephine must have been flattered by the glances and hovering presence of the young prince.

But even if she felt something for him in return, she was hardly in a position to begin a friendship, much less a flirtation, with Prince Frederick with her every movement watched and reported on, and her heart heavy with melancholy.

She was still mourning little Napoleon. She kept a lock of his blonde hair in a glass frame, and wept over it from time to time.[1] And while at Fontainebleau she received the news that her mother had died in Martinique. She had known for many years that most likely she would never see her mother again, yet with Rose-Claire Tascher's death a last link to Josephine's childhood was broken; already feeling isolated, the loss of her mother and of the past she represented must have increased Josephine's sense of aloneness as, surrounded by crowds of people, she went from the hunt to the salon to the ballroom, playing her part in the grand court.

Being at Fontainebleau must have revived memories of the time, more than twenty years earlier, when the youthful Rose de Beauharnais went to stay with her aunt and followed the court of Louis XVI and Marie Antoinette. Then she had been exuberant, vigorous, overjoyed to be free of the oppressive life she had lived as Alexandre de Beauharnais's wife. She had ridden off into the forest with a crowd of guests and hangers-on, tearing along fearlessly after the royal coach, avid for a sight of the king and queen, caring nothing for the cold or the rain that soaked her riding habit.

Then she had been a daring young woman, little more than a girl really, with a new world opening before her. Then she had been Rose, "the little American," captivating to men and learning to allow herself to be seduced with grace, always in control of the seduction, and of the seducers. There at Fontainebleau she had begun to learn how to profit from love—to exploit, rather than to be exploited.

Now, half a lifetime later, she was Empress of the French, still profiting from love, it might be said, but paying a high price for her wretchedly uncomfortable exaltation. The fearless girl had become a deeply fearful woman, the girl who had controlled her lovers had become a woman overcontrolled, restricted, spied on and caged.

It had been at Fontainebleau, in her youth, that Josephine first saw Queen Marie Antoinette, plump but still a doll-like beauty with her blue eyes and blonde curls, and heard, not for the first time, the ugly gossip about how the queen's extravagance was causing the kingdom to totter on the brink of bankruptcy. Poised and stoic, Marie Antoinette had endured the searing blasts of criticism with fortitude, and had kept her dignity amid the buffetings of her critics.

Now Empress Josephine stood in the late queen's stead, living in her royal apartments, served by many of the same people who had served her, following her precedents as the head of her own imperial household. Now Josephine too was accused of extravagance and menaced by ugly gossip, and though the realm over which her husband reigned was far richer and seemingly far more stable than Louis XVI's had been, she too felt buffeted about by critical blasts, and she too struggled to keep her dignity.

Though she tried to appear cheerful and contented, Josephine could not keep the true state of her feelings from the women closest to her. Laure Junot thought that she was "overpowered with melancholy," made anxious by all the talk of divorce—every fresh nuance of which was repeated to her—and constrained from mentioning the subject to her husband in order to judge the state of his mind.

"Madame Junot," Josephine told her confidante, "they will never be satisfied till they have driven me from the throne of France. They are inveterate against me."[2] In this season of hunter and hunted, the empress felt as if she were the quarry, the Bonapartes and most of the courtiers the hunters; she was being hounded mercilessly, driven to ground.

Fouché approached her one morning as the court was returning from hearing mass. He was blunt and curt. "The public good and the cohesion of the present dynasty demand that the emperor have children," he said. Josephine ought to go before the Senate and, after receiving its support, approach the emperor and request that he "make the sacrifice most painful to his heart."

These were the words she had been dreading to hear. She was being asked to step aside, and she had promised the emperor that when the request was made, she would comply. But she had not expected the request to come from Fouché.

She was confused. Had Bonaparte asked Fouché to speak for him, finding the words too difficult to speak on his own? Or was Fouché carrying out some secret intrigue he alone had designed, of which the emperor knew nothing? What should she do? Fouché was minister of police, a powerful and dangerous man. She had to be careful.

She asked the minister if he had been sent by her husband, and if he was speaking on his behalf.

Fouché replied, evasively, that he was speaking in his capacity as a government servant and as a subject concerned with the welfare of the French Empire. But his manner was that of a messenger, and his forthrightness, and the tone of the conversation, made Josephine faint with apprehension.

When, risking her husband's grave displeasure, she went to him to ask whether he had sent Fouché to speak to her, and he denied that he had, she was still deeply upset. A letter from Fouché, reiterating the need for her to take the first step in giving up her crown and her status as the emperor's wife, soon arrived. In the letter the minister said that he was acting alone, that Bonaparte had no knowledge of what he was saying and would be displeased if he knew. The empress must keep his letter a secret.

Caught between the fearsome minister's pressure and her husband's assurances that Fouché spoke only for himself, she did not know what to do. Fouché's letter, coming as it did after her conversation with Bonaparte, could not be ignored. Was it conceivable that Fouché might be acting without Bonaparte's knowledge? The emperor knew all, controlled all.

She knew that she had to read between the lines—but how? There was no one to advise her, in such a vital matter no one at court was disinterested. She could trust neither her supporters nor her detractors. Eugene could be counted on to give her sound advice, though Eugene was invariably loyal to the emperor. But Eugene was in Italy, and she could not afford to wait until she wrote him and received a response. She had to decide very soon what to do.

Several months earlier she had written to Eugene, telling him about the efforts being made by her enemies to urge Bonaparte to divorce her. "Those who surround him think rather of themselves than of him," she told her son. They deceived him, flattered him—and gave him self-serving advice.

Eugene's response was measured and judicious. The emperor's political needs, and his place in history, required him to make a dynastic marriage; therefore his first marriage must be set aside.

"There has been much talk of divorce," he told his mother. "I've been made aware of it from Paris and from Munich." She must prepare her mind for it, as an inevitability, and make certain that when it came, she was given a sufficient settlement and allowed to live near him in Italy.

"We will remain no less attached to him," Eugene added, "because his sentiments need not change toward us, though circumstances oblige him to put our family aside." "You need not fear either events or intriguers," he wrote reassuringly. "Always speak freely to His Majesty."[3]

Josephine had not forgotten her son's advice, but it did not seem to apply to her present dilemma. Should she ignore Fouché's attempt to intimidate her, or should she do what he asked, trusting that it was her husband's wish, whatever he might say to the contrary?

As time passed, she became more upset and frightened. A few days after Fouché's letter arrived, she sent an urgent summons at midnight to Claire de Rémusat's husband, who was one of the emperor's chamberlains. When the chamberlain was ushered into her apartments, he found her in a state of disarray. She had evidently been overwrought for some time, for her tearstained face was full of distress, her hair unkempt and her appearance neglected. It must have been a shock for Rémusat, who never saw her other than perfectly gowned and coiffed, to view his empress without the protective carapace of her public persona.

"What shall I do?" Josephine asked the chamberlain.

He advised her to go to her husband, show him Fouché's letter, and make clear her displeasure at it. She should once again assure him that she would be willing to give up her position, but only if he himself required it of her. And, Rémusat cautioned, she must be careful not to let him think that anyone else was behind her, telling her what to say and do, for that would arouse his suspicions.

Fortified by Rémusat's advice, and remembering that Eugene had told her to speak freely to her husband, Josephine approached the emperor.

When she read the minister's letter to him he feigned indignation and told Josephine that Fouché had acted without instructions. But the truth was more complex. Bonaparte had disclosed to Fouché that he was thinking about ending his marriage, though he confessed to some ambivalence about it. He had made up his mind to act—but he had not yet been able to decide how. In speaking and writing to Josephine Fouché was merely attempting to act for him, to push the matter forward. Though he had not been given explicit authorization, he had indeed been acting on the emperor's behalf.

Bonaparte denied all—but since the subject was being aired, he took the opportunity to ask Josephine what she thought about it. The question must have dismayed her, for it implied that the issue of divorce was indeed in the forefront of his mind.

She answered as best she could, reiterating her determination to take at most a passive role, and to subordinate herself to his will. She alluded to the luck she had always brought him and the bad luck that might result if she left him.

The question was left in the air, and nothing more was said about it. Yet Josephine noticed that Fouché suffered no punishment as a result of his disturbing conversation with her, and she had to conclude that, on some level, he had been expressing his sovereign's views after all.

Certainly Bonaparte made no effort to dampen the ever-widening discussions of divorce that now spread from the court through the capital and out into the provinces. Police reports were full of accounts of conversations overheard between Parisians and provincials of all classes, endlessly debating the empress's fate. Many took pity on Josephine, believing her doomed to abandonment, but others, probably the majority, believed that if the emperor married the tsar's sister—she seemed the appropriate next wife—the result would be a lasting peace, and after many bloody battles and much sacrifice, they had come to long for peace. Surely, they told one another, the emperor would provide for Josephine in some way. A rumor spread that she would be created Queen of Naples, and sent to reign over that romantic city at the base of the great volcano, overlooking the beautiful bay.

By the middle of November in the forest of Fontainebleau, the yellow and orange leaves had begun to wither and die. The imperial hunt still thundered along the twisting paths between the great trees, stags and boar continued to fall to the huntsmen, but there was frost on the ground in the early morning, and a cold wind had replaced the crisp autumnal air. Winter was coming, and soon the great court was dispersed.

The emperor departed for Italy, alone, and when Josephine begged to be taken with him so that she could see her tiny granddaughter and namesake, he refused. She had to content herself with miniatures of the baby girl, sent by Eugene along with letters giving her additional sensible advice.

One guest stayed on in Fontainebleau after most of the others had left, and followed Josephine to Paris when she returned there at the end of November. Prince Frederick was reluctant to leave Josephine, having fallen under her spell; though she showed him the same benevolent amiability she showed everyone else, and nothing more, he continued to be near her as often as possible.

In Bonaparte's absence she invited him, along with others, to attend the theater with her—not one of the grand theaters where she sat in marmoreal splendor in a velvet-lined box but one of the small theaters, intimate and cosy, where she could enjoy the performance incognito. The prince accepted—and Fouché's spies, who reported everything the empress did, notified their employer, who in turn notified the emperor in Italy.

The response was a written reprimand. Had he not told Josephine to avoid the small theaters, as beneath her dignity? She had been indiscreet. He wanted her to enjoy herself, but not to cause idle talk. Her behavior in taking a group of guests, including Prince Frederick who people said was in love with her, was inappropriate, and she must correct it. He would be back with her soon to make certain she did.

Winter closed in, and with it, a tightening of the restrictions around the empress. "I never go out, I have no pleasure, and I lead a life to which people are surprised I can adjust, since I have been accustomed to being more independent and to seeing a lot of people," she wrote to Eugene in February of 1808.[4] "I entrust myself to Providence and to the will of the emperor. My only defense is my conduct, which I try to make irreproachable."

Her stock was falling, she said. She had many causes for grief, and still feared poison. Some of those to whom she confided her thoughts believed that she actually wanted her marriage to end, so that the climate of fear and uncertainty under which she lived could end with it.

"What unhappiness thrones bring, my dear Eugene!" she wrote at the end of her letter. "I would sign an abdication on behalf of all my family tomorrow without regret."

28

"As Though a Deadly Poison Were Spreading Through My Veins"

*B*onaparte was master of Europe, but the countries and peoples he had subjected were becoming increasingly rebellious.

With each new campaigning season he was facing more resistance, more defiance and more resentment on the part of those he had subdued. Once seen as the liberator of Europe, he was now viewed as her oppressor; both monarchists and radical patriots plotted his assassination.

And as the burdens and pressures of imperial dominance grew more intense, the emperor felt his physical powers waning. He had long dreaded turning forty, believing that once he entered his fifth decade he would become fat and feeble. In 1808 he celebrated his thirty-ninth birthday, and though still well able to endure the open-air rigors of campaigning he was growing stout, and he often suffered from stomach pain.

To fortify his empire, and to ensure that, whatever happened to him, the strong foundation he had built over so many years would endure, he needed to establish a dynasty—and soon, for his heir would need decades of careful preparation and grooming for rulership himself.

But while he faced so many challenges, while his enemies seemed to resurge with greater strength each time he crushed them, and while his popularity within France was waning, he did not dare to add to his difficulties by risking the criticism he would suffer if he divorced his popular wife and married a foreign bride. Besides, he continued to dread that without Josephine, he would fall prey to bad luck, and much as he tried to steel himself against his vulnerable, emotional side, it was often dominant where his dealings with his wife were concerned.

In the spring of 1808 Bonaparte managed to summon his courage and decide to proceed with the divorce, no matter what the risk. He informed the major court officials of his decision, and legal preparations were begun. But his resolve soon began to waver, for the very act of making the decision to put his wife aside triggered nervous spasms and, before long, severe stomach pains; in his anguish the emperor took to his bed, and he told Josephine, in tears, that he could not possibly leave her.

After months of coldness and distance he was suddenly overcome with his old passion for Josephine, and they spent the night together— "a night of love," Josephine told Claire de Rémusat, lest there be any misunderstanding.

Afterward, however, Bonaparte was once again aware of the pressures that had brought him to the brink of divorce, and the interval of passion proved ephemeral. Still, he rescinded his decision for the time being.

Secretly wishing for an end to her long ordeal yet fearful of the shame and loss a divorce would bring, Josephine languished, her life in abeyance while she awaited her husband's definitive command. She was like a prisoner already sentenced to undergo punishment, yet condemned to wait for an indefinite period for the punishment to begin. It was not an unfamiliar state; she had discovered, in the Carmelite prison, what it was to await death, not to know when it would come or whether, from day to day, she would be allowed to live a little longer. Then her life itself had been at stake, now it was not her life but her way of life, the surroundings in which she spent her time, her place in the imperial family, her role at the apex of society, the material abundance to which she had become accustomed.

Kept in suspense, in a tedious state of limbo, denied her usual company and her usual pleasures, she clung to her possessions, as if taking refuge in the things she had amassed and continued to amass as a bulwark against her future fate. During 1808 and 1809 she over-spent with abandon, as if compelled by her condition of anxious suspense into a renewed burst of acquisitiveness.

She bought plants, furniture, Sèvres vases and crystal chandeliers. She paid painters to paint her portraits and then gave them away to servants. She spent lavishly on charity—more than ten percent of her annual allowance went to support relatives or pay annuities to elderly or indigent supplicants, among them Laure de Girardin, once Alex-andre de Beauharnais's mistress and now an ill, elderly widow nearing sixty, who had caused the youthful Rose de Beauharnais so much grief.

Sometimes the empress was observed to spend ten or twelve thou-sand francs in a single appetitive spree, then turn her back on the things she had bought and forget about them.

She became a collector of art objects and curiosities—antique sculptures, cameos, chunks of Russian amber, fine paintings and many genre paintings of little or no artistic value, rare books, harpsichords, columns of marble and granite, colorful plumes and feathers and, from Egypt, mummified heads and hands and entire mummies stolen from ancient graves. Malmaison was full of her treasures, yet she bought so many more that, in 1809, a new gallery was built to house them. Skylights illumined its hundred-foot length, and extra servants were employed to dust the items laid out for display on long tables.

Though her wardrobes and chests already held more dresses and linens than any one woman could possibly wear, she ordered more and more of everything, gowns of velvet and satin, embroidered mus-lin and percale, fitted coats of velours and taffeta capes, court dresses with lace ruffs and low-cut bodices outlined in cloth of gold. She had lace gowns that cost fifty or even a hundred thousand francs apiece, and gowns that were elaborate fantasies, covered in rose petals sewn on by hand at the last minute before wearing. One dress ap-peared to be made entirely of bright toucan feathers, each tipped with a pearl.

Josephine loved large, light soft cashmere shawls, and wore them in the mornings over her peignoir. She had so many of them—at least four hundred, by one count—that she had them made into dresses or coverings for her bed, or used them to cover cushions for her Russian wolfhounds to lie on.

The scale of her buying, in 1808 and 1809, was profligate: nearly a thousand pairs of gloves, eight hundred pairs of shoes, several thousand pairs of silk stockings in a variety of hues (she changed them three times a day, a new pair each time), hundreds of embroidered chemises, muslin peignoirs, delicate camisoles, nightcaps and handkerchieves trimmed in costly Valenciennes or Malines lace. Boxes and baskets of beautiful garments were brought to her apartments nearly every day, only to be given away, unwrapped and unworn, days or weeks later.

She clung to her array of things, yet they only increased her loneliness. Her solitary footsteps echoed in the vast galleries filled with odd collectibles and shallow scenic pictures. She sat alone, admiring her gowns as her four wardrobe women brought them before her one by one. Once in a long while, in response to a special request, she ordered a large table brought into her salon and had all her jewels spread out for a visitor to admire. They were truly dazzling, the stones large and brilliant, the huge pearls perfectly shaped and glowing, the display of rubies, sapphires, emeralds, and opals surpassing in size, number and quality any other European collection. The splendor of the glittering display was breathtaking, and the empress smiled to see the impression they made on her guest, but she soon ordered the treasure locked away again. She rarely wore her fine jewels, preferring wreaths of fresh flowers for her hair and simpler ornaments for her neck and wrists. Admiring the spectacle of blooming flowers in her hothouses gave her far more pleasure than looking over her jewels, but there too she was lonely, wandering among the plants in the steamy warm air, feeling lost and anxious.

One day she walked with Laure Junot in one of the overheated Malmaison greenhouses, pulling her cashmere shawl tight around her and complaining that she felt cold. She made conversation about family matters for a time, then became serious. She knew that Laure, who was at that time in the household of Letizia Bonaparte, was in a position to know what was being said about the question of divorce, while she herself was being kept in the dark.

"I beg you, tell me what you have been hearing about me," she said to Laure, taking her hands. "I ask this as a special favor to me, for you know that they all want to ruin me, and my children too."

It was the cri de coeur of a condemned woman, and Laure, who was discreet but also sympathetic, was moved, as Josephine leaned on her arm, shivering, her hands cold and clammy with fear. Laure knew that the empress had been quite ill, her headaches once again increasing in intensity and frequency and an abscess erupting that had "made her suffer horribly."[1]

"Remember what I tell you today," Josephine said, her words melodramatic but her voice calm. "This separation will be my death, and it is they who have killed me."

The pronouncement was oracular, the tone dark with prophecy, like that of a soothsayer on Martinique. Josephine had in fact been consulting fortune-tellers often, much to Bonaparte's displeasure—he ordered her favorite prophetess, Mademoiselle Lenormand, put in prison for the second time in 1809. Anguished in her uncertain situation, and deliberately kept from knowing the state of her husband's mind, she reached out for help in the only place she knew to find it: the occult.

Now, however, she had at hand a more reliable oracle in the person of Laure Junot, but Laure, whose first loyalty was to her Bonaparte mistress, could say little.

Laure's eldest daughter came running up as the two women were walking among the flowers, and Josephine, who had never yet seen her own granddaughter and namesake in Italy, gave the little girl a hug.

"You cannot know how much I have suffered when one of you has brought a child to me," she said in tears. "Heaven knows I am not envious, but I have felt as though a deadly poison were spreading through my veins." She knew, for it had been explained to her often enough, that it was not solely her inability to have Bonaparte's child that was forcing her marriage to an end, but the fact that she did not belong to a great royal house. Her past, too, was against her, and her age, and her strong personality. Bonaparte had long since come to prefer the womanly softness of Marie Walewska—whom he brought to Paris to be near him—to Josephine's flashes of rebellion, emotionality and endless physical complaints. (Still, when her abscess was giving her pain he nursed her from time to time, looking in on her three or four times a night, loyal and tender though deeply ambivalent, his very solicitude confusing and stressing her further.)

In her heart of hearts she knew what must come, and that it could not be long delayed, but still she consulted her cards, and called in psychics in a vain search for reassurance, and begged old friends to have pity on her and tell her what they knew.

Late in October of 1809 Josephine was summoned to Fontainebleau to join the court. She went, full of dread, upheld and comforted in her apprehension by Hortense and her two children. (A third son had been born to Hortense and Louis early in 1808, named Charles-Louis-Napoleon.) She found her usual apartments waiting, and moved into them, but in every other respect nothing was the same. Paulette had taken her place as the emperor's hostess, presiding over meals, holding balls and parties every night from which Josephine was excluded, leading the ladies to the hunt, and in every way eclipsing her sister-in-law. Paulette had even provided her brother with a new blonde mistress, a companion to divert him during the last weeks of his marriage.

For the imperial marriage was, at last, coming to an end. There at Fontainebleau, in November of 1809, the emperor at last decided to cut his ties to his wife. The timing was propitious, and chosen with care; although Bonaparte faced increasing hostility from the British in Spain and Belgium, he had won a great and decisive victory at Wagram in July, and in October had forced Austria to sign yet another peace treaty beneficial to France. He had won renewed respect from his fickle subjects, and his standing among the powers of Europe was high. Consequently his hopes for a great dynastic union had risen. The time had come to marry a highborn bride.

A representative of the French court was sent to Petersburg to discover whether Tsar Alexander's sister Anne was mature enough for marriage, and if so, to ask for her hand. Should the Russian marriage prove unworkable, the choice would fall on the Austrian Archduchess Marie Louise, eighteen years old and eminently marriageable; for the Austrian emperor to refuse to bestow his daughter on the victor of Wagram and the conqueror of Vienna was unthinkable.

To be sure, there was another candidate. The Bonapartes, suspicious of a foreign marriage, wanted the emperor to marry within the family. Lucien's fourteen-year-old daughter Charlotte would make the perfect bride, they thought. She was intelligent, obedient, and above all, Corsican. The union of uncle and niece would heal the old breach between the emperor and Lucien, and ensure that all the imperial wealth would remain within the family into the next generation.

No matter whom Bonaparte chose, Josephine would have to bow out gracefully to make room for her. But the emperor could not bear to tell her himself that the time had come for her to go. He asked the arch-chancellor, Cambacérès, to tell her for him, and when he refused, he tried others, including Hortense, and he assumed that Hortense would do as he asked.

The court returned to Paris, and Josephine, after four miserable weeks of being ignored and insulted, or simply treated as if she were invisible, sensed that the moment had come for her to be asked to leave. Hortense may or may not have carried the emperor's fateful message to her, but Josephine continued to wait in mournful silence at the Tuileries for Bonaparte to speak to her directly.

On the night of November 30 she sat down to dinner with her husband and others as usual, Paulette presiding. Josephine was subdued and red-eyed, "the image of sadness and despair," Laure Junot thought. Bonaparte had been lashing out at her angrily for overspending her allowance, and was still fuming over a scene that had taken place a day or so earlier.

He had gone to her apartments and found there a man he had explicitly forbidden her to see, a popular German psychic who had cards spread out on a table and was telling her fortune.

Incensed, Bonaparte shouted that she was deliberately disobeying him. Surprised and nonplussed, Josephine tried to cover up her disobedience by lying, saying that she had not invited the fortune-teller, that he had come uninvited with a dressmaker recommended by Letizia. The dressmaker hid in terror, the German was defiant, and Bonaparte, disgusted and angry, stormed out, slamming the door behind him and ordering his prefect Duroc to have both the dressmaker and the fortune-teller thrown out.

The emperor's fury had less to do with the presence of a psychic in Josephine's apartments than with the fact that Josephine was being obtuse. He was impatient to proceed with his wedding plans; he had ordered that she be informed of his plans for her; he needed her out of his way. He expected her to understand, to be cooperative. Instead she was witlessly refusing to accept the obvious and make a graceful exit.

"There is a storm brewing," Duroc told Laure Junot. "It is all about the divorce. The empress, who has never grasped what her true position is, cannot see what is happening; even a dying man has second sight, but she remains blind. . . . Her stupidity has ruined everything."

The unhappy dinner proceeded, and afterward, when Bonaparte and Josephine were in the salon having coffee, the storm Duroc had alluded to began to break. Weeping, holding a handkerchief to her eyes, Josephine asked her husband the question to which she had known the answer for years.

"Why do you want to leave me? Are we not happy?"

The fatuous question, which was meant to be provocative, produced a tirade.

"Happy? Happy? Why, the lowest clerk of one of my ministers is happier than I! Happy? Are you mocking me?" He paced and fumed, listing his grievances: he had been tormented by Josephine's unreasoning jealousy, by her accusations, by her hysteria. He might have been happy, he said accusingly, if she had not destroyed his peace by her suspicions and her anger. But with her mistrustful nature, contentment was impossible—and besides, the interests of France demanded that he put aside the vain search for contentment and find a wife who could provide an heir to the throne.

"So all is over then?" she asked.

Exasperated, he told her again that the needs of the French people had to come first—adding that she had forced him into this position, and that he was suffering more than she was, since, as he put it, "it is my hand that is hurting you."[2]

Josephine had begun to cry once again, and soon her tears became inconsolable sobs. All her pent-up fears poured forth in wails of dismay, shock and apprehension.

"No, I can never survive it!" she cried, falling onto the floor in a fit of weeping that was half tantrum, half grief-stricken collapse.

With the aid of one of the palace prefects, Bonaparte managed to carry the now near-comatose Josephine to her own bedroom. He was clearly surprised by the extent of her reaction, having expected Hortense to prepare her several days earlier. "I pity her with all my soul," the emperor told the prefect. "I thought she had more character, and I was not prepared for the outburst of her grief."

Bonaparte had convinced himself, against all evidence he had ever had of her, that Josephine would take the news of the impending divorce calmly. He thought that she would have begun thinking about the life she would have following the divorce. He assumed that she would consider marrying again, and even suggested the prince of Mecklenburg-Strelitz as a suitable husband.[3] Her collapse unnerved him, and his subsequent conversation with Hortense unnerved him still further.

Hortense had been summoned, along with Doctor Corvisart, to stay with the desolate Josephine. She told the emperor that, once the divorce was accomplished, she and Eugene would feel obligated to leave court and join their mother.

Now it was his turn to be stricken.

"What!" he cried in a choked voice. "You are all going to leave me? You are going to desert me? Then you don't care for me any more?"

When, a few days later, Eugene arrived from Italy, he too told Bonaparte that he felt compelled to withdraw along with his mother.

Troubled at the thought of losing the two stepchildren he genuinely loved, Bonaparte wavered; perhaps a way could be found for Josephine to remain within the orbit of the court, he suggested, or perhaps a divorce was not the best thing after all.

Both Hortense and Eugene were firm. There could be no compromise, no half-measures. Now that the entire family knew his intent, Josephine could not go on living with him without anxiety. The divorce must proceed as planned. Nothing could be the same as it was before.

Over the next ten days the servants were occupied with packing the empress's possessions and loading them into carts to be taken to Malmaison which, she had been informed, she would be allowed to keep as her own private residence. It must have been painful for her, watching the procession of trunks and baskets and boxes parade past, until the elegant rooms—rooms whose furnishings she had chosen with such care—were emptied of everything that was hers. Her marble-topped tables and escritoires and dressing cases, her cabinets of fine inlaid woods that held her treasures—her keepsakes from Hippolyte, Alexandre's letters, mementos from her long marriage to Bonaparte—her few possessions from childhood, all were efficiently placed in trunks and taken away, even the few books on botany she had kept in her bedroom and the toy soldiers, doll's furniture, miniature carriage and wooden warship on wheels she kept for her grandchildren to play with when they visited her.

Her dogs and birds were taken last. The female wolfhound was about to have a litter of pups, and it was thought that the journey to Malmaison might harm her.

There were other leavetakings too. The empress's household of several hundred people was rapidly shrinking, amid much excitement and trepidation about who the new mistress of the Tuileries would be and which of Josephine's many attendants would serve her. Only a handful of servants would accompany the empress to Malmaison, and for these, the move would mean a considerable reduction in salary and rank. Having lived and served at the grandest court in Europe, they would be retiring to a comfortable but relatively modest private home, to serve an ailing mistress of only marginal importance to the state.

In the first weeks of December 1809, while the moving went forward and decisions were made about the legal and ceremonial aspects of the divorce, the empress continued to appear in public, wearing her crown but seated far from the emperor and unacknowledged by him. She drew much attention at the ceremony held at the Hôtel de Ville to celebrate the fifth anniversary of the emperor's coronation, for by now it was generally known that her marriage would soon end and her reaction was closely watched.

Her dignity was much remarked on at the dinners, concerts and other seasonal events she attended, for despite the strain she was under and her recent brief breakdown, she managed to retain her customary gracious persona. She ignored the many watchful stares, the smiles and snickers of the Bonapartes, the endless conversations she could not help but overhear about who the next empress would be.

She began to discover that, after all, she could survive, that what was truest and strongest in her was buoyant amid difficulty. Bonaparte had promised that he would remain her friend, that he would see her often, that the familial ties that had bound her and her children to him would not be severed, merely continued in another form. He had promised to provide generously for her, giving her not only Malmaison but the Elysée Palace and an allowance of three million francs a year. He had agreed to pay all her outstanding debts, and had offered to give her a small principality in Italy to rule as well—but this she declined. She had always wanted a private, secluded life; now she was to have it.

She would still be known as Empress Josephine, but she would be empress, not of the French, but of Malmaison. There would be no more stress, no more conflict, no more irritating, venomous in-laws, no more intrigues. Along with her sadness and grief, Josephine may have felt an unaccustomed sense of repose, even relief, in the last days before her divorce became official. Perhaps now she could re-cover the life of ease she had lost when her husband began his rise to prominence, the long languorous afternoons, the slow strolls through the greenhouses, the pleasant indolence that had felt so nat-ural to her as a girl in Martinique.

Hortense encouraged her to look ahead, not with trepidation but with pleasant anticipation, to the future that was opening before her. "For the first time in our lives," Hortense had told her, "far from the world and the court, we will lead a real family life and know our first real happiness."

29

"The Elder Sister of the Graces"

The ceremony was brief and dignified. Bonaparte had given orders to the arch-chancellor that he wanted nothing in it that would dishonor Josephine, or imply that she was being rejected. All was done with decorum, leaving the court with the impression that the divorce was a family decision—indeed a "family sacrifice," made for the good of the empire and the emperor's subjects.

The grand throne room of the Tuileries was prepared as if for a magnificent celebration, and the courtiers assembled there, gowned and robed in their formal best. Among them were the Bonapartes, or most of them: Elisa had not come from Italy, being pregnant and too near her time for travel, and Joseph was in Spain, but Caroline and Murat, Jerome and his new wife Catherine, Louis, Paulette and Letizia were all present, sleek with satisfaction, eager for the moment when the last document was signed and the emperor became a free man.

Josephine, in an unadorned white dress, wearing no jewels and without her crown, entered the emperor's private study leaning on Hortense's arm, and the rest of the family filed in, seating themselves on chairs and stools around the walls. Josephine appeared pale but calm, Constant recalled, as she sat in an armchair in the middle of the room; indeed the others present, especially Hortense and Eugene, seemed much more upset than she was. Eugene in particular, who stood beside his stepfather with his arms crossed, was trembling so violently that he looked as if he might have a fit.¹ Bonaparte sat immobile as a statue, staring wild-eyed at nothing.

As soon as Josephine entered the study the arch-chancellor arrived, bearing the divorce documents, and accompanied by another official, the secretary of state to the imperial household.

The emperor rose and began to read from a prepared statement, departing from the text to add his own words. He explained that, motivated by concern for his subjects and knowing that he needed to provide a successor to his throne, he had decided, with much anguish of heart, to give up the wife he loved. "Far from ever finding cause for complaint," he said, "I can to the contrary only congratulate myself on the devotion and tenderness of my beloved wife. She has adorned fifteen years of my life; the memory will always remain engraved on my heart."²

After avowing that he would always remain "her best and dearest friend," Bonaparte turned to Josephine, who remained calm, but wept quietly, the tears running down her pale cheeks. She had been given a speech of her own to read, and had gone over it a good deal, making changes and recopying it in her own handwriting.

She began to read.

"With the permission of our august and dear husband, I must declare that, having no hope of bearing children who would fulfill the needs of his policies and the interests of France, I am pleased to offer him the greatest proof of attachment and devotion ever offered on this earth." Her voice gave out. More tears ran down her face. She handed the paper to the secretary, who read the rest of it.

The short speech expressed her indebtedness to Bonaparte for crowning her, and referred to him as "a great man raised up by Providence to drive out the evils of revolution" and restore order in society. Her feelings remained the same, though her marriage was ending. She would remain the emperor's "best friend." The speech concluded with the sentiment that both spouses would find their satisfaction in the sacrifice they were making for the good of the empire.

It only remained for all present to sign the official documents, to be passed on to the Council of State so that they could be made law by the Senate on the following day.

With a trembling hand Josephine signed her name. She still was, and would remain, empress.

Rain poured down on the courtyard of the Tuileries the next morning as the empress's carriages were being loaded. Her departure was singularly unheralded, and her retinue modest in size; in the past she had never traveled without a cavalry squadron escorting her, along with outriders and a staff of thirty or forty officials and a long parade of footmen, pages, ladies-in-waiting and menial servants. Now she had only Hortense, half a dozen female retainers and several chamberlains, her parrot and her wolfhounds with their newborn puppies. She was a private woman once again, albeit one who still bore an exalted title.

Bonaparte came to say good-bye and kissed her chastely but affectionately, as he might have kissed a favorite aunt, before making a brusque departure. Servants came to say their good-byes also, and from a distance, beyond the palace courtyard, a crowd had gathered to watch the leave-taking.

Once at Malmaison, Josephine tried to settle in, but instead of discovering her first real happiness, as Hortense had predicted, she was overwhelmed by melancholy. Bonaparte, true to his promise, came to see her quite often, and sent her letters, and in other ways reminded her that he was watching intently to see how she was adapting to her new life.

Pathetically, she clung to him. Having become distant and estranged during the latter years of their marriage, now that they were divorced she became for a time emotionally dependent on him as she never had been before. She was like a child, fearful of being abandoned by a capricious parent. She ran to meet his carriage when she heard it coming along the road toward the house. Smiling through her tears, she took his arm and led him into the park, where they sat together or strolled under the leafless trees or walked in the greenhouses. Seeing him, spending time with him gave her the only contentment she knew in her first weeks as a divorced woman. He was solicitous, concerned, far more attentive than he had been as a husband. For her, it was as if all the cruelty, all the humiliation and torment to which he had subjected her during their marriage had been temporarily forgotten.

She could not envision any other life than the one she had begun to lead, there at Malmaison, dwelling apart from the emperor yet seeing him frequently. When Prince Frederick wrote to Bonaparte, formally asking his permission to marry Josephine, she refused to consider the proposal. Marrying the prince would mean moving to Mecklenburg, and she did not want to leave the emperor's side. Besides, it seems clear that she did not love her young suitor, or even have much regard for him. In her present state, crushed and sorrowful, and deeply fearful of what would happen to her if she lost Bonaparte's affection, she could think of nothing but how to maintain the status quo.

"My dear," the emperor wrote to her shortly after she left the Tuileries, "today I found you weaker than you should have been. You have shown courage in the past, you must find courage now to support you." He urged her not to give in to despairing feelings, but to resign herself to her new life, and guard her health. "You must never doubt my constant and tender friendship," he wrote in conclusion, "and you would greatly misunderstand all my feelings toward you if you imagine that I can be happy if you are not happy, or content if you are restless."[3]

He sent a number of courtiers to visit her, and she received them all, though not in a mood to do so, wearing wide hats to hide her tearstained face. Some of the visitors were sympathetic; to those she confided that she "greatly needed to keep up her courage," and did not try to hide her tears. Others came merely because the emperor requested it. Still others were unkind, even spiteful, telling Josephine that she was getting fat and looking at her disdainfully. She treated each of them with the same welcoming sweetness. She was, Claire de Rémusat observed, "truly as gentle and affectionate as an angel," without bitterness or resentment.

She took her guests into her new gallery where all her paintings and other treasures were on display. An unfinished portrait of her by the painter Isabey—a flattering, youthful portrait—was in evident contrast to her present strained appearance. "It was the work of a friend rather than a painter," she told them in response to their unspoken reactions.

Seeing old friends both cheered and saddened her. When Therese Tallien—now the Princesse de Caraman-Chimay—and Fortunée Hamelin came to Malmaison, she embraced them with a rush of sentimental feeling, for Bonaparte had forbidden her to see either of them for nearly a decade. Though both women were by now middle-aged, Fortunée was as vivid, outspoken and entertaining as ever, and Therese, who had borne at least eight children, was still beautiful. By their presence alone they reminded Josephine of all that she had lost: they were abiding reminders of a time, many years earlier, when she had been carefree, even reckless, when her pleasures had been keen and her health strong, her lovers numerous and her future unshadowed.

For six leaden weeks and more, while ceaseless rain fell from grey skies and the gardens of Malmaison were reduced to a quagmire, Josephine labored under the effects of her melancholy. She was constantly in tears, so that "it gave one pain to see her," Claire de Rémusat recalled. "Sometimes," Josephine admitted, "it seems as though I were dead and had only a vague awareness that I no longer exist."

Her nights were full of suffering, her days empty, even when she was surrounded by companions. Every time she heard that a hunt was to be held in the forest bordering the estate, she went to the window in her study from which the main road was visible, watching for the emperor's carriage to pass. Seeing it was the high point of her day, even when he did not make the detour to Malmaison for a brief visit.

Toward the end of January she moved back to Paris, to her other residence, the Elysée Palace. The capital was astir with excitement, for in February the emperor announced that he would be marrying Marie Louise, Archduchess of Austria. The Russian alliance had foundered, in part because of the stubborn opposition of the dowager empress, who referred to Bonaparte as "the bloody tyrant who rules Europe with his iron scepter," and in part, so Bonaparte believed, because Josephine had spread a rumor that he was impotent—a rumor that she was formally called upon to dispel.

While making lavish preparations for the wedding, Parisians whispered that it was bad luck for a French ruler to marry an Austrian— look what happened to Louis XVI after he married one!—and gossiped about Marie Louise, who was said to be as stolid, phlegmatic and graceless as Josephine was tremulous, enchanting and graceful. Those who had seen the Austrian archduchess pronounced her to be a blonde farm girl with a heavy tread (though with surprisingly small and dainty feet), and said that her only talent was an odd ability to manipulate the muscles of her jaw so that one ear turned around nearly in a circle.[4]

Still, Marie Louise was nineteen, healthy and promisingly fertile, and the daughter of an imperial house, and that was what mattered. She had been given a very large dowry by her father, and her trousseau was magnificent—indeed the emperor himself was said to be preoccupied with supervising the assembling of her many beautiful garments. Hortense, who after her initial decision to leave Bonaparte's court had agreed to return and to become one of the new empress's ladies-in-waiting, told her mother of the sweeping changes being made in honor of Marie Louise's arrival: the renovation of the Tuileries, the organization of a new household, the appointment of Josephine's former dressmaker and hairdresser to serve the new empress and no one else, the beautiful satin wedding gown being cut and sewn from measurements sent from Vienna, the waltzing lessons Bonaparte was valiantly taking so that he could conduct himself on the dance floor like a proper Viennese. (The waltzing lessons were a fiasco; Talleyrand observed to the emperor that "he danced perfectly—for a great man.")[5]

Far from taking offense or feeling wounded by all the reminders that she was being supplanted by another woman, Josephine did her best to give the impression that she was pleased by her former husband's choice, that she favored the Austrian marriage and had even taken a hand in sponsoring it. Her sacrifice had been made in order to serve this outcome—or so the rhetoric of the divorce ceremony had asserted.

Once she left Malmaison, Josephine cast off her gloom, her strong and even cunning instinct for survival beginning to reassert itself. Realizing that it was in every way in her interest to ingratiate herself with the new empress and her entourage, she invited Marie Louise's chamberlains to dinner and won from them a promise to "guard her interests" with the new empress.

Before Bonaparte's ascent to power, Josephine had always known how to attain her goals through gaining influence with key people, and she had not lost that skill. She needed it now, if she was to make a place for herself—not so prominent a place that Marie Louise felt threatened by her, yet not so inconsequential a place that she could be thrust aside or exiled with ease—at the emperor's court.

Late in March Marie Louise arrived at Compiègne one evening with her many carriages of servants and possessions, and Bonaparte, who had been beside himself with impatience, was gratified by the sight of the plump, girlish archduchess, her cheeks rosy and her demeanor pleasingly diffident. Ignoring protocol, he supped with her in private. Afterward, being assured by his Uncle Fesch that the proxy wedding that had taken place in Vienna several weeks earlier constituted a legal civil marriage, the emperor bedded his young wife despite her cold. The experiment was a success.

The wedding of Emperor Napoleon I and Archduchess Marie Louise of Austria was held amid an atmosphere of grand spectacle. The ceremony itself, performed under an immense canopy in the gallery of the Louvre, brought together crowned heads and dignitaries in a glittering ornamental cluster, and the brilliance of the imperial court had never been more resplendent. Heralds in bright livery blew a fanfare, and senators, ministers, princes, and officials took their places beside bejeweled ladies in satin gowns. In the palace courtyard masses of troops stood to attention, there were artillery salutes and peals of bells, and the spring weather was sunny and seemingly full of promise.

The emperor was seen to smile with satisfaction throughout the ceremony, and Marie Louise, though stiff and awkward, and uncomfortable in her heavy diadem which pressed too hard on her temples, managed an occasional wan grimace. The proceedings were not without complications; the church refused to sanction the marriage, and no cardinals were present, and some of the participants in the ceremony were offended in matters of precedence and protocol. But the banquet that followed was opulent, wine flowed from all the fountains and fireworks lit the night sky for hours.

All the mansions and public buildings of Paris were ornamented with colored lights—even the church towers were outlined in glowing fires that seemed to shoot upward into the darkness. Along the Louis XV bridge, tall columns, each surmounted by a beaming star, were bound together with garlands of shining colored glass, making the entire structure pulse with brilliant light. An immense star, faceted like a diamond, shone above the Observatory on its hill, and from the cupola of the church of St-Geneviève, high above the city, a leaping flame burst forth.

Paris was at its most enchanting that April, but Josephine was not there to see it. She had been asked to remove herself for a time, so that her presence might not blemish the reception of the emperor's new wife.

Typically, Bonaparte made Josephine's temporary exile from Paris seem like an increase in honor. He granted her the duchy of Navarre, a small territory in Normandy sixty miles west of the capital, with its annual income of two million francs—a substantial increase in her revenues. The château had beautiful gardens, for previous owners had turned the wooded slopes of its extensive grounds into a fantasyland of artificial canals, streams, and pools along whose banks trees and flowers were planted. Thinking that the gardens would appeal to Josephine, the emperor chose to overlook the defects of the dilapidated old mansion that stood on the grounds. He all but commanded his former wife to go and live on her new estate during the month of April.

For the fourth time in six months, Josephine and her diminishing retinue packed their trunks and set out for a new destination.

The people of Evreux turned out to welcome her on her arrival, yet her heart sank at the pitiful reception, so different from the grand ceremonies offered to her in earlier days. The speeches made by the town dignitaries were closer to condolences than congratulations, and the dispirited applause was a reminder that her status had changed permanently. "Doubtless they were sorry," Josephine wrote to Hortense, "that I no longer counted for much."[6]

When she reached her estate she was at first impressed. The house itself, of an archaic design with a baroque round tower and fanciful cupola, was situated at the end of an avenue several miles long, lined with mature elms—truly a stately entrance. A vast expanse of lawn, ornamented with two large pools, set off the house to advantage, while more mature trees flanked its wings. From a distance, the entire grand vista was both imposing and charming: the house, raised on its height and with its several terraces, on one side a small river, on the other an expanse of meadow bordered by a magnificent waterfall, wooded hills, and a distant village, all enclosed in a green valley.

Once the new occupant moved in, however, she was quickly dismayed by the deplorable condition of the interior. The mansion had been empty since the outbreak of revolution twenty years earlier, and had been neglected before that. The roof leaked, the woodwork was stained and warped, and mold grew along the cracked walls of the gilded salon. Worst of all, the drafty, high-ceilinged salon and small dark rooms were freezing cold, for the woodwork was so swollen that the windows would not close and the chimneys were too blocked to draw properly.

After days of great discomfort, repairs were begun, and the weather grew warmer. Josephine began to discover the pleasures of the sodden gardens.

One afternoon that May she guided her visiting cousin Maurice de Tascher through the labyrinth of canals and streams. Maurice, who was not one of Josephine's first cousins from Martinique but from a different branch of the Tascher family, was somewhat overwhelmed by the state in which Josephine lived; the large numbers of servants in the ornate salon, the sophisticated conversation among the empress's waiting women, the pervasive worldliness and savoir faire, all left him feeling inadequate and tongue-tied. He admired the charm of the estate, though he found it too manicured, the gardens too artificial to be truly appealing. Like the carefully chosen words and carefully modulated gestures he had observed in the salon, there was too much artifice, too little that was authentic and natural.

Josephine, however, he found to be all natural charm. When she appeared on the terrace in her morning gown, with her pretty cousin Stephanie, Princess of Aremberg and her niece Stephanie, Princess of Baden beside her, she was captivating.

"The most ingenious art, the most elegant simplicity were present in her toilette," Maurice wrote in his journal. The evidence of her advanced years was wiped away. "Her gracious smile, knowing and intelligent, made her lovable even before she spoke. Her glance was full of sweetness and charm, and the beauty of her soul was evident." She was good, attractive, her womanly appeal still strong.[7]

He followed his cousin through the Garden of Hebe, scented with the heady fragrance of lilacs in bloom, as they walked along the banks of swollen streams and across lush green lawns. Josephine had hired gardeners to tend the grounds and restore the paths, and Maurice remarked on the large number of them.

Leaving the Garden of Hebe with its leafy woods and rose bushes they came to the Garden of Love, an aquatic garden where artificial waterfalls cascaded into shallow pools. Here antique statues bordered the path, which here and there offered scenic vistas of the valley and surrounding hills. Maurice could not help admiring his cousin Josephine, "still beautiful and seductive," as he noted in his diary, "despite her forty-five years." In truth Josephine was approaching her forty-seventh birthday, and her dyed hair, heavily made-up face and rotted teeth all betrayed her age. Wide-brimmed hats and veils shielded her from the revealing glare of the spring sun.

Yet when she stood beside the waterfalls, framed by the blooming flowerbeds and overhanging willows, Josephine still exerted a powerful feminine charm. "One would have taken her this morning," Maurice de Tascher wrote, "without hyperbole, for the elder sister of the Graces."

30

"Alone, Abandoned, and in the Midst of Strangers"

*J*osephine was only too aware that she was in limbo. She occupied a very ill-defined position as the emperor's ex-wife, sundered from the court yet with her own titles and dignity, and possessing her ex-husband's declared good will and favor—at once her most valuable asset and her greatest vulnerability in her uncertain state.

She knew that, if Empress Marie-Louise became frightened or felt threatened by her continued presence in France, because of Bonaparte's good will toward her, she might receive official orders to absent herself permanently from the country. Her continuing celebrity, and her popularity with the French, were dangerous; in the long run it would be best for her to downplay both, in order to avoid giving offense to the new occupant of the Tuileries and her august relatives.

Visitors to Navarre brought her the latest gossip from Paris, which was ominous. It was said in the capital that Bonaparte, enchanted with his young bride and eager to please her, did everything she told him to do. Marie-Louise was said to be very jealous of Josephine and ill-disposed toward her. It was only a matter of time until she seized Malmaison, poisoned Bonaparte against his former wife, and insisted that Josephine retire to some far-off place—much farther away than Normandy.

Knowing how capricious Bonaparte could be, Josephine was made anxious by the rumors, and her anxiety was not entirely assuaged, even after she was allowed to return to Malmaison. Bonaparte visited her there in June of 1810, six months after the divorce, in the best of spirits and full of affectionate consideration; after an hour and a half spent conversing with him, Josephine felt reassured that, for the time being, he would not abandon her.

Nevertheless she thought it best to remove herself from the vicinity of Paris for a time—perhaps at Bonaparte's suggestion—and made up her mind to travel. For years it had been her habit to go each summer to Aix-les-Bains in Savoy, and in mid-June she set off once again for the spa, accompanied by Claire de Rémusat and several other ladies, her black servant Malvina, five chamberlains and a variety of footmen and grooms, and her dog Askim.

She traveled incognito, borrowing the name of a member of her household, Madame d'Arberg. She rented several houses at Aix, for herself and Hortense, and a cottage for her staff, and settled into a pleasant routine of bathing in the spa waters in the mornings, dining with her household, then driving out in a carriage in the afternoon.

For the former wife of the emperor to disguise her true identity was impossible. Everyone knew that "Madame d'Arberg" was in fact Empress Josephine. Each afternoon a crowd formed near her house to watch for her carriage, and people came from as far away as Turin and Grenoble to catch a glimpse of her and hand her petitions to pass along to Bonaparte. She accepted the petitions, and greeted the petitioners with patience and kindness, telling each one that she would do what she could to help.

Everywhere she and her companions went they encountered gawkers, attracted by the sight of her beautiful carriage and splendid horses, the liveried servants that accompanied the vehicle, and the expensively dressed ladies inside. Soon the people of Aix became accustomed to the sight of the town's most distinguished visitor, and recognized at a glance her plump figure, large feathered hats and bright cashmere shawls. She had become matronly, exchanging her customary elegance for an overdressed heaviness of style that, to a discriminating eye, verged on the vulgar. Instead of light, floating pastel muslins with a deep decolletage she now wore gowns of thick silk in bright blues and purples buttoned to the neck. The delicate harmony of tones that had always characterized her style of dress now gave way to mismatched, even clashing colors. At Claire de Rémusat's insistence, Josephine began wearing stiff boned corsets, cinched in tightly at the waist; in the months since her divorce she had indulged herself in overeating, with the result that, as Bonaparte said, she was becoming "as fat as a good Normandy farmer's wife."

She was eating more, and feeling much better. Though still troubled with anxiety, she was far more relaxed than she had been in her years as Bonaparte's wife. Her nerves were less on edge, her body less subject to constant strain. Her nervous symptoms—constant weeping, irritability, above all her terrible migraines—receded. Her daily excursions were evidence of her improved health. She was often to be seen picnicking on picturesque hillsides, sitting under an umbrella beside a mountain spring, or standing at a scenic point, looking through a telescope at distant sights.

One afternoon Josephine and her party were out in a boat when suddenly a storm came up and the lake was churned by a strong wind. The small craft was tossed so violently that many of the passengers said their prayers and prepared to die, clinging desperately to the boat and to each other and hoping fervently that the sailors could manage to row them ashore. To hearten each other they began singing, and two of Josephine's chamberlains, Pourtalès and Turpin, held her hands and protected her as best they could. While the sailors pulled at the oars, spectators gathered on shore, in the rain, expecting disaster. But the boat did not quite founder, and at last it reached shore, full of water but still afloat, and the limp, drenched passengers were taken to safety.

Though she complained of being "alone, abandoned, . . . and in the midst of strangers," Josephine in fact had a good deal of companionship at Aix during the summer of 1810. Eugene and Augusta visited her, along with her cousin Louis Tascher. Several of her chamberlains, especially the mild-mannered, pleasant young Lancelot Turpin de Crissé, were very good company, and another member of the household, Charles de Flahaut, was cheery and entertaining.[1]

Hortense came to Aix twice during the summer, bringing her children. When she arrived the first time she was exhausted and ill, permanently separated from her husband and in a state of nervous collapse. Josephine had been concerned about Hortense for months, and had remained in close contact with her as her unhappy marriage entered its final stage. Following Josephine's divorce, Hortense's Bonaparte in-laws had attempted to coerce her into rejoining her husband in Holland and declaring herself to be on the Bonaparte side of the widening gulf between Bonaparte and Beauharnais. But the attempt at coercion failed, chiefly because Louis, at odds with his imperial brother, abdicated as King of Holland and the kingdom was absorbed into France. In the aftermath of this political debacle, Bonaparte gave Hortense permission to separate from Louis for good.

While at Aix Hortense began to revive, healed by the warm sun and fresh air, by a rejuvenating love affair with Charles de Flahaut, and by her mother's encouragement. Josephine urged Hortense to look within herself and renew her strength.

"Try to find a little courage, my dear daughter," Josephine had told Hortense in a letter shortly before her arrival at Aix. "You know that we have great need of it, both of us. Often mine is too weak, but I have faith in time and our own efforts."

Josephine's letter reflected her own growing inner strength and confidence. She was slowly returning to herself, rediscovering parts of herself that had been in eclipse for years. Now that she no longer lived under the dark spell of Bonaparte's continual manipulations, her emotional equilibrium was returning, along with a measure of physical health. An unaccustomed robustness of spirit replaced her habitual timidity and dread. She saw things more clearly, understood them better, feared them less.

To be sure, she was still capable of being reduced to a state of tearful dependency when confronted by her former husband, either by letter or in person. But the symptoms of overwrought nerves—the frantic weeping, labile emotions, fretful worries and constant sense of impending doom—were not so severe as before, and as a result, the world and everything in it began to look brighter.

From Aix Josephine went on to tour Switzerland in the fall, staying at a lakeside hotel in Geneva where a water festival was held in her honor. Amid bursting fireworks and serenading musicians on floating barges, she rode out on the lake in a special boat drawn by two swans, escorted by hundreds of small craft decorated with waving pennons and garlands of flowers. Her reception by the Genevans pleased her. "It is so gratifying to be loved," she told the mayor, thanking him for all the attention.

Her days that fall were filled with short trips—to Voltaire's estate at Ferney, to Bern, to Interlaken. She entertained local dignitaries, attended theatrical entertainments with folk dancing, wrestling and concerts on the Alpine horn. She presided at banquets and watched parades of flower-draped, bell-laden cows come down from their mountain pastures.

On one memorable trip she set out from Chamonix, on horseback, with an entourage of eighty guides, porters and companions, and ascended the lower slopes of Mont Blanc. When her horse could go no higher she had herself carried in a sedan chair to the Mer de Glace, and despite the icy wind walked out across the glacier, wrapped in furs.

Such trips exhilarated her, and helped to take her mind off the fateful news she had recently received from Bonaparte: Empress Marie Louise was pregnant.

Now that an imperial heir was going to be born, Josephine felt her position to be more precarious than ever. Bonaparte wanted her out of the way during the pregnancy, and suggested, via Hortense, that she settle in Rome as French governor there, or go to Brussels, or, at the very least, arrange to stay with Eugene in Milan throughout the winter. Certainly she should not return to Malmaison, so close to the capital; her presence there would upset the pregnant empress.

The disconcerting news threatened to reverse all Josephine's gains. She lost weight and stamina, and felt overcome by fatigue. She worried that Hortense and Eugene would suffer when Marie Louise's child was born, Hortense because her own two sons would no longer be of even marginal importance to Bonaparte as potential heirs, and Eugene because the new baby would displace him as ruler of Italy. Eugene had been offered another kingdom, Sweden, but had turned it down. Josephine feared that he too would now be in limbo, his future and that of his growing family uncertain.

Unwelcome in France, and enjoying her stay in Switzerland, Josephine decided to prolong it by buying a modest estate just outside Geneva on the shore of the lake. There, during October of 1810, she rested and pondered her future, while she waited for further word from France.

The Prégny-La-Tour estate was a miniature world unto itself, with several orchards, a patch of woods, fields of grain and vines and a wide expanse of meadow. A small dock extended out into the lake. Each of the three terraces of the main house provided views of the lake and mountains, and each had its own garden. It was a quiet, restful place, the sort of place Josephine may well have had in mind when she told Eugene several years earlier that "a profound solitude" would please her most.[2]

After less than a month, however, Josephine ordered her household to pack once again for the return to Navarre. Perhaps Prégny was overly isolating, or possibly, with the first snow beginning to fall, Switzerland seemed less inviting than Normandy with its rain and fog.

"I need many distractions," she told Bonaparte in a letter shortly before she moved to Prégny, "and I find them only in a change of location."[3] Clearly she considered her new estate no more than a temporary diversion, a place to come to rest briefly before moving on.

Josephine's estate at Navarre had been made much more appealing—indeed almost welcoming—than it had been the previous winter. Renovations had proceeded in her absence, the roof had been repaired and all the chimneys swept and cleaned. The fireplaces no longer smoked, and the small rooms that radiated off the grand salon were warm, their walls newly plastered and painted and the windows made tight in their wooden frames. Hundreds of plants had been brought from the gardens and hothouses of Malmaison, so that Josephine could enjoy her palms and ferns and sugar cane during the cold Normandy winter.

Declaring that she would henceforth occupy herself with "botany and the arts," Josephine settled in toward the end of November 1810, and did her best to make a comfortable place for herself within provincial society.[4] She invited the leading citizens of Evreux to dine with her, impressing them with the array of footmen, stewards, and valets that hovered around her long dining table, several servants for each guest. After dinner there were card games, or a concert. On occasion Josephine herself sang, somewhat to the surprise of her guests; she knew arias from some contemporary operas by heart, and could follow along and sing harmony if stronger voices took the lead.[5]

Her evenings were full, but her days were long and empty, particularly when the cold and rain confined her indoors. She sat by the hour doing needlework while her chamberlains read aloud. She played billiards. She played endless games of patience. She told fortunes. And she brooded: about the fact that Bonaparte no longer visited her, about what would happen when Marie Louise's child was born, about the brilliant winter season in Paris, from which she was excluded, and the life of the revitalized court.

Tactless visitors to Navarre brought Josephine news of grand balls and parties in the capital, said to be the most magnificent in years, where an array of elegantly dressed courtiers and titled aristocrats danced and supped amid extravagant splendor. Ignoring Josephine's sensitive feelings, her guests informed her of the grand receptions and balls held at the Tuileries where Bonaparte and his new empress presided like demigods reigning over lesser mortals. For the first time since the days of Marie Antoinette a generation earlier a lady of royal blood graced the palace; Bonaparte spared no expense in providing a luxurious backdrop for her exalted presence—and basking in its glory.

The imminent arrival of an heir for the Bonaparte dynasty added the glow of anticipation to all the festivities. Marie Louise's pregnancy was advancing normally, it was said. Her child would be healthy. The baby was expected in March and naturally, everyone at court hoped for a boy.

Josephine was quite forgotten in the midst of all the excitement in Paris. Her former friends and acquaintances, all those she had benefited when they asked for her help, neglected her. Even those who had come to see her at Malmaison the previous winter did not pay their respects at Navarre, or even write her or send messages.

"Those who, in previous days, seemed so attached to me have given me no proofs of their former regard," she wrote to Eugene. "I forgive them with all my heart. I recall only those who have not forgotten me and I don't think about the others. . . . I have drawn the line which I must follow and I will not stray from it; that is, to live apart from everyone in retreat, but with dignity and without asking for anything but rest."[6]

That she had received no word from Marie Louise was only to be expected. "It seems Empress Marie Louise has not spoken about me," Josephine told her son, "and that she has no desire to see me. In that we are in perfect agreement; I would not have consented to see her except to please the emperor."[7]

Winter came, and Josephine's life became even more restricted. She told Eugene that the château had "something of the atmosphere of a convent," for the women in her household far outnumbered the men and the mood was muted and subdued. In truth she was bored— and more than a little embittered. She felt wronged. Although she did not complain to Eugene, knowing of his enduring loyalty and affection for his former stepfather, she opened her heart to Bonaparte's former secretary Bourrienne, with whom she had shared secrets in the early years of her marriage and whom she trusted not to betray her now.

"I have had my fill of misfortune," she confided to Bourrienne when he came to visit her. "He has left me, abandoned me. He gave me the empty title of empress only to make my shame more noticeable. Ah! How well we judged him!" She had always known that Bonaparte would eventually discard her, she told the former secretary. His ambition was so vast he would sacrifice anything to satisfy it, including his marriage.

But the way he went about ridding himself of her revealed a degree of fiendishness that neither she nor Bourrienne could have foreseen. "He did everything with a cruelty you could never imagine," she said. "You cannot conceive everything he has made me endure . . . I cannot understand why I haven't died. Can you envision what torture it has been for me to read descriptions of celebrating everywhere?"

She told Bourrienne how, when Bonaparte first came to see her immediately after his wedding, he had injured her feelings and caused her pain, and how, with his present wife expecting their child, he deepened her injuries with his blithe references to the heir he was about to have.

"It would be better," Josephine told Bourrienne, "to be exiled a thousand leagues from here, and yet a few friends have remained faithful to me and that is now my sole consolation whenever I am able to have one at all."[8]

Speaking to Bourrienne must have been a relief, for Josephine was rarely able to confide the true state of her feelings and attitudes to anyone. To her children she continued to express her devotion and loyalty to Bonaparte, for their sakes as well as for her own safety; her letters were opened and read, and there were spies in every household, hers and her children's especially. But to an outsider like the former secretary, a man who had been expelled from the court years earlier, she could speak frankly.

When she told Bourrienne that she would prefer far-off exile to her present situation, Josephine was being disingenuous, speaking out of rancor. In fact she knew that she was fortunate to be at Navarre, now that it had been made reasonably comfortable. She was far enough from Paris not to give offense to Marie Louise—at least for the moment—yet not so far that she felt cut off entirely. Bonaparte had not renewed his suggestion that she remove herself to Rome or Brussels.

Over the course of her long and eventful life, Josephine had learned to adapt, and to wait. She settled in to lead, as she told Eugene, "the life of a chatelaine," supervising her household, passing the slow hours as best she could, watching the rain fall on her gardens and waiting for letters from her children.

Just before Christmas Eugene wrote with the news that Augusta had given birth to her first son, Auguste-Eugene, on December 9, the first anniversary of Josephine's divorce.

"This news spread joy in my house," Josephine wrote in response. "It has been a long time since we felt so much joy." The holidays were happy, with Josephine organizing a lottery for her staff and awarding the prize, a ruby ring, to her almoner Archbishop Barral. There were other diversions—parties in Evreux, visits from dressmakers, jewelers, milliners and art dealers, rehearsals of an opera with a number of Josephine's servants in the chorus. Only occasionally, in letters from the capital, was a sour note struck to dampen the festivities.

Paris was absorbed in preparing for the birth of the imperial child. His staff had been assembled, his costly nursery suite prepared, his grand cradle ordered with its antique decorations in gold leaf and its royal canopy. Bonaparte had given orders for an architect to design a royal palace for the "King of Rome," as the newborn would be called, an edifice far grander than any built so far for a French ruler.

Josephine heard of these things with a shiver of dread. She tried not to think about them, wrapping herself in her solitude and doing her best to devote herself, as she had promised she would, to botany and the arts. But she was often to be found with her cards spread out on a table, her brow furrowed in concentration, searching for the key to her future in the arcane images of the tarot.

31

"A Profound Solitude Would Please Me Most"

isturbing stories were reaching Navarre from Paris. While the elite of the court and society were amusing themselves at extravagant entertainments, the economy was in sharp decline. The newspapers were full of lists of bank failures, announcements of factories closing and reports of food shortages. Thousands of people were out of work. The financial crisis spread rapidly, so that by February of 1811 merchants and bankers in Evreux were affected, and laborers unable to find work were setting up stalls in the streets, trying to sell their possessions. Soup kitchens were opened, temporary shelters built. But the number of hungry people increased faster than the means to provide for them, and they clogged the country roads, entire families with all their goods on carts, stopping at farms and houses to beg for food.

By the beginning of March, the deprivations and hardships were causing riots. Armed bands stole flour from warehouses and waylaid barges transporting sacks of grain and barrels of wine. The roads became unsafe, and people complained that the old chaos-ridden days of the 1790s were returning. Despite Bonaparte's efforts to crush the unrest and arrest the criminals, and despite the tons of food he ordered sent into the towns for relief, the protests and lawbreaking continued, and it was becoming clear that more fundamental fissures were opening in the once solid bedrock of imperial France.

The sudden wave of insolvencies and the discontent that arose from it came at a time when, to all outward appearances, France was at the zenith of its power. The empire had swallowed up much of the continent of Europe, and although warfare continued in Spain, and in the ports and on the seas with Great Britain, through most of the imperial lands there was peace. The Bonaparte dynasty was about to be made more secure by the birth of an heir. The imperial treasury was full, and the emperor's personal fortune enormous. Why then should difficulties of any sort arise?

To begin with, the very vastness of the empire bred discontent. Politically, the engorged France was unwieldy, and Bonaparte's attempt to enforce on client states compliance with his economic embargo against Britain led to hardships and increasing resentment. To keep the Grande Armée at full strength, the emperor had to demand fresh recruits from Italy, Poland, the German states and other areas as well as insisting on costly taxes to support them. The emperor's critics—brave souls, daring to challenge the all-powerful regime with its network of spies and its history of sending dissenters into harsh exile—continued to question whether France needed more warfare, more conquests; there was apprehension too about Bonaparte's growing rift with Russia and his grandiose aspirations to add its empire to his own.

With every new call for recruits, every rumor of renewed war, every added tax, the signs of dissatisfaction grew more alarming, and though Emperor Napoleon was still revered, he was at the same time resented and, in some circles, plotted against. Not a few among his former supporters, including members of his government, looked forward to his overthrow and were actively working to hasten it.

Living at Navarre, Josephine was not entirely immune to the effects of the economic crisis, and was often reminded of the hardships suffered by the local population. Beggars came to her door, as they did to the doors of every estate in the vicinity, and she was always generous. One day a shabbily dressed man presented himself at the château offering to provide some musical entertainment. Though his performance was worse than mediocre, Josephine insisted that he be allowed to complete it, and chided her attendants for laughing at the poor man, who, she said, "took such pains to please me at a time when he was dying of hunger." "Good Josephine," as she was sometimes called, was at her best when there were acute human needs to be filled.

Toward the end of January 1811 Josephine wrote to Eugene giving him a picture of her day-to-day life. Snow lay thick on the ground, and the leafless bushes and bare trees in the gardens of Navarre struggled under the weight of high-piled drifts, but a pale sun was shining on the day she wrote her letter. She had gone out for a walk, taking advantage of the brief respite from the storms, and then had returned to her desk. Hortense was visiting for a few days—"she is so thin and changed," Josephine wrote—before going back to her duties at the Tuileries as a member of Marie Louise's entourage.

The routine at Navarre did not alter much from one day to the next, Josephine told Eugene, and she was becoming accustomed to the sameness. "Tranquillity is such a sweet thing! Ambition is the only thing which can spoil it, and, thanks be to God, I do not suffer from the disease of ambition." She had everything she needed, except that the fabrics in the shops in Evreux were inferior. Could Eugene send her some lengths of crepe from Bologna? "I would like to see you," she concluded. "Few other things are lacking to me."[1]

She wrote with some difficulty, for her eyes were bothering her and she had been treated by a doctor who told her that the trouble came from her constant crying. "But for some time past I have only cried occasionally," she told Hortense. "I hope that the quiet life which I lead here, far from intrigues and gossip, will strengthen me, and that my eyes will get well."

Josephine gave a ball in March, timed to coincide with the expected delivery of Empress Marie Louise. As there was no ballroom in the château, she hired carpenters to construct a wooden dance floor on top of the tiled floor of the salon, and arranged for a grand supper to be served to the hundreds of invited guests. On the night of the ball, she received her guests while seated in a chair of state, wearing one of her many diamond parures—a return, after many months, to the grand style she had assumed before her divorce. The blaze of candlelight in the huge salon hurt her eyes, and she had to squint while greeting the parade of visitors that passed before her in their provincial finery, but it was agreed that she looked charming and was gracious to everyone.[2]

With the exception of a few minor mishaps, the ball was a success, but the occasion it celebrated caused Josephine chagrin. No doubt she would have preferred not to hear the cannons roaring from Evreux the following night, announcing the news from Paris that the empress's baby had been born. To be sure, she had to express joy when Bonaparte's messenger arrived at the château, telling her that his newborn son was fat and healthy. She had to send a congratulatory letter to the court in response to the message, and had to pretend, to everyone she met, that she was entirely content at the happy outcome of the empress's pregnancy.

But the pretense must have been difficult to maintain, and she must have been relieved when, after a few weeks of excitement, the initial burst of enthusiasm died down and the newspapers were once again filled with stories of economic distress, civil unrest and an increase in the suicide rate among laborers out of work and in despair.

There were symptoms of unrest in Josephine's household as well. She was a lax mistress, her servants took advantage of her leniency and empathetic nature and her unwillingness to set limits to their petty quarrels over precedence. They put on airs, and insisted on privileges; one self-important household officer refused to leave the château without a carriage and an escort of outriders, and others demanded to eat at special tables set apart when the staff dined all at one time. So entrenched had the hierarchy of Josephine's household members become that the chamberlains refused to eat with the grooms and valets, and the floor cleaners considered themselves too grand to mingle at the dining table with the men who stoked the fires. When the head of the household, Madame d'Arberg, attempted to intervene, more conflict resulted.

The situation grew worse as the year advanced. Josephine's servants were deceiving her, stealing from her and exploiting her. They stole food and sold it for their own profit. They stole candles, lengths of cloth and objets d'art. They sold the valuable horses from the stables and replaced them with broken-down old nags. They even spirited away Josephine's fine carriages, had cheaper imitations built, and sold the originals—all without arousing her suspicions.

She was unwell again. Her headaches had returned, and with them there was a maddening buzzing in her ears that convinced her at times that she was going deaf. Throughout much of the summer of 1811, while verdant life returned to the gardens and the hundreds of new plants brought from Malmaison bloomed and thrived, Josephine stayed in her darkened room, in pain. Doctors attached leeches to her arms and feet to draw out her blood, and applied plasters to her neck, as they often had in the past, in order to raise blisters and relieve the pressure on her temples and sinuses. But these remedies did little to give her ease, and with the coming of autumn she determined to return to Malmaison—with Bonaparte's permission—hoping the move would improve her health.

By the fall of 1811 Josephine's relations with Bonaparte had changed. He had promised his young wife that he would never again visit Malmaison, so his communications with Josephine were all by letter or through messengers. He sent word to her that her mounting debts had to be paid before she would receive any additional funds from the treasury. He was displeased by the disorder and thieving among her servants, and by her unrestrained spending. He knew, for his spies told him, that she was exceeding the three million francs of her annual income; she bought with enthusiasm, she gave to those who needed money, she sent money and gifts to her grandchildren and her Tascher cousins.

"Look after your financial affairs and stop giving to everyone who asks for something," he wrote her. "If you wish to please me, behave so that I will know that you have a large surplus."[3] Josephine did her best to comply, but she felt constrained, and worried that the reprimand in Bonaparte's letter was a harbinger of harshness to come.

Still, he was allowing her to remain at Malmaison, and she was much happier there than at Navarre. At Bonaparte's insistence, a rather stiff etiquette was maintained at Malmaison, with the women of Josephine's household wearing uncomfortable court gowns with long trains when visitors were present. Often the visitors were dull, longwinded members of the (largely ceremonial) legislature or elderly, self-important councillors sent by Bonaparte to keep watch on his former wife. The conversation was stultifyingly correct, polite, and utterly lacking in spontaneity or interest. The dishes created by Josephine's excellent Italian chef Ruccesi were praised, as were the rich milk and butter produced by the estate's herd of Swiss cows and the Cheshire cheese and muffins made by the English wife of the care-taker. But when these conventional compliments had been delivered, there was little else to say. Everyone present knew that the conver-sation would be reported, word for word, to the emperor by the captain of the guard, who was known to be his spy, or by Josephine's reader Mademoiselle Gazzani, who repeated everything to Talleyrand; therefore only the most innocuous comments were exchanged.

On days when her health permitted, Josephine never seemed to tire of walking the length of her picture galleries or making her daily tour of her extensive greenhouses. (Her ladies, however, soon learned by heart her lexicon of comments on the art works and her recitation of the names of her plants, and found the repetition tedious.) The estate offered a variety of diversions. In fine weather one could take a boat out on the canal, and float amid the black swans and other water birds. Josephine had her own small boat, painted and decorated and fitted out with cushions trimmed in gold lace, with a waterproof cover that could be hoisted in the event of a sudden shower.

The zoo continued to grow larger with each passing year, and by 1811 it had expanded to include ostriches, flying squirrels, gnu, ante-lope, gazelles, and a female orangutan that wore a camisole and had been trained to curtsey. In the autumn one could watch the Mal-maison white wine grapes being pressed, in the spring the fields being prepared and planted. In all seasons one could visit the stables and barns, or ride through the many acres of woods and fields.

Malmaison, Claire de Rémusat wrote, was "a place of enchant-ment," and the gardens in particular had been made enchanting by landscape architects Josephine had hired. There were picturesque ar-tifacts at every turn—an imitation Greek temple, tall obelisks of red marble marked with hieroglyphs brought from Egypt, a grotto with a tomb, even the entire façade of a medieval chapel, its wooden doors intricately carved, brought from the Rhineland and reassembled at the top of a low hill.

As at Navarre, the gardens of Malmaison had waterfalls, streams, ponds and lakes, with overhanging willows, thick clumps of pink, white and red rhododendrons and small islands covered entirely in flowers. Fountains played, statues loomed up from amid the foliage, and mature trees shaded the smooth green lawns.

Josephine redecorated some of the interior rooms of the house, redesigning her own bedroom in severe yet ostentatious Roman style, with the walls swathed in purple cloth suspended between slender columns, the ceiling in another dramatic sweep of purple with a bold gold filigree design, and a gold-fringed muslin canopy over the bed. Carved wooden swans decorated the headboard. It was a vivid, self-dramatizing room, the boudoir of royalty. Except for the bed, it might have been taken for a throne room, so regal was the tall canopy and so formally arranged were the gilded ebony cabinets and purple-upholstered chairs.

Bonaparte's bedroom and study were not renovated, but kept as they had always been, with every detail intact, down to the tiger skins under the platform bed and the military tent covering the walls. There were few enough reminders of the emperor at Malmaison; it had always been Josephine's house. But visitors to the zoo who walked past the aviary heard a parrot shriek out "Bonaparte! Bonaparte!" at all hours of the day.

The retired life Josephine now led, her ailments—she was complaining of a "humor in the head" along with her other symptoms—and the bleak winter season brought on low spirits. Profound solitude did not, after all, please her as much as she had hoped. "I am a stranger to everything," Josephine told Eugene, complaining that she had been forgotten by the emperor—though in fact she knew full well, for the newspapers kept her informed, that Bonaparte was preoccupied with building up his army and intent on attempting his greatest military feat: the conquest of Russia.

The lull in war-making that had lasted for several years was coming to an end in the winter and spring of 1812. The nervous accord between the expansive French Empire and the only remaining great power on the continent, Russia, had been unraveling for several years.

Bonaparte felt betrayed by Tsar Alexander, for the latter, having pledged to make war on France's enemy Great Britain, had made only a lackluster effort and was sabotaging the French strategy of bottling up British exports by allowing British goods to enter Russian ports. Alexander, for his part, felt threatened by Bonaparte's seizure of Polish lands—territory the Russians claimed as belonging to their sphere of influence—and was affronted by the aggressive French posture toward the Balkans, where Russia sought to expand. Bonaparte's

Austrian marriage was another source of grievance. In the five years since the two emperors met at Tilsit, it had become increasingly clear that before long there would be a test of strength between the two sovereigns and their armies.

Toward the end of April, 1812, the Russian ambassador delivered to the Tuileries a message declaring that a state of war existed between the two empires. The Russian forces, modernized and trained in imitation of the French, had never been stronger, and the king of Great Britain and the crown prince of Sweden (Bonaparte's former marshal Bernadotte) were now supporting the tsar. Bonaparte had assembled and equipped an enormous fighting force that included large numbers of Austrian and Prussian troops—truly an overwhelming array of military strength. With this juggernaut he meant to crush the Russian opposition once and for all, and become the ruler of the entire continent—after which he envisioned marching further east to conquer India.

Bonaparte's focus was intense, his determination boundless. He was nearly forty-three, balding and stout, his stomach troubled him frequently and he had reached the stage of life where he lacked the stamina for arduous military campaigning. But his active, imaginative brain was still clear and sharp, and he still inspired fierce loyalty in his troops. He shrugged off as the chimeras of inferior minds predictions that he would have bad luck in his coming venture against Russia. His success in battle did not depend on whether or not he was married to an Austrian, he told himself, nor did he need Josephine by his side in order to be victorious.

All the same, he went to Malmaison, breaking his promise to Marie Louise, and had a long visit with Josephine before leaving for the east.

They walked in the gardens, and sat together under the flowering trees. No record of what they discussed has been preserved, but Josephine was no doubt concerned about what would become of her, and of those dependent on her, if Bonaparte should not return from Russia alive. She was also apprehensive about Eugene, who had been put in charge of one of the three divisions of the army. Bonaparte, full of his plans, may well have tried to reassure her by telling her that the campaign would be short—only five weeks—and that his Grande Armée of over six hundred thousand superbly trained troops, many battle-hardened, seasoned veterans, was certain to triumph over the Russian force that was less than half as large.

Eugene's wife Augusta was pregnant with her fourth child, and due to be delivered in July. In Eugene's absence Josephine made the journey to Italy to offer Augusta help and support and to supervise the household—though given her own experience at Navarre, her supervision was likely to be a liability.

Leaving Malmaison in mid-July, and traveling in considerable discomfort because of her head pains, Josephine arrived in Milan on July 27 and met, for the first time, the three grandchildren she had never seen.

Affection poured forth on both sides. The children, who had been receiving gifts from their grandmother all their lives—cases of dresses, wheeled toys, lead soldiers and stuffed animals had been sent to them nearly every month from wherever the empress was living—responded at once to her warmth and sweetness, and she returned their love.

"Your children are adorable," Josephine wrote to Eugene, hoping that the courier who took her letter would find him in Poland or Russia. "There are no more handsome or amiable ones in the world." Though she had only known them a few days, she already loved them "to the point of folly." "Augusta is marvelous," she added. "Her health is so good and her pregnancy is so splendid that it is an omen of a very easy delivery. I entreat you not to be anxious. I will look after her with the greatest care."[4]

Staying in Eugene's rooms, surrounded by reminders of him and hearing him spoken of constantly by his wife and children, Josephine thought often of her son. In her eyes, he was a paragon. A capable if not great commander, liked by his men, a successful ruler of his Italian principality, a good husband and father: Eugene was, at thirty-one, what most men hoped to be. His blithe temperament and high spirits made him good company, and his strength of character, his sense of duty and loyalty, his reliability and responsibility, made him admirable.

But Eugene's very virtues put him in danger. Dutiful as he was, Josephine knew that Eugene would sacrifice himself rather than betray or abandon his men. Many years earlier, in the Egyptian campaign, he had been called upon by Bonaparte to take great personal risks during the siege of Jaffa; he had not spared himself and in conse-

quence had returned home with a severe head wound. That he survived the heat, disease and hardship of Egypt when so many others,
officers and men both, had died was fortunate indeed. Like Bonaparte, Eugene had been through many campaigns and had always
escaped death or crippling injury.

"I think constantly of the dangers to which you are exposed,"
Josephine wrote Eugene, while sitting in his room. No doubt she
told his fortune over and over with her cards, trying to push out of
her mind the fear that rose whenever she imagined the worst. France
was full of widows and orphans, the men of Eugene's generation had
become few in number. Many women Josephine's age had lost sons
to war. So far, she was among the lucky ones. When she embraced
her grandchildren, her lovely namesake Josephine ("a beauty," she told
Hortense), the charming second daughter Eugénie ("lively and intelligent" as well as pretty), and the sturdy toddler Auguste-Eugene ("an
infant Hercules"), she must have clung to them lingeringly, her passionate concern for their father bringing tears to her eyes.

Augusta went into labor at midnight on July 31, and Josephine sat
by her bed, holding her hand and reassuring her when she cried out
for Eugene.[5] The labor soon became intense, Augusta's pains strong
and her suffering acute. Hour after hour she struggled, under the
watchful eye of the accoucheur, her cries growing louder and more
prolonged, while Josephine did her best to calm her. It was an exceptionally painful delivery, but a safe one; just before dawn, a tiny
girl was born, and began to cry lustily.

To Josephine's great relief, both mother and daughter survived the
ordeal, and appeared to be thriving. The baby was strong, her small
body solid and well made, and Josephine was convinced, before she
was an hour old, that she would be pretty. She was given the name
Amélie.

Thoroughly exhausted from her long night's vigil, but "content
and happy," as she wrote to Eugene later that day, Josephine went to
bed, a grandmother for the seventh time, and fell sound asleep.

32

Recessional

he Villa Bonaparte lay baking in the August heat, the geraniums and lemon trees on the terraces wilting and thirsty, the lawns yellowing and the grain in the nearby fields golden with ripeness. Peasants were harvesting clusters of purple grapes, and had already begun to trample the juice from them, and the vintners were predicting an excellent year.

It was difficult to imagine, amid the somnolent heat of Italy, that hundreds of miles to the northeast the Grande Armée was on the march, engaged in what Bonaparte had promised would be a brief but glorious campaign. Each day Josephine and the recovering Augusta waited eagerly for news from Russia, but when none came they were content to wait another day, napping in the hot afternoons, sitting outside surrounded by the children in the long warm evenings, watching for fireflies.

Josephine was continuing to complain of head pains, eyestrain and the persistent buzzing sound in her ears, and after a month she left for Aix, where she hoped that a regimen of swimming, socializing and afternoon excursions into the countryside would improve her health.

Through most of September 1812, while she continued to wait for news from Russia, Josephine visited with the crowd of titled ladies at the spa, among them her former sister-in-law Julie Bonaparte and Julie's sister Desirée Bernadotte, whom the emperor had once wanted to marry. They made an odd trio, the former mistress of the Tuileries, the Queen of Spain—for Julie's husband Joseph Bonaparte had been given the kingdom by his brother—and the Crown Princess of Sweden, whose husband, Jean Bernadotte, had been one of the emperor's marshals but was now heir to the Swedish throne and allied with Russia against the Grande Armée. All three women were as good-hearted as they were well bred, and they treated one another cordially.

Paulette Bonaparte, now Princess Borghese, who was also at Aix, was haughty and distant. She ignored Josephine, withholding her company from all but a few sycophants—she took several new lovers that summer—and obsessed with taking milk baths and listening to the advice of her three hovering physicians. Paulette and her siblings were locked in enmity with Empress Marie Louise, who dismissed them as lowborn Corsican riffraff and ignored their petty assaults; they had been displaced, to an extent, in Bonaparte's affections by his baby son, and they were nursing their injured vanity.

When in October Josephine left Aix for her lakeside estate at Prégny, she heard good news: Bonaparte had defeated the Russians at the Battle of Borodino. The campaign was lasting longer than he had intended, but evidently the delay was beneficial. A letter from Eugene telling her that he was well and that he had successfully commanded the left wing in the battle comforted her. ("We have all done our duty," Eugene wrote, "and hope that the emperor will be satisfied.")

Feeling relieved, Josephine celebrated the French victory at a reception in Geneva, and went on to hold receptions of her own in her flower-filled, hastily furnished house. Her guests were charmed by her informality; while she looked on, they played blind-man's-buff, running across the lawn like children. Although she was nearing fifty, Josephine still looked charming. At one ball she wore a low-cut gown of pink crepe embroidered in silver, with a necklace of large pearls. Her dyed hair was elaborately dressed and threaded with bands of silver—a youthful style that became her.[1]

Expecting to hear any day that the Grande Armée had begun its victorious return to France, Josephine left Prégny for Malmaison on October 19, only to learn, en route, that there had been a disruption in Paris. A French general, Claude-François de Malet, had taken advantage of the emperor's absence to seize power, and had quickly gained the support of a large number of important people. The Malet coup was short-lived. A week after his sudden overthrow, the general was deposed and shot as a traitor. But the incident revealed how thin the veneer of imperial power was, and how easily it could be stripped away, to lay bare the discontent and potential chaos beneath.

News of the events in Paris left Josephine shaken, and revived her misgivings about the campaign, and Eugene's safety and Bonaparte's. Had she known the truth of what was happening in Russia, her apprehension would have increased manyfold.

For the Grande Armée, having gone much deeper into Russia than anticipated, in pursuit of the retreating enemy, had been greatly reduced in numbers and strength. By the time the Battle of Borodino was fought on September 7, the French had fewer than a hundred and fifty thousand men, so many had been lost to desertion and disease. The battle was closer to a draw than a victory, and the Russians, made ferocious by their devotion to their sacred motherland, proved to be as stalwart in battle as they were clever.

Determined never to yield to the French, the Russian commanders made the fearsome decision to sacrifice their capital rather than offer battle again or—unthinkable alternative!—surrender and ask the French for peace terms. Their tactics were devastatingly simple: to allow the French to occupy Moscow, but to burn the city to the ground, so that the French could find neither supplies nor plunder there, nor refuge from the cold. In time, they reasoned, the combined effects of hunger and the cold weather would send the Grande Armée back to the west.

The Russian commander General Kutuzov ordered the evacuation of Moscow and, on the day the French entered the city, ordered hundreds of incendiaries to set it ablaze. They waited until nightfall, then lit torches and went through the crooked narrow streets, setting fire to the wooden houses and shops and stables. One by one the neighborhoods caught fire and blazed up like tinder, until the entire city was alight. Black smoke rose into the night sky, which was lit orange by the glow of thousands of small fires merging into a single giant conflagration. Though the French tried to douse the flames, the incendiaries had done their work too well. The great fire burned virtually unchecked for nearly a week, at the end of which most of the city lay in ruins, the stench of smoke and charred wood everywhere. Only the stone churches, their venerable interiors gutted, their ancient stones blackened, still stood defiantly in the midst of the destruction.

It took Bonaparte a long time to grasp the most essential truth about his situation—that he had been defeated, not by a confronting army, but by a retreating one. For weeks he sat amid the desolation, waiting for Tsar Alexander to send a message of capitulation and bewildered when no message came. He ignored the increasingly urgent voices—among them Eugene's—telling him that food supplies were running out and that there was no time to waste, the army had to reach its supply depots at Smolensk, more than three hundred miles away to the west, before the first snow fell.

Finally on October 18 the emperor ordered his troops to begin their departure from Moscow. There were fewer than a hundred thousand of them now, French, Poles, Germans, and Italians, their once splendid uniforms—the thin uniforms of summer—dirty and bedraggled and their gaunt horses spavined and slow. With the army marched tens of thousands of camp followers, wives, mistresses and children of the soldiers, grooms and laundresses, cooks and blacksmiths and engineers.

They set out from Moscow, spread out for miles along the line of march, all but defenseless against the troupes of Russian cavalry and Cossacks that galloped out of the forest on all sides to assault them. Murat's cavalry stood up poorly against the marauding Russians, while Bonaparte himself came very near to being captured in one raid late in October.

With each passing day the hours of daylight grew markedly shorter, the air more chill, the nights terribly cold. Snow began to fall early in November, piling in deep drifts, turning to ice along the road, blanketing the starving Grande Armée in its frozen embrace. Many succumbed. The slippery road was littered with fallen men, dead and dying horses. Bonaparte was among his men, walking miles at a time, scorning the relative comfort of his carriage. Only half the army that had left Moscow survived to reach Smolensk, and once there the famished remnant, maddened with hunger, smashed the food stores in their eagerness and wasted much of the precious supplies.

There was no respite from the savage Russian attacks—and no respite from the worsening weather. Withdrawal to winter quarters being impossible, because of the constant harassment of the Russian troops—strengthened in numbers by fresh forces from Finland and Moldavia—the shrunken Grande Armée had no choice but to go on, through the deepening snow and increasingly harsh storms, in hopes of reaching safety in Poland.

Now there was no army, only frostbitten, gray-faced stragglers, bony and wild-eyed and all but leaderless. Having eaten the last of their food, they slit open the bellies of the few horses that still lived and drank their warm blood, ate their warm raw flesh. In their desperation, they even ate the flesh of their fallen comrades. Each day more died, falling soundlessly into the high-piled drifts.

Numb to the tragedy around them, aware only of the cold, the constant pain and hunger, and the need to keep on going forward, the hardiest among the soldiers and camp followers clung to life, only to be decimated by a massed Russian force as they attempted to cross the Berezina River in the last days of November. Finally, in mid-December, those left alive staggered across the border into the Grand Duchy of Warsaw, famished wraiths covered in hoar frost and all but unrecognizable.

Parisians had been aware for weeks that the Russian campaign was not going well—otherwise the soldiers would have returned or would have sent word that they were safely established in winter quarters. The ominous silence was worrisome, and rumors spread that the emperor had been captured or killed, and that the government was about to collapse.

Then two weeks before Christmas, 1812, the worst possible news arrived. An official army bulletin announced that the Grande Armée had been demolished. Not only had it been defeated but it had melted away, disappeared into the depths of the Russian winter. Over a hundred thousand fathers, husbands, brothers, cousins were dead, their bodies left unburied along the roadside, food for wolves and birds of prey. Another hundred thousand and more of their families, servants and other camp followers had perished as well.

The few survivors who began to return to the capital early in the new year were shockingly altered. Many had wooden limbs, nearly all had lost fingers and toes (and often noses) to frostbite. Their cadaverous forms and pale, gaunt faces, the imprint of suffering in their deep-set eyes, above all the stories they told, stories of almost unendurable deprivation and suffering, made every room they entered, every gathering they attended, turn somber.

Paris was in mourning, and Josephine too put on black for though, to her relief, Eugene had returned alive and well her cousin Henri Tascher had not. His story was typical of many. With his brother Louis, Henri had started out from Moscow on the long retreat. Both men were wounded and ill and Henri, determined to save his brother from falling by the wayside, half-carried Louis for many miles, day after day, succeeding in keeping him alive. Once they reached safety, Henri entered a German hospital and died there.

Gradually the full implications of the terrible defeat became apparent to the grief-stricken Parisians. Bonaparte, once thought to be invincible, was no longer immune from disaster. Ruin stalked him; no longer could he safely be entrusted with men's lives. Always, or nearly always, in the past when soldiers in his armies had died, they died gloriously, in the course of winning an ultimate victory. But the deaths in Russia were inglorious, meaningless. Because the emperor could no longer win battles, several hundred thousand lives had been thrown away.

With that same streak of ghoulish humor that had led Parisians to hold "Victim's Balls" in the aftermath of the Terror, they now held "Wooden Leg Balls" at which the guests danced with wooden stumps clamped over their legs. Jokes about Bonaparte's defeat at the hands of "General Winter" made the rounds of dining tables, and there was much black humor in evidence along with the funeral black garments of mourning.

But even as they indulged their taste for macabre jokes, the Parisians were aware that Bonaparte's defeat had put France in danger. For the Russians, heartened by the annihilation of the Grande Armée, were sweeping westward, gathering allies as they came, determined to reconquer the lands Bonaparte had conquered and to give their populations an opportunity to take revenge on the French.

The tall, blond young Tsar Alexander saw himself as the avenger of Europe, appointed by God to destroy Bonaparte and overthrow his entire empire. He retook the Grand Duchy of Warsaw and moved on to Berlin, persuading the Prussian king to join him in his crusade.

Helped by large English subsidies, the Russians and Prussians moved on again, into the territories of the Confederation of the Rhine, preparing for an ultimate confrontation that would end the hegemony of imperial France.

Meanwhile Bonaparte, seemingly unaffected by the physical and emotional ordeal he had been through, and to all appearances hardened to tragedy, directed all his energies to reversing the effects of the military calamity. With remarkable speed he raised a new army, called up eighty thousand men from the National Guard, and had the fresh troops instructed in the routines of drilling and forming squares and in handling weaponry. Incredibly, the men responded eagerly to Bonaparte's inspiring messages and to his leadership—a tribute to his charisma, which was strong enough to make the men forget, or ignore, the fate of his last army.

By April of 1813 the emperor was ready to take the field with a new army of over two hundred thousand men, intending to regain the momentum in the coming conflict and to drive the Russians and their allies back eastward. Eugene, who had raised new forces in Italy, was at his stepfather's side. Early in May the French succeeded in overcoming Alexander and his troops at Lützen and again at Bautzen, but were unable to press their advantage; their losses were too heavy, and their supplies of arms, ammunition and other materiel too meager. An armistice was negotiated—in itself something of a triumph, given the overall disadvantages of the French—and both sides settled down to the tasks of preparing for a fresh engagement in the fall.

At Malmaison, Josephine tried to distract herself from the continual shocks and reverberations of the unstable military situation, occupying herself with collecting pictures for her gallery and extending her gardens to include a lake and artificial waterfalls. Her gardens, in the summer of 1813, drew more visitors than her salons, and it gave her pleasure to see Parisians by the dozens walking along the paths under the trees, among the blooming plants, admiring their variety and profusion.

But her efforts to distract herself could not quieten her nerves, which kept her jumpy and apprehensive. At night she was wakeful; she had always liked staying up late, playing cards or talking, but now, when midnight came, and then the early morning hours, she was agitated, restless, unable to relax or get to sleep.

It was all but impossible to still her apprehensions. Ever since the beginning of the year she had dreaded that 1813 would bring bad luck; years with the number thirteen were invariably years of disaster. The predictions of the seasoned imperial soldiers, who had said that if Bonaparte divorced "the old one" he would meet with catastrophe, were coming true. The times were unsettled, reminiscent of the volatile days of the revolution when everything was in flux, and no one could say, from one day to the next, where certainty was to be found.

During those far-off days of the 1790s Josephine had always been able to find a way to cope with the ever-shifting currents of change. She had adapted herself, found friends and allies to help her, used her ingenuity to discover the means to live. But now, having reached her fiftieth birthday, and with her aging body rebelling against the constant strain of the uncertain times, she was less able to come to terms with all that was happening—and happening swiftly. Every new bulletin from Paris, every new rumor brought by visitors, sent her more off balance, and gave her more to worry over in the shadowy predawn hours when she paced and fretted and called up images of disaster.

Her plump contours shrank, she became thin and there were dark circles under her eyes from lack of sleep. Worry lines creased her forehead, and in repose her mouth, usually smiling, became a grim line. Doctors were often called to Malmaison to consult about her increasingly severe migraines, and when they conferred together, they took note of the evident severe effect of Josephine's continuing anxiety on her general health.[2]

They had to acknowledge, however, that her anxiety was well founded, for major changes were coming, and it was by no means certain that the empress would survive them without great difficulty.

For as most of the French were beginning to realize, even if Bonaparte managed to keep the forces allied against him at bay, he could not do so for long. He was adroit, daring, brilliant, but his resources, both personal and political, were not infinite. More and more of his subjects had begun to hope for his defeat, and a few were trying to hasten it by quietly working with the Bourbon royal family in exile to bring about a restoration of the monarchy. In Josephine's own household there were those who spoke in hushed but optimistic tones of the coming fall of imperial France and of the beginning of a new era, an era of peace and stable government, under a Bourbon king.

What worried Josephine most was what would become of her when Bonaparte fell from power. True, he had divorced her, but she would forever be associated with him. She owed all her security to his protection and patronage, she had always publicly supported him—indeed in past years she had been responsible, through her network of friends, for promoting his advancement. Whatever happened to him would also happen to her, by association. Her fate was bound up with his. When he met his final defeat, however near or far-off that might be, she would not escape the consequences.

She sat in her purple-draped bedroom, her head throbbing, her mind a tumult of fears and dark imaginings. Many nights of scant sleep distorted her thinking, and exaggerated her fears. Of one thing she was certain: that, even though love no longer bound them, she and Bonaparte were united by unbreakable ties. She was part of his past, as he was part of hers; whatever happened to him would happen, in some measure, to her.

When the war resumed in August of 1813, it soon became clear that France's position had worsened. Bonaparte's enemies offered to make peace if he would give up most of his empire, and agree to rule over territory greatly reduced in size and no longer a threat to the stability of Europe, but he refused to accept this compromise. Austria now entered the coalition against him, and the crumbling of his once vast empire continued. In a three-day battle at Leipzig in October, the French forces were overwhelmingly defeated and Bonaparte had to retreat across the Rhine with an army of only sixty thousand men, many of them ill with typhus, all of them inadequately equipped.

Parisians began to prepare for the worst, arming themselves, storing food and water, turning their homes into fortresses. Those who could, made plans to escape into the western provinces when it appeared that the enemy could not be kept from invading.

The troops that had been guarding Josephine and her household at Malmaison were called away to join Bonaparte's thinning army, and were replaced by sixteen wounded men, none of them fit to mount much of a defense if foreign soldiers appeared in the gardens or in the nearby village of Rueil. Each day Hortense, who was with Empress Marie Louise at the Tuileries, sent a courier to Malmaison with the day's army bulletin. Josephine had it read to her by Madame Gazzani, with Claire de Rémusat and another of her women, Princess Giedroyc, listening eagerly, both of them wearing the white Bourbon cockade and cheering silently for the allied coalition.

The entire household was occupied in making bandages for the army. Food supplies were dwindling, though there was always enough milk from the white Swiss cows, and cheese, and bread and muffins made from Malmaison grain and wine made from Malmaison grapes. Fewer transport barges passed the estate along the river, and there were other disruptions—commerce ebbed, banks closed and, as always in unsettled times, people began selling goods along the roadsides and in hastily erected street markets.

Rumors flew: the enemy had been seen at Reims, at Soissons, at Versailles. Bonaparte had been killed. The government had fallen. No one knew what to believe, yet everyone knew that the end had to be near—the end, not only of imperial France, but of an entire era, an entire way of life. The thrusting spirit of the French, that spirit that had overturned the old monarchy and embarked on a long and bloody experiment in popular government, an experiment that had led to the advent of General Bonaparte and to French dominion over the rest of the continent, had run its course.

Josephine knew better than to believe all the rumors, but she could not prevent her servants from repeating them, nor could she alleviate their mounting panic. Often, as she sat by candlelight cutting strips of linen and winding them for bandages, she wept over her work. Her tears were for the dead and dying soldiers, for her own unknown future and that of her children, for all that rose up in her mind to frighten her and make her feel weak. And there were tears too for the past, for all that she had seen and lived through over the course of her singularly eventful, singularly favored life. With trembling hands she lifted the linen strips to her face from time to time and wiped away the tears, willing herself, whatever happened, to go on.

33

"*I Have Never in My Life Lacked Courage*"

In the greatest possible haste, Josephine gathered her possessions and gave orders for all her servants and staff to ready themselves to leave Malmaison the following morning. Earlier that day, March 28, 1814, an urgent message had come from Hortense. The capital was unfortified, and could not be defended, she said. The Russian and Austrian armies were only a day or two away. Empress Marie Louise was leaving the Tuileries for Blois. Josephine had to abandon Malmaison immediately and flee to Navarre. Hortense and her children would join her there as soon as possible.

For days the booming of enemy guns had been growing louder as the armies of Generals Blücher and Schwarzenburg came closer. Refugees from towns east of Paris clogged the roads into the capital, and peasants fleeing enemy patrols and marauding Cossacks began appearing in Rueil, pulling carts loaded down with sacks of grain and chickens and wide-eyed children.

Unlike many of her neighbors, Josephine had not panicked. "I have never in my life lacked the courage to meet the many dangerous situations in which I have found myself," she wrote to Hortense. All through the winter she had resisted the urge to leave the vicinity of Paris, keeping herself informed by reading the daily military bulletins and hoping that somehow the emperor, with his dwindling army, could hold firm against the superior numbers of the enemy.

By the last days of March, however, he had fought his last battle, and realizing that it would not be possible to mount a defense in Paris itself, had gone to Fontainebleau with the last of his troops, hoping to negotiate peace with the forces of Russia, Austria, Prussia and Great Britain from there. For a few days Parisians had rejoiced to learn that a diplomatic envoy was on his way from London, bringing a peace treaty—but then the story proved to be false.

It was only prudent for Josephine, relatively isolated and unprotected at Malmaison, to go to safety in Normandy. Cossack marauders had been looting and burning estates throughout Champagne and in the Loire valley; messages came shortly before Josephine's departure that the Russian cavalry was in Bondy, only a few miles from the center of Paris. They could not be expected to spare Malmaison.

There was little time to prepare, and only a few things could be taken. Josephine had her most valuable gems sewn into the wadding of a thick padded gown, and wore the gown on her journey. If the worst happened, and there was chaos or civil war, her jewels could be traded for food.

She set out with her servants and companions on the rainy morning of March 29, taking all the remaining horses in her stables (for horses were scarce, the army had seized most of them) and all of her carriages. "I am so unhappy at being separated from my children that I am indifferent to my fate," she wrote to Hortense. To Eugene, who was vainly fighting on in Italy, the only remaining one of Bonaparte's deputies not to desert him, she sent a letter saying that she was "tormented" by her knowledge of his situation and that she hoped for peace.[1]

The road that led northwestward out of Paris along the Seine was muddy and pockmarked with deep ruts made by the hundreds of vehicles that crowded it. Thousands of people walked among the slow-moving carts and wagons and carriages, driving their cattle, sheep and even geese before them, scurrying forward with each reverberating boom of the none-too-distant cannon. The travelers did not stop to eat or rest, fearful as they were of enemy scouts, highwaymen, above all the dreaded Cossacks. The fact that very few of the French had actually seen a Cossack made them even more feared; in the popular mind Cossacks were larger than life, shaggy, fur-covered bogeymen wielding huge swords and riding fire-breathing steeds, galloping suddenly out of the mists and killing everyone in their path.

At one point a servant in Josephine's household cried out "the Cossacks!" and immediately the travelers became vigilant. Josephine was so alarmed that she threw open her carriage door, jumped to the ground, and began to run, slowed by her bulky padded skirt with its freight of gems. When after a few moments it became evident that no Cossacks were near, she was brought back and reassured.

After a long sleepless night spent at Mantes, where the horses were fed and rested, the travelers went on, both dejected and frightened by the word being passed along from Paris that the enemy was about to enter the city. Guns continued to boom, alarm bells rang, there were transient panics when highwaymen were glimpsed—or imagined—and shouts of frustration when heavily laden vehicles broke down or became enmired in the mud and blocked the way until they could be dragged off the road.

Toward evening on the second day Josephine and her companions reached Navarre, only to discover that there was almost as much disruption and fear in Normandy as there had been in Paris. Everyone was desperate for news, and unable to receive any as the post from Evreux was temporarily discontinued and no letters or newspapers could arrive. Apart from a few hand carried letters, and the tales of frightened travelers, no reliable word was to be had.

"I cannot tell you how unhappy I am," Josephine wrote to Hortense on the night she arrived at her estate, not knowing when, or how, her letter might reach her daughter. "I have had courage in the painful positions in which I have found myself, I shall have courage to bear the reverses of fortune; but I have not enough courage to endure my children's absence and the uncertainty of their fate."[2] She urged Hortense to send her news of herself and her children—and of Eugene if she had received any word from him. She heard many rumors, she said, but she did not know what to believe. She was concerned about Malmaison—was it true that the enemy had occupied the Neuilly bridge? If so, they would be very close to the estate.

Josephine said nothing in her letter about Bonaparte. No one knew what had become of him, whether, as they swept toward the capital, the Russians or Austrians had captured him, or whether once again, with the odds overwhelmingly against him, he had managed to outwit his opponents and find a way to escape.

The initial days at Navarre were full of confusion and commotion. The house was in a state of disorder, and it was all but impossible to find food for the kitchens and coal for the fires, as no market days were being held in Evreux and deliveries of fuel had ended. To add to all the upheaval, refugees began arriving at Navarre, looking to Josephine to provide them with an oasis of peace and rest. A number of women from the imperial court found their way into Normandy, all of them worried and harassed, tearful and frantic for news from the capital. ("And all without a man," one of them wrote, "without any idea what to do!")

With banks closed and the usual flow of funds through financial channels interrupted, Josephine was severely short of money. She borrowed twenty-five thousand francs from the head of her household, and with it, did her best to provide hospitality to her anxious guests. Wrapped in several of her shawls against the chilly, rainy weather, her voice hoarse and her head aching, she did her best to cope with the food shortages and all the chaos and clutter. Worry took away her appetite, and it was difficult to sleep when every room was full of shrill treble voices, arguing, commiserating, sobbing.

In the midst of all the agitation and hubbub Hortense arrived, with her children, and everyone crowded around her to learn what she knew.

Having been with Empress Marie Louise during the last days before the surrender of the capital, Hortense had seen and heard much, and she described it now to her rapt audience. She told how, with the enemy approaching, handfuls of Parisian militiamen armed with long pikes had assembled on the hills of the city, determined to defend it to the last; how at the Tuileries, Joseph Bonaparte and the other members of the Regency Council, convinced that imperial power could not be salvaged, ordered the burning of all public records and the evacuation of the palace; how General Marmont, given the responsibility of protecting Paris with twenty thousand troops, had turned his forces over to the Russians and, in the early hours of March 31, signed the document of capitulation.

She described the scene when the conquering armies, with Tsar Alexander and King Frederick William III of Prussia in the lead, marched unopposed into Paris, the tramping of the soldiers' boots loud on the cobblestones, the crowds along the streets silent and watchful. There were no cheers for the conquerors, no nosegays thrown to the troops. Parisians were numb with shock; they had never before seen foreign armies in their streets. They could not yet comprehend the extent of the transformation unfolding before their eyes.

In the first week of April, the shape of the new government began to become clear. The emperor, who was still at Fontainebleau, was forced to abdicate, and a provisional government, with Talleyrand at its head, came into being. A new constitution was drawn up, and it was understood that within a month or two, the Bourbon monarchy would be restored. Fears of civil war retreated, markets sprang up, banks were reopened, and life began to return to normal.

So abrupt was the swift change in public mood that within days the newspapers were full of criticisms of Bonaparte. Overnight the former hero became a pariah, and no one had anything good to say about him. Many of those who had been servants and officials in Bonaparte's government flocked to Talleyrand's grand residence in hopes of finding places in the new regime; some in Josephine's retinue left her to look for better opportunities.

The fear, the turmoil, the discomforts, the constant upsets and surprises distressed Josephine and left her haggard with strain. "What a week I have spent, my dear Eugene!" she wrote to her son on April 9. "How I have suffered at the way they have treated the emperor! What attacks in the newspapers, what ingratitude on the part of those upon whom he showered his favors! But there is nothing more to hope for. All is finished, he is abdicating." She urged Eugene to consider himself absolved from his oath of fidelity to the former emperor, and to do whatever was expedient for the interests of his family.[3]

Like the rest of Bonaparte's former subjects, Josephine had to make an adjustment to the prevailing realities. She had done it before—how many times!—and knew well how to go about it. She wrote to Talleyrand, reminding him that, since her divorce, she had been living on the generous annuity granted her by the Senate. "I wait for the Senate to act anew, and I place my interests and those of my children in your hands," she wrote. "Counsel me in these circumstances, and I shall follow your advice with confidence."[4]

She was concerned about Eugene, who as Bonaparte's most loyal deputy stood to bear a heavy share of the new government's retaliation. And about Hortense, who was not only Bonaparte's stepdaughter but also his sister-in-law, and who, in the earliest days of the provisional government, was thinking of taking the extreme step of moving to Martinique, to live at Trois-Ilets, away from the upheavals of Paris.

Josephine professed relative unconcern about her own future, but all her actions indicated that her instincts for political and social survival were as strong as ever. She wrote to her superintendent at Malmaison, Bonpland, and told him to arrange for a protective guard to be set up around the estate, adding that he ought to "be sure to have the officer dine with you and provide food for his soldiers."[5] It was the sort of gesture that came naturally to her, to smooth relations and ensure loyalty through the alchemy of the personal touch. She had made her way through the labyrinth of power for decades by this light, gracious, devastatingly effective means, and would go on doing so.

No one recognized and appreciated Josephine's talent for self-preservation more than Talleyrand, himself a successful survivor of many regimes and a master of adapting himself to the prevailing political situation. He saw at once that Bonaparte's former wife, with her large acquaintance and long experience at and near the court, and with her reputation for goodness and helpfulness to all who approached her, would make a valuable ally for the provisional government. He wrote to her at Navarre, reassuring her that her annuity of a million francs a year would be continued under the new regime, and that Hortense would receive four hundred thousand francs a year as well.

Josephine's political instincts were still serving her well, but it was evident to everyone who saw her that her health was declining. She was thinner than ever—when her dressmaker came to take her measurements for new spring gowns, the alteration in her size was startling—and she no longer needed corsets to make her waist slender. Her complexion was pale, her voice hoarse, and she had a persistent cough. It was hard to escape the conclusion that the intensity and emotional impact of recent events were wearing heavily on Josephine's stamina. She was empathetic, she was suffering with those who suffered, including Bonaparte.

When an envoy came to Navarre, sent by the former emperor to give Josephine a full account of all that had happened to him in the last days before the capitulation of Paris, she listened tearfully. It pained her to learn how Bonaparte had tried, in vain, to retake Paris, how most of his servants and former supporters had abandoned him, how Marie Louise had gone back to Austria, above all how he had been condemned to enter a lonely exile on the small island of Elba. (He had wanted to be sent to Corsica, but the conquering powers had thought this far too dangerous.)

As she listened to the envoy Josephine seemed almost to suffer physical blows, her thin tired body reacting visibly to the buffetings of her spirit. She envisioned her former husband, once so feared, the ruler of millions, the master of vast armies, now rendered insignificant, a lone prisoner banished to a bleak exile.

"If it were not for his wife I would go lock myself up with him!" she cried impulsively when she learned what Bonaparte's sentence was to be. The impulse was generous, and compassionate—and, no doubt because of her exhausted state, exaggerated—but it was only an impulse. She would not have gone to Elba with Bonaparte, even if that had been possible, if for no other reason than that she wanted and needed to be near her children and grandchildren. They had become her principal concern, and she was doing her best to talk Hortense out of going to Martinique.

But there were other calls on Josephine's attention beyond those of family: by the middle of April she was being invited—indeed all but summoned—to return to Malmaison to serve as unofficial hostess to the new regime.

She was needed—and when she felt needed, she invariably did her best to respond. The masters of the transition regime—Talleyrand, Metternich, above all Tsar Alexander—sent messages to Josephine requesting her presence in the capital. Alexander offered to send a detachment of troops to guarantee her safety. The king would return soon, the messages said, and he was favorably disposed toward "the good Josephine." It would serve his gracious pleasure if she were to resume her residence at Malmaison.

The emperor was gone, the king was coming. Events were moving too fast, bringing too many demands, worries, emotional adjustments. Josephine knew that she had to respond to the urgent summons to return to Malmaison, and that once she arrived, she would be called upon to receive a parade of dignitaries, not once but many times. She would have to supervise the organization of the household for these receptions and entertainments, she would need new clothes, she would have to familiarize herself with the social configuration of the new regime—a configuration she herself would be called upon to mold. And she would have to preside, graciously, hour after hour, at an exhausting succession of events.

On a cold, blustery day in mid-April, the Countess of Navarre—it was no longer appropriate to call herself empress—left her estate in Normandy for the return to Malmaison. As the carriage rattled along the high road, she tried to rest, lying back against the cushioned seat and closing her tired eyes. But the incessant swaying and lurching of the vehicle disturbed her, as did her troublesome cough, and all the way to Paris her mind was on the unknown future, and all the tasks, great and small, that lay ahead.

34

Restoration

$\mathcal{A}$s soon as he could, the new king Louis XVIII intended to leave his home in England and cross the Channel to claim his kingdom. For the time being, however, he was confined to his bed, his foot purple and swollen with gout, his heavy, clumsy body so cumbersome that he could not walk without two servants supporting him, one on each side.

Louis-Stanislas-Xavier, Count of Provence, had been calling himself King Louis XVIII for nineteen years, ever since the son and heir of his brother, the late King Louis XVI, died in a revolutionary prison in 1795, making Louis-Stanislas next in line for the throne. In 1814 he was fifty-nine, a saurian figure from another age, having spent most of his adult life at the margin of events. He had held court in exile in Germany, Russia, Poland and most recently England, waiting with remarkable forbearance for his subjects to come to their senses and abandon the revolutionary madness that had bewitched them; the sham reign of "Emperor Napoleon" had been, to King Louis, nothing more than a delusion, for the emperor had no royal blood and his military conquests, however dazzling, had proved to be ephemeral.

The emperor's first wife Josephine, however, had been the real thing, in the king's view: a genuine aristocrat, both by birth and by marriage, a peripheral member of the old court of his brother King

Louis XVI and Queen Marie Antoinette, a gracious lady presiding over a crowd of upstarts, opportunists and ruffians. (The king tactfully overlooked Josephine's own opportunism, along with her Directory escapades.) Throughout the long decades of delusion Josephine had preserved, in her manner and personal elegance, something of the flavor of the old court, and the king was eager to honor her and to show her his royal favor now that he was about to ascend his rightful throne.

He sent his envoy the Duc de Polignac to visit Josephine at Malmaison, to present his compliments and to thank her for the efforts she had made years earlier on behalf of the emigrés. Louis's nephew the Duc de Berry also came to see Josephine, and before long the château was a magnet for the new king's courtiers and members of the provisional government.

Josephine's most distinguished and admiring visitor was Tsar Alexander, who in the absence of King Louis was by far the most celebrated person in Paris.

Tall and blue-eyed, with white-blonde thinning hair and an abundance of suave charm, the tsar was succeeding in melting the Parisians' icy reception of him and was on his way to becoming a popular hero. He left the palace frequently to walk the streets and mingle with the citizens of the capital, surrounded by his entourage of broad-shouldered Cossacks in thick fur coats and fur hats, and his hearty, open manner and excellent French soon won over the skeptical Parisians. They admired his good looks and his utter lack of regal pomposity, his eager curiosity about their city and themselves. Having adopted a hostile attitude toward their former emperor—condemned in widely circulated pamphlets as "the greatest criminal that has ever appeared on the earth"—they could hardly fail to applaud the man who had vanquished him, and welcome him as their deliverer.

And if the Parisians were enamored of Alexander, Alexander was enamored of Josephine, and went to see her often at her estate. Accustomed as he was to the ways of the Russian court, where despite the liberalizing influence of his grandmother Catherine the Great, women were regarded as decorative breeders, the tsar was fascinated by the phenomenon of the French salon hostess, independent, free-thinking, a cultural icon, a peer, in some sense, of the men who were her friends and lovers.

Germaine de Staël was a truer exemplar of that phenomenon than Josephine, and Germaine was in Paris in April of 1814, holding forth in her salon and attracting growing numbers of visitors. But Alexander much preferred Josephine to the brilliant but mannish Madame de Staël; the latter was domineering and hardened, accustomed to intellectual browbeating, while the frail, gentle Josephine in her delicately embroidered white muslin gowns was the picture of vulnerable feminine allure, her lack of control as ensorceling as Madame de Staël's overcontrol was forbidding.

The tsar not only enjoyed making himself at home at Malmaison, he concerned himself with Josephine's wellbeing. "It is with the keenest regret that I noticed your majesty had some anxieties," he wrote to her after their first meeting, "but I have every reason to hope that you will convince yourself they have no foundation."[1] He took an interest in Hortense and her children, asking Josephine what he could do for them and pledging to "look after their interests." He called Josephine "your majesty," and never presumed on his own rank, always asking permission to visit her and waiting for her to invite him to return.

The solicitude of the tsar, and the assurances from Talleyrand that her annuity would be continued, must have alleviated some of Josephine's worries, but she continued to look haggard and careworn, her eyes shadowed with dark circles and her complexion sallow. Though she could not speak of it to any of her guests, there was a constant sad undercurrent to her thoughts: she knew that very soon Bonaparte would be embarking for Elba, and she may have known that he had tried unsuccessfully to kill himself by swallowing poison.

He had written her a long letter from Fontainebleau, telling her that he "congratulated himself" on his situation. "My mind and my heart are free of an enormous burden," he wrote, "my fall is great, but at least, so they say, it serves a useful purpose."

He intended to dedicate his retirement on Elba to writing a history of his reign, he told Josephine. It would be a surprising story, for, as he said, "people have only seen me in profile, and I shall show myself full face."[2] He sought to be objective and analytical, but he was clearly wounded and embittered by his former subjects' lack of loyalty, and his letter was full of recriminations.

"I have showered benefits on thousands of wretches! What did they do, in the end, for me? They have betrayed me, yes, all of them. I except only our dear Eugene, so worthy of you and of me."

Now that Bonaparte was a forlorn figure about to embark on a humiliating exile, all Josephine's extragavant sympathies were with him. She had always been tenderhearted toward supplicants in need; now that her former husband was in a position of dishonor and disgrace, her heart went out to him as it never had in his days of power. It was compassion she felt, not love, but the emotional tie was very strong nonetheless; though others were betraying him, she, at least, wanted to remain loyal. To the tsar and her many other visitors she maintained an appearance of support for King Louis, but she felt the constant tug of sentiment toward Bonaparte and his plight, and the conflict between her inner anguish and her outward appearance of satisfaction often left her overwrought.

On May 4, King Louis made his joyous entry into Paris, and the citizens, who only a scant five weeks earlier had been in an uproar to defend their city against the invader, now accepted the monarch the invaders installed with open arms and loud cheers of "Vive le roi!"

A visitor to Malmaison brought news of the king's slow triumphant progress through the streets in his coach, of the white pennons, flags and sheets hung from balcony windows and the white cockades worn in thousands of hats as a token of support for the Bourbons, of the portraits of the king's jowly aging face hung in many windows and the songs sung and speeches delivered in tribute to the opening of his glorious reign.

It was all a feast of celebration—yet at the same time faintly comic, because of the gouty king's grotesque appearance and general air of inebriated good will. Louis XVIII was anything but regal, and in truth, the frenzy of merrymaking shown by the Parisians was anything but heartfelt—rather it was shallow and brittle, an ephemeral delirium rather than a deep and true response to the restoration of the monarchy. Many observers felt an undertone of disquiet beneath the froth of celebration, a moody restlessness that could easily threaten the peace of the new regime.

Josephine listened to her visitor's account of the day's events in Paris, laughing with the others at the dinner table when the king's appearance was described, interested to hear of the Parisians' fickle disposition. Laughing made her cough, and her cough was harsh and ragged. Putting her linen handkerchief to her mouth, she excused herself in a soft scratchy voice and left the table until she recovered.

The advent of King Louis, and the many kind words he spoke about Josephine to his courtiers, increased the flood of visitors to Malmaison. Day after day they came, Tsar Alexander and his aide Prince Tchernicheff, Grand Duke Constantine, Prince Leopold of Austria, Marie Antoinette's brother, the King of Prussia and his two sons, the Grand Duke of Baden, Prince Maximilien Joseph of Bavaria, Augusta's father, and even Prince Frederick of Mecklenburg-Strelitz, the handsome young man who had wanted to marry Josephine six years earlier. Many languages in addition to French were heard around the long dining table at Josephine's suppers, German, Russian, Polish (Countess Walewska, whom Josephine had befriended, was a frequent guest), Italian, even English, for a number of British aristocrats came to Paris for the diplomatic negotiations that ended the war. The babble of tongues, the constant comings and goings of carriages, the toing and froing of servants and tradesmen delivering food and drink created ceaseless noise and stir; there was no rest for the weary hostess, and by the time Eugene arrived, on May 9, he was alarmed at how ill his mother looked.

Neither Eugene nor I Hortense could persuade her to slow the pace of her entertaining, however. It was clear to Josephine's children that she needed peace and leisure. She needed, at the very least, the relaxed environment of Plombières or, even better, of her estate at Prégny. But having been chosen, as it seemed, by the tsar and the king to stand at the apex of society, she was unwilling to relinquish her position, even for a short time, fearful as she was that if she did not keep Malmaison open to all comers she would lose all her credit with the powerful and she and her children would face ruin.

It was an irrational fear, fed by exhaustion and illness, akin to the fear that had preyed on her years earlier when she became convinced that Bonaparte was poisoning her. In her imagination the demons of deprivation and poverty stalked her, she risked persecution, harshness, cruel revenge. The king, whom she had yet to meet, became, in her mind's eye, not a corpulent buffoon but a vengeful tyrant, banishing her from France forever and condemning her children and grandchildren to starve.

When in mid-May she confided her fear to Tsar Alexander at a gathering at Hortense's estate of St-Leu, he did his best to reassure her, scolding her for listening to the ill-advised remarks of "intriguers and go-betweens" and telling her to have confidence in the king's good will.

"No one has any thought of making you leave France or of disturbing your peace," he told her. "If necessary, I shall be your guarantor." She had many friends in high places, he reminded her. He himself was only one. And had he not offered her a palace in Petersburg, with a household of servants and all the money she would ever need?

That afternoon Josephine's thin face, usually pale, was flushed with fever, and the dampness in the air seemed to worsen her cough. When the family went out for a drive, she felt too weak to join them. She stayed inside and drank her preferred restorative, orangeflower water, and then lay down until suppertime.

The evening passed pleasantly, with Madame Ney, who had a lovely singing voice, entertaining the company and Hortense singing some of her own songs for the tsar. Josephine had no appetite for supper, but she did listen to the music, her cheeks an unhealthy pink and a haunted look on her face.

The following day, at Malmaison, she did her best to meet her numerous visitors as usual, but her spirits were low and her nerves exceptionally on edge. In this tense state she was ill prepared to confront Germaine de Staël, who came to call and was escorted into the picture gallery. Taking no notice of Josephine's fragile composure, the formidable Madame de Staël began to interrogate her hostess about her life with the former emperor. What had he really been like, what had his personal habits been, how many mistresses did he have—the questions went on and on, with Josephine becoming, as one who saw her immediately afterward remarked, more and more upset, with "an air of great agitation and emotion."

After Madame de Staël had left, Josephine, worn and anxious, approached several of her other guests. "I have just had a very painful meeting," she told them in her scratchy voice, hardly above a whisper. "Can you imagine that, among other questions which Madame de Staël was pleased to put to me, she asked if I still loved the emperor?

She seemed to want to analyze my very soul in the presence of great misfortune."

Shaken by her interview with the tactless Madame de Staël, her illness worsening, Josephine was forced to rest, and for the next week or so she struggled to carry out her social obligations while growing visibly weaker. No one could intervene; she simply would not listen or take advice. She had been invited to come to the Tuileries on the twenty-sixth of May to be presented to the king, and the prospect of meeting him both alarmed and animated her. Each day she drove herself until she collapsed, then, minimally refreshed, got up and began to drive herself again.

As the day of her expected visit to the Tuileries approached, her energy waxed and waned. She was well enough to take the King of Prussia and his sons on a complete tour of the gardens and menagerie, but afterward she had to rest, and appeared to Eugene more tired and ill than ever. On top of her severe cough and hoarseness, she developed a cold, but tried to shake it off, telling Hortense that she "never paid attention to a cold," and going ahead with her entertaining. She managed to dance with the tsar at a ball, but developed yet another fever afterward, her entire body enveloped in a painful rash and her cough so persistant that she was unable to sleep.

She was far too ill to go to the Tuileries, and on the day following her missed appointment with the king, Friday, May 27, Hortense became alarmed when the tsar's personal physician cautioned her that her mother was severely ill and needed immediate treatment.[3]

Hortense summoned three specialists from Paris, but the patient was by this time in the grip of an acute infection—the doctors' diagnosis was quinsy, or tonsillitis—and was at times delirious, and there was little they could do.[4]

Josephine lay in her bed under the gold-fringed canopy, tossing uneasily and at times gasping for breath. The plasters applied to her neck and feet were useless; her body, worn down by stress and overwork, was laboring under an increasing load of grave symptoms, and could no longer fight the infection that was gradually closing her throat. Disoriented and weak, she tried to fight against the enervating force that dragged her down, her exhausted mind struggling in vain for clarity. A confusion of images, memories, sensations crowded in:

the scent of sugar on the sea breeze, the smiling face of Hippolyte Charles, the reek of the Carmelite prison and Bonaparte's voice calling her name. Hortense, sitting by her bed, heard her mother call out "Bonaparte . . . the island of Elba . . . the King of Rome."

On Sunday morning, May 29, Hortense and Eugene went to their mother's bedroom and were shocked at the change in her. Her face was drained of color, and grotesquely swollen, her throat red and her neck enlarged. She tried to speak but could not, instead she held out her arms and embraced her children, all three of them in tears. The servants too were in tears, and when Hortense and Eugene went to the chapel to attend a brief mass, the entire household was there, praying for the Good Josephine.

Eugene asked Abbé Bertrand to give his mother the last rites, and when they had been administered he knelt beside her bed, holding her wasted body in his arms, until she quietly died.

Epilogue

he little church at Rueil was full of mourners. Though the early June weather was warm, and the breeze off the river smelled of flowers and the fragrant grass that flourished among the tombstones in the cemetery, the mood inside the sanctuary was somber, and the large crowd gathered outside the church—for it was far too small to contain all those who wanted to attend Josephine's funeral—waited in restrained silence for the funeral mass to begin.

Inside the church, lit by hundreds of flickering candles, the leaden coffin lay in state, covered by a simple black pall. There were no coats of arms, no insignia of any kind—nothing to indicate that the woman whose life had ended had for five years been Empress of France.

There were no monarchs among the mourners, for sovereigns did not attend funerals. Tsar Alexander and the King of Prussia sent deputies to represent them, and King Louis sent a letter of condolence. Even Hortense and Eugene were prevented, by the etiquette then prevailing, from being present at their mother's funeral mass. But the members of Josephine's household were there, and Hortense's two sons, who were the chief mourners, and a number of generals and dignitaries, along with laborers from the estate and peasant farmers from the vicinity. A delegation of the poor, representing all those Josephine had aided over the years, wept quietly at the back of the small church.

Frederick of Mecklenburg-Strelitz was there, much moved, but Hippolyte Charles was not—or if he was, no one thought to leave a record of his presence. Most likely Marie Walewska was there, for she had grown fond of Josephine during the many afternoons they spent together at Malmaison. Fortunée Hamelin and the Princess de Caraman-Chimay may well have been among the mourners, but Paul Barras was not; he was in Rome, kept there under guard by government order, and in any case he had nurtured a grudge against Josephine for years.

The archbishop of Tours ascended the low pulpit and eulogized Josephine, being careful to avoid any reference to Bonaparte, or to her life during the revolutionary years. He remembered her kindness and generosity, her loveliness and warmth. He recalled her assistance to the emigrés and her willingness to intercede with the authorities on behalf of relatives of guillotined aristocrats. These were the things it was safe to say in the France of Louis XVIII.

The choir sang, the host was distributed and after paying their final respects, the mourners filed out into the summer sunshine. Josephine's death had taken them by surprise; it had been yet one more startling change in a season of surprises and sudden reversals of fortune. They had lost Bonaparte, and his empire, and in his place they had gained the dull but safe King Louis. How enduring and stable his reign would be remained to be seen.

In the bookshops and stalls along the Seine, pamphlets were for sale commemorating Josephine's life, and offering details of the secret scandals in which she had been involved. Already the reality of her story was being distorted, and within a very few years, imaginative memoirists, journalists and gossipmongers would distort it further, until the real Josephine was all but undiscoverable. Bonaparte, on Elba and afterward on St. Helena, spoke disparagingly of his former wife and trivialized her contribution to his career.

But Josephine's children and grandchildren remembered her with great fondness, as did all those who had known her and served her, and in the little church of Rueil, where so many had gathered to remember her on that June day, Hortense and Eugene put up a monument to their mother, a sculpted image of her as she was in her prime, with sweet, timid features and hands clasped in an attitude of hope.

Notes

1: INTO THE WIND-HOUSE

1. Several of Josephine's biographers have assumed that, because the Taschers lived in the refinery following the great hurricane of 1766, they took refuge there during the storm. There is no documentary evidence of this, and indeed it was customary on Martinique to take shelter in a wind-house when storms struck. I think it more likely that Joseph Tascher and his family and house slaves followed this practice.

    That Rose-Claire's mother and Joseph's mother were present is a reasonable conjecture; both spent a great deal of time at Trois-Ilets and both were likely to have been there in August of 1766 with Rose-Claire about to give birth. If the two senior women of the family were on hand, then Alexandre was too, though this is also conjecture. Some biographers erroneously state that Alexandre returned to France in 1765, but Frédéric Masson, *Joséphine de Beauharnais, 1763–1796* (Paris, 1903), p. 89, the most reliable secondary writer, dates Alexandre's return to France as late 1769, long after the hurricane. In 1769 Alexandre was nine years old.

2: THE SCENT OF SUGAR

1. Though he claimed the title of Marquis de la Ferté-Beauharnais, François de Beauharnais did not in fact have either the extensive lands or the income to go with his empty title; he did have a fairly substantial government pension, granted in the aftermath of his naval service in the Antilles. François had three thousand livres income from rents due him

as seigneur de Mauroy-Prouville and from three estates in Santo Domingo which he co-owned with his younger brother.

2. While in France, before being assigned to Martinique, Renaudin had been imprisoned for four years, accused of poisoning his father; though the accusation, based on the testimony of a highly unreliable witness, was probably false, Renaudin continued to bear its stigma.

3. Masson, *Joséphine de Beauharnais*, p. 89.

4. In the 1720s, black sorcerers on Martinique were burned at the stake by the French authorities for being in league with the devil.

5. Jean Gabriel de Montgaillard, Comte de Rocques, *Mémoires diplomatiques extraits des Archives du Ministre de l'Intérieur* (Paris, 1895), p. 277. He added that she was "of a frivolity, a coquettishness, to say no more, that was astonishing, even in the colonies—capricious and extravagant."

Montgaillard was writing after little Yeyette had become the celebrated Empress of France, and no doubt her subsequent fame colored his memories of her to a degree.

6. Masson, *Joséphine de Beauharnais*, p. 103.

7. Ernest John Knapton, *Empress Josephine* (Cambridge, Mass., 1963), p. 19.

8. Masson, *Joséphine de Beauharnais*, p. 106.

9. *Ibid.*, 105.

10. Jean Hanoteau, *Joséphine avant Napoléon: Le Ménage Beauharnais d'après des correspondances inédites* (Paris, 1935), p. 50.

3: A Troubled Passage

1. Hanoteau, *Le Ménage Beauharnais*, p. 28.

2. *Ibid.*, 57–59.

3. It is sometimes incorrectly stated that on her wedding journey in 1779 Josephine was fearful of capture because she knew of the fate of her relative Aimée du Buc de Rivery, who was kidnapped at sea by Barbary pirates. However, Aimée's capture did not take place until 1784. Knapton, p. 14.

4. Hanoteau, *Le Ménage Beauharnais*, p. 51.

5. André Castelot, *Joséphine*, trans. Denise Folliot (New York and Evanston, 1967), p. 14.

6. Hanoteau, *Le Ménage Beauharnais*, p. 78.

7. Knapton, p. 26.

4: A Cankered Bond

1. Masson, *Joséphine de Beauharnais*, p. 112.
2. When Rose applied for a formal separation from Alexandre, she told the commissioner who heard her case that Alexandre was prone to "great dissipation." Knapton, p. 55. Certainly he had been accustomed to long nights of pleasure-filled inebriation before he married Rose; it would seem that he continued these habits afterward.
3. Laure de Girardin's husband died a few days before Alexandre and Rose were married. It is possible that Alexandre knew of his death before the wedding ceremony, but more likely he found out afterward.
4. Hanoteau, *Le Ménage Beauharnais*, pp. 114–115.

5: "The Vilest of Creatures"

1. Hanoteau, *Le Ménage Beauharnais*, pp. 138–139.
2. *Ibid.*, 137.
3. *Ibid.*, 155–156.
4. *Ibid.*, 158.
5. Knapton, p. 51.
6. Hanoteau, *Le Ménage Beauharnais*, pp. 177–178.
7. Knapton, p. 48. The correct date of Alexandre's letter is July 12, 1783. It is incorrectly dated in Masson, *Joséphine Beauharnais*, pp. 138–141.
8. Knapton, p. 49.
9. Hanoteau, *Le Ménage Beauharnais*, pp. 176–177.
10. *Ibid.*, 178.

6: "The Little American"

1. Castelot, p. 34.

7: Liberation

1. On the question of when Rose began to have sexual liaisons outside her marriage the biographer must tread warily. Bonaparte said that she was involved with the Duc de Lorge during her years in Fontainebleau, and that this involvement caused friction between Rose and Alexandre. Rose had many detractors who claimed, providing no written proof,

that she was promiscuous and that her promiscuity began in her early twenties, if not earlier. But because these writers were hostile to the Bonaparte regime, and were looking back at it, and at Rose's life, through the lens of the restored monarchy, their statements must be considered so biased as to be unconvincing.

Still, Bonaparte's assertions carry some weight, and Rose's personality and later behavior, the mores of the era and of the court, her financial extremity and the social circles in which she moved during her years at Fontainebleau combine to make it plausible that she began to take lovers during this time.

8: Transformation

Chapter 8 has no endnotes.

9: A Turn into Madness

1. In his memoirs General Lamarque wrote that Rose "had been brought up" with Desirée Hosten in Martinique. Philip W, Sergeant, *The Empress Josephine, Napoleon's Enchantress* (New York, 1909), p. 20.

10: Citizeness Beauharnais

1. The memoirist Claire de Rémusat, who in 1793 was a girl of thirteen or fourteen living at Croissy with her family, received a visit from Hortense who was absorbed in examining and inventorying the older girl's collection of jewelry. *Mémoires de Madame de Rémusat, 1802–1808*, ed. Paul de Rémusat (Paris, 1893), I, 138.
2. Masson, *Joséphine de Beauharnais*, pp. 219–220.
3. L. Bigaud, "Joséphine de Beauharnais à Croissy," *Revue des Etudes Napoléoniennes* (Mar–Apr 1926), p. 112.

11: The Days of the Red Mass

1. Alexandre Sorel, *Le Couvent des Carmes et le Séminaire de Saint-Sulpice pendant la terreur* (Paris, 1864), pp. 370–437.
2. Castelot, p. 56.

3. The prisoner Beugnot, a survivor of prison life under the Terror, wrote of this fervent eroticism, and noted that "France is probably the only country in the world, and Frenchwomen the only women, capable of offering such singular intimacy and displaying themselves at their most attractive and voluptuous in the midst of the most repugnant and horrible circumstances...." Cited in Castelot, p. 56.

A propos of the lovemaking in the filthy corridors of the Carmelite Prison, with its slop pails and overflowing chamberpots, one cannot but think of the lines of Yeats, "Love hath pitched his mansion/In the place of excrement."

4. Rose's prison romance with Lazare Hoche is recorded in the memoirs of General Montgaillard and the venomous memoirs of Barras, as well as being generally recognized by Rose's contemporaries. The spurious memoirs of the Englishwoman Grace Elliott, *Journal of My Life*, which purported to describe Rose's romance and to give other details about her detention at the Carmelite Prison, are sheer invention. Grace Elliott was never a prisoner herself, and her memoirs are full of errors. Sorel, p. 267.

5. It has been suggested that, as a result of her prison ordeal, Rose suffered from amenorrhea, the absence of menses, and that after her release her reproductive system was permanently damaged, hence her inability to conceive a child in her second marriage. I find this argument compelling, though no evidence exists.

6. Eugene de Beauharnais wrote in his memoirs that Tallien was "the man to whose kindness we owed this good deed"—i.e., the rescuing of Rose from the peril of death and the arranging of her release. "I have always been grateful to him for this," Eugene wrote, "and fortunately I have been in a position to give him repeated proofs of what I felt." *Mémoires et correspondance politique et militaire de Prince Eugène...*, ed. A. du Casse (Paris, 1858–60), I, 30.

7. An eyewitness recorded details of Rose's leavetaking. C. A. Dauban, *Les Prisons de Paris sous la Révolution* (Paris, 1870), p. 375.

12: A NEW LIFE

1. Knapton, p. 96.
2. *Ibid.*
3. Masson, *Joséphine de Beauharnais*, p. 253.
4. Laure Junot, Duchesse d'Abrantès, *Mémoires* (Paris, n.d.), II, 41. An official pass Rose obtained in July of 1795 described her as "age twenty-

nine years [in fact she was thirty-two], height five feet, nose and mouth well made, eyes orange, hair and eyebrows dark brown, face long, chin somewhat prominent." G. de Sainte-Croix de la Roncière, *Joséphine impératrice des français* (Paris, 1934), p. 98.

Laure Junot wrote that Rose was "still charming" at this time, and that apart from her decayed teeth "she had the appearance, especially at a few paces' distance, of a young and pretty woman." Abrantès, *Mémoires*, II, 51. The literary writer Frénilly said of Rose that she was the sort of woman who would continue to look thirty until she was forty-five.

13: "She Offered Her Entire Soul in Her Eyes"

1. Knapton, p. 93.
2. The young Buonaparte had proposed unsuccessfully to Adelaide de St. Germain when still in his teens. In Paris, in 1795, he approached Madame de la Bouchardie with marriage in mind, but sensing no welcome, did not propose to her. He told Joseph that he feared falling into the grip of a sort of "marriage mania," and according to Ouvrard, even proposed to the married Therese Tallien, who laughed at the offer of marriage and ignored him. Knapton, p. 110.

   Although the Clarys made it clear that they did not want Desirée to marry Nabuleone, as late as September 1795 he had not entirely given up hope and was still attempting to discover, through Joseph, whether or not Desirée had any interest in becoming his wife. "Either we settle this affair or we break it off," he told his brother.
3. Joseph Bonaparte, *Mémoires et correspondance politique et militaire* (Paris, 1855), I, 142–143.
4. Cited in Evangeline Bruce, *Napoleon and Josephine: An Improbable Marriage* (New York, 1995), p. 133. Barras's jaundiced view of Rose was no doubt influenced by his own hostility toward both Bonaparte and his wife. After Bonaparte's rise to power Barras was offered minor government appointments, but refused them all, and bore the brunt of Bonaparte's extreme disfavor. He lived in resentful retirement during Bonaparte's rule, much of the time outside of France.
5. Rose's somewhat tardy attention to Bonaparte, whom she seems to have ignored until he was showered with financial benefits by the Directors, lends some weight to Barras's assessment of her venal nature. In cultivating Bonaparte, she was certainly thinking, first and foremost, of her own advancement; it seems likely, in view of the lies she told him about

her own financial expectations, that as early as October or November of 1795 she began to think of him as a potential husband, and to do all she could to encourage him to propose to her.

6. François Gilbert de Coston, *Biographie des premières années de Napoléon Bonaparte* (Paris, 1840), I, 433.

7. In his memoirs Bonaparte said that he first saw Rose de Beauharnais in the summer of 1795, and this would seem to be corroborated by Barras's recollection that he took Bonaparte to the important salons of Paris, including that of Therese Tallien, that summer. Henri d'Alméras, *Barras et son temps* (Paris, 1930), p. 302 and note. According to Andoche Junot, in 1795 Bonaparte spent his time "calling on anyone with influence, and knocking on every door." He was infamous as an indefatigable perpetual guest. He could hardly have avoided meeting Rose on a number of occasions. Rose's note to him on October 28 implies a friendship of months rather than days or weeks.

The romantic story that Rose met Napoleon through Eugene, when the latter went in mid-October, 1795, to see Bonaparte to request that he be exempted from turning in his father's sword to the authorities—all weapons in his section having to be given up—is probably apocryphal. Eugene may have wanted, and requested, to keep his father's sword, but that was not the issue that occasioned the meeting of Rose and her future husband.

8. Gaspard Gourgaud, *Sainte-Hélène: Journal inédit de 1815 à 1818* (Paris, 1899), II, 329.

9. Louis Hastier, *Le grand amour de Joséphine* (Paris, n.d.), p. 36.

10. Long afterward, in his exile on St. Helena, Bonaparte spoke cynically about Josephine and the circumstances under which he decided to marry her. "I really loved Josephine," he told Bertrand, "but I had no respect for her. She had the prettiest little cunt in the world, the Trois-Ilets of Martinique were there. Actually, I married her only because I thought she had a large fortune. She said she had, but it was not true."

This was the recollection of a hardened and embittered man, remembering his first passion in the light of its subsequent souring and the strife it led to. It does scant justice to the flights of feeling experienced by the Bonaparte of twenty-six.

11. Rose told the Comte de Ségur in 1804 that she had "inner struggles and long reluctance" before she could bring herself to agree to marry Bonaparte. Sergeant, p. 86.

12. Rémusat, *Mémoires*, I, 102–103.

13. Gilbert Stenger, *La Société Française pendant le Consulat* (Paris, 1903–1908), I, 60. This was precisely the sort of advocacy the general counted on

Rose to carry out on his behalf. Josephine's biographers have frequently repeated the salacious insinuation of contemporaries who, viewing Josephine as nothing more than an erotic object, assumed that "the price of the Italian command" was that Bonaparte take Josephine off Barras's hands. In this view, the assumption is made that Barras tired of Josephine, could not easily free himself of her, and so resorted to bribery to be rid of her. In actuality, Josephine was only one of Barras's lovers, and there is no evidence that she clung to him or made herself disagreeably dependent on him. On the contrary, it was precisely because Josephine had influence with Barras, and with many others, that she was valuable to Bonaparte.

14: "The Lubricious Creole"

1. Eugene de Beauharnais, *Mémoires*, I, 32.
2. In March of 1796, the month Bonaparte and Josephine married, the assignat reached the nadir of its value, and new paper notes called "territorial mandates," issued against property owned by the government, had to be put into circulation.
3. Some of Josephine's biographers have suggested that she used her youngest sister's birth certificate, but Manette was born September 3, 1766, while Josephine gave her birth date as June 23, 1767. It is unclear why the ages of the spouses were changed. The facile explanation that it was a gesture of gallantry, to disguise the bride's seniority in age, is less persuasive than that it had to do with providing legal proof, or a facsimile thereof, of birth and citizenship.
4. This account of the badly arranged wedding of Bonaparte and Josephine—clearly a last-minute affair, almost an afterthought, put together while Bonaparte was in the throes of planning and preparing for the Italian campaign—draws on the journal of Jean and Therese Tallien's daughter Thermidor, summarized in Goerges Mauguin, *L'Impératrice Joséphine: Anecdotes et Curiosités* (Paris, n.d.), pp. 15–16.

    Thermidor tells a story about being present when Collin-Lacombe was brought to Malmaison in 1809 to see Josephine, who remembered him well. She greeted him "with feeling," Thermidor recalled, "and told him, "Eh! bien, Collin, remember the long nose of the candle?"

    It seems clear that Josephine and the witnesses were kept waiting not only by Bonaparte but by the municipal official Leclercq, so that the wedding did not take place until sometime between nine and ten in the evening. But like the ceremony itself, the surviving accounts of it are somewhat confused.

5. Proof of sexual intimacy is, of course, elusive if not impossible to discover. However, since Josephine was Barras's mistress in 1795 and early 1796, and was more than likely his mistress later on, after her return from Italy, in 1797–1798, and since her other habits did not alter following her marriage, it seems overwhelmingly likely that she continued her liaison with him in the early months of her marriage. Certainly she saw a great deal of him. Hastier, *passim.*

6. In his memoirs Bourrienne described how Josephine was constantly consulting "prophetesses of good fortune." Mauguin, p. 67.

7. Among the saddest legacies of Directory promiscuity was the remarkable increase in numbers of foundlings, not only in Paris but throughout France. Presumably the majority of these unwanted babies grew up to become the solid citizens of the Restoration era.

8. Josephine's long affair with Captain Charles, which called forth from her a degree of ardor comparable to that which Bonaparte felt for her, is unfortunately scantily documented. Hastier, *op. cit.*, discusses what is known of their involvement. Unfortunately, Charles requested that after he died, Josephine's numerous letters to him be burned, and his heirs carried out his wishes. Five letters escaped the destruction.

9. Jacques Bourgeat, ed., *Napoléon: lettres à Joséphine* (Paris, 1941), pp. 31–32. Josephine wrote a number of letters to her husband in the spring of 1796 (he alludes, in his letters to her, to having received them) but they have not been preserved; she saved those he wrote to her.

10. Bourgeat, *Lettres*, p. 39.

11. *Ibid.*, 34–35.

12. de Coston, I, 466.

15: ITALIAN SOJOURN

1. Bourgeat, *Lettres*, pp. 30–31.

2. In attempting to reconstuct the sparsely documented liaison between Josephine and Hippolyte Charles, one wonders to what extent Hippolyte was motivated by opportunism. To be sure, Josephine was still very attractive, but her status as wife of the rising star of the Directory, her access to Bonaparte, and her promise of profits from army contracts may have been equally strong, if not greater, attractions for the much younger man.

3. Laure Junot wrote that Josephine "was attached to [Hippolyte] with

the liveliest interest. . . . It was something known to everyone in the army and the city of Milan." *Mémoires*, IV, 244.

4. Bourgeat, *Lettres*, pp. 50–51.

16: "I Don't Like the Honors of This Country, and I Am Often Bored"

1. Bonaparte described Josephine's state in Castiglione as "melancholy, troubled and half-ill." Sergeant, p. 104.

2. Joseph Aubenas, *Histoire de l'Impératrice Joséphine* (Paris, 1857–1859), I, 348–349.

3. If, as has been suggested, Josephine suffered from amenorrhea, or the absence of menses—the result of the extraordinary stress she was under in prison during the Terror—then she was deceiving Bonaparte into believing that a pregnancy was possible. Her increasing nervousness, frequent weeping and overemotionality, which became worse as she aged, may have been due to a hormonal imbalance, of which amenorrhea would also have been a symptom. But these conjectures cannot be substantiated from existing documents.

4. During the winter of 1797, Josephine was very concerned about Bonaparte's safety. General Berthier wrote her reassuring reports from the field, telling her that the general was "miserable over these fancies and delusions which lead you to believe that he is dead." Knapton, p. 140.

5. Sergeant, pp. 110–111.

17: "Our Family Shall Want for Nothing"

1. Stenger, III, 164 note. The French expression is "poule mouillée," or "wet hen."

2. Claire de Rémusat remarked in her memoirs that Josephine "was exceedingly fearful of deep and prolonged feeling." "The strong emotions of the soul were a bit foreign to her." Rémusat, *Mémoires*, I, 317.

3. When Bonaparte returned from Italy he was dumbstruck by the extent of the renovation, and by the degree of luxury it attained. The bill came to three hundred thousand francs. G. Bord and L. Bigard, *La Maison du "Dix-huit Brumaire"* (Paris, 1930), pp. 107–111.

18: "The Most Unfortunate of Women"

1. *At the Court of Napoleon: Memoirs of the Duchesse d'Abrantès* (New York, 1989), p. 45.
2. Jean Bourguignon, *Napoléon Bonaparte* (Paris, 1936), I, 138.
3. Stenger, I, 69 note.
4. Hastier, p. 160. As noted above, because Hippolyte Charles gave orders that Josephine's letters to him be destroyed after his death, only a few notes such as this one survive.
5. Hastier, pp. 185–186.
6. *Ibid.*, 152.
7. *Ibid.*, 152–153.
8. *Ibid.*, 154.

19: "All I Do Is Cry"

1. Hastier, p. 165.
2. *Ibid.*, 161.
3. While she excelled at dancing and needlework, and played the harp fairly well, Hortense placed only fourteenth in her class of twenty-two at dictation and composition ("seldom correct" was the official judgment). Caroline Bonaparte, who was a year older than Hortense, could scarcely read or write when she began attending Madame Campan's school. Caroline took an immediate dislike to Hortense, no doubt reflecting her family's view of Josephine. Aubenas, II, 19–21 lists Hortense's highborn classmates, among them Madame Campan's nieces Eglé and Adèle, the daughters of the Duc de Mouchy and the Duc de Valence, and other emigré daughters and nieces.
4. Hastier, p. 171.
5. Despite his expressed cynicism about women and sex, there was an ingenuous, almost innocent quality in Bonaparte's emotional nature. One of his later mistresses, Mademoiselle George, found him to be "so good, so simple, tender, delicate..." Henri d'Alméras, *La vie Parisienne sous le Consulat et l'Empire* (Paris, n.d.), p. 210. One of his companions on the Italian campaign noted that he "referred to his love [for Josephine] with the openheartedness, the impetuosity, and the delusions of a very young man." Auguste-Frédéric de Marmont, *Mémoires du duc de Raguse* (Paris, 1857), I, 187–188. In the earliest weeks of the Egyptian campaign, before

receiving the revelations that broke his heart, Bonaparte was preoccupied with thoughts of Josephine and frequently spoke to his secretary Bourrienne about her, day after day.

On the other hand, it is worth noting that Claire de Rémusat, a very acute and insightful observer, was of the opinion that Bonaparte "had no heart. That faculty or organ that allows us to love and be loved was simply missing in him." According to her, he was capable of amour, grand passion, but not of devotion. Rémusat, *Mémoires*, I, 110.

6. Rémusat, *Mémoires*, I, 274.

7. As noted above, Bonaparte had always had a penchant for slipping into a trance-like dream state. Even as a young man he loved "all that led into reverie," according to Claire de Rémusat, who knew him well. He loved twilight, melancholy music, the hypnotic effect of dim lights and soft voices, especially Josephine's. Rémusat, *Mémoires*, I, 102–103.

"What is the future?" he wrote in a letter to Josephine, in one of his trance-like moods, "What is the past? What are we? What magical fluid surrounds us and hides from us those things we most need to know? We are born, we live, we die in the midst of the marvelous." Stenger, III, 230.

8. In late winter of 1799 Josephine wrote in a letter to Hippolyte that if he agreed to see her one last time, he "would no longer be tormented by her letters, or by her presence." "The honest woman," she added, "when betrayed, retires and says nothing." Hastier, p. 184.

Neighbors at Malmaison saw Josephine in her customary white gown walking along the road in the moonlit evening, leaning on the arm of a young man, "two shadows" in the dusk. The young man, one presumes, was Hippolyte. Hastier, pp. 190–191.

9. Jean Hanoteau, *Les Beauharnais et l'Empereur. Lettres de l'impératrice Joséphine et de la reine Hortense au Prince Eugène* (Paris, 1936), p. 126.

10. Hastier, p. 194.

20: A Fissured Marriage

1. Josephine's account of her climactic confrontation with Bonaparte is in Rémusat, *Mémoires*, I, 147–149. "I have this from Madame Bonaparte herself," Rémusat wrote.

2. Laure Junot noted in her memoirs that when Bonaparte returned from Egypt he was "much attached to Eugene." *At the Court of Napoleon*, p. 66.

3. Sergeant, p. 141.

4. *At the Court of Napoleon*, p. 70.

5. *Mémoires de Constant, Premier Valet de Chambre de Napoléon Premier*, ed. Arnould Galopin (Paris, 1909), p. 85.
6. d'Alméras, pp. 252–253.
7. *Mémoires de Constant*, pp. 32–33; *At the Court of Napoleon*, p. 135.

21: A Ride Through the Forest

1. The episode narrated in this chapter is described in considerable detail in *At the Court of Napoleon*, pp. 159ff. No exact date is assigned to these events but to judge from the context, they probably occurred in 1801.
2. *At the Court of Napoleon*, p. 160.
3. *Ibid.*, 140.
4. Laure Junot recounted how, at about the same time as the episode in the woods of Bûtard, Josephine became fearful when some veteran soldiers appeared in the park at Malmaison, intent on seeing their commander. Any odd or unexpected sound—the cry of an animal, a broken dish, a sentry firing off his gun accidentally—set her nerves on edge and made her weep helplessly with anxiety. *At the Court of Napoleon*, p. 158.
5. *Ibid.*, 162.
6. Hastier wrote that Josephine saw Hippolyte Charles for the last time in 1799, and dated their "definitive separation" to 1801. She told a friend that she was "truly unhappy" over their breach. Even if he had continued to love Josephine, Hippolyte was no doubt too self-protective to take the risk of carrying on an involvement with the wife of the first consul. Hastier, pp. 184–185, 213.
7. Josephine's letter of October 18, 1801 is in Aubenas, pp. 571–573.

22: "Luxury Had Grown Abundantly"

1. Stenger, I, 384.
2. *At the Court of Napoleon*, p. 60; Harrison Brent, *Pauline Bonaparte: A Woman of Affairs* (New York, 1946), pp. 54–56.
3. Sergeant, p. 162. Earlier in his life Louis had wanted to marry Josephine's niece Emilie Beauharnais, but this hope had been squelched.
4. Rémusat, *Mémoires*, I, 157ff.
5. Still earlier, while Josephine was at Plombières, a possible marriage between Hortense and a son of Director Rewbell was discussed.
6. Rémusat, *Mémoires*, I, 160. Laure Junot wrote that Hortense's "gaiety, good humor and spirit of pleasing imparted the same qualities to all

around her. The young people grouped about her, looked at her, and loved her." *At the Court of Napoleon*, p. 238.

7. Rémusat, *Mémoires*, I, 157–159. Hortense confided many details about her unhappy marriage to Madame de Rémusat.

8. Descriptions of Madame de Montesson's ball, including the names of Hortense's dancing partners, are found in several contemporary memoirs, summarized in Stenger, III, 283. The magnificent amateur dancers of the consulate are described in A. Laquiante, *Un Hiver à Paris sous le consulat 1802–3, d'après les lettres de Johann F. Reichardt* (Paris, 1896), p. 269, *At the Court of Napoleon*, p. 128, and *The Journal of a British Chaplain in Paris During the Peace Negotiations of 1801–2*, by Rev. Dawson Warren, ed. A. M. Broadley (London, 1913), p. 117.

Although it is often stated that the waltz did not become socially acceptable until after 1815, many Napoleonic journals record waltzing as a common social pastime, indeed a fad, in the early years of the century.

23: "A Violent and Murderous Ambition"

1. Bourgeat, *Lettres*, p. 112.

2. Laure Junot observed Bonaparte's paradoxical nature. "He concealed his feelings under a rude and dry exterior," she wrote, "till this rind became a part of his character." Yet he was so sensitive he "could not, without emotion, hear the sound of the evening bells" and was always moved by women's tears and by anyone earnestly attempting to assert the claims of family loyalty. As the years passed, his outer rind hardened and thickened, and his native cynicism overcame his romantic sensibilities. On St. Helena, looking back over the course of his life, he asserted that he was dominated by a feeling of contempt for others, and that he kept others near him only as long as they were useful to him.

3. Rémusat, *Mémoires*, I, 206.

4. Bonaparte "responded [to Josephine's complaints] sometimes with violence whose excesses I dare not describe," Claire de Rémusat wrote, implying physical abuse, which was not uncommon at the consular court. Rémusat, *Mémoires*, I, 206.

5. *Ibid.*, I, 203–204.

6. *Ibid.*, I, 207–209, 212.

7. The story of the contretemps is in Rémusat, *Mémoires*, II, 44–48ff.

8. *Ibid.*, II, 49–50.

9. Stenger, III, 230.

10. *Lettres de Napoléon à Joséphine . . . et lettres de Joséphine à Napoléon et à sa fille* (Paris, 1833), II, 222–223.

24: "MAY THE EMPEROR LIVE FOREVER!"

1. Rémusat, *Mémoires*, II, 43.
2. *Ibid.*, II, 58. Corvisart confided the details of this secret scheme to Claire de Rémusat after Josephine's divorce.
3. *Ibid.*, II, 92–93, 87–88.
4. During his exile on St. Helena, Bonaparte claimed that by 1804 he was determined to divorce Josephine, and that her participation in the coronation was no indication to the contrary.
5. Rémusat, *Mémoires*, II, 71.
6. Stenger, I, 335–336.
7. Frédéric Masson, *Madame Bonaparte* (Paris, n.d.), pp. 367–368.
8. *Mémoires de Constant*, p. 93.

25: "JOSEPHINE EMPRESS OF THE FRENCH"

1. Hanoteau, *Les Beauharnais et l'Empereur*, p. 7.
2. *Ibid.*, 5–9.
3. *Ibid.*, 16–17.
4. *Mémoires de la reine Hortense, publiés par le prince Napoléon* (Paris, 1927–8), I, 233. Rémusat, *Mémoires*, I, 158–159 describes Louis's contemptuous treatment of Hortense.
5. Rémusat, *Mémoires*, II, 301–302.
6. *Ibid.*

26: "I WILL BEHAVE LIKE THE VICTIM I AM"

1. Madame de Rémusat (*Mémoires*, II, 279) thought that following the Austerlitz victory Bonaparte imposed a more intense despotism on those around him. "One sensed something heavier in the yoke he placed on each citizen," she wrote. "One almost forcibly bowed to his glory." Impressed by the stiff etiquette of the German courts, he surrounded himself with new pomp which put greater distance between himself and others.
2. He swore, Claire de Rémusat recalled, that his anger went only to his

neck, and not above it, but those who witnessed it were convinced
otherwise. *Mémoires*, I, 120 note.

3. Hanoteau, *Les Beauharnais et l'Empereur*, pp. 28–29.

4. Rémusat, *Mémoires*, I, 152–154. Claire de Rémusat noted with some acer-
bity that Hortense "was a perfect judge of her mother, and did not
dare confide in her." Josephine loved her children, but was notoriously
indiscreet; Hortense knew that anything she told her mother would
soon become public knowledge. Despite this, she did in fact tell her a
great deal.

5. Gossip suggested that Eléonore was unchaste, and that Murat could
have been the father of her child; however, her son Léon Denuelle
resembled Bonaparte and was acknowledged by him. There seems to
be no reason to doubt Léon's paternity. No certain evidence exists that
Josephine knew of Eléonore Denuelle's pregnancy at the time, but because in the past Bonaparte had always boasted to her of his erotic
conquests, and because nothing could have pleased Caroline Murat
more than to reveal news of the impending birth of Bonaparte's child,
it seems likely that Josephine did know.

6. Rémusat, *Mémoires*, II, 117–118. Josephine had three equerries on her staff.
Her partiality toward Corbineau was noted from January 1806 on. Rémusat, *Mémoires, loc. cit.* and Hanoteau, *Les Beauharnais et l'Empereur*, pp. 37–
38.

7. Pierre-Louis Roederer, *Journal* (Paris, 1909), p. 214.

8. Sergeant, pp. 266–267.

9. Rémusat, *Mémoires*, II, 283.

10. Josephine complained of migraine frequently in letters from February
to May, 1807. Hanoteau, *Les Beauharnais et l'Empereur*, pp. 36, 38, 42. She
complained to Eugene of "an attack of melancholy I cannot seem to
shake off."

11. The ball is described by Marco de Saint-Hilaire, quoted in *Les Petits
Appartements des Tuileries, de Saint-Cloud et de la Malmaison* ... (Paris, 1831), II,
234.

12. Hanoteau, *Les Beauharnais et l'Empereur*, pp. 37–38; *Lettres de Napoléon à Joséphine* ... (Paris, 1833), II, 266.

13. Bourgeat, *Lettres*, pp. 127–128.

14. Hanoteau, *Les Beauharnais et l'Empereur*, pp. 34–40 *passim*. Josephine's
granddaughter and namesake married Oscar I, King of Sweden and
Norway. She died in 1876.

15. *Ibid.*, 43–44.

16. *Ibid.*, 45.

27: "They Are Inveterate Against Me"

1. *At the Court of Napoleon*, p. 333.
2. *Ibid.*, 332.
3. Hanoteau, *Les Beauharnais et l'Empereur*, pp. 49–50 note 1.
4. *Ibid.*, 52.

28: "As Though a Deadly Poison Were Spreading Through My Veins"

1. Hanoteau, *Les Beauharnais et l'Empereur*, pp. 54–55.
2. Sergeant, pp. 286ff.
3. "He proposed to me himself, at the time of the divorce," Josephine told Claire de Rémusat, "that I should take as husband the Prince of Mecklenburg-Strelitz—you remember that handsome young man who paid me such attentions at Fontainebleau, and then in Paris at the Tuileries." Rémusat, *Mémoires*, III, 257.

29: "The Elder Sister of the Graces"

1. Details of the ceremony are given in *Mémoires de Constant*, pp. 214–215. Constant tells a melodramatic anecdote about Josephine going to Bonaparte's room later that night, distraught, and spending a last anguished hour in his arms, but the story does not ring true; Bonaparte had been careful to keep his distance from his wife for many months, and would have spared himself the emotional pain of such an intimate parting.

    The Constant memoirs, like many others published during the Bourbon restoration, were "collaborations" between their reputed authors and novelistic writers who invented, elaborated, and rearranged with abandon. As historical sources they must be used with great caution.
2. Frédéric Masson, *Joséphine repudiée* (Paris, 1900), p. 80.
3. Bourgeat, *Lettres*, p. 192.
4. *At the Court of Napoleon*, p. 356.
5. d'Alméras, p. 308.
6. *Lettres de Napoléon à Joséphine* (Paris, 1833), II, 298–300.
7. Maurice de Tascher's reminiscence of Josephine is in *Le Journal de campagne d'un cousin d'impératrice* (Paris, 1933), pp. 286–290. Although a number of Josephine's biographers have assumed that Maurice de Tascher was one of the sons of Josephine's uncle Baron Robert de Tascher from Mar-

tinique, he belonged in fact to a distant branch of the Tascher family, a branch whose members had not emigrated to the New World.

Josephine's cousins from Martinique were Charles de Tascher, an officer in the grenadiers who returned to Martinique after several years of service in France; Henri de Tascher, who died in the Russian campaign of 1812 after service under Joseph Bonaparte in Spain, and who was married to a niece of Joseph's wife; Louis de Tascher, who was aide-de-camp to Eugene and married to the daughter of the Princesse de la Leyen; Saint-Rose de Tascher, an ordnance officer who was unwell and lived with his sister Stéphanie after her marriage was annulled; Numa de Tascher, who remained in Martinique; and Stéphanie de Tascher, a beauty in fragile health unhappily married to the Prince d'Aremberg. Aubenas, pp. 578–579; Rémusat, *Mémoires*, II, 350–352.

30: "Alone, Abandoned, and in the Midst of Strangers"

1. Contemporary gossip said that the good-looking Lancelot Turpin was Josephine's lover, and Josephine's more sensational biographers repeated the gossip as fact, but no known evidence supports the supposition. It is possible that Josephine had one or more lovers in the years following her divorce, and was discreet enough to disguise her liaisons, but because she was subject to so much public scrutiny—and to the surveillance of Bonaparte's spies—it seems likely that if she had lovers, something more substantial than gossip would have survived to testify to them.

2. Hanoteau, *Les Beauharnais et l'Empereur*, pp. 48–49. In September of 1807 Josephine had written to Eugene that "I have no ambition about anything but his [Bonaparte's] heart. If others were able to separate me from him, it would not be the rank [of empress] I would regret; a profound solitude would please me most."

3. *Ibid.*, 78–79 note.

4. Hanoteau, *Les Beauharnais et l'Empereur*, p. 81. "I shall occupy myself with botany and the arts," Josephine told Eugene in a letter on November 19, 1810.

5. Madame Ney, until early in 1810 one of Josephine's attendants, had a voice of operatic quality and Josephine often sang along with her in informal evening concerts. A German composer who visited Paris in 1803 was pleasantly surprised to find that Josephine knew, and could perform, scenes from several of his operas. *Un Hiver à Paris*, p. 314.

6. Hanoteau, *Les Beauharnais et l'Empereur*, p. 81.

7. *Ibid.*
8. Castelot, p. 443.

31: "A Profound Solitude Would Please Me Most"

1. Hanoteau, *Les Beauharnais et l'Empereur*, pp. 87–88.
2. A woman who saw Josephine in the fall of 1810 wrote that "she is so thoughtful that one forgets the empress and thinks only of the woman who wishes to please everyone, and it is impossible not to like her.... She has had a charming face and still looks well." Castelot, p. 442.
3. Bourgeat, *Lettres*, pp. 215–216.
4. Hanoteau, *Les Beauharnais et l'Empereur*, p. 104.
5. Josephine's letter describing Augusta's labor is in Hanoteau, *Les Beauharnais et l'Empereur*, p. 106.

32: Recessional

1. Eugene's letter from Russia informed Josephine that she was "adored in Milan," as she was everywhere. "People have written charming things about you," he wrote, "and you have turned the head of everyone you have approached." Knapton, p. 311.
2. After Josephine's death her principal doctor, who had cared for her over the entire course of her final illness, told Bonaparte that he thought she died of "anxiety" and "grief." Castelot, p. 482.

33: "I Have Never in My Life Lacked Courage"

1. Hanoteau, *Les Beauharnais et l'Empereur*, p. 117.
2. Sergeant, pp. 340–341.
3. Hanoteau, *Les Beauharnais et l'Empereur*, p. 118.
4. Knapton, p. 318.
5. Masson, *Joséphine repudiée*, p. 330.

34: RESTORATION

1. Mauguin, p. 87.
2. Bourgeat, *Lettres*, pp. 216–217.
3. This account of Josephine's last illness and very sudden death relies on Aubenas, pp. 553ff and ancillary sources. The surviving contemporary evidence is scant, and sketchy. According to the official autopsy, Josephine died of pneumonia and a "gangrenous sore throat," and her lungs were choked with blood. It has been suggested that she had cancer of the throat; if so, it was most likely complicated by an acute infection that developed rapidly and caused her windpipe to close.

   Dr. Horeau told Bonaparte that Josephine died of "anxiety and grief." It seems certain that her depression and anguish made her vulnerable to illness, and unable to resist it once the acute infection set in. Clearly she was unable to prevent her fears from coloring her perceptions and judgment in her last weeks; she was not herself, and her mental world was clouded. "Must I again see my children wanting and destitute?" she cried out to a confidant. "The idea is killing me!" Sergeant, pp. 348–349.
4. Dr. Horeau said that Josephine's "head was affected as though she were in a state of intoxication."

Works Cited

Note to the reader: The bibliography on the ancien régime and Napoleonic era is vast, though most books on Josephine herself are either fanciful, romanticized, unscholarly, or distorted by the author's bias toward Napoleon. The following list of titles includes only those works cited in the footnotes.

Alméras, Henri d'. *Barras et son temps.* Paris: Albin Michel, 1930.

———. *La vie parisienne sous le consulat et l'empire.* Paris: Albin Michel, n.d.

Aubenas, Joseph. *Histoire de l'impératrice Joséphine.* 2 vols. Paris: Amyot, 1857–1859.

Beauharnais, Eugène de. *Mémoires et correspondance politique et militaire de Prince Eugène,* ed. A. du Casse. 10 vols. Paris: Michel Lévy, 1858–1860.

Beauharnais, Hortense de, Reine. *Mémoires de la reine Hortense, publiés par le prince Napoléon.* 3 vols. Paris: Plon, n.d. (Déposé Bibliothèque Nationale, 1928).

Bord, Gustave, and Louis Bigard. *La Maison du "Dix-huit Brumaire."* Paris: Hachette, 1930.

Bourgeat, Jacques, ed. *Napoléon: lettres à Joséphine.* Paris: Guy Le Prat, 1941.

Brent, Harrison. *Pauline Bonaparte: A Woman of Affairs.* New York and Toronto: Rinehart, 1946.

Broadley, A. M., ed. *The Journal of a British Chaplain in Paris During the Peace Negotiations of 1801–1802,* by Rev. Dawson Warren. London: Chapman and Hall, 1913.

Bruce, Evangeline. *Napoleon and Josephine: An Improbable Marriage.* New York: Kensington, 1995.

Castelot, André. *Joséphine.* trans. Denise Folliot. New York and Evanston: Harper and Row, 1967.

Mémoires de Constant, premier valet de chambre de Napoléon premier, ed. Arnould Galopin. Paris: Albin Michel, 1909.

Coston, François Gilbert de. *Biographie des premières années de Napoléon Bonaparte.* 2 vols. Paris and Valence: Marc Aurèle Frères, 1840.

Dauban, C. A. *Les prisons de Paris sous la révolution.* Paris: Plon, 1870.

Gourgaud, Gaspard. *Sainte-Hélène: Journal inédit de 1815 à 1818.* Paris: Flammarion, 1899.

Hanoteau, Gabriel, and Alfred Martineau. *Histoire des colonies françaises.* 6 vols. Paris: Société de L'Histoire Nationale/Plon, 1929.

Hanoteau, Jean. *Joséphine avant Napoléon: Le ménage Beauharnais d'après des correspondances inédites.* Paris: Plon, 1935.

———. *Les Beauharnais et l'empereur. Lettres de l'impératrice Joséphine et de la reine Hortense au prince Eugène.* Paris: Plon, 1936.

Hastier, Louis. *Le grand amour de Joséphine.* Paris: Editions Correa Buchet/ Chastel, 1955.

Junot, Laure, Duchesse d'Abrantès. *Mémoires.* 4 vols. Paris: Albin Michel, n.d.

———. *At the Court of Napoleon: Memoirs of the Duchesse d'Abrantès.* New York: Doubleday, 1989.

Knapton, Ernest John. *Empress Josephine.* Cambridge, Mass.: Harvard University Press, 1963.

Laquiante, A. *Un hiver à Paris sous le consulat 1802–1803, d'après les lettres de J.-F. Reichardt.* Paris: Plon, 1896.

Marmont, Duc de Raguse, Auguste-Frédéric de. *Mémoires du duc de Raguse.* Paris: Perrotin, 1857.

Masson, Frédéric. *Joséphine de Beauharnais, 1763–1796.* Paris: Société d'éditions littéraires et artistiques, 1903.

———. *Joséphine répudiée.* Paris: Société d'éditions littéraires et artistiques, Librairie Paul Ollendorff, 1900.

———. *Madame Bonaparte.* Paris: Albin Michel, n.d.

Mauguin, Georges. *L'impératrice Joséphine: Anecdotes et curiosités.* Paris: J. Peyronnet, n.d.

Montgaillard, Comte de Rocques, Jean-Gabriel de. *Mémoires diplomatiques extraits des archives du ministre de l'intérieur.* Paris: Paul Ollendorff, 1895.

Mémoires de Madame de Rémusat, 1802–1808, ed. Paul de Rémusat. 3 vols. Paris: Calmann-Lévy, 1893.

Roederer, Pierre-Louis. *Journal.* Paris: H. Daragon, 1909.

Sainte-Croix de la Roncière, G. de. *Joséphine impératrice des français.* Paris: Chez l'Auteur, 1934.

Sergeant, Philip W. *The Empress Josephine, Napoleon's Enchantress.* New York: Hutchinson's Library of Standard Lives, 1909.

Sorel, Alexandre. *Le couvent des Carmes et le séminaire de Saint-Sulpice pendant la terreur*. Paris: Librairie Academique, Didier, 1864.

Stenger, Gilbert. *La société française pendant le consulat*. 6 vols. Paris: Perrin, 1903–1908.

Tascher, Maurice de. *Journal de campagne d'un cousin de l'impératrice, 1806–1813*. Paris: Plon, 1933.

Index